THE GLORIOUS CROSS

OF SAINT JOHN

The Key that unlocks the Book of Revelation.

One Day At A Time.

Gordon Dean Johnson

The Glorious Cross of Saint John
The Key that Unlocks the Book of Revelation

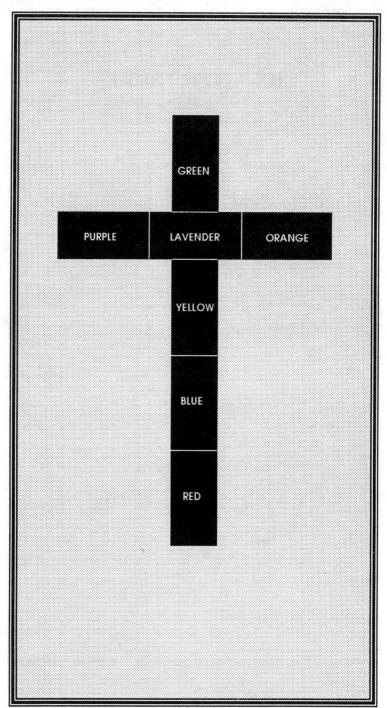

THE SEVEN THEMES

1. Testimony/Preparation
a. 1:19-34   c. 12:1-11
b. 3:22-36   d. 20:1-7

2. Faith/Betrothal
a. 1:35-51   c. 12:12-50
b. 11:1-27   d. 20:8-10

3. Life/Marriage
a. 2:1-12   c. 13:1-38
b. 11:28-57   d. 20:11-16

4. Homecoming/Abiding
a. 2:13-25   c. 14:1-31
b. 7:1-8:59   d. 20:17-18

5. New Birth/Fruitfulness
a. 3:1-21   c. 15:1-27
b. 9:1-10:42   d. 20:19-29

6. Nurture/Holy Spirit
a. 4:1-42   c. 16:1-33
b. 6:1-72   d. 18:1-19:42

7. Healing/Prayer
a. 4:43-54   c. 17:1-26
b. 5:1-47   d. Between chs.
19 and 20

THE COLOR SCHEME

1. Red is the color of Testimony/Preparation
because it is the color of blood. The word testimony in the Greek
has the root "martus," from which our word martyr is derived.
A martyr is one who is willing to shed blood for what he or she
believes.

2. Blue is the color of Faith/Betrothal because it is the color
of the sky, which speaks of the faithfulness of God that over-
arches us. We say "true blue," and truth in Old English is pronounced troth, which means faithfulness.

3. Yellow is the color of Life/Marriage because it is the color
of the sun that brings life to the earth. It is also the color of gold,
symbolizing that which is most precious. (The three dominant
themes are represented by the three primary colors from which
the others are derived.)

4. Lavender is the color of Abiding/Homecoming because
it is the product of light blue (unbelief) and a touch of red (blood).
The unbelief of the Jews obliged Jesus to go home to his heavenly Father by way of the cross. It is the way of the cross which
leads us home as well.

5. Green is the color of Fruitfulness/New Birth because it
betokens the presence of fruit. Jesus, seeing the fig tree in leaf,
anticipated the presence of winter fruit. Since there was none,
he cursed it, as Judaism was cursed for being unfruitful for God.

6. Purple is the color of Nurture/Holy Spirit because it is
the color of the grape, which we eat. We also drink the juice of
the grape when we partake of the cup of communion, which is
the New Covenant in Christ's blood.

7. Orange is the color of Healing/Prayer because it is the
product of red (emblematic of the shedding of blood/death)
mingled with yellow, which symbolizes life. In answer to prayer
God is pleased to bestow healing and life to those who are in the
grip of disease and death. On the lighter side, oranges are a
source of vitamin C, beneficial in warding off sickness.

DEDICATION

This book is dedicated to the members of the churches I have served, from whom I have learned so much.

Fort Calhoun Presbyterian Church, Fort Calhoun, Nebraska. Pierce Memorial Presbyterian Church, Farmingdale, New Jersey. Dundee Presbyterian Church, Omaha, Nebraska. Trinity Presbyterian Church, Wichita, Kansas. First Presbyterian Church, Clinton, Missouri. Brandt Memorial Presbyterian Church, St. Louis, Missouri.

ACKNOWLEDGEMENTS

To Rita, my beloved wife and co-laborer, without whose assistance and encouragement this book would not be.

To William Robert Bonds, who created the cover design.

To Professor Otto A. Piper, who taught me the New Biblical Theology at Princeton Theological Seminary.

PREFACE

As a student at Princeton Theological Seminary from 1950 to 1953, I was privileged to study under Professor Otto A. Piper, who taught the New Testament in the original Greek. The good professor had departed from Hitler's Germany in 1933, when he saw the writing on the wall. Arriving in England, he was approached by a stranger, who told him that a position was awaiting him at a certain place, so he went there. They said, "Yes, a position opened just today, but how did you know?" The professor realized that an angel had told him.

I believe that God directed me to Princeton, where I studied under his tutelage the Gospel According to St. John. He began by saying that John was a master architect, and that this gospel was some thirty years in composition under the leading of the Holy Spirit. Ten years after taking the course, I was reflecting on the fact that John 2:1 says, "On the third day there was a wedding at Cana in Galilee." I knew that it was the third day after Jesus had said to Philip, "Follow me." But it occurred to me that "the third day" could have a deeper significance. Perhaps it was "the third day" as we have it in Genesis chapter one, where we read of the six days of creation, followed by the seventh day, when God rested. Then I looked at John's expression of the Gospel from the standpoint of themes, or motifs. When I did, it exploded in my face. I took our youngsters' building blocks and reconstructed the gospel episode by episode in the form of a cross. Each block fell automatically into place. This book attempts to show the underlying structure of the gospel. In addition it gives a verse by verse analysis. In the prologue John lays the foundation. The seven themes occur in verses 11 to 17. Then he constructs upon it an edifice four stories high. The last chapter is the roof, where the seven motifs are found again.

Which came first, the chicken or the egg? In John's narrative they occur together. We understand the whole only as we comprehend the parts. By the same token, we understand the parts only as we come to grips with the totality. It is crucial that we realize that John gives us a different perspective from that of the first three gospels. They view the ministry of our Lord from the standpoint of Peter, whose testimony underlies the Gospel According to Mark, to which Matthew and Luke add their material. St. John is symbolized by the eagle, which sees ten times more keenly than we. Let us avoid the error of trying to harmonize John and the other evangelists, as most scholars do. If John's chronology differs from that of the others, let us attend to what he says without being upset. John views the ministry of Jesus from the perspective of eternity, whereas the other evangelists see it from the standpoint of time. As the result we enjoy depth perception.

In chapters 12 to 17 we encounter the seven themes in their original order. John says that Mary of Bethany anointed Jesus as Messiah "six days before the Passover," which coincided with the Jewish sabbath. John 19:31 This placed her deed on the first day of Holy Week. So according to John the triumphal entry occurred on blue Monday, the second day of the week. Blue is the color of faith. But Jesus' attempt to woo and win official Judaism met with failure. So for a symbolic reason this gospel is silent about what happened on the third, fourth and fifth days of holy week. But, praise God, the themes of the marriage, homecoming, and new birth actually did take place in association with his followers at the last supper. The narrative gets more exciting when we realize that the book of Revelation is structured after the same manner. Commencing on November 18, we survey the book of Revelation.

G.D.J.
7100 Cheshire
St. Louis, Missouri 63123
January 18, 1991

THE GLORIOUS CROSS

OF SAINT JOHN

The Key that unlocks the Book of Revelation.

One Day At A Time.

Gordon Dean Johnson

A GOOD BEGINNING

*"**I**n the beginning was the Word, and the Word was with God, and the Word was God." John 1:1*

We begin the New Year looking to Him who was with God the Father before the world was made. His name is "the Word" (the Logos, from which we get our word logic. So the gospel is emminently logical). He was with God before the universe was fashioned. But more exactly in the original Greek text, he was toward God. Two people may sit alongside one another on a park bench and remain complete strangers. Should one turn toward the other and strike up a conversation, they would then be in fellowship. Well, the Word was toward God, speaking to Him, in fellowship with him, before creation.

All things were made through the Word, who imparted his essential nature, that is to say, his "toGodwardness" to everything that was made. We buy items marked "Made in USA." Every creature bears this mark, "Made by God through the Word." And this toGodwardness, this stamp of deity, is the life of every creature. Everything in the universe from the tiniest snowflake to the most immense galaxy has a toGodwardness about it that points to the God who created it. This life, this toGodwardness, is the light of men. We see in the world about us order and beauty. Indeed the Greek word "cosmos" (world) means order, orderliness, harmony. What we see around us turns on the light within us, and we know instinctively that there is a God who is responsible for it all.

We differ from the other creatures on earth in that we are able to respond in a personal way to the God who has fashioned us with a God-shaped vacuum in our hearts. As we praise and thank him for all the good we see about us and within us, our lives take on the toGodwardness which is life. The darkness and evil in the world cannot overcome the light that shines within us, nor can they put it out. Light conquers darkness. You see that every time you turn on the lights.

❧

A POWERFUL, GOOD NAME

"There was a man sent from God whose name was John."

John 1:6

There came into existence through the creative activity of God and the Word a man whose message is contained in his name. John means "God is gracious." His name tells us that God deals with us in a kindly, gracious way. God sent him for testimony. Testimony is needed in a courtroom situation where a claim is contested. There are those who contend that God is not gracious. But John takes the witness stand to testify to the light. "God is light. In him is no darkness nor shadow due to change." James 1:17 The goal of John's message and ministry is that all people everywhere might believe. His work has universal scope. It is essential that we in our generation attend to what he did and said. He was not himself the light, as some of his disciples believed, but he came to bear witness to the light.

The reason for his work was that the true light that enlightens every man was coming into the world. The source of all energy and revelation from God was moving away from the presence of God into the universe. When he who is the light arrived, the very world that was made through him, strange as it seems, did not recognize him. The world was in the dark, and in the grasp of the prince of darkness. Mankind was not only ignorant of God, but rebellious against him.

The eternal Word came to his own home. But his own people, who, from the time of Abraham some 2000 years before, were being prepared for his arrival, received him not. Remember, "there was no room at the inn," where he might have been born. So his mother delivered him in a stable and cradled him in a manger. But, praise God, there is room in our heart for him. So come into my heart, Lord Jesus. Come in now, this very moment. Really, but invisibly, he has come in. He is a gentleman. He never barges in. He comes only where he is welcome.

❧

WHOSE CHILDREN ARE WE?

*"**B**ut to all who received him, who believed in his name, he gave power to become children of God."* John 1:12

Most of the people to whom he came rejected him, but, praise God, there were noble exceptions. And to those who did receive him, and to receive him involved believing in his name, he gave something. His name, Jesus, means "The Eternal One Saves." He is the "I am who I am" come to rescue us from the darkness of our ignorance and rebellion against God. To all who so <u>believe</u> he gave the right to become something they were not by nature, "children of God." We are by nature children of the evil one; creatures of God, yes, but God's off-spring, no. The way in which we become the offspring of God is through being born, not of blood, (human ancestry), nor of the will of the flesh (sexual desire), nor of the will of man to have a child, but <u>born of God</u> (literally, out of God himself). We learn more of this in Jesus' conversation with Nicodemus beginning in chapter 3:1, where Jesus tells about new birth.

"And the Word became flesh." Here is the Christmas story in a sentence. The Eternal Word, through which the universe and every individual in it was created, stepped down to the level of mortal man. The Infinite became finite. The Eternal became temporal. The Almighty became weakness, for "the flesh is weak," he said.

This one "pitched his tent" among us. This was written in a day when the people lived in stone houses. A tent is a temporary dwelling. He was to be among us as man just a very short time. He died in his thirties. But what a life he lived: "full of grace and truth." Now we realise that the tent was actually a tabernacle inhabited by God. Only God in human flesh is filled to overflowing with grace and truth. The rest of us are afflicted by the works of the flesh: immorality, impurity, jealousy, anger, selfishness, etc. Galatians 5:19

❦

GLORY

"*We have beheld his glory, glory as of the only Son from the Father.*" *John 1:14*

At the wedding in Cana his disciples for the first time beheld his glory. Glory means weightiness, heaviness. They watched him without effort turn water into wine. By this creative act, he let his supernatural weight down for the first time. They perceived then that he was on the side of Creator, not creature. Such stupendous weight and splendor was that of an only Son from the Father. A Father who has an only son focuses all his love and attention upon his one offspring. There is no one else like him. He has the life of God within.

He is the incomparable one, the overflowing source of grace and truth, as we have seen. Grace has forgiveness in it. It is kindness bestowed upon us who are not entitled to it. Were justice to prevail we would not have a leg to stand on. But in his tender mercy we are accepted just as we are in all of our unworthiness. We have broken covenant with God, but in his grace he does not abandon us. He allows the covenant to stand even so, holding up his end when we have let ours fall. He is also full of truth. That is to say, through him a power is released in the universe that will enable us to become true men and women. He reproduces his own likeness in us, so that ultimately we shall be just like Jesus, who said, "He who has seen me has seen the Father." Talk about a remarkable future.

John bore witness to him, and cried, "This is he of whom I said, `He who comes after me ranks before me, for he was before me.'" Though Jesus came after John in time, and evidently followed him for a short time as John's disciple, John recognized that Jesus was his chief. He knew that Jesus was the Eternal One, who was infinitely superior to himself. John had a beginning in time. Jesus, on the other hand, is the One without beginning or end, the Alpha and Omega. He is everything to us from A to Z.

FULNESS

"*And from his fulness have we all received, grace upon grace.*"

John 1:16

The earth is the Lord's and the fulness thereof." Psalm 24:1. The fulness of the earth is its productivity. Every year there comes a new harvest. There is no end to it. Jesus is like that. The more we receive from him, the more there is coming. He is like a battery that never runs down. His grace and his truth are the living properties of his nature. Every human being, whether she knows it or not, has been the recipient of the grace that flows through Jesus Christ from God. Like the waves of the sea washing in upon the shore, grace upon grace flows over us continually. There is no end to it. It is without limit.

"For the law was given through Moses; grace and truth came through Jesus Christ." The straight-edge of the law of Moses shows us how crooked we are, but the living properties of Jesus Christ (grace and truth) gradually straighten us out. They transform us and turn us into God's property.

"No one has ever seen God," not even Moses. He may have seen the glory of his backside, but that is all. "The only Son (the only begotten God, in another rendering) who is in the bosom of the Father, he has made him known." Jesus' place from before creation has been and is the place of intimate love at the Father's side. He and he alone is in the position to make God clear to us. As God's Eternal Word, he has declared the love of God to the entire universe. God is love, because He is the personal process of self-giving. It is his nature to have begotten out of himself a Son through whom He has fashioned even you and me.

We have come to the end of the prologue, which is like the overture of an opera, in which all the main themes are sounded forth. We have encountered the motifs of testimony, faith, life, home coming, new birth, nurture and healing. The rest of the gospel is merely a development of what we have already heard. ❧

THE FIRST DAY OF THE NEW CREATION

And this is the testimony of John, when the Jews sent priests and Levites from Jerusalem to ask him, 'Who are you?'" John 1:19

This is the first day of the new creation. The new creation is "the called out ones" (the church). There are seven days underlying this new week of creative activity. The first day is the day of the testimony of John. John the Baptist by his testimony and his ministry is preparing the people for the coming of the Lord. His work finalizes the Old Testament. The Old Testament is the book of preparation. We must be prepared for the coming of our God.

A minister received a phone call from a man who asked, "Can you tell me where it says in the Bible 'Prepare to meet thy God?'" "I will be pleased to tell you," answered the minister, "but why do you ask?" He answered, "Forty years ago I heard a sermon on that text, and I just got to thinking about it." See Amos 4:12.

The Jewish ruling circle in Jerusalem sent this delegation to John with the question, "Who are you?" He confessed, he did not deny, but confessed, "I am not the Christ." He did not wait for them to ask if he were the Christ. He denied categorically that he was. Get that thought out of your heads. I am most certainly not the long-expected Redeemer. And they asked him, "What then? Are you Elijah?" He said, "I am not." The last book of the Old Testament foretold, "Behold, I will send you Elijah the prophet before the great and terrible day of the Lord comes." Malachi 4:5. John tells them that he is not Elijah returned to earth, though he did come in the spirit and power of Elijah. Elijah did come to Jesus together with Moses less than a year before his crucifixion when they discussed on the Mount of Transfiguration the Exodus (departure) that Jesus was about to accomplish at Jerusalem. Jesus experienced the great and terrible day of the Lord's wrath for us on the cross, that we might not have to experience it for ourselves.

WHO ARE YOU?

*"**A**re you the prophet?" And he answered, "No.'*　*John 1:21*

Moses had written some 1400 years before, "The Lord your God will raise up for you a prophet like me from among you, from your brethren - him you shall heed." Deuteronomy 18:15. John said he was not that prophet, because Jesus was that one. Jesus is our heavenly Moses (meaning "He draws"). He draws us by the cords of his love through his greater and higher Exodus to our Promised Land on high.

They said to him then, "Who are you? Let us have an answer for those who sent us. What do you say about yourself?" He said, "I am the voice of one crying in the wilderness, `make straight the way of the LORD,' as the prophet Isaiah said." Isaiah 40:3

The important thing about me, says John, is not who I am, but what I have to say. He is not interested in having his name appear on the front page of the New York Times, or his picture on the cover of Time Magazine. He says, I am nothing. My message is everything. God uses mere nobodies to accomplish his work. I am only a voice, but an historically important voice. I declare that one step more and the Eternal God will be here. You must prepare for his coming by making straight his way, and by cleaning up your act.

Isaiah chapters 40 to 48 has as its theme the Imminent Coming of God. The coming of Jesus is the coming of God to meet the needs of his people. John recognizes who Jesus is - Emmanuel, God with us. He is also aware of the eternal significance of his own ministry as the forerunner. The astonishing thing is that Jesus said that his humblest disciple has a greater role in history than John the Baptist had, that he who is least in the Kingdom of God is greater than John. True greatness is measured by genuine humility. "What have you that you did not receive? If you received it as a gift, then why do you boast?"

❧

THE GOSPEL OF THE SECOND CHANCE

"Now they had been sent from the Pharisees. They asked him, 'Then why are you baptizing, if you are neither the Christ, nor Elijah, nor the prophet?'" John 1:24,25

The delegation in 1:19 had been sent by the Sadducees. (One reason they were so "sad-you-see" was because they had no belief in the resurrection). The present delegation was from the Pharisees. Their concern was not so much the person of John as his ministry. The only candidates for baptism in their religion were "gentile-dogs." Gentiles were baptized that they might fraternize with Jews. By demanding that Jews be baptized, the Baptist was in effect excommunicating the whole nation, treating them like hated heathen. What right had John to do such a thing, especially if he was not one of the aforementioned personages?

John answered them, "I baptize with water, but among you stands one whom you do not know, even he who comes after me, the thong of whose sandal I am not worthy to untie." By referring to Jesus as the one who "comes after me," he was indicating that Jesus was for a short time his follower. Even so, John was saying that he was not worthy to be Jesus' slave. A disciple would never be required to untie his rabbi's sandal; that was the task of a slave. The Apostle Paul identified himself in his letter to the Romans as a "slave of Jesus Christ." He was thrilled to be the slave of the Master of the universe. The Baptist considered himself to be unworthy of such a high office.

"This took place in Bethany beyond the Jordan, where Jesus was baptizing." He was calling the Judeans to the east bank of the Jordan, from whence their ancestors had followed an earlier Jesus (Joshua) across the river to possess the land. They had failed in this task through disobedience. Now they were given a second opportunity to possess not merely the Promised Land but also the whole earth in the name of the Lord: the Gospel of the second chance.

❦

THE LAMB OF GOD

"The next day he saw Jesus coming toward him, and said, 'Behold, the Lamb of God, who takes away the sin of the world'" John 1:29

Jesus is returning from the wilderness where he had been tempted by the devil for forty days and nights. In the wilderness he had hammered out the course of his ministry. He would not use his divinely given power merely to meet the physical needs of people, nor would he dazzle people into submission by miracles. Furthermore he would make no compromise with evil, as though the end justifies the means. No, he would sacrifice himself upon the cross as the sin-offering to God for fallen humanity. This job-description was confirmed by the Baptist. "Behold, the Lamb of God, who takes away the sin of the world."

What is the root sin which bears fruit in sinful behavior? The first sin, of course, which is unbelief. Adam and Eve refused to believe God. Instead they believed the devil's lie that, eating the forbidden fruit, they would not die; they would become like God himself, knowing good and evil. But they did die spiritually and then physically. The product of their unbelief is our birth in the dark about God. We do not know God by nature, neither do we have fellowship with him. Spiritually we are the offspring of the evil one, the father of lies and death. But Jesus would carry our sin and death upon the cross as the Sacrificial Lamb provided by God.

In Genesis Abraham was willing to sacrifice his son, Isaac, but at the last moment his hand was stopped. A ram caught in the thicket was the substitute for his son. It was put to death in his place. Isaac was the ancestor of Jesus Christ. What Abraham was not obliged to do, God himself did. He sacrificed his Son to take away the sin of unbelief which has infected all humanity. His resurrection on the third day has dispersed the darkness of unbelief. By our faith in the Risen Christ we are brought back into a personal relation with our Creator.

JESUS' CONFIRMATION

"*This is he of whom I said, 'After me comes a man who ranks before me, for he was before me.'" John 1:30*

John is aware of the fact that Jesus is essentially superior to him, because Jesus existed before him. "I myself did not know him," he says. He knew Jesus as his cousin from years gone by, but he did not know that Jesus was God in human form until it was revealed to him. "But for this I came baptizing with water, that he might be revealed to Israel." He realized that his ministry of baptizing with water would draw the Messiah/Saviour into the public eye, as indeed it did.

God had told him that one whom he would baptize would receive the Holy Spirit from heaven. This would signify that one to be the Messiah. He would, indeed, be anointed by God with the Spirit. "And John bore witness, 'I saw the Spirit descend as a dove from heaven, and it remained on him.'" The Holy Spirit came on this occasion in the form of a dove. The dove was used as a sacrificial victim by the poor. It was regarded as a sacred bird in Israel that might not be hunted. It symbolizes divine love and a humble spirit. When you hear the voice of the dove, you may hear it say to its companion and to you, "I love you, you, you." The Heavenly Dove remained on Jesus. It did not depart until that horrible day in which he was nailed to the cross and took the curse of sin upon himself.

"I myself did not know him; but he who sent me to baptize with water said to me, 'He on whom you see the Spirit descend and remain, this is he who baptizes with the Holy Spirit.' And I have seen and have borne witness that this is the Son of God.'" You may believe with John that Jesus is the Son of God, but do you know him as your baptizer in the Holy Spirit? I must confess that I did not know Jesus as my baptizer until I was 39. Then I didn't stop counting birthdays like Jack Benny, because for me life began at 40.

ONE GOD AND ONE BAPTISM

"He who sent me to baptize with water said to me, 'He on whom you see the Spirit descend and remain, this is he who baptizes with the Holy Spirit.'" John 1:34

There is one true and living God, but he is three persons: Father, Son, and Holy Spirit. By the same token there is only one baptism, but there are three expressions of it: water, Spirit, and blood. And these three agree, even as the three Persons of the Godhead do.

Jesus was baptized in water by the hand of John. He thus identified himself with sinful mankind. But Jesus had no sins to confess. In one sense the baptism of Jesus is the beginning of the passion story. By his water baptism he became a public figure with his face toward the cross. Everything he did and said would take him a step closer to Calvary.

Just after his baptism in water, he was baptized in the Holy Spirit by God the Father. He was indued with power from on high. This power would enable him to minister to others with telling results. He did not need to be born of God as we do, since he was conceived by the activity of the Holy Spirit. He had Holy Spirit within him from conception on. But, even so, he did not minister until he was clothed with the person and power of the Holy Spirit. When we are born of the Spirit, we are inclined to begin ministering to others. We would be wise to allow Jesus to baptize us in the Holy Spirit first. Let us seek our own personal Pentecost with the resultant manifestations of the Holy Spirit occurring through us. I Cor. 12:8-10 Only after we are baptized by Jesus in the power of the Holy Spirit will we be prepared for the highest expression of baptism, which is the baptism of blood. Jesus was baptized in his own blood by the hands of sinful men instigated by the devil. We also will discover that our personal Pentecost will come at "plenty of cost." We will find that we are targets in the devil's shooting gallery.

❦

THE DAY OF FAITH

"The next day again John was standing with two of his disciples; and he looked at Jesus as he walked, and said, 'Behold, the Lamb of God!'" John 1:35

We have come now to the second day of the new creation, the day of faith. In this section (35 to 51) we learn what faith means. First we learn that faith comes through hearing the word of God. The two disciples of the Baptist hear his testimony about Jesus being the Lamb of God. John is standing. His ministry is now at a stand-still. He has gone as far as he can go. Jesus is in motion. His ministry is just beginning. He is on his way back to God the Father, and wants to take others with him.

"The two disciples heard him say this." How do we know? "And they followed Jesus." All who have heard in their hearts the testimony of John will also follow Jesus. John was a great teacher, but he could not satisfy the inner yearning of these two disciples. Though they had been baptized by John, they were still unsatisfied. Since he again pointed them to Jesus, they took the hint and followed him.

"Jesus turned, and saw them following, and said to them, `What do you seek?'" The first word of Jesus in this gospel is a question: what is your motive in coming after me? What do you hope to gain? When we express an interest in Jesus, he takes notice of us. He challenges us to examine our hearts as to why we follow after. If we follow for the wrong reason, we will fall away. "And they said to him, `Rabbi' (which means Teacher), `where are you staying?'" They were following Jesus because they wanted to learn from him. The Baptist had taught them all he could; now they want Jesus to be their teacher. Jesus, where do you stay? What is your foundation? "He said to them, `Come and see.'" Here he invited them to become his students with the promise that they will see the Foundation under him, which is none other than the Creator himself.

❦

AN IMPORTANT HOUR

"They came and saw where he was staying; and they stayed with him that day, for it was about the tenth hour." John 1:39

We are not told where they stayed with Jesus that day. Was it at an inn, in the home of a friend, or did they sit under a tree? We are not told, because it is not important where he takes us. The important thing is that we are with Jesus. This is the day of faith. Faith is the head side of the coin. The other side is courtship. Jesus is wooing and winning them into a personal allegiance to himself. When a fellow begins courting a girl and they start dating, it makes no difference whether they go to a movie or to the park. All that matters is that they are together.

Years later, one of the two, John the son of Zebedee, could remember the exact hour when he first stayed with Jesus. It was ten o'clock in the morning. Ten is the number symbolizing divine order. From that hour his life began to be ordered by God. He could see it in retrospect. And that hour came to be the most important hour of his life. Those of us who are married in all likelihood can remember the very hour when we first met the one who became our mate.

"One of the two who heard John speak, and followed him, was Andrew, Simon Peter's brother. He first found his <u>own</u> brother Simon, and said to him, `We have found the Messiah' (which means Christ)." We have underlined "own" because, though it is in the original Greek text, it is omitted in our version. RSV The implication is that while Andrew was testifying to his brother, the other disciple was simultaneously securing his own brother, James. Realise that faith expresses itself in the urge to share our knowledge of Jesus with another, usually with someone close to us. Why is that? Because impression plus expression equals exhilaration. On the contrary, impression without expression leaves depression. And who wants to be depressed? ❧

PETER, PETER, PUMPKIN EATER?

"*He brought him to Jesus.*" *John 1:42*

Notice that Andrew brought his brother to Jesus. He did not send him. Some parents send their children to Jesus and Sunday School. They are giving their children mixed signals. Mommy, Daddy, if Jesus is so wonderful, why don't you want him too? Example is apt to win out over precept. Andrew brought Simon to Jesus because he wanted more of him too. He could never get enough of Jesus. Who can? We start hungering and thirsting for him who is the righteousness of God.

Jesus looked at him, and said, "What a mixed-up, vascillating character you are!" He might have said that, but he didn't. No, instead he said, "So you are Simon the son of John? You shall be called Cephas" (which means Peter). The key to this event is to know that Simon is a Hebrew name which means "he listens." He who listens to Jesus is on his way to becoming Cephas. In the language that Jesus spoke it means a stone. Jesus himself is the Cepha, bedrock. Jesus is the divine mountain come down from heaven. Whoever listens to Jesus and obeys him will be changed little by little from a mixed-up, weak, vascillating character into a stone.

Jesus has the ability to impart his divine nature to anyone who will listen to him and obey him. Obey in the Greek means literally "to hear under." The words of Jesus are heavy words like gold. They are not intended to go in one ear and out the other. Rightly heard they sink down into the innermost recesses of our being where they accomplish a miracle within us. They transform us into new creatures, children of God. Jesus Christ is the stabilizer of this universe. As we let our weight down upon him, we too become stabilizers. By his presence within us, we steady those about us who wobble. Simon became in fact the first living stone to be laid upon the Foundation. Jesus' promise to him was fulfilled in Matthew 16:15-20.

GALILEE, HERE WE COME

"*The next day Jesus decided to go to Galilee.*"   *John 1:43*

What motivated his decision to go to Galilee? He had to attend a wedding at Cana in Galilee three days later. "And he found Philip and said to him, `Follow me,'" Philip, like Jesus' first four followers, had been a disciple of the Baptist. To be invited to follow Jesus was an enormous privilege. When a rabbi told a young man to follow him, it meant that the rabbi would train up the youth to become a highly honored professional like himself. He would pour into his students all that he knew about God. What a thrilling prospect to have Jesus as our Teacher. The implication is that one day we will know God as well as Jesus knows him.

"Now Philip was from Beth-saida, the city of Andrew and Peter." So Jesus' first followers were all from the same town. They had grown up together and were doubtless buddies. Out of this native soil sprang the beginnings of the church. Jesus chose men who had an affinity for one another, a point worth remembering when beginning a congregation.

"Philip found Nathanael, and said to him, `We have found him of whom Moses in the law and also the prophets wrote, Jesus of Nazareth, the son of Joseph.'" We learn in 21:2 that Nathanael was from Cana, where Jesus was heading. A small world. When we look closely, we find that all the pieces fit neatly together. It is evident that Philip does not see what the Baptist saw in Jesus. Philip calls him "the son of Joseph." It is encouraging to know that Jesus is able to use us in his service despite our faulty knowledge of him. We don't have to have perfect theology to be used by God. Only Jesus' theology is perfect. Jesus had found Philip, but Philip says, "We have found him." When the shepherd finds the lost sheep, he hears it say, "I am sure glad I found you." At least Philip was right in his assessment that the Old Testament points to Jesus.

❦

A GIFT OF GOD

"**N** athanael said to him, `Can anything good come out of Nazareth?'"   *John 1:46*

Since Nathanael's hometown of Cana was close to Nazareth, he was inclined to disparage anyone who came from that "God-forsaken place." They were rival towns. Isaiah 53:2 compares Messiah to "a root out of dry ground." Root is pronounced in the Hebrew "nacer," which is why Matthew 2:23 says, "He shall be called a Nazarene." Philip didn't argue. Instead he said to him, "Come and see." Come and see for yourself if he is good for you. Let us not theorize about Jesus. Let us experience him.

"Jesus saw Nathanael coming to him, and said of him, `Behold, an Israelite indeed, in whom is no guile!'" "Nathanael" is a Hebrew name which means "gift of God." So Jesus regards everyone who is brought to him by the leading of the Holy Spirit as God the Father's gift to himself. Needless to say, he is eager to receive us and care for us. Jacob became Israel when he was broken at the Jabbok, having wrestled all the night. By that experience his guile and deceit had been wrested from him. He was no longer "Jacob" (heel-grabber), but "Israel" (a wrestler with God.) Nathanael is one of his spiritual descendants. So are you and I once we have been broken and had our pride dispersed.

"Nathanael said to him, `How do you know me?'" I am to you an open book, though we have never met. "Jesus answered him, `Before Philip called you, when you were under the fig tree, I saw you.'" This display of supernatural knowledge evoked from Nathanael the response, "Rabbi, you are the Son of God! You are the King of Israel!" His faith had transcended the faith of Philip, who had brought him. Evidently Nathanael had been pondering under a fig tree the Baptist's message, and was wondering if it could possibly be so. Jesus had read the thoughts and intentions of his heart before their encounter. He did the same with you and me.

GREATER THINGS THAN THESE

"**Jesus** *answered him, 'Because I said to you, I saw you under the fig tree, do you believe?'" John 1:50*

After Jesus had been baptized in the Holy Spirit, he was the beneficary of spiritual gifts. He had "a word of knowledge" concerning Nathanael. It was supernaturally imparted information. This heavenly display had shocked Nathanael into an affirmation of faith. So Jesus assured him, "You shall see greater things than these."

"And he said to him, `Truly, truly, I say to you (which is plural), you (and your associates) will see heaven opened, and the angels of God ascending and descending upon the Son of Man.'" It is established, it is established (beyond the shadow of a doubt) that you will have the same experience Jacob had that night at Bethel. Genesis 28:10 Remember how he used a stone for a pillow, and dreamed of a ladder reaching to heaven, and how the Lord God made a covenant with him. This same God is going to make a covenant with you in your own hometown, Nathanael.

He will do it at a wedding. On that occasion, you will come to see that I am infinitely greater than you imagine me to be, a far greater King than my ancestor David. You will see that I myself am the ladder let down from heaven, and that angels accompany me. I am the ladder joining heaven and earth. As you establish your life upon me and my faithful dealings with you, you will find me to be an escalator conducting you heavenward. Ultimately you will see heaven, which has been closed to mankind because of sin, opened wide. The angels of God will bear the beloved of my Father into their heavenly habitation. You, Nathanael, and those who share your faith, shall one day experience the glory of God's love. God is love, and you will experience through countless ages his infinite, eternal, and unchangeable love for you. How is that for a bright future?

🍎

THE THIRD DAY

"**O**n the third day, there was a marriage at Cana in Galilee, and the mother of Jesus was there." John 2:1

It was the third day after Jesus told Philip to follow him that this wedding took place. On a deeper level it was the third day of the new creation. The new creation is the Church. Galatians 6:15 Here we have the great love story. It is the story of God's love for this world. Underlying the narrative are seven themes, seven mighty acts.

The first is the day of the ministry of John the Baptist. The ministry of Jesus is rooted in that of John. The second day of this new week of creative activity is the day in which Jesus gathered his first disciples about him. By their faith they became his betrothed, and were engaged to belong to him.

Now on the third day there was a marriage at Cana. The mother of Jesus is never mentioned by name in this gospel because she is a symbolic figure. She symbolizes the chosen people of old. Jesus comes to us as the Son of his mother, not out of the blue. We can understand him only when we see him against the background of the Old Covenant Community of believers, of whom his mother is one. She is their spokesperson. She was present at the wedding because she was a celebrant, probably the mother of the bride. This explains her authoritative role. Had she not been a principle, she would not have been in a position to give orders to the servants. Her husband, Joseph, is dead; so she is a widow. She is now about to claim the blessing in Isaiah 54:4,5: "You will forget the shame of your youth, and the reproach of your widowhood you will remember no more. For your Maker is your husband, the Lord of hosts is his name..." She had endured the shame of being found pregnant before her marriage to Joseph. Who would believe that it was the work of God's Spirit? The Jews maintain to this day that Jesus' father was a Roman soldier.

❦

THE SIMPLEST SOLUTION

"**J**esus also was invited to the marriage, with his disciples."

John 2:2

If Jesus was the brother of the bride, we can understand why he would travel some 80 or 90 miles from the fords of the Jordan, where John was baptizing, to attend the wedding on the third day. It was a long way to go in such a short time. He came with his six disciples, who were tired, hungry and thirsty. They were welcomed to the marriage because they were his companions. He and his disciples were now inseparable. You can't have him and not accept them. They are engaged, and belong together. The fact that his disciples were invited to the marriage at the door when they arrived with Jesus, combined with their excessive thirst, created a problem. "The wine gave out."

The rabbis had a saying, "Without wine there is no joy." The failure of the wine was no small tragedy. It cast a pall upon this most joyous event in their natural life. The bridegroom most especially felt the shame, as it was his responsibility to provide for his own wedding party, and as lavishly as possible. "The mother of Jesus said to him, 'They have no wine.'" She is blaming him. Why did he bring his disciples? Had he dropped them off someplace the problem would have been averted. His brother-in-law, the groom, was not counting on so many. She speaks for the people of the Old Covenant. For them the wine, the joy, was always failing. It happened to Job, who blamed the Lord for his plight, though he refused to curse him for it.

"Son, the only decent thing to do is leave. Get up and go; take your disciples with you. When the other guests see you leave, they will realize it is getting late. They will follow your example and depart also. Then who will know that the wine has failed? By taking my advice, you will save your sister and brother-in-law needless embarrassment on their wedding night. You wouldn't want to do that!"

❦

HIS HOUR OF DEPARTURE

"*And Jesus said to her, 'O woman, what have you to do with me? My hour has not yet come.'" John 2:4*

What hour has not yet come? According to John 13:1, his hour is his hour of departure: "Now before the feast of the Passover, when Jesus knew that his hour had come to depart out of this world to the Father, having loved his own who were in the world, he loved them to the end." He will not leave this world without first doing something to solve its basic problem. It is the problem of sin that has brought upon humanity the curses listed in Deut. 28. Vs. 47, for instance: "Because you did not serve the Lord your God with joyfulness and gladness of heart by reason of the abundance of all things, therefore you shall serve your enemies whom the Lord will send against you, in hunger and thirst, in nakedness and want of all things."

He will not depart without first shedding his precious blood to wash away our sins. So also he will not leave the bridegroom in his perplexity and shame on his wedding night. He has come to save the world from sin. He has come also to restore joy to the wedding that has suddenly experienced a minor calamity. In his dealings with the particular situation, he expresses his loving concern for the totality.

His mother now knows that he is not going to leave. Since he is going to stay, he is evidently going to do something to resolve the situation. So she says to the servants, "Do whatever he tells you." She is speaking now for the entire Old Testament. Its message may be summarized in one brief statement: "Do whatever he tells you." Simple isn't it? Do you want to experience victory in your life? Then do whatever Jesus tells you. He is the power of God released in this universe which can turn tears into shouts of joy, frustration into success. All you need to do is to listen carefully to him, and then do exactly what he says.

❦

SIX STONE JARS

"*Now six stone jars were standing there, for the Jewish rites of purification, each holding twenty or thirty gallons.*" *John 2:6*

The gospel is literally true and also figuratively so. Six is the number for imperfection, for that which is incomplete. He brought six disciples with him to the wedding. Apart from him they were nothing, but with him in their midst they were seven, the number of perfection and heaven. There were also six stone jars standing there. Is it just a matter of chance that there were six disciples and six stone jars? I don't believe that anything in this gospel is just by chance. Quite the contrary, everything is providential, and part of the plan. In the Bible our bodies are likened to vessels that will be filled ultimately with the Spirit of God or the devil. An empty mind and an empty heart are dangerous things. They are the devil's playground.

He had already said that Simon would be called a stone (Peter). Indeed all who persist in hearing and believing the gospel are in the process of becoming living stones. They had already undergone the water treatment (baptism) at the hands of the Baptist. They were about to become vessels fit for the Master's use, as symbolized by the waterpots. Peter and John were 30 gallon vessels; the others were 20 gallon vessels, of lesser capacity.

"Jesus said to the servants, `Fill the jars with water.' So they filled them up to the brim." If I asked you to please fill my glass with water, and you filled it up to the brim, I would say, "Literalist! Now I'm going to spill some on my shirt." But they did exactly what he told them, because his mother had so instructed. As the mother of the bride, she was someone to be taken seriously and heeded. She represents the scriptures, which command us to be filled with the Holy Spirit (Ephesians 5:18), even as Jesus commanded that the jars be filled with water.

HAS GOD EVER SPOKEN TO YOU?

"He said to them, 'Now draw some out, and take it to the steward of the feast.' So they took it." John 2:8

If you want to experience a miracle in your life, listen very carefully to Jesus, and then do whatever he tells you. "They took it." Faith is acting on the word of God. But you must hear his word before you can act upon it.

Rev. Richard Wurmbrand of Rumania tells of tearing pages out of Russian Bibles and giving them to the Russian soldiers during World War II. The next day a soldier came to him and said, "You gave me a page of Jeremiah. Just who is this Jeremiah? He wrote, 'The word of the Lord came to me.' From this I learned that the Lord is a God who speaks. I asked him to speak to me, and he has been speaking ever since.'" Has God ever spoken to you? He speaks in many ways and in many dialects. The simplest way for God to speak is by quickening to us a verse of scripture.

"If you want more of the Holy Spirit, go to where the Holy Spirit is." Acting upon this word I went to a Pastors' Conference where I knew the Holy Spirit would be. As I was driving home, within my heart I heard the Spirit say, "There has been ignited within you a long slow-burning fuse that is going to explode with glory." I wondered what the glory would be. A few minutes later the explosion occurred. The glory turned out to be the Holy Spirit's burning love for Jesus.

A pastor friend had preached six times after graduating from seminary. A parishioner said, "You haven't said anything yet." It really shook him up. He said to his seminary professor, "I would give anything to help people hear from God." "They can if they will watch their dreams." He took a doctorate in dream interpretation. Forty signed up for his first seven week course. When it was over, all forty said that God had spoken to them through their dreams.

IN THE KNOW

"When the steward of the feast tasted the water now become wine, and did not know where it came from (though the servants who had drawn the water knew)." John 2:9

The man in charge of the wedding party did not know the Source of the wine. He was a VIP, a very important person, but Jesus had not spoken to him. Frequently very important persons are not in the know. They do not know as much as the so-called "flunkies" know, because they have not had a personal encounter with the Lord. He had tasted the wine of the Lord's kindness (everyone has), but he did not trace it back to Jesus. How many people have? Comparatively few.

However the servants who had drawn the water knew that the wine had come from Jesus. They had what in the Hebrew is called "yadah," inner knowledge, the knowledge that stems from personal experience. We may say to those who have strange opinions about Jesus, "I would rather have my experience than your opinion." Opinions carry no weight in a court of law. People bear witness to what they have experienced.

When did the water become wine? Did you notice? "The servants who had drawn the water." They had filled the jars with water. What they had drawn out was still water. It became wine as they took it to the steward. "Do whatever he tells you." In the process of doing, the miracle occurs. It doesn't always happen at first blush.

A woman said to her pastor when the worship was over, "I read that passage of scripture just before the service, and I did not see what you brought out." He said to her, "I didn't see it either the first 500 times I read it." That is literally the case in what we have just said about when the water became wine. Peter did not walk upon the water until he had stepped out of the boat in response to the Lord's invitation: Come. Then came the miracle.

❧

THE KING'S WINE

"*The steward of the feast called the bridegroom and said to him, 'Every man serves the good wine first; and when men have drunk freely, then the poor wine; but you have kept the good wine until now.'*" John 2:9,10

Why did the steward congratulate the bridegroom for providing the wine? Because the bridegroom was responsible for the wedding feast. It was his affair. By providing the wine on this occasion, Jesus has become for the initiated the true Bridegroom. He stands silently in the shadows, allowing the young husband from Cana to take the credit for serving the best wine last. How gracious Jesus is. He refuses to steal the show. He lets the young groom enjoy the lime-light. He doesn't make a speech saying "I did that." How humble, how self-effacing he is.

Yes, every <u>man</u> serves the good wine first. Then when the taste buds have been somewhat numbed, man serves up the poorer vintage. But not so God. He saves the best for last.

A taxi driver in Washington, D.C. was asked by a passenger, who was a tourist, the meaning of the inscription on one of our Federal Buildings: "What is past is prologue." He responded, "That means, `You ain't seen nothing yet.'" Praise God, the best is yet to be. We do not know what the immediate future holds, but we do know Jesus who holds the ultimate future. And it is glorious!

The Apostle Paul alludes to this in 2 Cor. 4, where he writes: "We have this treasure (Christ in us) in earthen vessels, to show that the transcendent power belongs to God and not to us. We are afflicted in every way, but not crushed; perplexed, but not driven to despair; persecuted, but not forsaken; struck down, but not destroyed.... Though our outer nature is wasting away, our inner nature is being renewed every day. For this slight momentary affliction is preparing for us an eternal weight of glory beyond all comparison."

❦

THE FIRST OF HIS SIGNS

"This, the first of his signs, Jesus did at Cana in Galilee, and manifested his glory; and his disciples believed in him." John 2:11

The word "first" in the Greek is "arche" (from which we derive our word "arch.") This was not merely the "protos" sign, the first in a sequence of signs; it was the arch sign that holds the building (the gospel) together. It is the beginning, ruling, principle or chief sign. It is the key sign that unlocks the hidden meaning in the signs that follow. All the other signs recorded look back to this one, which manifested his glory, his weightiness. For the first time Jesus had let down his weight. His was a divine heaviness. It was creative.

His disciples had been prepared for this. They had been ministered to by the friend of the bridegroom, or in our terminology, the best man, and collectively had become the bride-to-be. They had believed him to be the Messiah of Jewish expectations. In the previous chapter they had believed about him. But now they believed in him, as the woman believes in the man when she becomes his wife. Now they believed in him with the faith of full surrender. They perceived him now to be essentially different from themselves, mere mortals. There was something of God about him. He is not on the side of creature, but on the side of Creator. This revelation commanded their allegiance. As husband and wife are in the process of becoming "one flesh," Jesus and his disciples were now in the process of becoming "one spirit." "He who is united to the Lord becomes one spirit with him." I Corinthians 1:17

Just now on TV women were telling about their first sexual experience. They didn't seem to realize that by giving themselves to a man they had established with him an indissoluable link. He had solved for them the riddle of their bodily existence, a never to be repeated event.

THE HONEYMOON

"After this he went down to Capernaum, with his mother and his brothers and his disciples; and there they stayed for a few days."

John 2:12

Here we have the Divine/human honeymoon - the vacation following the marriage. Jesus took his "own ones" some twenty miles down the road to a beautiful seaside resort on the north-west shore of Lake Galilee, where they stayed for a few days. However this was a spiritual honeymoon. His disciples were now his bride, his new covenant community. He took his mother and brothers along also. But where were his sisters? Evidently they were now all married and so included in their husbands' families. This brings us to the conclusion that the wedding at Cana was that of his youngest sister. Had it been a brother's wedding it would have taken place at Nazareth.

We have already seen that his mother represents the Old Covenant Community of believers. But what about his brothers? We read in John 7:5, "For even his brothers did not believe in him." Like Jesus they were of the tribe of Judah, but they were unbelieving Jews. But the good news is this: Jesus' kinsmen after the flesh still belong in a special way to Jesus.

In our day there are Jews represented by his mother (Old Covenant believers), whose scriptures tell us to do everything Jesus says to us, though they themselves are not members of his community of love (his church). Most of the Jews in our day are symbolized by his brothers, who simply do not believe in him, nor in their Bible. Nevertheless, in a profound way they are objects of Jesus' love. We New Covenant believers are not true to Jesus if we do not express at every opportunity our love and esteem for the people from whom Jesus sprang. The confessing Church under Hitler opposed the holocaust of the Jews, many by the forfeiture of their lives. Are we expressing our love toward them? The least we can do is pray for the peace of Jerusalem.

❦

TESTIMONY + FAITH = LIFE

"**O**n the third day there was a marriage at Cana in Galilee."
John 2:1

The first day was the day of testimony. The second day was the day of faith. The third day (the day of the marriage) was the day of life. On this occasion Jesus performed his first sign; he turned water into wine. The water of baptism is changed into the wine of holy communion. When we get to heaven and experience the Marriage Supper of the Lamb, we will realize that it was anticipated by the wedding at Cana, which we have experienced in a measure every time we partook of the Lord's Supper.

What kind of life results from faith in the testimony? We see seven characteristics of the life. It is the joyous life as symbolized by the wine (the essential ingredient of the Jewish wedding). It is the life of power, for Jesus displayed his creative power for the first time on this occasion. It is the life of love, for marriage is the love relationship par excellence. It is the meaningful life, for humanly speaking meaning is imparted to our lives through the marriage relationship. We understand why God created us male and female, as he did. It is the abundant life, as expressed by the vast quantity of the best wine they had ever tasted. It is the glorious life, for Jesus manifested his glory for the first time at this wedding. It is also the heavenly life, for according to the Lord's Prayer heaven is where God's will is being done, and at the wedding at Cana in Galilee the divine will was expressed in a crystal clear way.

Jesus' ministry was characterized by children playing wedding. Wherever Jesus went, he brought the joy of the wedding. The ministry of the Baptist, on the other hand, was likened by Jesus to children playing funeral. His message sounded like a funeral dirge. See Matthew 11:16-19. Let us delight in the fact that testimony plus faith equals life.

❦

HOMECOMING

"*Take these things away; you shall not make my Father's house a house of trade.*" *John 2:16*

After the marriage Jesus takes his own ones home with him. He takes them not to Nazareth and the house of Joseph. He takes them to Jerusalem to his heavenly Father's house, where he would abide with them. When he arrives, he rolls up his sleeves and goes to work. He cleans house. "Making a whip of cords, he drove them all, that is to say, the sheep and oxen, out of the temple." (The word "with" in the R.S.V. is not in the Greek text.) This is the way in which John tells us that sinners are welcome in the place of worship. He hates the sin but loves the sinner. After my wife and I were married, we moved into an apartment where two bachelors had lived before us. The place was filthy. Immediatelty we did what Jesus did. We cleaned house.

"Who can endure the day of his coming (to his Father's house) and who can stand when he appears? For he is like a refiner's fire and like fuller's soap." Malachi 3:2. Jesus purifies the dwelling place of God. He comes with his divine detergent (his precious blood and the fire of his Spirit) and does a mighty work within us. You shall be holy, for I am holy, says the Lord. "Beloved, do not be surprised at the fiery ordeal which comes upon you to prove you, as though something strange were happening to you. But rejoice in so far as you share Christ's suffering, that you may also rejoice and be glad when his glory is revealed." I Peter 4:12,13

The first day of the gospel was preparation, as the Baptist prepared the people for the coming of the Lord. The second day was the courtship. On the third day was the marriage. Now on the fourth day we have the day of homecoming, as Jesus takes us to his Father's house, where he would abide with us. Are we following the pattern in our individual lives?

❧

CONSUMED

"**H**is disciples remembered that it was written, 'Zeal for thy house will consume me.'" *John 2:17*

This verse quoted from Psalm 69:9 goes on to say, "And the insults of those who insult thee have fallen on me." They were insulting God and his Son, whom he claimed to be, by calling the temple "my Father's house." They had turned the courtyard of the Gentiles into an oriental market and stockyard. To worship in such a setting would be impossible. By doing this they expressed their contempt for the heathen nations, which God had called their mission field. The purpose of worship is to glorify God. Instead they had perverted worship into a money-making affair. We are somewhat reluctant to bring up what is going on today in the church world. The bingo, the bazaars, the multitude of money raising operations that have proliferated are to be seriously questioned. Later Jesus said, "My house shall be called a house of prayer for all the nations, but you have turned it into a den of robbers." Mark 11:17 Do we draw near to God for what we can get out of it? Or do we approach him that He may get something out of us? He would extract from us our sin, and draw out of us praise for his holy name.

It was his zeal for the pure worship of his Father that would result in his being consumed by death upon the cross. There his body was broken and his blood poured out. Hence he has become our food and drink. We consume him so that he might live his life in and through us.

In cleansing the temple he did something that no prophet or priest (not even John the Baptist, who was a priest) had dared to do. You can't fight city hall, they say. Jesus says, "Oh yes you can, if you are willing to die for your convictions." Let us take note of the fact that Jesus' first and last public deed was the cleansing of the temple. He began and ended his public ministry with a challenge of the authorities.

❧

THE CHALLENGE

"*The Jews then said to him, 'What sign have you to show us for doing this?'" John 2:18*

You are not a priest of the tribe of Levi. You are only a layman of the tribe of Judah. You have no authority in the temple. Give us some sign, some miracle to demonstrate that you have authority here.

Jesus said in effect, "By cleansing the temple and calling it 'my Father's house,' I have come with the claim of divine authority. Meet me at my level. Destroy this temple, and in three days I will raise it up." What an awesome challenge. What a spectacular throwing down of the gauntlet. They said, "It has taken forty-six years to build this temple (and it was not finished yet), and will you raise it up in three days?" They naturally thought he was referring to the building standing there in its magnificence. They did not realize that he spoke of the temple of his body. Had they demolished their building, they would have seen that he could reconstruct it in three days with the assistance of twelve legions of angels.

Without realizing that they were doing so, they did accept his challenge three years later. They destroyed his body upon the cross. He did come alive on the third day, as he had maintained he would, to demonstrate that he does exercize the authority here on earth. He would also have us know that his body is the temple, the place where God dwells here below. When he breathed his last, the Holy Spirit left the temple building on Mount Zion, that he might enter our hearts after Easter, and make us living stones in the new temple of God, his body the Church. We see here an eighth characteristic of the life Jesus brings us: the authoritative life. Hitler claimed that his Third Reich would last for a thousand years. He was wrong, because power without authority quickly wanes. Authority resides ultimately in the Author of the universe, who has shared it with Christians.

❧

SIGN SEEKERS

"*Now when he was in Jerusalam at the Passover feast, many believed in his name when they saw the signs which he did.*"

John 2:23

"Jews demand signs," said Paul. But faith that rests on signs and wonders is not what Jesus is looking for. Such faith is self-centered, saying, "What's in it for me?" Jesus had given the Jews a sign: the cleansing of the temple. What enormous courage he had displayed. It would cost him his life. But it was not the sort of sign they were looking for. The question is, do we have the right to demand what a sign must be, or are we willing to recognize the sign that God gives us? The religion of the Bible is a religion of signs, as everyone who has read it must realize.

Take for instance the birth narrative in Luke 2. The shepherds were told, "This will be a sign for you: you will find a babe wrapped in swaddling cloths and lying in a manger." To everyone but the shepherds it had no significance, but to them it was proof positive that the Baby Jesus was the Savior. They had not even asked for a sign, let alone demanded what it must be. This the devil did though, in the wilderness, when he urged Jesus to do certain miracles.

Doubtless Jesus healed many people and cast out many demons in Jerusalem on this occasion. So many placed their trust in him, and believed him to be the savior of their nation. Jesus, however, did not confide in them, because he could read their motives. He could see into their hearts. Jesus does not need someone to tell him about us. He knows us through and through. This is illustrated in his conversation with Nicodemus which follows. We, though, do need someone to tell us about him, since faith comes through hearing about Jesus, not through seeing signs. We have learned that faith is a two-way street. We trust in Jesus, but he also must confide in us. After the marriage the bride and groom abide together. Next comes the birth of offspring in chapter 3.

❦

A FIVE TALENT MAN

"**N**ow there was a man of the Pharisees, named Nicodemus, a ruler of the Jews." John 3:1

If anyone had everything going for him, it was this five-talent individual. In the first place, he was a man. In that sexist culture every man thanked God daily that he was born a male. Secondly, he was a Pharisee (a separated one, literally). There were never more than 6000 of these individuals, who took it upon themselves to live by the letter of the Law, the strictest sect of Judaism. They were the super-religious. Thirdly, his name was Nicodemus, a Greek name meaning "victor over the people." His family had evidently assimilated the best of the Greek culture. The name had the ring of Rockefeller about it. As the cream of the society, he was bound to rise to the top. Fourthly, he was a ruler of the Jews. He was a ruling elder, one of the seventy members of the Sanhedrin in Jerusalem. In our frame of reference, he would be called a Senator, a man of political prominence. Fifth, he was a Jew (literally a Judean). He was born into the most prominent tribe of Israel, the tribe from which Messiah was to come. "The scepter shall not depart from Judah, nor the ruler's staff from between his feet, until he comes to whom it belongs; and to him shall be the obedience of the peoples." Genesis 49:10

In addition to all this, he had an interest in Jesus. His interest was so great that he came to Jesus by night. He wanted to talk to Jesus privately. He desired to know Jesus personally. He stepped out of the shadows and came to him who is the Light. From this moment on he will never be the same. Goliath fell stunned before David when the stone struck him in the forehead. A greater than David is about to stun Nicodemus with a word of truth. Revelation 2:6,15 speaks of the Nicolaitans, whose works and teaching God hates. The name also means "victor over the people". Can it be a veiled reference to what Nicodemus represents?

A POLITE GENTLEMAN

*"**R**abbi, we know that you are a teacher come from God; for no one can do these signs that you do, unless God is with him."*

John 3:2

Nicodemus is so polite to Jesus, calling him a rabbi, a teacher like himself. He calls Jesus a teacher despite the fact that Jesus was not trained in the schools as he had been. He is accepting Jesus as his equal because of the signs that Jesus did. Of course, any rabbi come from God could pray and see people healed, Nicodemus would say. "A rabbi come from God" was one who came with true doctrine.

"Jesus, you are one of us. I accept you. You are every bit as much a man of God as I myself. I appreciate the courage you displayed in cleansing the temple. But I question the wisdom of it. Our big problem is the Romans. We must rid ourselves of their tyranny over the land. The important thing, therefore, is that we maintain peace between us Jews. United we stand; divided we fall. By coming to you at night, I acknowledge that I have a divided heart. I hold out a hand of peace to you, but I also must hold the hands of the ruling circles of our people. Don't divide our nation. We leaders will play ball with you, if only you will be reasonable with us. The differences between us are not irreconcilable. Let us reason together and come to terms."

The problem is that Nicodemus does not realize that what he said to Jesus was literally true. He does not know that Jesus is not a teacher come from God, but that Jesus is the one and only Teacher come from God. Jesus came from God in what we call "the incarnation." He is the Word become flesh. This stunning truth has not yet dawned upon Nicodemus, but, praise God, it is about to hit him between the eyes.

Recently an elder statesman in our Presbytery said to several of us that a person can be a communist and a Christian. He is attempting to be a super-diplomat like Nicodemus.

DO YOU SEE THE KINGDOM?

"*Jesus answered him, 'Truly, truly, I say to you, unless one is born anew, he cannot see the kingdom of God.'" John 3:3*

Nicodemus, when I cleansed the temple I came with the claim of divine authority. You are trying to sweep my claim under the rug. You cannot do it. You do not realize that my presence here on earth means that history has come into a new phase. It is called the Kingdom of God. Before my ministry began people could call upon God by name, realizing that He knows them by name, as He called young Samuel by name. But now God's reign has come to earth in the person of the King. As God's Son, I have taken up the scepter and begun to rule.

As the result of who I am and what I am doing, individuals are called upon to make a new response. Prior to this time a natural response to God was good enough, but now a supernatural response is required. That response is new birth. When you were born physically, as the product of your parents' love for one another, you became their child. Now you must be born from above, if you would become a child of God. Now, as the product of my advent and ministry, it is possible for you to receive a new nature, the nature of God himself. If you do not receive a new nature, you will never understand what I am talking about. You will never see who I really am. You will not see that God is present with you now in the person of the King.

Nicodemus, your big mistake is to approach me as though you and I were equals. If you could see spiritually, you would realize that we are on different levels. I am on the level of God; you are on the level of man. When it dawns on you to whom you are talking, you will prostrate yourself before me. The dialogue will end and the worship will begin. Nicodemus was in the place where Moses was when he saw the burning bush. He was told to take off his shoes, for he was standing on holy ground.

NICODEMUS' MISTAKE

"*Nicodemus said to him, 'How can a man be born when he is old? Can he enter a second time into his mother's womb and be born?'*"

John 3:4

Jesus, I am trying to understand you, but it is difficult. When you are as old as I am, you will realize how heavy are the words you speak. Now I am wise. I can see the mistakes I have made, the wrong turns I have taken. But I am obliged to carry the weight of who I have become, and what I have done with my life. I have painted myself into a corner. But then don't we all. Sure, it would be nice to begin again with a fresh start. I would do many things differently with the advantage of hind- sight. Would that it were possible to enter a second time into my mother's womb and be born again. Yet life has been so rough that I doubt if I would have the courage to have another go at it. Your riddle is a poor one. Just thinking about it makes me all the more melancholy.

Nicodemus' mistake is that he is looking at the requirement of new birth from a totally human perspective. He has forgotten that he was passive in his natural birth. He didn't say to himself, "Now I have got to get out of here." It was something that happened to him. When the time was ripe and he was ready, the contractions started, and he was on his way. He was just along for the ride. So it is with our spiritual birth. It is not something that we do. It is something that God does for us, if we will allow him. The good news is that the kingdom of God has come. Another way of saying it is: God is at work, doing something new. What is new is Jesus. Jesus has come. He is the creative Word. Listen to him very carefully. Then do what he tells you. He will turn the water of your natural life into the wine of that which is altogether new. This is God's doing, and it is marvelous in our eyes.

TWO PREREQUISITES

"Jesus answered, 'Truly, truly, I say to you, unless one is born of water and the Spirit, he cannot enter the kingdom of God.'"

John 3:5

Nicodemus, unless you are born anew you will not even see the kingdom of God. You will not even get a clear idea of what the kingdom is. But it is one thing to see the kingdom, to recognize it. It is an altogether different thing to enter it, to participate in it. Everyone in our society has seen airplanes passing over head. Not everyone, though, has entered into one and flown in one.

There are two prerequisites to enter the kingdom. The first is the requirement of being born of water. You heard the Baptist preach, saying, "Repent and be baptized," but you refused. Remember how the Baptist excoriated you Pharisees, calling you a brood of vipers. He warned you to flee from the wrath to come. He refused to baptize you because you were trusting in your physical ancestry, connecting you with Abraham. Repent means "change." The change that is called for is so radical that it really means change from one creature into another. Become a new creation. Water baptism is God's way of offering you cleansing and the assurance of pardon. By it He cleanses you. Rejecting water baptism, you rejected God's plan for your life. The water cleanses you from past defilement, looking backward.

The second requirement is future oriented. It is being born of the Spirit. The Spirit takes you into the new life that God is offering. The Holy Spirit empowers you to resist your sinful urges. Sin defiles and ensnares. By the instrumentality of water God pardons your sin. By the instrumentality of the Spirit he gives you power over sin. You need both pardon and power, cleansing and deliverance. The coming of the kingdom means that God is now prepared to meet your deepest needs. The provision has been made. The only question is: are you willing to receive what God is offering?

LIKE GIVES BIRTH TO LIKE

*"**T**hat which is born of the flesh is flesh, and that which is born of the Spirit is spirit."*   *John 3:6*

Like gives birth to like. All flesh is born out of the horizontal. Only the Holy Spirit gives birth out of the vertical, out of God. "Do not marvel that I said to you, 'You must be born anew.'" Then Jesus compares the activity of the Holy Spirit with the wind. Both are invisible, and beyond human control. Both produce sound. The Spirit speaks intelligibly through the words and deeds of Jesus, and through our inner impressions and dreams. Our second birth comes about not through our own effort, but through the activity of the Holy Spirit, who enables the seeds sown by the living Word to germinate and flourish within us.

Nicodemus said to him, "How can this be?" The former know-it-all is now reduced to the level of a child, and this is progress. Jesus began by telling him the basic facts. He now knows them, though he cannot understand them. He wants to understand the process whereby the Spirit produces new life.

Jesus answered him, "Are you <u>the</u> teacher (literally) of Israel, and yet you do not understand this?" How can you call yourself a teacher of God's people when you do not comprehend even the A.B.C's of entering the Kingdom? Jesus compared entrance into the Kingdom with entrance into this world. We pass through the water of the placenta into the air of earth, through the water of baptism into the realm of the Spirit, that we may inhale the breath of God. The passage through the birth canal is arduous. So do we enter the Kingdom of God violently. Luke 16:16. The Kingdom is for the desperate. We must passionately desire God to take control over our lives even if it kills us. And, of course, it will. Entrance into the Kingdom is a death blow to our egocentricity.

❧

NICODEMUS' PROBLEM

"Truly, truly, I say to you, we speak of what we know, and bear witness to what we have seen, but you do not receive our testimony." John 3:11

The "we" of whom Jesus is speaking was in the original setting John the Baptist as well as Jesus. Subsequently it came to refer to all who have been born into the Kingdom of God.

Your problem, Nicodemus, is that you do not take seriously what John the Baptist and I are telling you. You and those who are like you think that you must understand something before you can accept it. "If I have told you earthly things and you do not believe, how can you believe if I tell you heavenly things?" Spiritual birth is comparable to natural birth in some respects. If you do not believe truths wrapped in the garments of natural experience, how can you believe truths that have no earthly counterpart? There is only One who can tell you heavenly things. That is the One whose origin is God and whose destination is God, Jesus, the Son of Man, who is in heaven even as he talks to you now. Heaven is more than a place; it is a condition. It is the condition of being in the center of the Father's will, as Jesus always was and is. Jesus takes the atmosphere of heaven with him wherever he goes. Only Jesus can tell you about God, who He is, what He is like, how He thinks and plans and purposes. No one has gone to heaven and come back with information from God. There is One, however, who was at home in the Father's bosom before creation. He can tell you all about God. But you must take his word for it.

Nicodemus was in a sense a twentieth century man before his time. He had a scientific mind. He wanted to understand how things work. If he could not understand the how of things, he had difficulty accepting them. I am thankful that I can throw on the light switch without having a degree in electrical engineering. We have learned to accept certain things by faith.

SNAKE BIT

"*And as Moses lifted up the serpent in the wilderness, so must the Son of man be lifted up, that whoever believes in him may have eternal life." John 3:14,15*

Jesus explains how it is possible to be born into the Kingdom of God by calling our attention to the key passage in the Old Testament. It is the story in Numbers 21:4-9, which tells how the people spoke against God and against Moses for bringing them into the wilderness to die. They were sick to death of the manna, which they called this worthless food. So the Lord punished them by sending a plague of poisonous snakes. Then they asked Moses to pray for them, confessing their sins. The Lord told Moses to make a serpent out of bronze and set it on a pole, that all who were bitten might look up and live. The bronze serpent on the pole was the divine antidote for snake bite. Those who looked lived. Those who refused to do so obviously died.

Jesus lifted up on the cross is the cure for all who realize they have within them the serpent's venom. The devil has pumped his evil nature into us. We are a fallen mankind. But Jesus, the innocent Lamb of God, became sin when he died the death of the damned: hanging on a tree. "A hanged man is cursed by God." Deuteronomy 21:23. As we look to Jesus, having been crucified for us and in our place, a miracle takes place. It is the miracle of new birth. We hear him say, "Father, forgive them, for they know not what they do." We have been forgiven unconditionally by Jesus and by our loving heavenly Father.

Jesus writhed like a serpent nailed to a pole. He became sin upon the cross, that we through faith in him might become the righteousness of God. II Corinthians 5:21. Believe the good news, and you are at peace with God. Looking back, you will find that the Holy Spirit has taken up his residence in your body, now a temple of God.

❧

THE "WHY" OF NEW BIRTH

*"**F**or God so loved the world that he gave his only Son, that whoever believes in him should not perish but have eternal life."*

John 3:16

Nicodemus asked, "How can this be?" How is it possible for an old man to be born again? The how of it Jesus explained in the passage about the serpent lifted up. Jesus, lifted up on the cross, will eventually draw all flesh to himself. He is the reconciling center of the universe, the only mediator between God and man. Now Jesus wants Nicodemus to know something more profound than how it can be. He wants him to know why it is possible for a human being to be born into God's Kingdom. The why of it is the love of God. God loves sinful mankind so much that he gave his only son, Jesus, to die as the substitute and sacrifice for us all. A sacrifice is that which makes sacred. God has made us holy in his sight by our faith in the sacrificial blood of the Lamb of God.

To be born of God is to believe in His son. God's love is for everyone, but only those who believe in His love are benefited by it. Can you believe that God loves you so much that he sent Jesus to die on the cross just for you? Can you believe that Jesus shed one such precious drop of blood just for you? An English chaplain was quoting John 3:16 to a condemned murderer as he was being marched to the place of execution. Suddenly the condemned man said to the chaplain, "Do you believe that? Do you believe that? Why if I believed that, I would crawl on broken glass over the whole of England telling people it was so."

The entire gospel is compressed into this one verse. It says it all, so simply that a little child can understand. Carol King said that she responded to the gospel preached by her father when she was four years old, and experienced new birth. The man who became her husband was also converted by her father. Rick too is now a minister. Exciting isn't it!

STEPPING STONES

*"**F**or God sent the Son into the world, not to condemn the world, but that the world might be saved through him." John 3:17*

Nicodemus had it all wrong. The Jews believed that the Savior (Messiah) would come to rescue them and destroy their heathen enemies. Here we learn that God sent his Son to rescue for God all nations. The Jewish nation was to be a stepping stone for God's love, that through it all the world might experience his embrace. Tragically they said no to this high calling. They wanted to keep God's love to themselves. They thought that their deliverer would come like another David and drive the hated Romans into the sea. We followers of Jesus must remember that we are obligated to share the good news with the whole human race. Otherwise we make the same mistake the Jewish nation did.

"He who believes in him is not condemned." On the contrary, he who believes in Jesus has been acquitted from the cross. "He who does not believe is condemned already, because he has not believed in the name of the only Son of God." Remember the meaning of his name? Jesus means "I am who I am, saves." It is the nature of the Eternal One to rescue us. Everyone who calls upon him will be saved. Think of the criminal crucified with him, who came to his senses. He acknowledged his guilt and Jesus' innocence, and asked Jesus to remember him when he came into his kingdom. Jesus assured him, "Today you will be with me in paradise." Turning to Christ crucified, he had turned to God come down from the highest heaven to save. Jesus' arms stretched out upon the cross here became the arms of God reaching to embrace the universe. The darkness through which we pass is but the shadow of his arms outstretched in love. The other day I talked to a man who came to the Lord in one of our meetings 14 years ago. It was decisive in his life, and he heard heavenly music that no one else could hear.

❦

THIS IS THE JUDGMENT

"*And this is the judgment that the light has come into the world and men loved darkness rather than light, because their deeds were evil.*" *John 3:19*

Jesus came to save us from our sins. That was his purpose. But we cannot stay neutral in his presence. If we will not love him, we will hate him. We will hate him because he is light, and light exposes. Evil deeds in his presence are revealed to be exceedingly evil. Those engaging in evil do so under the cover of darkness. "For every one who does evil hates the light, and does not come to the light, lest his deeds should be exposed." The basic question is what do you love, and what do you hate? Belief and unbelief are rooted in emotions. There is the logic of emotions that runs deeper than intellectual logic. Faith is a matter of the heart, not the head.

"But he who does what is true comes to the light, that it may be clearly seen that his deeds have been wrought in God." The truth is something you do, not something you merely believe. You express your belief by your life. Those who do what they know to be right, who live up to the highest that they know, will receive more truth. They will come to Christ, who is the truth, when they learn of him. By coming to him they declare that they have been following him all along.

A missionary to China was the first one to preach the gospel in that village. He said that after his first message the midwife in that community said, "Somehow I knew that God must be just like this Jesus you are telling us about." She knew the King and was part of his kingdom before she heard his name. She had been expressing her faith in him for many years by her selfless service to others. Without realizing it, she was serving him in her practical helpfulness toward those in need. "Inasmuch as you have done it to the least of these, my brethren, you have done it to me."

❧

THE FRIEND OF THE BRIDEGROOM

"He who has the bride is the bridegroom; the friend of the bridegroom, who stands and hears him, rejoices greatly at the bridegroom's voice." John 3:29

We hear again in this section the testimony of the Baptist. It amplifies and confirms what we have learned before. His disciples are jealous of the growing popularity of Jesus, whom they regard as John's rival. He allays their anxiety by reminding them that he is only Jesus' forerunner. Jesus' greater success is from God. He then underscores our understanding of the wedding at Cana. Sure enough, Jesus is the groom, and his disciples are his bride. John then identifies himself as the friend of the bridegroom.

When I was wed, my best man, also named John, saw to it that I was ready for the marriage, with ring and marriage licence in hand. He got me to the church on time. In the Hebrew culture, however, the best man had a different role. It was his responsibility to see to it that the bride was ready for the marriage. He was the groom's agent in his dealings with the bride prior to the marriage. And (get this) just before the marriage the bride-to-be underwent a baptism (an immersion) to purify her for the marriage relationship. It is called a mikva in Hebrew.

In light of this it is beautiful to see that the ministry of the Baptist was God's way of preparing a people to be the chosen bride of his only begotten Son. They were called to put off the filthy garments of their own righteousness, that cleansed by the washing of water (baptism) with the word, they might be presented to Jesus their groom in splendor, without spot or wrinkle or any such thing, that they might be holy and without blemish. See Ephesians 5:27. This throws a brilliant light upon the significance of our water-baptism, does it not? It also reveals how essential it is to approach the gospel from the perspective of the Old Testament people. 🌱

THE TESTIMONY OF THE TWO JOHNS

"**H**e *who comes from above is above all; he who is of the earth belongs to the earth, and of the earth he speaks.*   *John 3:31*

In verses 27 to 30 we heard the Baptist's testimony about Jesus: that Jesus must increase, but that the Baptist must decrease. May this be true in the lives of us all. In what follows (31- 36), we hear John the Son of Zebedee amplify what the Baptist said.

In a strange way our evangelist identifies his ministry with that of the Baptist. They enjoy the same first name (God is gracious). The son of Zebedee hides in the shadow of the Baptist. In a self-effacing way, he never draws attention to himself. He is aware, as was the Baptist, of the infinite greatness of Jesus, whose origin is God in heaven. He is astonished "that no one receives his testimony." But then how can we mere mortals with our puny understanding comprehend the thoughts of God? Only by the spontaneous open-mindedness that the Holy Spirit gives may we receive the truth about Jesus. The Father loves him so much that he has put everything in the universe under his jurisdiction. Yet such is the greatness of the human soul, that each individual decides for him or her self whether or not to receive Jesus as Saviour and obey him as Lord. Failure to obey means continuing to be blind to the meaning of life. It also means existing under the wrath of God. There is no life under wrath. There is only existence unto death. But the sad thing is that death is not the end; it is the prelude to judgment. Hebrews 10:27 says, "It is appointed for men to die once, and after that comes judgment."

Daniel Webster said that the greatest thought that ever occupied his mind was that of his accountability to Almighty God. Jesus said that we shall give account for every idle word that we utter. It is terrifying to consider this, living as we do in a generation characterized by a toilet mouth and a cesspool heart.   ❧

THE STAGE IS SET

"*Now when the Lord knew that the Pharisees had heard that Jesus was making and baptizing more disciples than John.*"

John 4:1

Jesus and John carried on simultaneous ministries about sixty miles apart. Jesus had his disciples baptize converts in his name, as John baptized at the behest of the Father. Jesus himself baptized no one in water; he baptizes us in the Holy Spirit, of which water is a symbol. If the Pharisees hated John's ministry, they hated that of Jesus even more, because he had become more popular than John. So as to prevent a premature collision with the Pharisees, Jesus left Judea and departed again to Galilee. He abandoned Judea because the authorities there had bristled at his claims.

He had to pass through Samaria (though normally Jewish pilgrims steered east of the Jordan River out of their disdain for the Samaritans), because he had an appointment with a woman at a well. There was a divine necessity behind his every course of action. He always took his directions from his Father. We are privileged to do the same.

So he came to a city of Samaria called Sychar ("place of a drunkard" in Hebrew) near the field that Jacob gave to his son Joseph. It is 39 miles north of Jerusalem. Jacob's well was there, and so Jesus, wearied as he was with his journey, sat down beside the well. It was about six o'clock in the evening. It had been a long day. No doubt Jesus had been teaching his disciples as they walked. Teaching was work. The word "wearied" also means "labor." There came a woman of Samaria to draw water. She came from the city about a mile to the north. After she had drawn her water from this 120 foot deep well (no small task in itself), Jesus said to her, "Give me a drink." For his disciples had gone away into the city to buy food. Had they been there he would have asked them. The stage is now set for one of the most amazing conversations ever recorded.

❧

PROPRIETY, BE HANGED

"The Samaritan woman said to him, 'How is it that you, a Jew, asked a drink of me, a woman of Samaria?'" For Jews have no dealings with Samaritans."   John 4:9

The woman did not take kindly to his request. In the first place, Judaism forbade a man to speak even to his wife in a public place like a well. A rabbi would lose his reputation for doing what Jesus had just done. We see here that Jesus refused to allow custom to hinder his personal concern for individuals. God's love for people is more important than the decrees of propriety. Furthermore Jews hated Samaritans as much as Christians hate Moslems. The Samaritans were heretics. They accepted as scripture only the five books of Moses and even twisted them. The Jews could have business dealings with the Samaritans, but no social contact. The disciples would buy eggs and fruit in Sychar, but unless Jesus allowed it, they would not eat their bread. It was regarded as unclean. The woman was astonished that Jesus would even drink from her vessel.

Jesus answered her, "If you knew the gift of God, and who it is that is saying to you, 'Give me a drink,' you would have asked him and he would have given you living water." The word gift here is "dorea." Only here in the gospels is the word used. In the book of Acts it refers to the gift of the Holy Spirit. It has reference to an enormously significant gift. "God so loved the world that he gave his only begotten Son." This love embraces women as well as men. It includes an influential man named Nicodemus and an anonymous half-breed woman.

Shortly we will see the shoe on the other foot. The woman will ask Jesus for a drink. Though she refuses him, he will not spurn her request. He is infinitely more generous than we. Eventually upon the cross he will say, "I thirst." He who as "the divine drinking fountain" bestows the water of life, must settle for vinegar to moisten his lips.

❧

PUT UP OR SHUT UP

"The woman answered him, 'Sir, you have nothing to draw with, and the well is deep; where do you get that living water?'"

John 4:11

With his second remark Jesus at least got her attention. She begins to show him a little respect, addressing him as "Sir." Now she is puzzled. He has no bucket with which to bring up the water, so where can he possibly secure it? Perhaps by "living water" he means spring water lying near the surface. But that cannot be, else why would Jacob have dug so deep for water. "Are you greater than our father Jacob, who gave us the well, and drank from it himself, and his sons and his cattle?" She doesn't realize that Someone greater than Jacob sits beside her.

Jesus said to her, "Everyone who drinks of this water will thirst again, but whoever drinks of the water that I shall give him will never thirst; the water that I shall give him will become in him a spring of water welling up to eternal life." One thing about water, we never get enough of it. We drink only to thirst again. Jesus has her completely baffled. She hasn't the foggiest notion what he is talking about. But she is from Missouri, the "show me" state. It is time to put up or shut up. "Sir," she says, "give me this water, that I may not thirst, nor come here to draw."

It certainly would be advantageous to have a spring of water flowing within one: never to thirst again, never to walk a mile just to get a drink. The fact of the matter is, we have the well of salvation within us. It is our inner man, our spirit. It was dug out by God when He fashioned us after his image. When we were born of the Spirit, our well began to flow. To draw to the surface this water of life, all we need to do is listen to Numbers 21:17: "Then Israel sang this song: 'Spring up, O well! Sing to it!'" Sing to your inner well. Sing songs of praise. Worship God, and the Holy Spirit within you believers will spring up! The joy of the Lord will be your strength.

❦

THE SEVENTH MAN

"**J**esus said to her, `Go, call your husband, and come here.`"

John 4:16

Jesus is proffering her a sip of living water. As the Great Physician, he is deftly reaching out to make contact with the sickness in her life. It must be brought to the surface. "The woman answered him,`I have no husband.`" Jesus might have responded, "You are a damned liar." (People who persist in lying are damned, you know.) Instead Jesus said to her, "You are right in saying `I have no husband`; for you have had five husbands, and he whom you now have is not your husband; this you said truly." Here Jesus was as gentle as a dove, but as wise as a serpent. He did not hit her over the head with the truth. He found a little corner of truth in her statement and built on that. We would do well to follow his example in our outreach. Congratulate others for the truth they possess, and afterward point out the shortcomings. Technically speaking, she told the truth when she said, "I do not have a husband." She was now living with a man to whom she was not married. He dealt with her sin so graciously that she hardly winced. He was so tender in touching the sore area in her life that she must have realized he accepted her just as she was in spite of herself.

A woman who has had five husbands could hardly have been the ugliest gal on the block. Quite possibly she was "a knock out," stunning! I believe that she was incapable of producing a son and heir. This would account for her many divorces. These repeated rejections took such a toll that finally she gave up on marriage altogether, and just started "living in."

Symbolically the five husbands could represent our five senses. They somehow never satisfy. So now she is exploring her sixth sense. This exploration runs the risk of getting us into the occult, unless we receive direction from the seventh man in her life: Jesus Christ, the man from heaven.

❦

MORE THAN A PROPHET

"The woman said to him, `Sir, I perceive that you are a prophet.'"

John 4:19

In other words, she said, "You have got my number. My life is to you an open book." Religion in Samaria had fallen so low that to her a prophet meant a fortune teller. Though she was kind in her response to Jesus, she had said the worst possible thing. In her darkened state she connected fortune telling with religion. Jesus had touched upon her moral problem. Perhaps he could shed some light upon her religious problem. "Our fathers worshiped on this mountain (they were standing at the foot of Mount Gerezim) and you say that Jerusalem is the place where men ought to worship." We would say that she didn't know what church to go to. Who's right? The Catholics? The Protestants? Who?

"Jesus said to her, `Woman, believe me, the hour is coming when neither on this mountain nor in Jerusalem will you worship the Father.'" It is not a matter of where you worship, but whom. The object of worship is the most important aspect of worship. Worship that is for real must be directed to the Father. Here we move into the deepest secret of the Bible. God is by nature Father because he is also Son. From before the creation of the universe God had engendered out of himself his only begotten Son. His Son, who is Jesus, is the only adequate expression of himself. To know God as he really is, to know him personally, intimately, one is obliged to receive the revelation that is given through Jesus Christ.

She had experienced through Jesus the divine love, which is understanding plus acceptance. Though he knew about her sinful life, he had accepted her even so. God does not play favorites. He has the same attitude of unconquerable benevolence toward you.

❦

THE SYMBOL FOR GOD

"You worship what you do not know; we worship what we know, for salvation is from the Jews." John 4:22

Samaritan worship is ignorant worship. A man when asked what came to mind when he thought of God, said: "an ill-defined, oblong-shaped blur." That is about as clear as God can be outside of the religion of the Jews. Salvation (restoration to God) is from the Jews. God is found in the ways taught in the Jewish scriptures. Jesus is the Saviour of the world because he fulfills what is written in the Old Testament, all 39 books, from Genesis to Malachi. The Bible is the record of a divinely guided history. It is called holy history, and it culminates in the coming of Jesus Christ.

"But the hour is coming, and now is, when the true worshipers will worship the Father in spirit and truth, for such the Father seeks to worship him." Holy history is the story of God the Father's quest for lost and fallen mankind. The goal of the quest is that we may worship aright. This involves two things. First, that we worship (kneel before) God not merely with our bodies and our minds, but also with our spirits, illuminated by the Holy Spirit. Second, that we worship in truth. To do so we must worship not the figment of our imagination, but God as he really is. God has come into focus for us only through the person and ministry of Jesus Christ.

Every religion has a symbol for God. He is symbolized in Buddhism by the "enlightenment" of its founder, who said, "In reality there is nothing." In Judaism he is represented by the divine mandate expressed in the Law. In Islam he expressed himself by "his prophet" Mohammed, who as one report has it, died while stuffing himself on roast pork (forbidden in the law). In Christianity God is symbolized by Jesus, who died praying, "Father, forgive them; for they know not what they do." You decide which symbol expresses the true nature of God.

❧

TRUE WORSHIP

"*God is spirit, and those who worship him must worship in spirit and truth.*" *John 4:24*

God as spirit is "the Father of spirits" we read in Hebrews 12:9. In Genesis 2:7 we have the story of God fathering the first human being, who was spirit, soul, and body. Like God man is also a spirit. He has a soul (mind, will and emotion). And he lives in a body. "The spirit of man is the candle of the Lord searching all the innermost parts." Proverbs 20:27. In this illustration, man's spirit is the candle and God's Spirit is the flame. When Adam disobeyed God his candle went out, as the Holy Spirit left him. Ever since human beings have been born in the dark concerning God. The Holy Spirit is not by nature within us.

Jesus said to his disciples at the Last Supper that "he (the Spirit of truth) dwells with you, and will be in you." John 14:17. The Spirit of truth was with them, because he was within and upon Jesus. After the resurrection on Easter evening, Jesus breathed on his disciples, and said to them, "Receive the Holy Spirit." John 20:22. Immediately their candles were lit, as the Holy Spirit entered into them. They were born of the Spirit. No longer were they natural men but supernatural. Now it was possible for them to worship "in spirit and truth."

Have you received the Holy Spirit from the risen Christ? You must believe that he was put to death for your sins and raised for your justification (that your life might be rendered meaningful). Now confess your sins; name them one by one. Say, "I hate them with perfect hatred, and turn my back upon them." Now accept by faith his forgiveness. Then ask him to breathe his Holy Spirit into you, saying, "I present myself and my members to you, Lord Jesus, as instruments of your saving activity. From now on I will seize every opportunity to bear witness to you and your love. Amen." In this setting, "amen" means "it is done."

❦

MESSIAH IS HERE

"The woman said to him, 'I know that Messiah is coming (he who is called Christ); when he comes, he will show us all things.'"

John 4:25

Balaam the prophet said, "I see him, but not now; I behold him, but not nigh: a star shall come forth out of Jacob, and a scepter shall rise out of Israel; it shall crush the forehead of Moab (the enemy of Israel.)" Numbers 24:17. This star, this scepter was the Messiah, the long awaited Deliverer and Saviour. The woman knew he was coming because it was revealed in the writings of Moses, the only scripture Samaritans accepted. Jesus had shown her many things. Messiah will show us all things.

"Jesus said to her, 'I who speak to you am he.'" I am the Saviour of mankind, and the revealer of God. Actually he made to her even a greater claim: "I who speak to you, I Am," is what he literally said. He who was speaking to her was the very one who spoke to Moses out of the burning bush, when Moses asked what his name was. "I AM WHO I AM," God answered. Exodus 3:14. Jesus was and is the Eternal One, Jehovah, Yahweh (in Hebrew). Jesus is the Eternal Word of God, whose very nature it is to speak to us. The God who created this universe is a God who speaks. He is still speaking to the present hour. How does he speak? Through His Eternal Word who became man, Jesus, the Anointed (Messiah or Christ). By a multitude of media God is communicating with us today: through the orderliness of the universe, the Bible, Christian literature, dreams, visions, prophecy, conscience, speaking in tongues and interpretation, a still small voice, an actual voice, angels, circumstances, impressions, intuitions, through friends and enemies. He who has ears to hear, let him hear.

We are living in a day when the so called New Age Movement is proliferating. Through "channeling" these people believe they are hearing from God. The god they are hearing from is the god of this world, the Devil.

A WOMAN ON FIRE

"**J**ust then his disciples came. They marveled that he was talking with a woman." John 4:27

The rabbis in those days did not talk to women. "Rather burn the words of the Law than teach them to a woman," they said. "But none said, `What do you wish?' or `Why are you talking with her?'" They knew that Jesus would explain in his own good time why he had talked with her. He did not live in an ivory tower. Eventually he makes everything clear to those who follow him. If we continue in his words, we will find that gradually he will make everything plain to us as well.

"So the woman left her water jar, and went away into the city." Her water jar was her most valuable possession. She could not survive without it. Even so, she left it behind for two reasons. In the first place, she planned to return. And in the second, she had already gotten her drink. She drank spiritual water, as she received from Jesus the revelation of the heavenly Father's seeking love for her. We drink as we hear the good news. It was too good to keep to herself. She was obliged to share it with others. "She said to the people, `Come, see a man who told me all that I ever did. Can this be the Christ?'" His supernatural knowledge of her combined with his kindly acceptance of her had set her feet a running. He had conquered her built-in reluctance to talk about her past, and given her a convincing testimony. Those who have encountered the living Christ inevitably spill out the good news. There is no way that they can keep it to themselves.

"They went out of the city and were coming to him." The city stands for tradition and prejudice, both of which we must leave behind if we would come to Jesus. Having come to him, though, we discover that he will go with us back into the city, that together, little by little, we may transform it into a habitation of God. Jesus plus one is always a majority.

❧

TIME TO EAT

"*Meanwhile the disciples besought him, saying, 'Rabbi, eat.'*"

John 4:31

You sent us to buy food. We have done as you said, and brought it, and you don't eat. We can't eat either until you offer the blessing. "But he said to them, `I have food to eat of which you do not know.'" We have learned about drinking the water of life; now we shall learn about eating the bread of life.

"So the disciples said to one another, `Has anyone brought him food?'" Perhaps the woman slipped him a lamb sandwich. (It wouldn't be ham, you know.) "Jesus said to them, `My food is to do the will of him who sent me, and to accomplish his work.'" It was the Father's will that his Son reveal the Father's love to the world. God's work of redeeming love would require Jesus to go to the cross, where he would die shouting, "It is accomplished!" He became sin upon the cross, that in his death sin would die. It's power over the race would be ended. As the woman heard the good news, she drank. As Jesus told the good news, he ate. We drink as we listen to the good news of the gospel, and worship in spirit and truth. Then we go out and bear witness to the One through whom we worship, and in so doing we eat.

"Do you not say, `There are yet four months, then comes the harvest?' I tell you, lift up your eyes, and see how the fields are already white for harvest." Coming across the fields, clothed in white, were the citizens of Sychar, eager to see Jesus for themselves. In giving them her simple testimony, the woman had sown the seed, and already the harvest is at hand. Natural agriculture requires several months between seed-time and harvest, but not so in Kingdom farming. The Lord is able to do a quick work upon earth. Let the wise take note: "He will vindicate his elect speedily" at the end of the age. Luke 18:8 We are in the position to hasten the coming of that day as we eat and drink, that we may grow thereby.

SCATTERING AND GATHERING

"*He who reaps receives wages, and gathers fruit for eternal life, so that sower and reaper may rejoice together."*   *John 4:36*

In those days it was customary for the farm hand to receive a share of the crop as his wage. His work provided his food. It should not surprise us, therefore, that as we work for the Lord, bearing witness to him, we find ourselves eating. One is never hungry immediately after teaching or proclaiming the gospel. A supernatural energy or fire is imparted in sharing the good news.

Not only does a worker for Jesus eat heavenly bread as he bears witness, but also he gathers fruit for eternal life, as people put their trust in Jesus. They are gathered into the granery of God, which means that they go immediately to heaven when they die. The teaching of purgatory is an invention of the midieval Church which had lost sight of the gospel of grace. Those who sow the seed of God's word (as Jesus had just done in the heart of the woman), and those who reap (as the disciples are about to do) may rejoice together. In Kingdom activity sowers and reapers tread on each other's heels.

"For here the saying holds true, `One sows and another reaps.'" It is comforting to know that we don't have to do it all. Jesus sowed the seed in the woman's heart. She in turn sowed her testimony into the hearts of her neighbors in Sychar. Now the disciples would have the joy of sharing their experiences of Jesus with the Samaritans, who are already ripe for committing themselves to Jesus also. Let us be like Johnny Appleseed who broadcast seeds far and wide. He didn't see the trees he planted, nor did he eat of their fruit, but he became renown throughout the land. Some enjoy the Christian tract ministry, others the placing of Gideon bibles. These are valid ministries. "I planted, Apollos watered, but God gave the growth," wrote Paul. I Cor. 3:6

OTHERS HAVE LABORED

"I *sent you to reap that for which you did not labor; others have labored, and you have entered into their labor."*   *John 4:38*

The pioneers had to clear out the forests, uproot the stumps, roll out the stones. Theirs was a back-breaking work, but they did not reap the great harvests that their descendants did. Missionaries have ventured into foreign fields where they have expended blood, sweat and tears with precious little results, but their labors were not in vain. Their successors are the beneficiaries of their labors. The first missionary to Southern Rhodesia (now Zimbabwe) was martyred. A generation later another missionary came to the same district. His first convert was the son of the chief, who as a child had witnessed the martyrdom. He had always wondered why the white man had come to his tribe only to forfeit his life for his trouble. The blood of the martyr turned out to be the seed of the church.

Adoniram Judson became the first missionary to Burma in 1814. Someone wrote him, "Adoniram, how is it going?" He wrote back, "I have labored diligently now for seven years without a single convert, but the prospects are as bright as the promises of God." That's the ticket. We are not held accountable for the success of our efforts. We are to be measured for our faithfulness. "It is required of stewards that they be found faithful." I Cor. 4:2.

The first church I served was Pierce Memorial Presbyterian Church in Farmingdale, N.J. Pastor Pierce, the first minister, had been a missionary to Africa, where his wife and child died of African fever, and his health failed. In 1870 he organized the church. When he died in 1892 he left his estate of $200,000 to Howard University in Washington D.C. for the purpose of training black students to go to Africa as missionaries. Remember Winston Churchill's ten word address: Never give up. Never give up. Never. Never. Never. Never.

MANY BELIEVED, BUT NOT ALL

"*Many Samaritans from that city believed in him because of the woman's testimony, 'He told me all that I ever did.'*" *John 4:39*

The Samaritans were heretics hungering and thirsting for God. They were so dry that a little spark from the woman caused faith to flare up. This may be said concerning a number of mission fields in the world today. The Christian faith is exploding in Africa. China also is a nation where the gospel is gaining ground by leaps and bounds. When the monks in a certain monastery heard this they leaped for joy, as they had been praying exclusively for China for some 30 years.

"So when the Samaritans came to him, they asked him to stay with them; and he stayed there two days. And many more believed because of his word." Some people will believe in Jesus if only we will tell them of our experience of him. Others will believe if we will take them to some meeting where the gospel is presented. They will hear his word expressed for themselves. "They said to the woman, `It is no longer because of your words that we believe, for we have heard for ourselves." Something happens when unbelievers hear the gospel in the presence of believers.

A missionary in Africa announced that a service was to be held out-of-doors. The believers sat around him as he preached. The unbelievers stood around him in a larger circle. What really got to them was not so much the words of the preacher, but the expression on the faces of the believers, who hung on his every word. "We have heard for ourselves, and we know that this is indeed the Savior of the world." Their faith had leap-frogged her faith. She had wondered if he could be the Savior of the chosen people. They had become convinced that he was the Savior of the entire human race. Years later Philip the evangelist would speak to this people and see a mighty revival break out. Acts 8 "Truly our labor is not in vain in the Lord."

❦

THE CONQUERING HERO RETURNS

"**A**fter two days he departed to Galilee. For Jesus himself testified that a prophet has no honor in his own country." John 4:43,44

"After two days" means on the third day, and the third day was the key day, the day of the marriage. So here we may assume that we will return to the theme of the miracle of Cana, as indeed we do. The third day is the day of life. Jesus is the source of life. But the new life he brings was rejected by Jerusalem, which was "his own country." Rejecting life brings us into judgment. Later Jesus will prophecy Jerusalem's doom. Matthew 24

"So when he came to Galilee, the Galileans welcomed him." His life from the time he was four or five years of age was lived in exile in the north. He was by birth a Southerner, a Judean. Judea had the reputation of killing their own prophets, as they would Jesus.

His reception back in Galilee reminds us of the welcome Charles Lindbergh received in New York City after his transAtlantic flight: the conquering hero returns. But Jesus' fame is insubstantial, resting as it does upon the signs he had done in Jerusalem. It is like the fizz in a freshly opened bottle of soda. It won't last long.

"So he came again to Cana in Galilee, where he had made the water wine." A burly truck driver gave his heart to Christ. He was chided by his old cronies, who said, "Don't tell us you believe that old wives' tale of Jesus turning water into wine?" He responded: "Whether Jesus turned water into wine I do not know. But this I do know, that in my house he turned beer into furniture. And that is a great enough miracle for me!"

My wife and I moved to Omaha, my old home town, when I was thirty. We were called to the staff of the church my folks joined when I was in seminary. God allowed us to be with them while my dad succumbed to lung cancer. God's gracious providence was self-evident. 🍂

THE WINE HAS FAILED AGAIN

*"**A**nd at Capernaum there was an official whose son was ill."*

John 4:46

The wine had failed at Cana nearly a year before. Now once again the joy was gone. The laughter had ceased in the home of this royal official, who lived some 25 miles from Cana. His little boy was dying. There was nothing he could do to prevent it. Or was there? Men ought always to pray and not to faint, not to lose heart, said Jesus. When there's life, there's hope; when there's hope, there's life.

"When he heard that Jesus had come from Judea to Galilee, he went and begged him to come down and heal his son, for he was at the point of death." There is nothing that so threatens us as death. Death robs our lives of meaning. If we are not living for the welfare of our children, for what then are we living? This man assumes that the death of his child will cause his world to crumble around him. He wants Jesus to keep his boy from dying. But the deeper question is this. Does your life have meaning even in the face of death? Is God the God of the dead as well as the living? If he is, then death is not as deplorable as we make it out to be.

Jesus therefore said to him, "Unless you see signs and wonders you will not believe." You and the Galileans, whom you represent, believe that should I refuse to keep your son from dying, "Life is a tale told by an idiot, full of sound and fury, signifying nothing." It is time for you to look death full in the face. It is time for you to stare it down. It is time for you to view death through my eyes, and realize that it is an enemy that has met its match. I, Jesus, am the Source of life. I will pin its shoulders to the mat. It will have its come-uppance. I am the death-knell of death, the last enemy that is to be destroyed. Don't worry that your son may die. Death must come to all. But it does not have the last word.

❦

WHO IS IN CHARGE HERE?

"$\mathbb{T}$*he official said to him, 'Sir, come down before my child dies.'"*

John 4:49

Jesus, I can't understand why you want to test me so. Why throw a road block in my way, bringing up this business of needing signs and wonders! I don't follow your logic. All I know is that my son is dying. Unless you come down with me to lay your hand upon him and pray, he will die. Perhaps, even so, it will be too late.

You must also realize, Jesus, how important I am. I am not your average flunky. I am a royal official, the right-hand man of the king in these parts, Herod Antipas. I can put in a good word for you in high places. On the other hand, I can get you into trouble, if you won't play ball with me.

My dear man, says Jesus, you don't seem to realize to whom you are talking. I am the Eternal Word of God. You don't tell me what to do, no matter how big your britches. I tell you what to do. And this is what I am telling you. Go. Go alone. I am not going with you. But your request has been granted. Your son lives.

Miracle of miracles, the man believed the word that Jesus spoke to him and went his way. As he was going down, his servants met him and told him that his son was living. So he asked the hour when he began to mend, and they said to him, "Yesterday at the seventh hour the fever left him." It happened instantaneously, when Jesus said the word.

The faith that pleases God is not the faith that demands signs and wonders, the faith that wants to scrutinize the miraculous. It is the faith that the official exemplified. Faith is acting on the word of God. This portion reminds us of the fact that we can't put on airs when we draw near to the Lord or try to impress him with our credentials. We can never get chummy with deity, nor can we commandeer him to fit in with our plans.

777

"*The father knew that was the hour when Jesus had said to him,
'Your son will live'; and he himself believed, and all his household.*"

John 4:53

The hour when Jesus said, "Your son lives" (not "will
live" in the original Greek) was the seventh hour, seven o'clock
in the evening. Seven in the Bible symbolizes completion,
perfection. We saw in the previous episode that Jesus was the
seventh man in the Samaritan woman's life. He is the man from
heaven, the place of fulfillment and perfection. Furthermore
this is now the seventh day in the Gospel, when we encounter
the theme of healing and wholeness in answer to prayer. Here
we have three sevens: 777. (The seventh man, the seventh day,
the seventh hour.) We have transcended in Jesus the mark of
the beast, three sixes: 666, which is as far as human nature
unaided by God can go.

The father believed in importuning prayer. His persis-
tence by the grace of God received a favorable answer. This
father loved his son. His love for his son is a pale reflection of
the Heavenly Father's love for his only begotten Son. And the
love our Heavenly Father has for Jesus is the same love that he
has for each of us. He does not play favorites.

"This was now the second sign that Jesus did when he
had come from Judea to Galilee." Each sign is greater than the
one before. It is a greater thing to keep a child from dying, than
it is to keep a wedding party from falling on its face when the
wine has failed. It is greater also because Jesus was present at
the wedding, but he healed the boy across the miles. Distance
is no obstacle to God. Jesus is now in heaven, but when he
speaks a word in our behalf, it takes effect. We don't have to see
him to experience his healing love. While the father went to
Jesus in prayer, the mother stood by caring for him, as the
church cares for the little ones in her charge.

❦

DO YOU SEE THE PLAN?

"*This was now the second sign that Jesus did when he had come from Judea to Galilee.*" John 4:54

We have now surveyed the Seven Days of the New Creation. On the first day we heard the testimony of the friend of the Bridegroom. He introduced us to the groom, and saw to it that we were groomed for the coming marriage by being bathed in the water of baptism. On the second day we saw the beginning of faith, and the initial gathering of "the called out ones," who were called to follow Jesus to the wedding. On the third day Jesus became the Bridegroom by providing the best wine supernaturally, and the disciples became his bride by the faith of full surrender. (Only one life; it will soon be passed; only what's done for Christ will last. He will be Lord of all, or not Lord at all.)

After the wedding Jesus took his disciples home with him to His Father's house, where he cleaned house, and would abide with them on day number four. The fifth day was the day of new birth. By abiding in Christ our lives become fruitful for God, and we find ourselves reproducing after our kind. On the sixth day we learned how the new born baby is nourished, and that we drink as we hear the good news in worship, and we eat as we bear witness concerning him whom we worship. Unfortunately, though, the babe in Christ gets sick and runs the risk of dying spiritually. What are we to do? We must go to the Lord in prayer, as the father did. We must also do as the mother did - give tender loving care - until the little one is restored to health.

The seventh day is the day of healing. Do you get the picture? Do you see the plan? What happens to us in our natural life points beyond itself to what happens in our walk with the Lord. This is a sacramental universe. The tangible realm illustrates the intangible and the eternal. And so we come to see that the Christian life is profoundly meaningful.

A GOOD PLACE FOR THE DISABLED

"After this there was a feast of the Jews, and Jesus went up to Jerusalem."   *John 5:1*

Jerusalem (possession of peace) is always up hill. Peace with God is a gift, but gaining possession of it requires effort. Any dead fish can float downstream, but it takes some effort to make headway against the current. The feasts of the Jews were celebrations of past history with God. Unless we are careful our religion will be nothing more than looking back with nostalgia, as is the case with Judaism. Christianity is future oriented. It looks forward with eager anticipation to the return of Jesus and the healing of this divided universe. A fatal flaw runs though the whole creation and every creature in it.

"Now there is in Jerusalem by the Sheep Gate a pool, in Hebrew called Bethzatha, which has five porticoes." Late in the 19th century this place was excavated by some friar monks. They found the columns under 30 feet of rubbish. It was nearly as long as a football field. The fifth porch divided the large pool into two. "In these lay a multitude of invalids." They lacked strength, because they were disabled. "King" in Hebrew means "the one who is able." The prefix "dis" means "separation from." Separated from King Jesus (the one who is able to meet our needs), we are disabled. The disability took three forms: blind, lame, paralyzed.

The folklore associated with this site was that periodically the water was disturbed by an angel. When this happened, the first one who stepped into the troubled water was supposed to be healed of whatever disease he had. This expression was not an original part of this gospel. It was added by the primitive Church to explain the crowd of sick people there. The situation might be likened to a hospital or a nursing home. Birds of a feather flock together. There is evidence that an intermittently flowing spring was the source of the disturbance.

❦

DO YOU WANT TO BE HEALED?

"*One man was there who had been ill for thirty- eight years.*"

John 5:5

Thirty-eight years was the length of time the Hebrews wandered in the wilderness under Moses, after they had disobeyed the Lord's command to go in and possess the promised land. In this particular case it seems that the man's sin brought on the malady that afflicted him. It was an exceptional situation. Indeed he possibly enjoyed seniority in this deplorable company, having been there longer than anyone.

"When Jesus saw him and knew that he had been lying there a long time, he said to him, `Do you want to be healed?'" Mind you, he had been in this miserable condition longer than Jesus had been on earth. Why wouldn't he want to be healed? Well, for one thing he had not done a lick of work in all that time. He had survived because of the generosity of God's people. They had been instructed by God to give alms to the poor. As long as he was incapable of working, he was privileged to live off of the compassion of the religious community. Should he be healed, he would have to go to work and become self- supporting. And, after all, he was getting up in years. Would he be able to find a job and hold on to it? It was worth thinking about.

Some years ago we prayed for a young woman who had an incurable illness. She was incapable of walking. Her ability to get about returned, but she did not reach out for total health because she had been receiving a disability pension, and would have lost her benefits had she taken advantage of what the Lord had done for her. How long have I been living a sick spiritual life? If the Lord should heal me, won't I be obliged to go to work for him? If I stick my neck out for Jesus, I will probably get hurt by those who enjoy the status quo. Perhaps like a turtle I would be more safe keeping my head under my shell, and leaving well enough alone.

NO MORE EXCUSES

"The sick man answered him, 'Sir, I have no man to put me into the pool when the water is troubled, and while I am going another steps down before me.'" John 5:7

In the midst of the five porticoes, symbolizing our five senses, is the sixth feature of this locale, the pool, which may represent our sixth sense. Apart from the guidance of scripture, our sixth sense gets us into the psychic realm, where magic and the occult operate. Such a plunge would create more problems than it would solve.

"My problem, Jesus, is the fact that my friends and family have all deserted me. Left to my own resources, I cannot possibly get into the pool unaided. As a matter of fact, far from helping me, people are always getting in my way." The good news is that Jesus is the man who can and will do for us that which no other man can do. He has come to the pool of Bethzatha (house of the olive) with that which the olive oil represents, the anointing of the Spirit. Plunge into the center of that pool, who is Jesus, (having the depth of eternity within him), and you will begin to experience the healing process that will enable you to become all that God designed you to be.

Enough of this foolishness and procrastination, says Jesus. "Rise, take up your pallet, and walk." The devil has knocked you down. Your inner man, your spirit, has been on the canvas long enough. Rise in the resurrection strength of God. I give you my help. "And at once the man was healed, and he took up his pallet and walked." Faith is doing what Jesus tells us. When Jesus, the Word of God, tells you to do something, even though it seems impossible, obey him. His Spirit, his word, and your obedience are an unbeatable combination. A famous evangelist said that the devil knocks him down about five times a week. He has to hear Jesus say, "Stand up on the inside and keep going, man," and do it.

❧

THE LAW OF THE SABBATH

"*Now that day was the sabbath.*" *John 5:9*

The sabbath (meaning "rest") was the day on which the Jews remembered the Creator. Sabbath observance had become the centerpiece of their religion, since their return from exile in Babylon. High-handed failure to observe it required death by stoning. By commanding this man to take up his mattress and walk, Jesus had set him on a collision course with his religion. It was part of the plan.

Jesus was truly laying his axe to the root of fruitless Judaism (Matthew 3:10). When he cleansed the temple he was severing the tap root of commercialism in religion. In attacking the love of money he had come against the root of all evils. By requiring this man to carry his bed on the sabbath, he was exposing the evil of legalism and of dead orthodoxy.

"So the Jews said to the man who had been healed, `It is the sabbath, it is not lawful for you to carry your pallet.'" A woman was not allowed to wear even so much as a brooch on the sabbath, as the bearing of it was considered work. It was debated whether or not a man might wear his dentures or his wooden leg on this sanctified day. He wouldn't dare pick his teeth with a toothpick. "But he answered them, "The man who healed me said to me, `Take up your pallet and walk.'" I am only doing what he told me. It was not my idea, but his. Don't blame me; blame him.

"They asked him, `Who is the man who said to you, Take up your pallet and walk?'" What man dare contradict the fourth commandment of God? Such a one is wearing shoes of divine dimension. He cannot get away with it! "Now the man who had been healed did not know who it was, for Jesus had withdrawn, as there was a crowd in the place." So often Jesus expresses God's grace anonymously. He refused to take the credit away from the bridegroom for providing the best wine. He blesses us, and then slips away unnoticed.

DAY SEVEN - HEALING

*"*𝕬*fterward Jesus found him in the temple, and said to him, 'See, you are well! Sin no more, that nothing worse befall you.'"*

John 5:14

You mean there is something worse than going through life an invalid and unable to work? Eternal damnation and exclusion from the presence of God would be infinitely worse. And this man was in danger of this. Should he misinterpret the healing he had received by considering God as some great Santa Claus, he could miss out on heaven.

God is not a nice Father who goes around doing good turns, expecting nothing in return. Such a sentimental idea of God will wind people up in hell. He is a holy God, eternally set apart from all that is unworthy of his companionship. From now on this man is obliged to live a life of gratitude, expressing itself in pure and noble living. "Don't continue to live in a self-centered way. Live a life that acknowledges God as your Lord, doing all that you can to please Him." This man now had the possibility of being more evil than he was before. Now he could even rob banks and commit adultery.

"The man went away and told the Jews that it was Jesus who had healed him. And this was why the Jews persecuted Jesus, because he did this on the Sabbath." Within the gospels there is the record of Jesus healing seven individuals on the sabbath. He made a point of doing so. The seventh day in the gospel is the day of healing. The waves of the sea come in sevens. Each seventh wave is the big wave. We are beginning to experience in our time the coming of the seventh wave of God. More and more the Holy Spirit in answer to prayer is touching people with the healing finger of God. "By his wounds you have been healed" wrote Peter. (I Peter 2:24) "Whatever you ask in faith, believe that you have received it, and it will be yours," said Jesus. Mark 11:24 You have got to believe you have got it, before you get it. ❧

SINCE GOD HAS NOT RETIRED, SHOULD WE?

"*But Jesus answered them, 'My Father is working still, and I am working.'*"   *John 5:17*

God created the universe. From this work he rested. But God has not gone into retirement, neither is he on vacation. Jesus tells us that he is working still. God is a Person with a purpose. He purposes that the universe should have fellowship with himself. Though much of it has turned its back on God, it has not been abandoned by God. He sent his eternal Word into creation to effect a reconciliation. The name of his eternal creative Word is now Jesus. Whoever calls upon the name of Jesus will be saved from futility and ultimate ruin.

"This was why the Jews sought all the more to kill him, because he not only broke the Sabbath but also called God his own Father, making himself equal with God." Anyone who would attempt to make himself equal with God would be guilty of the devil's sin. Isaiah 14:12-14. They were accusing Jesus of two crimes meriting capital punishment. The Jews were reluctant to call God "Father" because a father has children who share his nature. Should they worship a God having offspring, before long they could fall into the worship of more than one God. They would be guilty of turning from monotheism into polytheism. This they would never do.

Christians worship one God to be sure. But something happened within God before all creation that is akin to nuclear fission. A division took place within God. He divided into three. So there is a differentiation within God which He himself brought about before he fashioned time and space. The three persons who comprise the Godhead are Father, Son, and Holy Spirit. Each of the three is as much God as the others. But a remarkable change has taken place within the second person, in that since the incarnation, he is forever man as well as God. In the person of Jesus Christ, mankind has been elevated, at least potentially, to the level of God himself.

THE REPLY TO THE CHARGE OF REBELLION

"*Jesus said to them, 'Truly, truly, I say to you, the Son can do nothing of his own accord, but only what he sees the Father doing.'*"

John 5:19

Now Jesus defines with precision who he is, and why he has the authority to break the law of Moses, as they interpreted it. He is not, as they assume, a rebel against God. Quite the contrary, he is the dutiful Son of God, who does nothing from self-will. His will is in perfect harmony with the superior will of his Father. The story is told of a man who turned aside to go into a tavern. His little boy trailing behind, said, "Daddy, I'm walking in your footprints." Jesus always walked in the footprints of his heavenly Father.

"Whatever he does, that the Son does likewise. For the Father loves the Son, and shows him all that he himself is doing." The Father has such affection for the Son that he keeps no secrets from him. So also Jesus did not live in some ivory tower. He shared everything that he heard from the Father with his followers.

The incarnate Word become man was deprived of his omniscience, his innate knowledge of everything. Jesus experienced the limitations of us all. He had to learn to read and write just like the rest of us. Any supernatural knowledge he enjoyed came to him through the Holy Spirit as the Father's gift. Greater works than healing a man 38 years a cripple the Father will show him, that men may marvel.

"For as the Father raises the dead and gives them life, so also the Son gives life to whom he will." The Jews believed that only God could raise the dead and give life. By raising Lazarus from the dead at the end of his ministry, Jesus would prove conclusively that he, though a man, enjoyed the status of God. Such a thing was anathema to the Jewish theologians, who were locked into the notion that all the miraclous things happened centuries before. Many theologians today are like-minded.

❧

JESUS IS OUR JUDGE, NOT THE FATHER

"The Father judges no one, but has given all judgment to the Son, that all may honor the Son even as they honor the Father."

John 5:22,23

When the judge comes into the courtroom, he requires that everyone stand, and that he be addressed as "your honor." To show any disrespect toward the judge is to be in contempt of court, for which a penalty is meted out. Those who dishonor Jesus are dishonoring the Father who sent him. It is only through the Son that we come to know the Father. If you will pardon the expression: He is the spittin' image of his Dad.

"Truly, truly, I say to you, he who hears my word and believes him who sent me, has eternal life; he does not come into judgment, but has passed from death to life." To hear Jesus' word is to recognize that what he says is authoritative. His words are not idle or empty. They have the weight of eternity in them because they come from the Creator of the universe. Failure to perceive the weightiness of what Jesus says is rejection of God, but to believe Jesus is to receive the life of God. We accept thereby the judgment of the cross on our sins, and pass out from the realm of death into the realm of life.

The Greeks believed that by thinking ideal thoughts our minds were rendered immortal. The Bible teaches that our minds and bodies are by nature in the realm of death. By receiving Jesus and through him God, our bodies and our minds enter into a totally new realm. It is like passing across the border from Mexico into the United States. I am the same person, but now I am under a different jurisdiction. Trusting in Jesus gets me out from under the government of death into the government of life. Under Jesus all that I do and say that is in keeping with his will has an unending influence. Eternal means unending. Death is that power that causes everything to come to an end. In Christ death has been defeated.

❦

THE TWO RESURRECTIONS

"**T**ruly, truly, I say to you, the hour is coming, and now is, when
the dead will hear the voice of the Son of God, and those who hear
will live." *John 5:25*

Are you among those who are now hearing the voice
of the Son of God? A minister I know and respect once said that
he had to live for five years without hearing from God. He had
to derive support for five long years on what God had previously
said to him. That may be difficult, but infinitely worse off are
those who say that they have never heard God speak to them.
They are spiritually dead, because God is One who speaks.

"For as the Father has life in himself, so he has granted
the Son to have life in himself, and has given him authority to
execute judgment, because he is the Son of man." Here the
original says "Son of man" without the definite article "the." The
reason Jesus gives for God imparting to him the authority to
judge us is because he is a son of man, a human being. No one
can say on Judgment Day, "But you do not know, Lord, what I
was up against, or how exceedingly difficult was the row I had
to hoe." His glorified body will still bear the marks of slaughter.
Yes, our Judge is touched by the feelings of our infirmities; he
has experienced them all, in a far greater measure than we.

"Do not marvel at this; for the hour is coming when all
who are in the tombs will hear his voice and come forth, those
who have done good, to the resurrection of life, and those who
have done evil, to the resurrection of judgment." One thousand
years will separate the two resurrections. The first is for
believers, the second for unbelievers. See Revelation 20:4-6 for
the resurrection to life, and Revelation 20:11-15 for the resurrection to judgment. Today let us make sure that we will be
among those resurrected unto life by yielding ourselves totally
to Jesus Christ.

THE TOTALLY DEPENDENT ONE

"*J can do nothing on my own authority; as I hear, I judge; and my judgment is just, because I seek not my own will but the will of him who sent me.*" *John 5:30*

A close relative used to ask me if I had self-confidence yet. I kept saying, "No, my confidence is in Christ." If Jesus said that he could do nothing on his own, how much more are we obliged to say the same? Whose will are we seeking? My last will and testament will be read by others after my death. Those mentioned in it will receive precious little. The last will and testament of Jesus Christ is the one that interests me. To think that he mentioned me in his will is a stupendous thought. The twenty- seven books of the New Testament express the will of Jesus for the human race. To be a beneficiary of his will faith is called for. If I believe in him, I am included in his will. If I persist in disbelief, I exclude myself from all the benefits he came to bestow. His will is the will of the Father who sent him.

Are we students of God's will? If we ignore the Bible, we are missing out on much that is our birthright in the here and now. Let us resolve to spend a little time reading the Bible every day. It ought to have priority over the morning newspaper.

"If I bear witness to myself, my testimony is not true." Who trusts a person who goes about patting himself on the back? "There is another who bears witness to me, and I know that the testimony which he bears to me is true." This other one is Jesus' heavenly Father. Jesus was without sin, and so he enjoyed a clear connection with the Father's throne. Have you ever had a long-distance call with a bad connection, where there was interference on the line? Sometimes we cannot hear from God because of the static produced by unconfessed sin. The Holy Spirit within Jesus always gave him immediate access to his Father, who continually communicated with him.

❧

A BURNING AND SHINING LAMP

*"**Y**ou sent to John, and he has borne witness to the truth."*
John 5:33

John the Baptist is the first of four objective witnesses to Jesus, in addition to the witness of the Father within Jesus by the Holy Spirit. The Jews cannot receive the inner witness of God the Father, because they neither see him nor know him. The testimony of the Baptist, on the other hand, they had already received. He would seal the truth of his testimony with his life blood. Miguel de Unomuno said, "I will not accept the testimony of any man who will not have his throat cut open for the sake of his testimony." Nor should we.

"Not that the testimony which I receive is from man; but I say this that you may be saved." The value of John's witness was marginal because he was a mortal man like the rest of us, and he was their contemporary. Prophets are invariably dismissed by their own generation. They are out of step with their peers.

"He was a burning and shining lamp, and you were willing to rejoice for awhile in his light." It is evident that John had already been thrown into prison by Herod. His opportunity was brief but significant. Quality lords it over quantity in the service of God.

While in Seminary, I attended the funeral of a fellow student who was killed in an automobile accident several months before his graduation. As a matter of fact, it was a triple funeral in the Seminary chapel. His wife and unborn infant were also killed. The memorial service had the aspect of an Easter service. Resurrection hymns were sung. Eternally in joy for a day's exercise on earth. This young man's ministry was over before it was officially begun. Are we a burning and shining lamp, alight with the love of God? We do not have forever. Perhaps today is my final day. If the Lord has laid upon my heart to bear witness to someone or to do a particular good deed, may God give me the grace to do it today.

A WITNESS GREATER THAN JOHN

"*But the testimony which I have is greater than that of John; for the works which the Father has granted me to accomplish, these very works which I am doing, bear me witness that the Father has sent me.*" *John 5:36*

The second external witness to Jesus, greater than that of John, was the miracles he performed. The Targum of the Jews (which expresses the official teaching of their religion) says that Jesus did work miracles but that he did them by means of black magic. Tragically they held that Jesus was in league with the devil. The good news is that Jesus is the same today as he was then. He is still working miracles in the lives of those who trust him. A hundred thousand miracles are happening every day if we only had our eyes open to recognize them.

"And the Father who sent me has himself borne witness to me." God did this on the occasion of Jesus' baptism: "This is my beloved Son with whom I am well pleased." "His voice you have never heard, his form you have never seen; and you do not have his word abiding in you, for you do not believe him whom he has sent."

The Baptist heard and understood the Father's voice. No doubt those who responded to the Baptist's ministry also understood, but those who had their heels dug in could not comprehend the meaning of what they heard. To them it was merely the sound of thunder. The fact that God has form indicates that he enjoys a body. The meaningful life requires a body. Eventually we who believe shall put on our spiritual, glorified bodies. Our bodies of flesh are tents (temporary). At the second coming of Christ we will inhabit buildings (our permanent dwelling places). Believers have God's word within them. As a seed contains germinal life, so God's word has within it the life of God. This life of God within us is that which enables us to believe that Jesus is the One sent by God.

THE PEOPLE OF THE BOOK

"*You search the scriptures, because you think that in them you have eternal life; and it is they that bear witness to me.*" *John 5:39*

The Jews were and are the people of the book. Their religious leaders have through the centuries been students of their Bible. They call their Torah (the Law - the first five books of their Bible written by Moses) the Derek (the Way in Hebrew). Jews say: the Law is the Way. Jesus says: I am the Way. The religious Jews think that pondering their scriptures gives them eternal life, if they believe there is such a thing. Some Jews believe there is life beyond the grave and some do not.

Jesus says that the third objective witness to himself is the Old Testament. Spiritually understood every page of the Jewish Bible discloses something of the face of Jesus Christ. The subject of their scriptures is Jesus and his saving activity. When we were children, we enjoyed studying pictures with multiple faces hidden in the landscape. We should approach the First Testament looking for Jesus in every nook and cranny.

"Yet you refuse to come to me that you may have life." Judaism today is a sinful religion because it perpetuates the rejection of Jesus as Messiah. I heard a Jewish leader say, "A Jew who accepts Jesus is no longer a Jew." From his standpoint a Jewish Christian is a traitor, an enemy of all they hold dear. We do them an injustice by patting them on the back and ignoring our differences. Should we say, "Let's kiss and make up," we would betray the gospel of Jesus Christ. We love the Jewish people, but in Christian love we beg to differ with them. On several occasions the Lord has allowed me to lead Jews to Jesus. These have been among the most momentous occasions of my life. We should seek opportunities to tell these dear people about their Saviour. One mode of evangelism is through friendship. Why not befriend one of Jesus' kinsmen?

WHOM AM I TRYING TO PLEASE?

"**J** *do not receive glory from men.*" *John 5:41*

Do you know why Jesus does not receive glory from men? It is because he speaks to us the truth, and the truth hurts. The trouble is that the people who hear the gospel don't understand the gospel. And if they understood it they wouldn't like it. Do you know why? Because when Jesus calls a man he bids him come and die. He calls us to deny our natural ambitions, and to seek first the Kingdom of God and his righteousness. Do you seek above all the mastery of Jesus over your life, and to be the object and instrument of his saving activity? Jesus called his disciples evil. "If you who are evil know how to give good gifts to your children, how much more will the heavenly Father give the Holy Spirit to those who ask him!" Luke 11:13. He called a spade a spade. He always spoke the truth in love, and the truth kills our egocentricity. It hurts like hell. So instinctively we fight against it.

"But I know that you have not the love of God within you." How did he know that? Answer: "I have come in my Father's name, and you do not receive me; if another comes in his own name, him you will receive. How can you believe, who receive glory from one another and do not seek the glory that comes from the only God?" We are eager to be approved and applauded by men. We are sensitive to what people think of us, because we want to be promoted and held in high esteem. But we forget that in the final analysis it is not what people think of us, but what God thinks of us.

Jesus said, "I always do those things that please the Father." The big question is: whom am I seeking to please? The Apostle Paul wrote: "If I were still pleasing men, I would not be a servant of Christ." "Let those of us who are mature be thus minded; and if in anything you are otherwise minded, God will reveal that also to you."

THE FRIEND OF SINNERS

"*Do not think that I shall accuse you to the Father; it is Moses who accuses you, on whom you set your hope.*"   *John 5:45*

One of the greatest things ever said about Jesus was that he is "the friend of sinners." "All have sinned and fallen short of the glory of God." Romans 3:23   But we have an Advocate with the Father, who is interceding for us. He is not against us; he is for us, whether we are Jew or Gentile. The tragedy is that the Jews were setting their hope on Moses, the Lawgiver, instead of on Jesus, the Savior. James 2:10 says: "For whoever keeps the whole law but fails in one point has become guilty of all of it." 613 laws were laid down through Moses. If I kept 612 my whole life long, but on one occasion broke one little law, then I am a lawbreaker and am guilty before God.

God's standard is perfection. "You shall be perfect, even as your Father in heaven is perfect," said Jesus. If this is a new law, then for sure we have had it. But, praise God, this is a promise. Through faith in Jesus, we are washed in his precious blood. We are rendered perfect in the eyes of God. That is good news, not good advice.

"If you believed Moses, you would believe me, for he wrote of me. But if you do not believe his writings, how will you believe my words?" The Jews searched the scriptures, but tragically they did not believe them. That is why they did not believe in Jesus. Someone remarked, "I believe the Bible from cover to cover." To this the answer was made, "That's just the trouble. Get beyond the covers into the pages." Even so, the ink on the pages won't help us; it is the Spirit that inspired the written words that must work in our hearts. "The letter kills, the Spirit gives life." Some people use the Bible to bludgeon others. We should aspire to so assimilate its message that we can present the truth of it in our own words in a winsome way - that we may win some.

❦

THE NURTURE QUESTION

" *After this Jesus went to the other side of the Sea of Galilee, which is the Sea of Tiberias."*   *John 6:1*

"After this" looks back to chapter 5, where the main theme was healing. We have learned that Jesus heals those who are young in the faith in answer to the prayer-support of others. We also know that Jesus heals directly those chronically ill who have no one to assist them. In chapter six we return to the theme of the sixth day, the day of nurture. In this chapter John gives us the significance of the Lord's Supper. Though we were not there, we may still benefit in an extraordinary way from what occurred in the upper room the night before his crucifixion.

"And a multitude followed him, because they saw the signs which he did on those who were diseased." He is the One who heals us still in spirit, emotions, mind, body and relationships. "Jesus went up on the mountain, and there sat down with his disciples," seeking rest. Now the Passover, the feast of the Jews, was at hand." On this occasion Jesus did not go up to Jerusalem for the feast. Next year he would go up to offer himself to the nation as the Passover Lamb.

The significance of his dying upon the cross is spelled out in what now occurs. "Lifting up his eyes, then, and seeing that a multitude was coming to him, Jesus said to Philip, 'How are we to buy bread, so that these people may eat?' This he said to test him, for he himself knew what he would do." He asked the nurture question not out of ignorance. He wanted to see how practical Philip sized up the situation. "Philip answered him, 'Two hundred denarii would not buy enough bread for each of them to get a little.'" In other words, they did not have the resources to provide for each one even a mouthful. It was a hopeless situation. Perhaps you are facing a hopeless predicament. Remember that our extremity is God's opportunity.

❦

WITH JESUS NOTHING IS IMPOSSIBLE

"One of his disciples, Andrew, Simon Peter's brother, said to him, 'There is a lad here who has five barley loaves and two fish; but what are they among so many?"   John 6:8-9

When faced with an impossible situation, don't wring your hands in despair. Present to Jesus whatever you have got. Let him decide what to do with it. Jesus didn't answer Andrew's question; instead, he acted. "Jesus said, 'Make the people sit down.'" A missionary in China told how trucks of grain were brought in to feed the starving masses. They were about to stampede. Then he remembered what Jesus had done on this occasion. He too commanded them to sit down. Order prevailed then in an otherwise chaotic situation, thanks to the practical wisdom of Jesus, he said.

"Now there was much grass in the place; so the men sat down, in number about five thousand." Counting women and children they may have numbered twenty-five thousand. The good Shepherd makes his sheep lie down in green pastures, because he wants to feed them. "Jesus then took the loaves, and when he had given thanks, he distributed them to those who were seated; so also the fish, as much as they wanted." When we come to the Lord's Table for Holy Communion, we receive a tiny bit of bread, and wine in a very little cup. We are tempted to ask, "What is this, as our need is so vast?" We must remember the secret of the multiplication of the loaves and the fish. It is this: Jesus is adding of himself in the breaking. It points to the cross, where he was broken in dying. A little goes a long way, when Jesus adds his divine life to what is distributed.

It happened in an Episcopal Church. The pastor told that a lady with a withered arm reached out to receive the communion element. Her arm was immediately healed. This sort of thing ought to happen from time to time.

A MIND-STRETCHING GOD

"**A**s much as they wanted."   *John 6:11*

As Jesus broke the bread and the fish, a miracle took place. "Of the increase of his government there will be no end." Isaiah 9:7. In a similar fashion the boy's sack lunch increased in his hands as long as he continued the breaking. He imparted of himself, as the One who is full of grace and truth. Jesus enjoyed the creativity of God. The word create (bara in the Hebrew) means to bring into existence out of nothing. He who could have turned stones into bread found it a little thing to turn bread into more bread, fish into more fish. "With God all things are possible," said Jesus. If we think something is impossible for God to do, we have too small a concept of God.

The astronomers have now reached out into space 15 billion light years. Light travels at 186,000 miles per second. The earth we are told is between 4 and 5 billion years old. So the light now reaching earth from outer space started its journey some 10 billion years before the earth came into existence. A star named Betelgues is so immense that were it our sun, which is 93 million miles away, the earth would be rotating within its circumference. To reach the nearest star a ball of spider web the size of the earth would have to be unrolled. The Creator transcends (goes beyond) all this, the time/space continuum (our material cosmos). He occupies that which the Bible calls "the third heaven," the realm of spirit. In this context the second heaven is the material universe, and the first heaven is our sky, or the atmosphere of earth.

We are saying all this to make more evident the fact that nothing is too difficult for God. And since we believe that God was in Christ Jesus, we should not be staggered that Jesus could feed twenty thousand people effortlessly, so that they had "as much as they wanted." He has come to meet the needs of his people, including you and me, today.

KING OF HEARTS

"And when they had eaten their fill, he told his disciples, 'Gather up the fragments left over, that nothing may be lost.'"   John 6:13

In Vietnam the troops were told on occasion, "Waste them." That was devil (damned-evil) talk and the devil (ultimate evil) is damned, you know. God does not will that any should be lost (wasted). It is a sad thing to see anything wasted. That is why some of us are charter members of the clean plate club. A little boy, when asked his definition of having it made, said: "Not to clean my plate without being reminded of all the starving orphans in India."

"So they gathered them up and filled twelve baskets with fragments from the five barley loaves, left by those who had eaten." The disciples, who distributed the food to the people, ate last, and each had enough to feed his face for a week. But for Jesus there was no basket. He depended upon them for his meal. Today we cannot proffer Jesus a fish sandwich, but we can do something that will give him greater satisfaction. We can praise him and thank him. "Thank you, Jesus, for feeding us and caring for us." A sacrifice of thanksgiving is to thank the Lord when we are blue (the color of faith) and don't feel like it. When we are in the pink, we are inclined to walk by feeling, not faith.

"When the people saw the sign which he had done, they said, 'This is indeed the prophet who is to come into the world.'" They regarded him as the king they were seeking. "Perceiving then that they were about to come and take him by force to make him king, Jesus withdrew again to the mountain by himself." Jesus refused to allow them to force him into their mold. He would not be a bread-king, one who would satisfy only their physical appetites. No, he would mold us into his likeness, that we may become individuals after his own heart. He is not king of stomachs, but King of hearts.

THE SURPRISING CHRIST

"**W**hen *evening came, his disciples went down to the sea, got into a boat, and started across the sea to Capernaum.* " *John 6:16*

In his fourth sign (the multiplication of bread and fish) we saw the secret of the cross. It is the secret of brokenness. Only by being broken in death could he impart his divine life to us in holy communion. He adds of himself to the elements that they may supernaturally nourish the life he has given us when we committed ourselves to him. If the feeding of the multitudes points to his death upon the cross, the sign of his walking on the water anticipates his resurrection. We may think of these two signs as twins, not identical but fraternal. You can't have one without the other.

Since Jesus was no longer at hand, the disciples on their own decided to return to headquarters. "It was now dark, and Jesus had not yet come to them." We are inevitably in the dark when the Light of the World is not with us. "The sea rose because a strong wind was blowing," and the wind was against them. When we are getting farther away from Jesus, we find to our dismay that the going gets rough. "When they had rowed about three or four miles, they saw Jesus walking on the sea and drawing near to the boat. They were frightened (thinking they saw a ghost), but he said to them, `It is I; do not be afraid.' Then they were glad to take him into the boat, and immediately the boat was at the land to which they were going." When we receive the supernatural, risen Christ into our circumstances, we have arrived. His real name is Journey's End. In his sovereign freedom, he comes to us when we least expect him. He is the surprising Christ.

Remember the three companions of Daniel, who were hurled alive into the fiery furance. The king saw in astonishment Another with them. It was Jesus, centuries before he became flesh.

CONSOLATION

"*On the next day the people who remained on the other side of the sea saw that there had been only one boat there, and that Jesus had not entered the boat with his disciples, but that his disciples had gone away alone.*"   John 6:22

When people come to Jesus for the wrong reason, they discover him to be as evasive as quick-silver. We must come to him on his terms, not our own. "However, boats from Tiberias came near the place where they ate the bread after the Lord had given thanks." The Lord's Supper is called "the giving thanks," literally "the eucharist" in the Greek text. Every time we break bread (eat a simple meal, be it just a sandwich) after bowing our heads to give thanks, we may realize that we are taking communion. It is every bit as sacred as communion in church.

The tragedy is that the denominations have separated Christians from one another by insisting upon their own particular interpretation of Communion. (Though we realize that denominations are part of God's plan for the Church, we are tempted at times to think of them as damnations, especially when they say, "We are in and you are out.") Interpretations are beside the point. Transubstantiation, consubstantiation, no substantiation - it is enough to make the good Lord weep. We are not called to squabble. We are called to "do this in (grateful) remembrance of Jesus," who was put to death for our sins and raised for our justification. He shares himself with us despite our interpretation or lack of it.

"So when the people saw that Jesus was not there, nor his disciples, they themselves got into the boats and went to Capernaum, seeking Jesus." Capernaum means "village of Nahum" (Consolation). Everyone from time to time needs consolation. At such times, whether they realize it or not, they are seeking Jesus. He is the true Consoler. Let us come to him, and so find rest for our weary souls.

OUR BIGGEST PROBLEM

"*When they found him on the other side of the sea, they said to him, 'Rabbi, when did you come here?'*"   *John 6:25*

"When" is a whisker word. It has no substance. What is the difference when he came there. It would be more significant to ask how he got there. But had he told them he walked across the lake, they would have laughed him to scorn. Concerning him Job 9:8 says: "who alone stretched out the heavens, and trampled the waves of the sea."

Jesus answered them, "Truly, truly, I say to you, you seek me, not because you saw signs (the significance of what I did), but because you ate your fill of the loaves. Do not labor for the food which perishes, but for the food which endures to eternal life, which the Son of man will give to you; for on him has God the Father set his seal." God sealed him with the Holy Spirit at his baptism.

Then they said to him, "What must we do, to be doing the works of God?" Jesus answered them, "This is the work of God," that you go out and turn the world right-side-up? No, but "that you believe in him whom God has sent." Who can do the work of God? Only God. And what is the one essential work of God? To engender faith in our hearts through the hearing of the gospel.

Our biggest problem is confusing ourselves with God. We have all eaten of the forbidden fruit, and somehow think that we are by nature divine. Nothing could be farther from the truth. What effrontery to suppose that we can do the works of God! Who do we think we are? Let us humbly receive the words of Jesus. Perhaps the Holy Spirit will give us the grace to believe them. Our trust in Jesus will give evidence of the work of God in our lives. Ephesians 2:10 says, "We (Christians) are his workmanship (poem, literally, or creative artestry) created in Christ Jesus for good works, which God prepared beforehand, that we should walk in them."

YOU HAVEN'T MATCHED MOSES YET

"*So they said to him, 'Then what sign do you do, that we may see, and believe you? What work do you perform?'*" John 6:30

Sure, we know you turned that lad's sack lunch into a feast for the multitudes, and we ate our fill. But who likes barley bread? Yuk. "Our fathers ate the manna in the wilderness; as it is written, 'He gave them bread from heaven to eat.'" Manna is the Hebrew word for "what is it?" We might have called it Angel Food Cake. It rained down out of the skies. They were demanding that Jesus duplicate the miracle of manna, which they attributed to Moses.

Jesus then said to them, "Truly, truly, I say to you, it was not Moses who gave you the bread from heaven; my Father gives you the true bread from heaven. For the bread of God is that which comes down from heaven, and gives life to the world." The manna they were referring to came not from Moses but from the Father of Jesus. That "what is it?" was not the real thing. It was a pale reflection of the real thing. The real thing is not a thing at all, but a Person, the Eternal Word of God. He came down in his incarnation, and he is still coming down. He is raining upon us, and desirous of reigning over us. Only so can he give us his eternal life. They said to him, "Lord, give us this bread always."

At first they called him teacher. Now they are calling him Lord, which is some progress. They have come as far as the woman at the well had come when she said, "Sir, give me this water, that I may not thirst, nor come here to draw."

James 4:2 says, "You do not have because you do not ask. You ask and do not receive, because you ask wrongly, to spend it on your passions." So the Lord must get us to the place where we ask. Then he must get us to ask for the right reason, a more difficult task than the first. Don't you agree?

WHOSE SON IS HE ANYWAY?

"Jesus said to them, 'I am the bread of life; he who comes to me shall not hunger, and he who believes in me shall never thirst.'"

John 6:35

Up to this point Jesus had been speaking symbolically. Now he spells it out clearly. Surrender yourself totally to me, he says, and I will satisfy your cravings for life that is life indeed. It is reported that a southern California funeral home advertised during the depths of the depression in the 1930's, "Why walk around half dead when we can bury you for $30." A famous preacher used as his topic , "How to Stay Alive As Long As You Live." That's the ticket. And that is what Jesus offers us: he brings us back to God alive.

"But I said to you that you have seen me and yet do not believe." The reason he then gives for their unbelief is that they are not the Father's gift to himself. Those whom the Father gives him, he will never cast out. "For I have come down from heaven, not to do my own will, but the will of him who sent me; and this is the will of him who sent me, that I should lose nothing of all that he has given me, but raise it up at the last day."

"The Jews then murmured at him, because he said, 'I am the bread which came down from heaven.' They said, "Is not this Jesus, the son of Joseph, whose father and mother we know? How does he now say, 'I have come down from heaven?'" Here the saying, "Familiarity breeds contempt," has application. When we think we know Jesus, we do not know as we ought. There is the realm of mystery about him that we never fully fathom.

Obviously Joseph had kept secret between himself and Mary the story of Jesus' miraculous conception. Had he not, who would have believed it anyway? Only those whom the Holy Spirit enlightens. How about you? Mary conceived him in her womb when the Holy Spirit overshadowed her. When he overshadows us, he engenders Jesus in our heart.

❧

DO YOU HAVE BUILT-IN SHOCK ABSORBERS?

"Jesus answered them, 'Do not murmur among yourselves.'"

John 6:43

One of the things God can't stand is murmuring. Under Moses the chronic complainers all died in the wilderness. "No one can come to me unless the Father who sent me draws him; and I will raise him up at the last day." Your inclination to Jesus is your primary experience of the love of God, who is passionately desirous of your living in his presence forever.

Jesus then quotes Isaiah 54:13, "All your sons shall be taught by God." The verse goes on to say, "And great shall be the prosperity of your sons." Do you want to prosper? Then start learning from Jesus. "Everyone who has heard and learned from the Father comes to me." In our day many are claiming to have heard from God. They lie, if they do not point enthusiastically to Jesus, as John the Baptist did. And it cost him his life.

"Not that anyone has seen the Father except him who is from God; he has seen the Father. Truly, truly I say to you, he who believes has eternal life." On the contrary, he who believes and then withdraws his trust forfeits eternal life. Jesus concludes his teaching on this point by saying, "The bread which I shall give for the life of the world is my flesh."

This shocking statement caused the Jews to dispute among themselves, saying, "How can this man give us his flesh to eat?" Jesus answered by identifying his flesh and blood that must be eaten as that of the Son of man. He alludes to Daniel 7:13, where the Son of man is the Heavenly Man. "I saw in the night visions, and behold with the clouds of heaven there came one like a son of man, and he came to the Ancient of Days and was presented before him. And to him was given" (in summary) unending mastery of the universe. He is intentionally offending the literalists, who reject his claim of a heavenly origin.

❦

THE FLESH IS OF NO AVAIL

"*Many of his disciples, when they heard it, said, 'This is a hard saying; who can listen to it?'*" John 6:60

The literalists, even among his disciples, were enormously offended thinking that he was telling them they had to become cannibals, and feed upon his fingers and ears. Years ago I saw on TV Hugh Downs interview a French anthropologist, who had inadvertently eaten human flesh while living among a cannibalistic tribe in Africa. Hugh asked him, "What did it taste like?" He answered, "It was delicious. It tasted like a cross between beef and pork."

Just reading this has offended and disgusted you, I am sure. Jesus said to them, "Do you take offense at this? Then what if you were to see the Son of man ascending where he was before?" Unfortunately, those whom he had just offended would not be among those who would witness his ascension forty days after his resurrection from the dead. "It is the spirit that gives life, the flesh is of no avail; the words that I have spoken to you are spirit and life."

Here Jesus clearly reveals that he was speaking symbolically. We appropriate his flesh and blood (his divine humanity) as we avail ourselves of the Spirit that motivated his self-giving love, and as we allow his life to imprint itself upon our actions and endeavors. His example we cannot emulate. It is too high for us. But we can by faith harness a fragment of his love. "Make love your aim." We can at least aim in that direction. "'But there are some of you that do not believe.' For Jesus knew from the first who those were that did not believe, and who it was that would betray him." Before he called the twelve he spent the night in prayer. Why? Because he was getting Judas Iscariot as an answer, demonstrating the integrity of prayer. Father, you certainly don't want me to call Judas? Yes, Judas, that he might cross you.

A FRIGHTENING THOUGHT

"*After this many of his disciples drew back and no longer went about with him.*"　　*John 6:66*

This verse anticipates the falling away that will precede the day of the Lord's wrath. See 2 Thessalonians 2:3 which says, "For that day (the day of wrath) will not come, unless the falling away comes first, and the man of lawlessness is revealed, the son of perdition" (another Judas Iscariot, the numerical value of whose name will total 666.) Is it merely coincidental that our verse is John 6:66?

Chapter six begins with the multitudes thronging after him, and concludes with all but the twelve deserting him. Revelation sifts the chaff from the wheat and separates the sheep from the goats. Yet in a strange way that is progress. It is growth, not in numbers, but an increase in purity. Remember the story of Gideon. He started out with 32,000 men. But they were too many. After the thinning out process, he was left with 300. They were more than enough to get the victory. "Give me some men, who are stout-hearted men, who will fight for the right they adore. Start me with ten... and I'll soon give you ten thousand more."

Jesus said to the twelve, "Do you also wish to go away?" Simon Peter answered him, "Lord to whom shall we go? You have the words of eternal life; and we have believed, and have come to know, that you are the Holy One of God." Even Peter had missed it. He had regarded Jesus' words as the important thing. He did not get the point: that Jesus himself is eternal life.

Jesus answered them, "Did I not choose you, the twelve, and one of you is a devil." By calling Judas to be his disciple in the beginning, Jesus made the cross inevitable. Judas was the devil's agent, a thorn in his side for three long years. He performed miracles in Jesus' name, but never yielded him the affection of his heart. Is it possible that there is a little of Judas in us all?

ARE YOU A JUDEAN OR A GALILEAN?

"*After this Jesus went about in Galilee; he would not go about in Judea, because the Jews sought to kill him.*" *John 7:1*

There were two types of people in the land of Jesus. There were the Galileans, the countryfolk, who wanted to have the easy and comfortable life. They were content if their basic needs were met: food, clothing, and shelter. Jesus was relatively safe in Galilee, but Judea had an altogether different atmosphere. The Judeans were driven by the ambition for success and power. That is the nature of city life. It is acquisitive and aggressive. When we were children we enjoyed the game called "King on the Mountain." That was the game they played in Judea and Jerusalem.

John chapter six developed the sixth theme in this gospel, the theme of nurture. It began with the feeding of the multitudes, followed by Jesus' meditation about himself as the Bread of Life. He gradually revealed the hidden meaning of the feeding, as well as the mystery of the Lord's Supper. It resulted in the vast falling away. All those who were hanging on for what they could get out of it departed, with the exception of Judas. He would be weeded out one year later at the Last Supper.

John chapters seven and eight belong together. They develop the fourth theme, which is homecoming. Remember how Jesus, after the marriage, took his own ones home with him to his Father's house, where he would abide with them, where he cleaned house. Here he goes again.

Everyone is seeking Jesus, whether he or she knows it or not. We seek Jesus that we may derive life from him, or we seek him that we may destroy him. It depends upon our motivation. Is our personal life constructive, or is it destructive? If we derive our spiritual life from Jesus, we will benefit humanity, but if we refuse Jesus we destroy him, others, and ultimately ourselves.

BEWARE OF DIRECTIVE COUNSELING

"*Now the Jews' feast of Tabernacles was at hand.*" *John 7:2*

Six months have elapsed since Jesus fed the multitudes on the occasion of Passover. The great fall festival called Succoth in Hebrew was at hand, when the people inhabited temporary shelters made of branches and foliage in commemoration of the 40 year sojourn in the wilderness under Moses. We too are abiding in these frail temporary bodies of flesh, as we make our pilgrimage to our heavenly Jerusalem, which has its foundations in eternity, whose maker and builder is God.

"So his brothers said to him, `Leave here and go to Judea, that your disciples may see the works you are doing. For no man works in secret if he seeks to be known openly. If you do these things, show yourself to the world.' For even his brothers did not believe in him." How do we know? When you pray do you tell Jesus, "Now I want you to do this, and then I want you to do that?" If you pray like this, you are an unbeliever. Unbelievers think they know better than Jesus what he ought to do. They are quick to give him advise out of their vast knowledge and wisdom, speaking tongue in cheek.

Believers, on the other hand, are like little children. We are reminded of the prayer of Solomon in I Kings 3:7: "And now, O Lord my God, thou hast made thy servant king in place of David my father, although I am but a little child; I do not know how to go out or come in." Well I am so simple that I scarcely know how to come in out of the rain. That is the humility and honesty that God respects.

God said in response to Solomon, "Behold, I give you a wise and discerning mind." If you are so wonderfully wise, you don't need Jesus, and him crucified - the divine foolishness which is wiser than men. Watch out for those who like to play God by always telling others what to do, as the brothers of Jesus told him what he ought to do. My major task is figure out what I ought to do.

❦

TIMING IS OF THE ESSENCE

"**J**esus said to them, 'My time has not yet come, but your time is always here.'" John 7:6

To Jesus timing was of the essence. He would not take one step in the direction of Jerusalem until he got the green light from his Father. His brothers could go to Jerusalem any time. "The world cannot hate you." As unbelievers you are part and parcel of the world. "But it hates me because I testify of it that its works are evil." He had not even heard of Dale Carnegie's course on "How to Win Friends and Influence People." He buttered up no one. He always called a spade a spade in love, which, by the way, was why they crucified him. All who follow his example will fare no better. Remember, though, you who criticize, that Jesus was perfect and sinless. Example accomplishes more than criticism.

"Go to the feast yourselves; I am not going up to the feast, for my time has not yet fully come." So saying, he remained in Galilee. But after his brothers had gone up to the feast, then he also went up, not publicly but in private."

Wait a minute! Whoa, Nellie! Have we caught Jesus in a fib, a white lie? First he says he is not going, and then all of a sudden he goes. What is going on here? Well, he didn't go up to the feast when his brothers went. They would have made a public demonstration, and ballyhooed his arrival. They wanted some fame, at Jesus' expense, for the expansion of their egos.

Jesus could not be party to that. So he waited until his Father said, "Now!" When the time was ripe, exactly right, he went up almost secretly after the pilgrims had departed. His public presentation of himself must take place not in conjunction with the Feast of Booths but with Passover, when he would go up to be slaughtered as the Lamb of God in fulfillment of all the Old Testament scriptures. Jesus fulfills all the Jewish feast days. He will fulfill Tabernacles at his second coming.

❧

THE RETURN TO THE FATHER'S HOUSE

*"**T**he Jews were looking for him at the feast, and saying, 'Where is he?'" John 7.11*

As Messiah Jesus fulfills the deep meaning of all the Jewish feasts. It is inevitable that his own people would look for him on such an occasion. "And there was much muttering about him among the people. While some said, `He is a good man,' others said, `No, he is leading the people astray.'"

Jesus did not come to bring peace on earth in his first coming, but to separate people from one another on the basis of their appraisal of himself. He came to separate the sheep from the goats. Goats have horns that hurt, and they love to butt. "Yes, but. Yes, he may appear to be good, but he is leading people in the wrong direction, away from trust in the establishment." "Yet for fear of the Jews (the religious establishment) no one spoke openly of him." To the present day people fear to speak openly of Jesus. Talking about Jesus may get you into trouble. You are in danger of being deemed a fanatic.

"About the middle of the feast Jesus went up into the temple and taught." About the fourth day Jesus fulfilled the theme of the fourth day (homecoming) by leading his disciples a second time to the temple, where he had cleaned house. When I was fifteen years old I was baptized. From then on I began frequenting the Father's house that I might learn more about Jesus and what he taught, and that I might partake of the Lord's Supper. The water of baptism became for me the wine of Holy Communion. To follow Jesus involves one inevitably in frequenting the house of worship.

"The Jews marveled at it, saying, `How is it that this man has learning, when he has never studied?'" When I graduated from college, I went to Theological Seminary to study, not to teach. But Jesus, the carpenter, went to Jerusalem as Teacher. He had learned at the feet of his heavenly Father.

WHO HAS THE DEMON?

"*So Jesus answered them, 'My teaching is not mine, but his who sent me.'" John 7:16*

Jesus did not claim to be self-taught. The heavenly Father who sent Jesus to earth is the source of his teaching. "If any man's will is to do his will, he shall know whether the teaching is from God or whether I am teaching on my own authority." As soon as I willed to do the Father's will for my life, I immediately received in my heart confirmation that Jesus is from God.

"He who speaks on his own authority seeks his own glory; but he who seeks the glory of him who sent him is true, and in him there is no falsehood." He who speaks on his own (from himself, literally) is out to enhance his own reputation, to make a name for himself. But Jesus made himself of no reputation that his Father might become everything to everyone. He is eager to forgive all who blaspheme and insult himself, but he said that no one can defame the Holy Spirit and get away with it.

"Did not Moses give you the law? Yet none of you keeps the law." No one can keep the law perfectly, because it is of heavenly origin. It is too high for us. "Why do you seek to kill me?" Our lives are destructive of Jesus because we are by nature rebels. His gospel is designed to destroy our egocentricity, the one thing we seek to preserve at all costs. "The people answered, 'You have a demon! Who is seeking to kill you?'" They do not know what spirit they are of. They have the demon of unbelief within them, so inevitably they project their own evil upon Jesus. The thing we hate in ourselves we see in those about us, whether it be there or not. In our egocentricity, we go about in a house of mirrors. In this benighted condition, we nearly drive ourselves mad.

Someone said, "The trouble in the church today is that there are too many spirits of unbelief standing behind pulpits." A little old lady said to her preacher, "In spite of all you said today, I still believe in God."

APPEARANCES ARE DECEPTIVE

"Jesus answered, 'I did one deed, and you all marvel at it.'"

John 7:21

More than a year earlier Jesus had healed the man thirty-eight years an invalid on the Sabbath day, and they still hadn't gotten over it. How could he, a violater of the Sabbath law, do such a thing? "Moses gave you circumcision (not that it is from Moses, but from the fathers - Abraham, Isaac, and Jacob), and you circumcise a man on the Sabbath (should the eighth day from birth fall on the Sabbath). If on the Sabbath a man receives circumcision, so that the law of Moses may not be broken, are you angry with me because on the Sabbath I made a man's whole body well?"

The law requiring circumcision on the eighth day had priority over the Sabbath law. Medical science has confirmed that there is less risk of excessive bleeding on the eighth day than any other. Eight is the number of new beginnings. How beautiful to receive in one's flesh the sign of the covenant on that day. Circumcision was regarded as having therapeutic value as well. So it pointed to complete wholeness, which Jesus had granted the invalid on the Sabbath.

"Do not judge by appearances, but judge with right judgment." "Appearances" is literally "according to face." Beauty is only skin deep. According to Isaiah 53:2 the suffering servant (Jesus) "had no form or comeliness that we should look at him, and no beauty that we should desire him." We must look beneath the surface or we will be deceived every time.

God looks at the heart. He knows the secrets that lurk therein. The devil himself comes to us as an angel of light, without pitchfork or barbed tail. To be a Christian obliges one to think more deeply than non-Christians. Reality is complicated by reason of the fact that there are two supernatural spirits operative in the world. Those who pretend that there is no Devil have made Jesus out to be a liar, whether they realize it or not.

🍒

WHERE DO YOU COME FROM?

"**S**ome *of the people of Jerusalem said, `Is not this the man whom they seek to kill?'"* John 7:25

We seek Jesus to derive life from him, or we seek to kill him, depending upon whether we are moved by the Holy Spirit or by the devil. Tragically a spirit of religion is not the Spirit of God. "Religion" in the Latin means "return to bondage." Only when we surrender to Jesus does it take on its more profound meaning, "to reconnect." Jesus, as the only Mediator between God and man, reconnects us with our Creator. Though they seek to kill him, "here he is, speaking openly, and they say nothing to him! Can it be that the authorities really know that this is the Christ?"

The last parable Jesus told, as recorded in Mark 12:1-9, discloses the fact that Jesus' enemies rejected him because they knew exactly who he was, not out of ignorance. "Yet we know where this man comes from; and when the Christ appears, no one will know where he comes from." So Jesus proclaimed, as he taught in the temple, "You know me, and you know where I come from?"

It is important to know where a person comes from. They called him Jesus of Nazareth, because that is where he lived for most of his life. Actually he should have been called Jesus of Bethlehem, because that was the place of his birth. I myself have lived in Missouri for 24 years now, but I was born in Nebraska, where I lived for my first 18 years in Omaha, an Indian word meaning "upstream." I am at heart an upstreamer, a word which characterizes my life. It has been uphill all the way. To know someone, you must know from where that one is coming. To know Jesus, you must know that he comes from heaven by way of Bethlehem, "House of bread." Only so is he entitled to be called "the Bread of Life." Bread has been called the staff of life. We lean upon it for existence itself. A little girl prayed the Lord's Prayer, "Give us this day our jelly bread."

THE GREATEST LIE IMAGINABLE

"**B**ut I have not come of my own accord; he who sent me is true, and him you do not know." John 7:28

The most important thing a person can know is who Jesus is. It is not what you know, but who you know. To know Jesus personally and intimately is to know the One who sent him. The One who sent him is true and incapable of lying. "Let God be true, though every man be found a liar," wrote St. Paul. Jesus accused the most religious people who ever lived of not knowing God.

Today the Moslems appear to be the most religious people on earth. Many of them gladly die for their religion. Even so, they do not know God. They call God Allah. But Allah is not his name. His name is Abba - in the English "Daddy" or "Papa." He is the Papa of our Lord and Saviour Jesus Christ. The Moslems pretend that Mohammed is God's prophet. Actually Mohammed is the most significant false prophet who ever lived. He has led more people astray than anyone in history. He taught in the Koran that Jesus is not the Eternal Son of God, but only a prophet. He uttered the greatest lie imaginable in saying that "Jesus did not die upon the cross, but ascended to heaven without dying." He wrote that "Judas Iscariot died in Jesus' place." If you believe the teaching of Mohammed you will die in your sins. Every teaching that is not 100% on target in regard to the Person, Nature, and Work of Jesus Christ is demonic. Jesus is God become man. And he died upon the cross in our stead that we, through faith in him and his mighty resurrection, might not die and go to hell, but live with him forever.

We were worshiping the Lord in songs of praise on temple mount near the Golden Gate, through which Moslems say Jesus will enter Jerusalem upon his return to earth. A Moslem police officer interrupted, saying it was unlawful for us Christians to worship at this sacred site. We left amazed, but undaunted.

❦

ARREST, IF YOU CAN, THE ARRESTING ONE

"**J** *know him, for I come from him, and he sent me.*" *John 7:29*
          It is one thing to know about someone, but quite another thing to know the individual personally. Theologians know quite a bit about God, but do they know him? Professor Piper at Princeton knew the Lord to be a miracle working God to the present hour. I thank God for that. He opened the door for me to experience God on a deeper level. "So they sought to arrest him; but no one laid hands on him, because his hour had not yet come."

          What hour had not yet come? Why his hour to depart from this world to the Father. Until his hour of Exodus (the "way out" literally) arrived, he could be seized by no one. The expression "his hour" occurs time and again like the tolling of a bell. For whom does the bell toll? It tolls for you and me. Our hour of departure is approaching whether we are ready or not. "Be prepared" is the motto of the Boy Scouts. It is a good motto for us all. "Until God is through using me, I am immortal," someone said. The only trouble is I do not know when God is through using me.

          "Yet many of the people believed him; they said, 'When Christ appears, will he do more signs than this man has done?'" In this gospel Jesus' miracles are always called signs. The most important thing is not the display of divine power, but that which is thereby signified. Signs are windows into heavenly reality. Jesus never performed signs on demand. He took his instructions only from his heavenly Father.

          "The Pharisees heard the crowd thus muttering about him, and the chief priests and Pharisees sent officers to arrest him." At the beginning these two groups sent separate delegations to interrogate the Baptist. Now their common hostility to Jesus brought them together. Jesus is the peacemaker. Because of him even his enemies make peace with one another.

WHERE I AM YOU CANNOT COME

"**J**esus then said, `I shall be with you a little longer, and then I go to him who sent me; you will seek me and you will not find me; where I am you cannot come.'"　　　　　*John 7:33,34*

Joseph Policastro had the salty tang. I met him at Presbytery in New Jersey. He was an elder in the Presbyterian Church in Asbury Park. He told how he used to preach to his fellow workers in a manufacturing plant about Jesus, thereby making himself unpopular. One night at work they gathered around him to beat him up. He stood his ground and preached the gospel. When he had finished, he was told by a big hulk of a man, "Policastro, we know you are of God. We were going to beat up on you, but all the time you were speaking, we could not take a step toward you. Get out of here, and never come back." He did leave, and never came back. Where Joe was they could not come, because he was divinely protected. This was why they could not arrest Jesus. The Holy Spirit or angels had evidently ringed him round.

"The Jews said to one another, `Where does this man intend to go that we shall not find him? Does he intend to go to the Dispersion (the Jews) among the Greeks (the heathen) and teach the Greeks?'"

This is exactly what he intended to do. Ten years after his death and resurrection, he sent Peter to preach to the heathen in the house of Cornelius. Not long after he flung Paul and his companions out among the Jews of the Dispersion. When the majority of the Jews in the gentile cities rejected the gospel, Paul and his companions shook the dust off their feet and went to their heathen neighbors. Now the Jews cannot find him because he is a Greek-speaking Christ, and seems to them a foreigner. It will require a special revelation at the end of the age before the Jews as a people will be able to embrace their Messiah, who seems to them so strange. This will happen after the opening of the sixth seal in Rev. 6:12-17.

❦

IS YOUR CUP RUNNING OVER?

"*On the last day of the feast, the great day, Jesus stood up and proclaimed, 'If any one thirst, let him come to me and drink,'*"

John 7:37

The last day of the Feast of Tabernacles, the eighth day, is called Simhat Torah (Happy Law). It is the most joyous day in the Jewish religious calendar. The populace celebrate and dance in the streets much of the night. When the temple stood, the high priest carried water in a golden pitcher from the pool of Siloam to the altar in front of the temple, where before the religious procession he poured it out. Then amid the splendor of the lamps the dancing began.

In 1970 I observed this celebration in the ultra-orthodox section of Jerusalem, where Zwe Rose and I were privileged to share our faith in Jesus with a few English-speaking Jews. It was a night to remember. We were interogated by the police for breaking the law against proselyting. We were in danger of being expelled from the country, I learned later. Talking about Jesus can get you into trouble in many places.

On the occasion of this rejoicing, Jesus said, in effect, if all this religious pageantry and falderal still leaves you strangely unsatisfied, come to me. "He who believes in me, as the scripture has said, 'Out of his heart (belly) shall flow rivers of living water.'" Now this he said about the Spirit, which those who believe in him were to receive; for as yet the Spirit had not been given, because Jesus was not yet glorified. At Pentecost the river began to flow from the temple of Christ's body that the thirsty world might be watered by God. We are reminded of the vision of Ezekiel 47:1-12, where water was issuing forth from below the threshold of the temple in ever increasing measure, until it sweetened the Dead Sea. This is a parable of the ministry of the Church through the centuries. Through us the water of God's Spirit is bringing life to the world.

CAN A COMMUNIST BE A CHRISTIAN?

"*When they heard these words, some of the people said, 'This is really the prophet.'*" *John 7:40*

The prophet was to be one like Moses. See Deuteronomy 18:15-19. Moses struck the rock in the wilderness and out gushed the water for the people to drink. Jesus, it turns out, is the Rock, who was struck by the rod of the law, that we who thirst may drink of his life-giving stream (God's Spirit).

"Others said, 'This is the Christ.' But some said 'Is the Christ to come from Galilee? Has not the scripture said that the Christ is descended from David, and comes from Bethlehem, the village where David was?' So there was a division among the people over him. Some of them wanted to arrest him, but no one laid hands on him." We remember how Jesus said, "I did not come to bring peace but a sword." He forces us to choose up sides. A minister I know said that he believes it is possible to be a communist and a Christian. I beg to differ with him. The communist dictum is, "There is no God." But "the fool says in his heart, 'There is no God.'" (Psalm 14:1). Only the damn fool will say it with his lips.

Years ago I heard a Metropolitan of the Russian Orthodox Church tell that he was in Red Square in 1918 and heard Lenin address three million Russians. Lenin said defiantly: "We have defeated the earthly powers. Now we shall dethrone the heavenly powers." And he shook his fist in the teeth of the heavens, declaring war against God Almighty. The Metropolitan then said that the divine answer to this is found in Psalm 2. "The rulers take soviet (literally) against the LORD." The divine reaction: "He who sits in the heavens laughs; the LORD has them in derision." Ultimately he "will dash them in pieces like a potter's vessel." I do not think it is possible to be against God and for God at the same time. It is an either/or. Don't you agree?

❦

THE DEATH THROES OF RELIGION

"*Then the officers went back to the chief priests and Pharisees, who said to them, 'Why did you not bring him?'*" John 7:45

"The officers answered, 'No man ever spoke like this man!'" Was that their way of saying, "He is the Word of God?" "The Pharisees answered them, 'Are you led astray, you also? Have any of the authorities or of the Pharisees believed in him? But this crowd, who do not know the law, are accursed.'"

Death has been defined as loss of control, or the ultimate weakness. If that be true, the religion of the priests and Pharisees was in its death throes. They were losing their grip even upon those whose job it was to implement their decisions. Now all that the Pharisees could do was to lash out at the common folk. They felt themselves superior by reason of their religious knowledge. "Knowledge puffs up; love builds up," wrote St. Paul. It is frightening to consider that the more religious knowledge we have, the more we are responsible to love people. It is easy to curse others. It is blessed to reach out a helping hand. We need fewer critics and more examples here below.

"Nicodemus, who had gone to him before, and who was one of them, said to them, 'Does our law judge a man without first giving him a hearing and learning what he does?'" Bias is inevitable, but prejudice is reprehensible. It means "to judge before the evidence has been presented." In attacking Jesus, his enemies were violating their own law, undermining the ground beneath their feet.

"They replied, 'Are you from Galilee too? Search and you will see that no prophet is to rise from Galilee.'" Proud in their knowledge of their scriptures, they had completely forgotten Isaiah 9:1,2: "In the latter time he will make glorious Galilee of the nations. The people who walked in darkness have seen a great light." Isaiah had prophecied the coming to Galilee of one much greater than a prophet, the Light of the world.

EACH TO HIS OWN HOUSE

"*They went each to his own house, but Jesus went to the Mount of Olives.*" *John 7:53-8:1*

During the days of his ministry, unlike the birds and the foxes, Jesus had no place to lay his head, so he slept out of doors on the Mount of Olives. The Mount of Olives represents the anointing of the Holy Spirit. The second mountain in Jerusalem is Temple Mount (Moriah meaning "the Lord will provide.") Gordon's Calvary north of the city wall is an extension of that mountain, where the Lord provided the Lamb of God as the vicarious sacrifice for the sins of the world. The third mountain of Jerusalem is Scopus, a word meaning "see." To me it speaks of God the Father who sees the end from the beginning and oversees the whole of creation. So, the three Persons of the Godhead are symbolized by the mountains of Jerusalem. It was from the Mount of Olives that the Holy Spirit caught up Jesus and carried him back to heaven.

"Early in the morning he came again to the temple; all the people came to him, and he sat down and taught them." Remember that Chapters 7 and 8 develop the theme of home-coming. Upon this earth Jesus felt most at home in the place where his Father was worshiped. This was where his claim to be the Son of God was contested and rejected.

"The scribes and Pharisees brought a woman who had been caught in adultery, and placing her in the midst, they said to him, 'Teacher, this woman has been caught in adultery.'" The question that comes to mind is where was the man? It takes two to tango, as we say. Today we call it sexism. The woman was the guilty party, while "boys will be boys." God, on the other hand, does not play favorites, as legalists are prone to do. Two men were going through a cemetery where they saw the epitaph, "Here lies a lawyer and an honest man." "What do you know," said one to the other, "Two men in one grave." Don't be offended; it is only a joke.

❧

HE SAVED HER LIFE

"**Now** *in the law Moses commanded us to stone such. What do you say about her?'"*   *John 8:5*

"This they said to test him, that they might bring some charge against him." A young Jew, Art Katz, had read this far in the gospel, and was much enamored of Jesus. Now he saw that his hero was trapped. If Jesus said, "Release her," he would be stoned to death as one who enjoined the violation of the law. If he commanded her to be stoned, he could no longer be regarded as "the friend of sinners," and would forfeit his reputation as the compassionate one.

"Jesus bent down and wrote with his finger on the ground," stalling for time in his quandary, thought Art. "And as they continued to ask him, he stood up and said to them, `Let him who is without sin among you be the first to throw a stone at her!'" This word struck Art right in the heart. Immediately he knew that Jesus is God. Only God in his wisdom could so quickly turn the situation about to impale his adversaries on the horns of their own dilemma. "And once more he bent down and wrote with his finger on the ground." It has been suggested that he looked at one accuser and wrote, "Thief," at another and wrote, "Idolater." He may have identified the particular sin of each.

"But when they heard it, they went away, one by one, beginning with the eldest, and Jesus was left alone with the woman standing before him. Jesus looked up and said to her, `Woman, where are they? Has no one condemned you?'" Since he was without sin, he might have. "She said, `No one, Lord.' And Jesus said, `Neither do I condemn you; go, and do not sin again.'" He would be condemned for her upon the cross. He did not condone her behaviour, but charged her to express her gratitude by living a life that would not engage in adultery again. Someone said, "It is perfectly all right to make a mistake, just so it is always a different one." ❦

LIKE FATHER, LIKE SON

" *Again Jesus spoke to them, saying, 'I am the light of the world; he who follows me will not walk in darkness, but will have the light of life.'"*   *John 8:12*

We saw in Chapter 7 that Jesus is the spiritual Rock, which followed Israel in the wilderness, from which all drank the same supernatural drink. I Cor. 10:4 Now we learn that Jesus is the supernatural Light that guided and warmed them by night, and directed and sheltered them by day. Following Jesus, we experience the truth concerning the life of God.

"The Pharisees then said to him, 'You are bearing witness to yourself; your testimony is not true.'" People make exaggerated statements about their own importance continually, but when you, Jesus, make such a claim in the Temple of God, you go too far.

"Jesus answered, 'Even if I do bear witness to myself, my testimony is true, for I know whence I have come and whither I am going, but you do not know whence I come or whither I am going. You judge according to the flesh, I judge no one.'" Isn't it remarkable? "We must all appear before the judgment seat of Christ" (2 Cor. 5:10), and yet our judge does not judge us in his first coming. "Yet even if I do judge, my judgment is true, for it is not I alone that judge, but I and he that sent me. In your law it is written that the testimony of two men is true; I bear witness to myself, and the Father who sent me bears witness to me." They said to him therefore, "Where is your Father?" They probably thought that he was referring to some great rabbi who had indoctrinated him. Jesus answered, "You know neither me nor my Father; if you knew me, you would know my Father also." Like father, like Son.

I didn't see my father from the time I was 4 until I was 40. When I saw him, I thought I was seeing his father. They looked so much alike. It is exciting to realize that our knowledge of Jesus translates into the knowledge of the Great Creator.

❦

WHO DIED?

"**B**ut no one arrested him, because his hour had not yet come."
                                                            John 8:20

"Again he said to them, `I go away, and you will seek me and die in your sin; where I am going, you cannot come.'" Do you remember what that singular and heinous sin is? The sin of unbelief. Faith in Jesus makes us righteous (right with God). Persistence in disbelief keeps us estranged from God. "Then said the Jews, `Will he kill himself, since he says, `Where I am going, you cannot come?'" They had the notion that those who killed themselves went into torment, and they certainly didn't intend to follow him there.

"He said to them, `You are from below, I am from above; you are of this world, I am not of this world. I told you that you would die in your sins, for you will die in your sins unless you believe that I am.'" (The "he" is not in the Greek text). It is not enough to believe that Jesus is the greatest teacher of religion who ever lived, nor that he is the most important person in history.

"They said to him, `Who are you?' Jesus said to them, `Even what I have told you from the beginning.'" Another possible rendering: Even the One speaking to you from the beginning. (I am the One whose very nature it is to speak to you from the beginning of creation - the Eternal Word of God.) `I have much to say about you and much to judge; but he who sent me is true, and I declare to the world what I have heard from him.' (Jesus is God addressing us in this zone of conflict and death, the world). They did not understand that he spoke to them of the Father (God). So Jesus said, `When you have lifted up the Son of man, then you will know that I am, and that I do nothing on my own authority but speak thus as the Father taught me.'" After they had lifted him up upon the cruel tree, they would gradually begin to see that he died as no man has ever died. A Jehovah Witness once said to me, "You are saying that God died." "Exactly," I responded, "for you and for me."

THE SUPREME ADDICTION

"*And he who sent me is with me; he has not left me alone, for I always do what is pleasing to him.*" *John 8:29*

How can the One who sent Jesus be with him, unless that One be God? The Jews have a saying, "As the soul fills the body, so God fills the universe." The reason Jesus gives for the Father's presence with him is his sinlessness. To displease God is sin. We please God by acknowledging that we are created by God, (and therefore depend on him), for God, (and therefore pursue his plan for our lives). We do both when we trust in Jesus and follow him. "As he spoke thus, many believed in him." Faith comes through hearing, and hearing through a "rhema" (a particular word) of Christ, wrote St. Paul in Romans 10:17.

"Jesus then said to the Jews who had believed in him, `If you continue in my word, you are truly my disciples, and you will know the truth, and the truth will make you free.'" In other words, they had started running the race of faith, but they must continue to do so. He who finishes the race receives the prize. Those who drop out along the way receive nothing. "They answered him, `We are descendents of Abraham, and have never been in bondage to anyone. How is it that you say, `You will be made free?'" They felt that Jesus was insulting them in saying that they were not free. They took pride in their independent spirit which they had inherited from Abraham.

"Jesus answered them, `Truly, truly, I say to you, everyone who commits sin is a slave to sin.'" The tyranny that Jesus was talking about is not external but internal. Sin is a deceitful power that enslaves us, preventing us from doing good at all times. One expression of sin's power is addiction in its many forms. We will refrain from citing any, lest we stop teaching and start meddling. I am adept at detecting yours, as you are mine. We are all standing in our own blind spot. Jesus alone was addiction free, as he was consumed by the love of God.

❦

FREE INDEED

"*The slave does not continue in the house forever; the Son contin-ues forever.*" *John 8:35*

God said to Abraham, "Cast out the slave woman (Hagar) with her son (Ishmael),... for through Isaac (the son of promise) shall your descendents be named." Genesis 21:10-12. Jesus, the ultimate Son of promise, continues in God's family forever. "So if the Son makes you free, you will be free indeed." We credit Abraham Lincoln with making the Emancipation Proclamation. He struck the institution of slavery a mighty blow. The war to liberate the black slaves cost hundreds of thousands of lives including Lincoln's own. But who can say that that race is totally free? Every black will tell us that they have a long way to go.

Years ago I heard a black Presbyterian minister say that he was serving a church in Philadelphia when Dr. Edler Hawkins was elected Moderator of our denomination's General Assembly. From the pulpit he waxed eloquent over this black minister being chosen for the highest office in our Church, and said, "I can envision the day when a black man will live in the White House." There was a snicker in the choir loft. After the service his wife, who sang in the choir, told him, "When you said what you did, a choir member said, 'The day a nigger gets in the White House is the day I'm leaving.'" The pastor then informed us that in our country every black person is born feeling inferior to whites and every white is born feeling superior to blacks.

A church in Boston was served by two ministers, Rev. Black and Rev. White. On Sunday morning Rev. White preached and would blackball the saints. On Sunday evening Rev. Black preached and would whitewash the sinners. When I feel too saintly, I need to have my sins pointed out to me. When I feel too sinful, I need to be sprinkled afresh with the precious blood of the Lamb. When he declares me free from sin, I am free indeed.

❧

THE ACID TEST

"I *know that you are descendants of Abraham; yet you seek to kill me, because my word finds no place in you."* John 8:37

The extraordinary thing is that Jesus is speaking to the Jews who had believed in him (8:31). I talked the other day to a man who considers himself a Christian, and yet the things he said revealed there to be murder in his heart. Lord, give us the grace to see ourselves as you see us. But perhaps we could not bear it. Does your heart make room for Jesus' word? Certainly not, if the only time you allow for it is the sermon on Sunday morning. They said concerning an individual that he was a holy Joe on Sunday, and a holy terror all the rest of the week.

"I speak of what I have seen with my Father, and you do what you have heard from your father." Now Jesus is getting down to the root of the matter, the question of origin. "They answered him, `Abraham is our Father.' Jesus said to them, `If you were Abraham's children, you would do what Abraham did, but now you seek to kill me, a man who has told you the truth which I heard from God; this is not what Abraham did.'"

Remember how Abraham welcomed the messengers sent by God and killed for their meal the fatted calf? Genesis 18:1-8. It never entered his mind to kill God's messenger. "`You do what your father did.'" Now they had their backs against the wall. "They said to him, `We were not born of fornication; we have one Father, even God.'" They still claimed Abraham to be their father, and went up a peg, claiming to be even the offspring of God.

"Jesus said to them, `If God were your Father, you would love me, for I proceeded and came forth from God; I came not of my own accord, but he sent me.'" Big question: Do you and I love Jesus? "If any one has no love for the Lord, let him be accursed (devoted to destruction)." I Cor. 16:22 If we have no love for Jesus, we are still in our sins.

❦

WHY DON'T I GO TO CHURCH?

"**W**hy do you not understand what I say? It is because you cannot bear to hear my word." John 8:43

Someone said, "There are three reasons why I do not go to church: because I don't have to go, because there are some things in my life that ought not to be there, and because I don't want to be reminded of them. Another common excuse: there are too many hypocrites in church. Answer: there is always room for one more. Friend, you are hiding behind a hypocrite (phony). You have got to be smaller than something to hide behind it.

"You are of your Father the devil, and your will is to do your Father's desires." These words expose their root problem. They have got the wrong father. We are sinners not because we sin. We sin because we are by nature sinners. The good news is, as the little girl said, that Jesus died for cinders. We are cinders in God's eye, making him cry. When we surrender to Jesus Christ, the cinder leaves God's eye, and we become at once the apple of his eye. Speaking of the devil, Jesus went on to say, "He was a murderer from the beginning, and has nothing to do with the truth, because there is no truth in him."

The devil murdered our first parents in the garden of Eden. He lied in accusing God of knowing experientially good and evil. But God is light. There is no darkness or evil in him. He knows about evil, but can have no personal contact with it. That is why unrepentant sin separates from God. God hates sin and is repelled by those who cling to it. "When (the devil) lies, he speaks according to his own nature, for he is a liar and the father of lies." When the devil told Eve, "You will not die," if she ate the forbidden fruit, he lied. He knew that upon eating their spirits would immediately die, just as his spirit died when he disobeyed God in seeking to be his equal. Someone said that our trouble began with that "apple" on the tree. No, it began with that "pair" on the ground.

❧

DO YOU BELIEVE IN THE DEVIL?

*"***B***ut, because I tell you the truth, you do not believe me."*

John 8:45

In other words, if Jesus lied they would have no trouble believing him. Some people do not believe there is a devil. They are calling Jesus a liar. They are saying that Jesus sinned. Jesus told of the devil's three temptations. If those thoughts were not suggested to him by another, then they came out of his own unconscious. If so, then he originated thoughts displeasing to God, and he is a sinner like you and me. Jesus said, "Which of you convicts me of sin?" No one ever has.

"If I tell the truth, why do you not believe me?" He already made that plain - because they were deceived by the devil and were believers in the liar. Hans Hoffman was asked, "Do you believe in the devil?" "No," he answered, "I believe in Jesus Christ." "He who is of God hears the words of God." If you are born of God, you delight in hearing time and again all that the Bible says. It is your spiritual nourishment.

"The reason why you do not hear them is that you are not of God." You are of your father the devil. The Jews answered him, "Are we not right in saying you are a Samaritan and have a demon?" Since they had lost the argument, all they could do was resort to name calling. "Sticks and stones may break my bones, but names will never hurt me." Don't be so sure. Name calling is the devil's brew. Diabolos (the Greek for devil) is the word from which diabolical is derived, and it means accuser, slanderer. Jesus, ignoring the charge that he was a Samaritan (a self-evident lie), answered, "I have not a demon; but I honor my Father, and you dishonor me." They were approaching the unforgivable sin. The spirit which he had was the Holy Spirit. He was always careful to honor his heavenly Father. We should be equally careful to honor Jesus. Those who take his name in vain are bringing shame upon themselves. They are disclosing the cesspool in their hearts.

❦

HOW NOT TO WIN FRIENDS

"*Yet I do not seek my own glory; there is One who seeks it and he will be the judge." John 8:50*

Because Jesus did not seek his own glory, he was free to go to the cross, the most ignominious fate imaginable. Since he went the way of the cross, he placed himself in the position for his Father to glorify him by exalting him to his right hand. Furthermore God judged the nation that rejected him by turning their city over to the Roman power a generation later. "Truly, truly, I say to you, if any one keeps my word, he will never see death." The word "see" is "theoreo" from which theorize is derived. The person who obeys Jesus will never contemplate death nor gaze into the eyes of the fallen angel who bears that name. Rev. 6:8.

The Jews said to him, "Now we know that you have a demon. Abraham died, as did the prophets, and you say, `If anyone keeps my word, he will never taste death.'" Notice the subtle change in terminology. Jesus did not say the believer would not taste or experience death in the sense of going through it, only that he would not be obliged to endure it as an ongoing experience. The Jews then said, "Are you greater than our father Abraham who died? And the prophets died! Who do you claim to be?" Jesus answered, "If I glorify myself, my glory is nothing; it is my Father who glorifies me, of whom you say that he is your God." Jesus refused to make any pretentious claims as to his own greatness. He would allow his Father to vindicate him. "But you do not know him," that is your problem - your ignorance of God. "I know him. If I said, I do not know him, I should be a liar like you." How tactless!

As a youngster I asked my teenage sister which of the four boys on the porch she loved. I had 3 suckers: 1 for me, 1 for her, and 1 for that special friend. She quickly ushered me off the porch. They will be quick to usher Jesus off the face of the earth for being so "tactless."

❦

HISTORY'S MOST EXTRAORDINARY
CONVERSATION

*"**If** I said, I do not know him, I should be a liar like you; but I do know him and I keep his word." John 8:55*

The more intimately one knows God, the more he is bound and obliged to do what he says. "Your father Abraham rejoiced that he was to see my day; he saw it and was glad." The first time Abraham saw Jesus' day was on the occasion of the birth of Isaac, who was born to his ancient parents in fulfillment of God's promise. Jesus' birth of the virgin Mary was even more remarkable. The primary time he saw Jesus' day was the time he was going to sacrifice Isaac, when the Lord provided the ram caught in the thicket as the substitute. The ultimate substitute, of course, was Jesus, who died upon the central cross. Do you know for whom that cross was made? For Barabbas. But at the last moment Jesus was substituted for Barabbas.

Romans 6:6 says: "We know that our old self was crucified with him so that the sinful body might be destroyed, and we might no longer be enslaved to sin." That verse tells me that I am Barabbas. Think about it. Romans is the sixth book in the New Testament. So that verse may be regarded as 666, the number of the antichrist (Revelation 13:18). My "old self," my sinful nature, is every bit as much a rebel as was Barabbas (a name which means "son of a father"). We remember that Jesus had just said "your father is the devil." Until we are born of God, we are the spiritual offspring of the devil and imitate his behavior.

The Jews then said to him, "You are not yet fifty years old, and have you seen Abraham?" Just like their father, they twisted everything Jesus said. Though in the deepest sense, he, as the Eternal One, had seen Abraham. Jesus said to them, "Truly, truly, I say to you, before Abraham was, I am." So they took up stones to throw at him (for "this blasphemy"); but Jesus hid himself (rendered himself invisible?), and went out of the temple.

❦

A GOD WHO HIDES HIMSELF

"*But Jesus hid himself, and went out of the temple.*" *John 8:59*

As we have said, chapters 7 and 8 develop the theme of homecoming/abiding. It all took place in his Father's house, the temple in Jerusalem. "Thy way, O God, is in the sanctuary," wrote Asaph in Psalm 77:13. A moment ago a young man "down on his luck" knocked on the study door, seeking help. The house of prayer and praise is a good place to come for help. We were able to give him a few dollars, but above all he and I had prayer together. Through his prayer, I could tell he is a believer. I gave him a copy of this book (January through March) and of our other book about Dreams. God speaks to us externally through the Bible and internally through the Holy Spirit.

One of the easiest ways for the Spirit to speak to us is through our dreams, if we are willing to take the time and trouble to learn the language of our own dreaming. In Bible times they did. Is it possible that Jesus has been hiding himself in the temple of your body? If you are a Christian, you have his Holy Spirit in the unconscious of your heart. When I was a child, I delighted in hunting for Easter eggs. Now, as a man, I enjoy seeking God's guidance and encouragement inside of myself during the watches of the night. "He gives to his beloved in sleep," we read in Psalm 127:2.

How exciting it is to discover that God inhabits our bodies, thanks to our allegiance to Jesus Christ; that the Spirit of God is our drink when we are thirsty according to 7:37; that he is the light who guides us through the darkness according to 8:12; that he is the Word who speaks to us from within ourselves according to 8:25. No wonder our hearts are restless until we find our rest in him, and he in us. "You would not be seeking me had I not already found you," wrote Blaise Pascal of God. It is difficult to get into a room when one is already in it. By faith we realize that we are already in Christ.

❦

BLIND FROM BIRTH

"As he passed by, he saw a man blind from his birth." John 9:1

Chapter 9 develops the idea expressed in 3:3: "Truly, truly, I say to you, unless one is born anew he cannot see the Kingdom of God." Seeing the Kingdom is the concept underlying chapter 9. Chapter 10 develops the thought found in 3:5; "Truly, truly, I say to you, unless one is born of water and the Spirit, he cannot enter the Kingdom." Entering the Kingdom is the principle undergirding chapter 10. So together these chapters build upon what Jesus said to Nicodemus: You must be born anew.

"As Jesus passed by he saw a man blind from his birth." From the Greek word saw, "eiden," we get the word idea. Jesus had a clear idea of this man who was born blind. It would be good for us to have a clear idea too, because he represents you and me, and the entire human race. Because of original sin, we have all been born blind as far as the Kingdom is concerned. We will not be able to form a clear idea of it, unless we are born of the Spirit.

And his disciples asked him, "Rabbi, who sinned, this man or his parents, that he was born blind?" His disciples, brought up in traditional Judaism, had failed to learn the message taught in Job, that handicaps and misfortune are not necessarily the product of sin. Jesus answered, "It was not that this man sinned or his parents, but that the works of God might be made manifest in him." The "works of God" is another way of saying "the Kingdom of God." This man's blindness would provide an occasion for God to make evil to bless him.

"We must work the works of him who sent me, while it is day; night comes, when no one can work." There is a divine necessity laid not only upon Jesus but us as well to take part in what God is up to at the present time. The hour of darkness is approaching, when evil will have full sway. It is urgent, therefore, that we seize every opportunity to minister to those in need. We shall not pass this way again.

❧

THE WATERS OF SHILOAH

"As long as I am in the world, I am the light of the world."
John 9:5

Strictly speaking Jesus is no longer the light of the world, because he has gone back to heaven. Now we who believe in him are the light of the world, a city set on a hill that cannot be hid. Mt. 5:14. To illustrate the fact that while he was here in the flesh he was the world's light, "he spat on the ground and made clay of the spittle and anointed the man's eyes with clay, saying to him, `Go, wash in the pool of Siloam (which means sent).'" It is significant that Jesus, the Sent One (9:4), sent this man to the pool, the name of which means sent.

Eight centuries before Christ, Hezekiah had his workmen tunnel through Temple Mount to conduct the water of Gihon spring outside the city wall to the pool of Siloam within the city. Speaking of this stream, Isaiah 8:5,6 reads, "The Lord spoke to me again:`Because this people have refused the waters of Shiloah (sent) that flow gently,'" he was going to bring against them the great River Euphrates, symbolizing the Assyrian army. The water sent through the rock speaks of the Holy Spirit that flows gently into our lives through the Rock (Jesus) whose body was pierced and wounded. If we refuse Jesus and the gently flowing stream, we too shall not gain our sight.

"He came back seeing" (blepon). The word means simply to see the facts. Though he could see physically, he did not yet enjoy spiritual insight, as we shall observe. "The neighbors and those who had seen (theoreo) him before as a beggar, said, `Is not this the man who used to sit and beg?' Some said, `It is he'; others said, `No, but he is like him.' He said, `I am the man.'" Theoreo means to look carefully with contemplation, to ponder and reflect critically. People look at us quizically, when we have encountered Jesus. Are we the same person, or are we different? They can't make up their minds about us. One thing for sure, we can no longer sit and beg.

❧

HOW WERE YOUR EYES OPENED?

"They said to him, 'Then how were your eyes opened?'"

John 9:10

"How" is the scientific question. The more important question would be, "why" did he open your eyes? The answer, of course, is because of his love. Well how were your eyes opened to the love of God? As a high school freshman, I heard a blind evangelist tell of his former life as a member of a dance band. He had been living a dissolute life. Then while hunting, he was climbing a fence, when one of the barbs squeezed the trigger on his shot gun, which discharged in his face. Lying on his hospital bed, blind and in despair, he called upon the Lord, and surrendered what was left of his life to Jesus. Christ came into his heart. In seminary he tutored sighted students in Biblical Greek. His expression of the gospel was so powerful that I responded to the altar call.

He answered, "The man called Jesus made clay, and anointed my eyes and said to me, `Go to Siloam and wash;' so I went and washed and received my sight." It is evident that he has not yet seen the Kingdom, because he said, "The man called Jesus" did this for him. Jesus is just "the man." Earlier he had said, "I am the man." So Jesus is no more than a man like himself. He sees with his bodily eyes, but his spiritual eyes are still darkened. They said to him, "Where is he?" He said, "I do not know." He is at this juncture an agnostic. An agnostic is one who says, "I do not know who Jesus is." The Latin equivalent of the Greek word is ignoramus, nothing to be proud of.

"They brought to the Pharisees the man who had formerly been blind." I think of the Pharisees as `Far I sees'. They are the far-sighted ones. As Jesus said, they would traverse land and sea to make one convert, and then turn him into twice as much a son of hell as themselves. It is safer to be near-sighted spiritually, that we might see ourselves as others see us, and above all as God sees us.

❧

THE FAR-I-SEE AGAIN

"*Now it was a Sabbath day when Jesus made the clay and opened his eyes.*" *John 9:14*

Now we can understand why Jesus went to all the trouble of mingling the clay and spittle. He could have simply prayed or laid his hands on him as on other occasions of giving sight to the blind. But since it was the Sabbath, he intentionally engaged in this work to cross sabers with the legalists. It makes us think of God fashioning man out of dust from the ground in Gen. 2. Through Jesus we are in touch with our Creator. "The Pharisees again asked him how he had received his sight. And he said to them, `He put clay on my eyes, and I washed, and I see.'" He had told the story so often that he is getting tired of telling it. It is getting shorter and sweeter.

"Some of the Pharisees said, `This man is not from God, for he does not keep the Sabbath.'" Sabbath observance had been the central feature of their faith ever since the exile in Babylon. "But others said, `How can a man who is a sinner do such signs?'" Good question! "There was a division among them." The God of Creation at the beginning separated light from darkness; he divided the sea from the dry land. Divide and conquer, as the old saying has it.

"So they again said to the blind man, (notice he is still blind as far as the ultimate reality of Jesus is concerned), `What do you say about him, since he has opened your eyes?' He said, `He is a prophet.'" Wait a minute! He is no longer spiritually blind, at least not completely so. Jesus is no longer merely a man from Nazareth. He is now a spokesman for God. We are reminded of the blind man for whom Jesus prayed, and then he could see men, but they looked like trees walking. Everything was fuzzy, out of focus. Then Jesus prayed for him again, and he saw plainly. Well, this man is in the intermediate state. He now sees Jesus as more than an ordinary man, but not yet as God in our midst. How does Jesus appear to you? As a prophet, or more than a prophet?

DON'T GET ME INVOLVED IN THIS

"The Jews did not believe that he had been blind and had received his sight." John 9:18

"I believe, help my unbelief" pleaded the father of the tormented boy. So it is with us: half of us believes, the other half does not. We are like pregnant Rebekah with two nations warring within: faith and unbelief (Jacob and Esau). The unbelieving part of us is represented by the Jews, who require proof positive. "They called the parents of the man who had received his sight, and asked them, `Is this your son, who you say was born blind? How then does he now see?' His parents answered, `We know that this is our son, and that he was born blind; but how he now sees we do not know, nor do we know who opened his eyes. Ask him; he is of age, he will speak for himself.' His parents said this because they feared the Jews, for the Jews had already agreed that if any one should confess him to be Christ, he was to be put out of the synagogue. Therefore his parents said, `He is of age, ask him.'" To be put out of the synagogue was serious business. You would henceforth be treated like a social pariah, a leper. You could lose your job, and even starve to death.

A seminary classmate came into what I call the power dimension of the faith. It happened as the result of the Lord supernaturally healing his wife. Many members of his church followed him and his wife in this. They began raising their hands in worship, as we are enjoined to do in scripture. I Tim. 2:8. When the Presbytery got word of this, they clamped down on him. He was removed from his pulpit and forbidden to contact any of the church members until this matter had been thoroughly investigated. It is a serious thing to believe that "Jesus Christ is the same yesterday, today and forever." Heb. 13:8. People who believe this way are rockers of the boat. They turn over apple carts. They are much to be feared. I speak, as you may perceive, with tongue in cheek. Shall we laugh or shall we cry?

❦

GIVE GOD THE PRAISE

"So for the second time they called the man who had been blind, and said to him, 'Give God the praise; we know that this man is a sinner.'" John 9:24

What they meant by this was "Give God the praise by agreeing with our assessment." He answered, "Whether he is a sinner, I do not know; one thing I know, that though I was blind, now I see." What do you know for sure? What would you stake your life on? Some people know for sure only two things: death and taxes. Blessed are those who know for sure a third reality: the love of God. Blessed indeed! They said to him, "What did he do to you? How did he open your eyes?" He answered them, "I told you already, and you would not listen. Why do you want to hear it again? Do you too want to become his disciples?" The implication in the "too" is that the one who speaks is in the process of becoming Jesus' disciple. He is talking himself into the Kingdom of God. It happens when our contact with Jesus meets opposition. He is experiencing the pressure and contractions that will thrust him into the world as a believer in Jesus.

"And they reviled him, saying, 'You are his disciple, but we are disciples of Moses.'" They recognize in him something that he does not yet see in himself, that he is already Jesus' disciple (student). "We know that God has spoken to Moses, but as for this man, we do not know where he comes from." The man got sarcastic at this point, and answered, "Why, this is a marvel! You do not know where he comes from, and yet he opened my eyes. We know that God does not listen to sinners, but if any one is a worshiper of God and does his will, God listens to him."

Is it true that God does not listen to sinners? Perhaps the only prayer God will listen to from a sinner is a prayer of confession: "God be merciful to me, a sinner." If we worship God and seek to do his will, we may be sure that our prayers will be answered.

THEY CAST HIM OUT

"*Never since the world began has it been heard that any one opened the eyes of a man born blind.*"   *John 9:32*

This is the seventh time reference is made to "opened his eyes" in this chapter. Ever so slowly his eyes are being opened by Jesus and the Holy Spirit. As we continue in this gospel our eyes too are gradually being opened with dramatic results. Never before in history had it been heard of a person who was born blind receiving vision. This man epitomized hopelessness. There are no hopeless situations - there are merely hopeless people in them. "If this man were not from God, he could do nothing" he declared. So he has now convinced himself that as Jesus had sent him to the "sent" pool, Jesus had likewise been sent by God. Is his washing himself in the pool an allusion to water baptism? Is he inadvertently becoming a part of the baptism washed bride? The important thing is that he did as he was told. "Obedience is better than sacrifice" or anything else.

They answered him, "You were born in utter sin, and would you teach us?" They had a completely different evaluation of this man than Jesus had, who said, "It was not that this man sinned or his parents." In their frustration all they could do was defame him as they had Jesus. "And they cast him out." Out of what? Out of their religion, out of the temple and the synagogue.

What has been happening here? Inadvertently he had been passing through the birth canal. Now he has been cast out of his mother's body (the Old Testament "qahal" or assembly) into the world. He illustrates new birth. In our natural birth we were expelled from our mother's body as the result of her birth pangs. When we are born a second time, we produce a few strange sounds for Jesus outside of the church, where we were so cozy and comfortable. As a baby is not heard from until it is born, so it is with us. Suddenly we can't keep quiet about Jesus.

❦

DO YOU BELIEVE IN THE SON OF MAN?

"Jesus heard that they had cast him out, and having found him he said, "Do you believe in the Son of man?"   *John 9:35*

The original Greek text is even more explicit: Jesus heard that they cast him out outside. He is now an outsider, an outcast. Jesus seeks the rejects. He seeks until he finds. Have you experienced rejection from the authorities and from your peers? If so, rejoice. You are on Jesus' "seek until you find" list. Isn't that good news? Having found him, Jesus asked, "Do you believe in the Son of man?" Unfortunately, the King James Version utilizes time and again faulty manuscript evidence, and renders it "Son of God." But Jesus seldom calls himself the Son of God. He calls himself the Son of man (Adam). He knows that the Son of man is also the Son of God. He wants us to discover for ourselves who he really is. Actually it must be revealed to us by the Holy Spirit.

Several days ago I was visiting with an 88 year old man who told me that he did not believe in "the immaculate conception." I tried to explain to him that the Catholic doctrine of the immaculate conception has nothing to do with the conception of Jesus; it has to do with the conception of Mary, in the womb of her mother, "without the taint of original sin", as they pretend. What he meant was that he did not believe in the conception of Jesus by the overshadowing of the Holy Spirit and in the virgin birth. He did not believe in the clear teaching of the inspired scripture. No one can believe the story of Jesus' supernatural conception and birth, unless he or she is enabled to do so by the Holy Spirit.

I imagine someone saying, "Wait a minute. How about John 3:16? Didn't Jesus call himself the 'only begotten Son' there?" I gently submit to you that Jesus' conversation with Nicodemus ends with verse 15, in which he calls himself 'the Son of man.' Beginning with verse 16 we have the inspired words of John, our evangelist. ❧

HE WORSHIPED HIM

*"**H**e answered, `And who is he, sir, that I may believe in him?'"*
John 9:36

The blind are especially gifted at recognizing people by their voices, so we may be sure that the man knew that the One speaking to him was he who had given him his sight. Since he had rejected the theology of those who were the teachers of his former religion, and they had rejected him, he was open to believe whatever Jesus would now tell him. Jesus said to him, "You have seen him, and it is he who speaks to you." Here we encounter the fourth Greek word for "see" in this chapter: horao. It is the most profound of the four. It means to see in the sense of to experience in depth. It goes beyond theorizing, beyond getting a clear idea, into the realm of profound realization. Man, you have seen the sun come up like thunder on the road to Mandalay. The Son of man is the One who has brought you out of darkness into the Light of God's glorious presence.

"He said, `LORD, I believe' and he worshiped him." Literally "worship" means he knelt before him. Probably on this occasion he fell at Jesus' feet. He expressed bodily the faith of abject surrender, and was willing to be Jesus' slave. We are hearkened back to what Jesus said to Nicodemus, "Truly, truly, I say to you unless one is born anew (from above), he cannot see the kingdom of God." By worshiping Jesus, this dear man demonstrated the fact that he had actually seen the Kingdom. In Jesus he had experienced the saving activity of God.

In Revelation 22:8, John writes, "I fell down to worship at the feet of the angel, but he said to me, `You must not do that! I am a fellow servant with you and your brethren the prophets, and with those who keep the words of this book. Worship God.'" Angels of light reject our worship, but Jesus accepts our worship, as he did the worship of the man born blind. When we have been born of God, we find ourselves among those who offer Jesus worship.

THE BLESSING OF PLEADING IGNORANCE

*"**J**esus said, 'For judgment I came into this world, that those who do not see may see, and that those who see may become blind."*

                                                              John 9:39

Some of the Pharisees near him heard this, and they said to him, "Are we also blind?" A better rendering would be, we are not also blind are we? They actually believe that they see truth with 20/20 vision. Jesus said to them, "If you were blind, you would have no guilt (literally, no sin), but now that you say, `We see,' your guilt (sin) remains." What does he mean by that? Under law ignorance is no excuse. You may drive through a stop sign and be stopped by the police officer. You may say to her, "But officer, I did not see the stop sign." It will make no difference. She will write you a summons just the same. But, praise God, under grace ignorance is an excuse. Under grace you are not held accountable for what you neither see nor know.

Jesus has come to turn the tables. He came to give sight to the blind, but those who pretend that they see and comprehend the truth about God but really don't, he confirms in their blindness. Illustration: if you read a passage of scripture and then claim that you understand it perfectly, you have seen all that you are going to see in it. On the other hand, if you approach the passage with humility and a 'first time' attitude, there is no end to what you may eventually see in it. I once heard an evangelist speak on a scripture portion that I believed I understood thoroughly. To my utter astonishment he taught on the passage for an hour without mentioning one of my insights. It was for me a lesson in humility.

The sequel to John 9 is Acts 9. There we learn of a young Pharisee, Saul of Tarsus, who thought he enjoyed perfect spiritual vision. Then he encountered the exalted Christ, and was struck blind. As the result he began to see the Kingdom and was born into it.

❦

GOD'S DEALINGS WITH HUMANITY

"*Truly, truly, I say to you, he who does not enter the sheepfold by the door but climbs in by another way, that man is a thief and a robber." John 10.1*

John chapter 9 (seeing the Kingdom) depicts new birth subjectively, what it is like to go through the birth canal. John chapter 10 (entering the Kingdom) describes the same experience objectively, looking at the process from the perspective of the King (Jesus). The key idea in chapter 9 is "opened his eyes." The key word in chapter 10 is "enter." It is one thing to have your eyes opened as to who Jesus is, the divinely appointed King. It is quite another thing to enter his Kingdom. None of us would be permitted to enter the Kingdom of God had not Jesus first of all entered the sheepfold by the door. The door through which he came into the place where God's sheep were was the door of humility and obedience. See Philippians 2:8.

To understand what is happening here we must know something about the four phases of God's dealings with humanity. The first phase is called natural revelation: God has revealed something of himself through the world without (nature) and the world within (conscience). The second phase is the revelation of the divine name, by which God entered into a personal relationship with the old covenant people. The third phase is the Kingdom of God ushered in by Jesus, who brought God's power to earth, enabling believers to make a supernatural response to God, called new birth. The fourth phase is the coming glory. This will happen when Jesus reveals himself at his second coming. When this occurs, our faith will give way to sight. Our relationship with the invisible God will no longer be contended by the powers of evil, but will be direct and unhindered. This final phase will not occur until after the gospel has been proclaimed to all nations. It has been said that 95% of the earth has been exposed in some measure to the gospel. What are we doing to hasten his appearing?

EVERYONE NEEDS A GUIDE

"**B**ut *he who enters by the door is the shepherd of the sheep.*"

John 10:2

Jesus, the shepherd of the sheep, once he came into the world from the Father, continued to be humble and obedient by going through the door of baptism. Though he had no sins to confess, he identified himself with the sinners in baptism. The religious leaders who refused to enter the sheepfold through the door of baptism were all thieves and robbers. Remember that Jesus said in 3:5 that one must be born of water (baptism) to enter the kingdom. "To him the gatekeeper opens; the sheep hear his voice and he calls his own sheep by name and leads them out." During the winter the shepherds would herd their sheep into community barns, where they would leave them under the charge of the gatekeeper that they might spend the nights with their families. In the morning the gatekeeper would allow the legitimate shepherd into the barn to call out his own sheep. In this setting John the Baptist is the gatekeeper. He allowed Jesus to call to himself those who had responded to his message of the coming kingdom by repenting and being baptized. Jesus called his first disciples all by name. Then he led them out of the fold of Judaism into the Kingdom of God. He leads us out of religion into a personal relation with God. To be born of the Spirit is to be personally related to God.

"When he has brought out all his own, he goes before them, and the sheep follow him, for they know his voice. A stranger they will not follow, but they will flee from him, for they do not know the voice of strangers." Sheep are timid, and shy of strangers. So should we shy away from teachers who do not allow Jesus to speak to his followers through the Bible - the whole Bible taught in context. A text without a context is a pretext for teaching error. "This figure Jesus used with them, but they did not understand what he was saying to them." Hopefully we have some comprehension of this "transparency" through these few words of interpretation.

THE DOOR OF THE SHEEP

"*So Jesus again said to them, 'Truly, truly, I say to you, I am the door of the sheep.'" John 10:7*

Jesus has led his followers out of the official religion of legalism into a new frame of reference symbolized by the pastures in the countryside. There is security in the communal barn in town, but no freedom. Many are reluctant to forsake their traditional religion for life in the Kingdom because they fear a loss of security. Could it be that their religion is primarily their security blanket?

In verse one we saw that the door through which Jesus entered the religious system of the Jews was humility and obedience. He expressed these two chief characteristics of his life by leaving the Father and coming into this world, and also by being baptized by John. Now he has conducted his followers out of their mother's body, Judaism, into the Kingdom of God, where he himself has become the door. In the countryside there were innumerable sheepfolds, enclosures surrounded by rocks piled loosely upon one another. Of course the opening would have no gate. After the shepherd had herded his sheep into the fold, he himself would lie down across the opening. So his body would serve as the door.

"All who came before me (claiming to be the Saviour/ Messiah) are thieves and robbers; but the sheep did not heed them. I am the door; if anyone enters by me, he will be saved, and will go in and out and find pasture." As the door by which we enter the Kingdom, Jesus affords his follower three basic benefits. First, he will be saved; that is to say, he will find security, the same security he enjoyed in his old religion. Second, he will go in and out - an expression referring to freedom, the freedom to come and go. He is no longer locked into a fortress- like system. "For freedom Christ has set us free," wrote Paul in Galatians 5:1. Third, she will find pasture, total provision for all of her needs. "Seek first his kingdom and his righteousness and all these things (what shall we eat, drink, wear) shall be yours as well." Matthew 6:33.

❦

THE ARCHTHIEF

"The thief comes only to steal and kill and destroy; I came that they may have life, and have it abundantly." John 10:10

The archthief, of course, is the devil, of whom Jesus spoke in chapter 8. He is totally evil, and he has three great ambitions. He wants to rob us of our faith. Then he intends to kill us. Finally, he desires to destroy us with himself in hell, which was prepared for him and his angels. Hell is the lake that burns with fire and brimstone; it is the second death. Since the first death is not extinction, it is wishful thinking in the extreme to suppose that the second death is obliteration. If the devil is 100% evil, Jesus is 100% good. He came to earth that he might share his toGodwardness with us, and that we might experience it to the full. "I am the good shepherd. The good shepherd lays down his life for the sheep." As the shepherd, when night approached, would lie down across the opening into the fold, so Jesus would lay down his life upon the cross, where at noon it became dark as night. Upon the cross he took unto himself all the barbs of outrageous fortune. Indeed he became sin, that we through faith in him might become the righteousness of God - the most profound riddle ever propounded.

"He who is a hireling and not a shepherd, whose own the sheep are not, sees the wolf coming and flees; and the wolf snatches them and scatters them. He flees because he is a hireling and cares nothing for the sheep." Jesus had contrasted himself with thieves and robbers. Now he contrasts himself with a hired-hand, whose only motivation is to collect his wage. He is strictly a mercenary, who runs for his life when danger threatens. At the arrest in the garden, as we shall see, Jesus allows the wolf to seize him by the throat, that his sheep may be spared. He would literally sacrifice himself that their lives might not be forfeited. Only those overseers who share in the spirit of the good shepherd are able to stay with the sheep when the evil day comes. Apart from supernatural assistance they too would hightail it to save their skin.

THE IMPORTANCE OF DISTINGUISHING A FLOCK FROM A FOLD

"**I** *am the good shepherd; I know my own and my own know me, as the Father knows me and I know the Father; and I lay down my life for the sheep." John 10:14,15*

You cannot know Jesus experientially until you realize that you belong to him. You actually belong to him for three reasons: because through him you were fashioned, by him you are sustained, and by his precious blood you were purchased. Through the years I have loaned books to people. They have my name in them. They belong to me, but I do not possess them. Once it dawns on you that you are not your own, you are privileged to surrender yourself totally to Jesus that he may possess you. Ultimately every human being will be possessed by Jesus or by the devil. "I lay down my life" is the refrain in this portion dealing with Jesus as the good shepherd. It is rooted in the 23rd Psalm, the most positive psalm in the psaltry.

"And I have other sheep that are not of this fold (the Jewish nation); I must bring them also, and they will heed my voice." It happened for the first time in the house of Cornelius (Acts 10), when the gentiles heard the gospel, believed, and received the Holy Spirit, even speaking in tongues. This was ten years after Pentecost. "So there shall be one flock, one shepherd." Tragically the Latin vulgate, translated from the original Greek by Jerome, reads amiss, "one fold, one shepherd." This error crept into the King James version, and even into the Book of Mormon, demonstrating that Joseph Smith had plagarized from the King James Bible. So the Mormon religion sinks quietly beneath the waves. The Catholic Church built its doctrine of the Church upon this manuscript error, pretending that there is only one fold (or structure) and that they are it. Thank God, we know better. There are many folds, but only "one flock." The chief characteristic of those who are members of Jesus' flock is that they recognize Jesus' voice, and that they will not follow strangers.

❦

A MIRACULOUS DEATH

"*For this reason the Father loves me, because I lay down my life, that I may take it again.*" *John 10:17*

Should Jesus have changed his mind, as the devil tempted him to do through the voice of Simon Peter in Matthew 16:22 ("This shall never happen to you"), he would have disobeyed his Father, and become a sinner like you and me. He was the beneficiary of the Father's love, because of his rock-ribbed determination to endure the cross no matter what. Now he indicates the aftermath of that decision, "that I may take it again." As the shepherd became the door by lying down across the opening of the fold, so in the morning he would rise up to lead the sheep elsewhere. Similarly Jesus laid his life down upon the cross, and it became night at noon. Then bright and early on Easter morn he stood up again, that he might be Lord of the dead as well as of the living.

"No one takes it (my life) from me, but I lay it down of my own accord. I have power to lay it down, and I have power to take it again; this charge I have received from my Father." Even more remarkable than his power to arise from the dead on the third day was his ability to die of his own volition. The crucified customarily lingered on crosses for several days. Jesus, on the contrary, died after six short hours. He died with a shout, "It is finished." It was a victory cry. Then he exhaled, and refused to inhale. A man 100 years old was asked the secret of his longevity. He answered, "Oh, just keep breathing." What could be simpler? Yes, but do you know anyone who stopped breathing of his own volition, after saying, "Father, into your hands I commit my spirit?" This is in fulfillment of Psalm 31:5.

By enduring the cross Jesus revealed his radical obedience to God, he made atonement for sin, and he defeated all the evils that assail. How is that for accomplishment? Have you thanked him yet today?

130

WALL-EYED?

"There was again a division among the Jews because of these words."   *John 10:19*

Albert Einstein said, "God is the great mathematician." We have seen Jesus <u>multiply</u> the loaves and fishes. We have witnessed him <u>subtract</u> from his followers the same multitude who watched him multiply. On the occasion of Pentecost he will <u>add</u> to the company 3000 souls who were being saved. Here he demonstrates again his ability to <u>divide</u> his hearers into two camps. "Many of them said, `He has a demon, and he is mad; why listen to him?' Others said, `These are not the sayings of one who has a demon. Can a demon open the eyes of the blind?'"

I have been privileged to witness the opening of blind eyes on two occasions. The first time was in Yugoslavia when we prayed for 5 year old Daniella, who was blind in one eye. Her grandmother, a prostitute in Pacras, exclaimed, "If they were to kill me tomorrow, I would still have to say there is a God." A week later she came to the Baptist Church in Daruvar and testified during the Sunday morning service as to what had happened. The second occasion was during a meeting in our church in St. Louis, when two of our elders prayed over 78 year old Florence Payken. About 15 minutes later someone asked her why she was crying. She said, "Because I can see the pastor out of my blind eye." Two months later I called upon her husband, George, in the hospital. He said to me, "It is the strangest thing. Florence was told by the doctors that there was no medical possibility of having her sight restored in her blind eye. Even so, she can see. But now she is wall- eyed." "Wall-eyed?" I asked. "What is that?" He said, "She has double vision. So she had to get glasses to cure the double vision."

All of our problems stem from our taking our eyes off of Jesus. If our eyes are focused upon him, our bodies will be full of light.

❧

DEDICATION TO DEATH

"It was the feast of the Dedication at Jerusalem; it was winter, and Jesus was walking, in the temple, in the portico of Solomon."
John 10:22,23

Three months have gone by since Jesus went up to Jerusalem in connection with the Feast of Tabernacles. Ch. 7 Now it is Hanukkuh, the season of winter solstice. The days are gradually getting longer. The Light of the world is getting brighter and brighter. This feast commemorated the desecration of the altar in 168 B.C. and was the occasion of ceremonies of purification and rededication three years later lasting for eight days. At this feast Jesus finally dedicated himself to death.

We see a parallel here in that Jesus three years before this had been baptized by John. In his baptism he had identified himself with sinful mankind, and taken upon himself the attack of the devil. In his three year public ministry he had been taking upon himself the sicknesses, pains, and sorrows of humanity. He was experiencing our devastation that we might experience his life. His passion (suffering) really began with his baptism. For three long years he had been the suffering servant spoken of in Isaiah 53.

"So the Jews gathered round him and said to him, `How long will you keep us in suspense? If you are the Christ, tell us plainly.'" They wanted him to identify himself as the Savior of their anticipation - the one who would divest them of the Roman yoke. Many became disillusioned with Jesus because he did not conform to their specifications. They secured a tailored suit and demand him to fit into it. He never does. We are the ones who must change to conform with his design. He is the standard and pattern for the new humanity. "Jesus answered them, `I told you, and you do not believe. (See again ch. 7 and 8) The works that I do in my Father's name, they bear witness to me; but you do not believe, because you do not belong to my sheep.'"

THE KINGDOM WITHIN

" **M**y sheep hear my voice, and I know them, and they follow
me. "
John 10:27

Are you one of Jesus' sheep? If so, you are doing two
things: you are listening to his voice, and you are accepting his
guidance. One of the ways in which I have been hearing from
the Lord and learning to follow after him is by attending to my
dreams. I put a pen and sheet of paper near my bed, and upon
waking immediately write down what I remember of my dreams.
I then pass them through a seven layered filter.

1) I give the dream material a <u>title</u>. Frequently it is
derived from the first sentence of what I have written down. 2)
I stand back and think of a <u>theme</u> that may underlie the
dreaming and express its continuity. 3) I write down a word or
two that indicates my emotional <u>attitude</u> or mood, be it fear,
surprise, frustration, pleasure or whatever. 4) I allow the
dreaming to formulate a <u>question</u> that it may be asking me. 5)
I try to determine the <u>context</u> of the dreaming. What may have
motivated or triggered them? Was it something that happened
to me the day before, something that is currently pressing in
upon me, or a decision that I must make? 6) I make a list of
<u>associations</u>. For example, the other day I dreamed I was in an
immense house where I found some money. I put down
"immense house = enlarged personal unconscious" (soul). "Money
= wealth within." 7) Now I seek to discover the <u>meaning</u> of what
I have dreamed. The dream just mentioned encouraged me to
believe that I am making progress in my inner journey. My soul
is growing. I think of the line of poetry, "Build thee more stately
mansions, O my soul." Also I am discovering wealth and power
within me placed there by someone else, whom I take to be the
Spirit of God. Spiritual growth for believers is primarily growth
in the awareness of how exceedingly rich we already are, as
those whose bodies are indwelt by the Spirit who manfiests
himself to us in the night.

❧

PERFECT SECURITY

"*And I give them eternal life, and they shall never perish, and no one shall snatch them out of my hand.*"   *John 10:28*

We have seen the two things we do as his sheep (hear his voice, and follow him). Now we learn what three things the shepherd does for us. First, he gives us continually eternal life, which flows to us from our close contact with him. Second, we will never ever be destroyed. Heaven and earth shall pass away, but we shall not. Third, no one can pry us out of Jesus' grasp. In other words, we enjoy perfect security as long as we confide in our Saviour. Here he amplifies what he said in 10:9 about our being saved, as those who have entered his Kingdom. "My Father, who has given them to me is greater than all, and no one is able to snatch them out of the Father's hand."

The Father of Jesus is the Creator of all. How great is he? The Westminster Catechism puts it this way: "He is a Spirit, infinite, eternal, and unchangeable in his being, wisdom, power, holiness, justice, goodness, and truth." He is all-powerful Love. Then Jesus affirms, "I and the Father are one." It is as though Jesus were saying, you are held firm in not one hand only, but two. One hand is the Father's and the other his own. The word "one" here is in the neuter gender. If it were masculine, he would be saying that he and the Father are identical, the same person. United Pentecostals hold this view. They are the so called "oneness" group, who pretend that Jesus is all there is of God. But Jesus here contradicts their view. He says that he and the Father are distinct from one another, as a husband is other than his wife. The husband and wife are one flesh. They enjoy the oneness of mutual indwelling. Well, Jesus and his Father are one in spirit. They have in common the same Holy Spirit. The Father is prior to the Son, who gives God priority in all things. His will is subservient to the will of the Father, so that the two wills are in perfect harmony.

❦

SPIRITUAL MILLIONAIRES

"The Jews took up stones again to stone him." John 10:31

Jesus answered them, "I have shown you many good works from the Father; for which of these do you stone me?" The Jews answered him, "It is not for a good work that we stone you but for blasphemy; because you being a man, make yourself God." They had it completely reversed. He, having been God, made himself man. He answered them, "Is it not written in your law, `I said, you are gods?' Psalm 82:6 If he called them gods to whom the word of God came (and scripture cannot be broken), do you say of him whom the Father consecrated and sent into the world, `You are blaspheming,' because I said, `I am the Son of God?'"

What a thrilling observation! When the Word of God speaks to you, you who hear and respond have been elevated to the status of the divine. The Word of God spoke to the woman at the well. By hearing and believing, she had been lifted to the level of him who had spoken to her. The same was true of the man 38 years an invalid. When the Word of God is heard by a person, that individual is treated as though she were on the level of God. We enjoy the potentiality of making a personal response to God. Isn't that what is meant by being made in the image of God? By speaking to them, Jesus was treating those Jews as though they were as divine as himself. What an enormous compliment! Tragically they couldn't see it. Their closed minds had blinded them. Another observation: "scripture cannot be broken." Change is the law of the universe. Everything is in flux except one reliable thing - Scripture. Jesus' body was broken upon the cross. But that did not break the Bible. On the contrary, the Old Testament promises were fulfilled by his death and rising. I would rather have a knowledge of the Bible than a college or seminary diploma. "The law of thy mouth is better to me than thousands of gold and silver pieces." Psalm 119: 72. Bible students are spiritual millionaires.

BELIEVE THE WORKS

"*If I am not doing the works of my Father, then do not believe me; but if I do them, even though you do not believe me, believe the works, that you may know and understand that the Father is in me and I am in the Father.*"   *John 10:37, 38*

Six works of Jesus have been detailed up to this point. The seventh will be described in the next chapter. The first and key sign was turning water into wine at Cana, thereby disclosing him to be the heavenly Bridegroom. The second was the healing of the official's son across the miles, that we may know there is no distance in prayer. The third was the healing of the man 38 years infirm, that we may know there are no hopeless situations for those who are ready to go to work for God. The fourth was the multiplication of the five loaves and two fish. Five parts word and two parts Spirit blended together provide a balanced spiritual diet for the multitudes, when they sit at Jesus' feet. The fifth was his walking across the sea to his laboring disciples, who are never beyond the reach of his kindly approach. Sixth was the opening of the eyes of the man born blind, illustrating new birth into God's Kingdom.

Sad to say, "Again they tried to arrest him, but he escaped from their hands." Yet the hour of his arrest was fast approaching. "He went away again across the Jordon to the place where John at first baptized, and there he remained." We have returned to the place where it all began. What goes around, comes around.

"And many came to him and they said, `John did no sign, (How could he, since he was unbaptized either in water or in the Holy Spirit? He had received, though, the highest form of baptism in his martyrdom: the baptism of blood.) ...but everything that John said about this man was true.' And many believed in him there." "God's word accomplishes the purpose for which he sent it out." Isaiah 55:11

TIME IS RUNNING OUT

"*ℛow a certain man was ill, Lazarus of Bethany, the village of Mary and her sister Martha.*"   *John 11:1*

Ch. 11 is significant symbolically. Eleven reminds us of the eleventh hour, which tells us time is running out. Something significant happens when the clock strikes twelve. The carriage turns back into a pumpkin, or something even more ominous happens. Eleven speaks of that which is incomplete, while twelve implies divine government - God takes charge. "Now a certain man was ill." The word "man" does not appear in the Greek text, so it should be rendered "a certain one." That certain one is you and me. I am ill, ailing with the sickness known as mortality. It is one thing to say "Man is mortal," but quite another to say "Death is for me." This certain individual was Lazarus, a name meaning "without help." Despite all that medical science can do, we are ultimately helpless in the face of our last enemy upon this earth - Death. "Without help" was from Bethany, "house of the destitute."

Years ago our little group spent six nights in the Handel Hotel in Bethlehem. Our waiter lived in Bethany. One evening he served us a table spoon of peas on our plates. It was such a skimpy portion that I realize he must have come from the "house of the destitute." In Philadelphia there was an orphanage named "The Home for Destitute Children." Apart from Jesus we are poor orphans in a vast, insensitive universe. Bethany was "the village of Mary and her sister Martha." The grand old name "Mary" means "bitter." "Martha" means "lady". They represent in the gospel two different types. Mary is the contemplative one, the feminine counterpart of John, our evangelist. She liked to think things out. Martha is the enterprising one, like Peter, the man of action. "Don't just sit there, do something," (even if it is the wrong thing) is their motto. Thank God for Martha, the Lady in the kitchen. Without her we would go hungry.

❧

HOW STRANGE HIS WAYS

"**It** *was Mary who anointed the Lord with ointment and wiped his feet with her hair, whose brother Lazarus was ill." John 11:2*

Here we have a preview of coming attractions. Mary is preeminent over her older more practical sister by reason of what she did as recorded in ch. 12. Her awesomely significant deed was the inevitable consequence of what Jesus is about to do for Lazarus. "So the sisters sent to him, saying, `Lord, he whom you love is ill,'" The word "love" is phileo, which indicates the strong emotional attachment at the base of all friendship. "Behold, your friend is ill." They would leave it up to Jesus as to what he would do about it. Perhaps a prayer across the miles would suffice. "But when Jesus heard it he said, `This illness is not unto death; it is for the glory of God, so that the Son of God may be glorified by means of it.'" In retrospect we perceive that when Jesus said, "This illness is not unto death," Lazarus was already dead. He died while the messengers were on their way. What Jesus meant was "This death is not unto death." There is physical death unto ultimate death. Also there is physical death unto ultimate life. Lazarus' death was of the latter. It was designed to give God the occasion to allow his Son to demonstrate his unique supremacy.

"Now Jesus loved Martha and her sister and Lazarus, so when he heard that he was ill," he immediately hastened to Bethany? Not so. Here the word "loved" is a form of agape, unconquerable benevolence, undefeatable good will. It is not emotional, but volitional. We cannot like our enemies, but we may agape them. Because Jesus had this deeper love for his friends, "he stayed two days longer in the place where he was." God's ways are not ours. His ways and thoughts are higher than ours as the heavens are higher than the earth. The children of Israel saw at the time of the Exodus God's mighty acts, but Moses was privileged to see his ways, a far greater blessing. Psalm 103:7.

❦

138

BACK TO JERUSALEM? YOU'VE GOT TO BE KIDDING!

" *Then after this he said to his disciples, `Let us go into Judea again!'"   John 11:7*

"Let us all go together!" In World War II a soldier who had won the Medal of Honor was asked why he had volunteered for such a dangerous mission. He said, "The commanding officer had described the mission, saying that the one who accepted the assignment could not expect to return alive. Then he asked the volunteer to take one step forward. The entire company, except for me, took one step backward. So I was volunteered." The disciples said to him, `Rabbi, the Jews were but now seeking to stone you, and are you going there again?'" Since they were as close to Jesus as the chicks to the hen, they would be endangered by the same stones. They were pleased to keep a safe distance between themselves and Judea.

"Jesus answered, `Are there not twelve hours in the day? If any one walks in the day, he does not stumble, because he sees the light of this world. But if anyone walks in the night, he stumbles, because the light is not in him.'" If we think of our allotted span of life as our twelve hour day, we must realize that we are safe during that interval. We enjoy the divine protection of the Son of God. But when our time of ministry here is over, night has come. Our temporal protection is lifted. It is a way of saying that we are kept out of harm's way until our mission on earth is fulfilled, and then who cares. After this comes glory.

A seminary classmate had surgery on the day I was wed. Then he returned to Princeton for his senior year. Within a year of graduation he died of cancer. A New York pastor conducted the wedding of a young couple on a Saturday. The following Saturday he officiated at their funeral. They were killed in a car accident while on their honeymoon. From a human standpoint these are tragedies. But viewed from the perspective of eternity, who is better off? We feebly struggle; they in glory shine.

❧

NOT DEAD BUT SLEEPING

"Thus he spoke, and then he said to them, `Our friend Lazarus has fallen asleep, but I go to awake him out of sleep.'" John 11:11

It is refreshing to realize that Jesus referred to death as sleep. He said to the Jews who were mourning the death of Jairus' daughter, "She is not dead, but sleeping." They laughed him to scorn, knowing that she was dead. But Jesus broke up every funeral he ever attended. For example: the funeral at Nain of the widow's son.

Bishop Benson Idahosa told how as a young man in his native Nigeria he heard his pastor read Matthew 10:7 - "Heal the sick, raise the dead." Afterward he asked the pastor if he could raise the dead. He said he could not, because he did not have enough faith. He then asked the minister if he, himself, could raise the dead. He answered, "If you have the faith." It was a Sunday morning when he went out on the street to find someone who had died. He was unsuccessful - until 4 in the afternoon when he learned of a 5 year old girl who had died at 9 that morning, and was to be buried at 5 p.m. He was welcomed into the house, where he asked if he could pray over her body. When he was given permission, he took her in his arms and offered a strong prayer that the Lord would raise her up. Nothing happened. Then he asked for a Bible and read how Jesus had said to Jairus' daughter, "Damsel, arise!" (Mark 5:21) Thinking that Damsel was the little girl's name, he asked for the name of this dead 5 year old. Learning her name, he called her by name, and commanded her in the name of Jesus to come back to life. She opened her eyes, and lived. Raising her from the dead was Brother Benson's first Christian experience. Since then the Lord has used him to raise six others from the dead and to establish thousands of churches. Those who think that miracles ceased with the death of the Apostles are tragically misinformed. "Jesus Christ is the same yesterday and today and for ever." Hebrews 13:8

❧

THE REALIST

*"**T**he disciples said to him, `Lord, if he has fallen asleep, he will recover.'" John 11:12*

They figured that Lazarus' fever had broken. "Now Jesus had spoken of his death, but they thought he meant taking rest in sleep. Then Jesus told them plainly, `Lazarus is dead.'" To be more accurate, Jesus said, "Lazarus died." He had stopped breathing, but had not thereby ceased to exist. He had entered into another realm, where his soul and spirit continued on. Remember how Jesus said in Matthew 10:28, "Do not fear those who kill the body, but cannot kill the soul; rather fear him who can destroy both soul and body in hell." I am a spirit; I have a soul; I live in a body. The frightening thing is that there is no mention of the destruction of the human spirit by God. Is it possible that the spirit of man, fathered by God, (Hebrews 12:9) is unending?

"Lazarus died; and for your sake I am glad that I was not there, so that you may believe." Had Jesus been there it would not have been possible for Lazarus to die. What was about to happen was destined to enrich the disciples' faith, and also ours. "Thomas, called the Twin, said to his fellow disciples, `Let us also go, that we may die with him.'"

Thomas could never be accused of being an optimist. Above all he was a realist with a sober-eyed view of life. Indeed he could be called the melancholy type. Peter was the choloric type whose blood ran hot. Matthew was the sanguine type who tended to look on the bright side of things. He threw a party for his buddies after he was invited to follow Jesus. Still another type of person is the phlegmatic, who tends not to get excited about anything. It was Thomas who encouraged the others to accompany Jesus back into the lions' den. He had the spirit of the martyr. Tradition tells us that eventually he carried the gospel into India where he established the Son of Thomas Church. He died in the East Indies killed by a spear in Cormandel.

YOUR BROTHER WILL RISE AGAIN

"*Now when Jesus came, he found that Lazarus had already been in the tomb four days.*" *John 11:17*

He had died shortly after the messengers had begun their day's journey to find Jesus, and was buried the same day according to custom. To appreciate the significance of what is about to happen, we should understand that the Jews were persuaded that after death the soul lingered near the body until the third day. Then when evidence of decomposition began to set in, the soul departed, since there was no longer hope of being revived.

"Bethany was near Jerusalem, about two miles off, (just east of the Mount of Olives) and many of the Jews had come to Martha and Mary to console them concerning their brother. When Martha heard that Jesus was coming, she went and met him, while Mary sat in the house." "Jesus is coming to earth again" we sing. We can go out to meet him by doing our utmost to publish the gospel to all nations in fulfillment of the great commission. He cannot return until the task is accomplished.

"Martha said to Jesus, `Lord, if you had been here, my brother would not have died. And even now I know that whatever you ask from God, God will give you.'" She knew that Jesus' prayers were always answered. The same may be said of every believer, unless we ask amiss. "Jesus said to her, `Your brother will rise again.'" That expression was colloquial upon the lips of those who sought to comfort the bereaved. She had heard it, doubtless, a hundred times. And so she responded with her proverbial answer, "I know that he will rise again in the resurrection at the last day." She had embraced the teaching of the Pharisees in this regard, but it was small comfort at the present hour, and did not relieve the pain of loss. "Jesus, we expected more of you on this occasion than the mouthing of pleasant platitudes. You have disappointed us." Don't be so sure!

❦

BELIEVERS NEVER DIE

"**J**esus said to her, `I am the resurrection and the life, he who believes in me, though he die, yet shall he live.'" *John 11:25*

A woman's husband had died suddenly, unexpectedly of a heart attack. What kept her going, she said later, was the word of a neighbor, who said: "You will see him again."

The Pharisees taught the resurrection of the dead. With great audacity Jesus affirmed that the principle of resurrection and life beyond was entwined around a personal relationship with himself. He who trusts in Jesus, though that one die as Lazarus had, yet shall he live. "And whoever lives and believes in me shall never die." You and I are living as we read these words. Believing as we do in Jesus, we shall never (by no means, literally) die. "Do you believe this?" Let us think twice before we answer.

The wife of a man with no church affiliation had died. We were seated at his kitchen table. I was reading to him this chapter, and had come to this verse, and the question, "Do you believe this?" Without hesitation he said, "Yes." Evidently he had never heard this scripture before, and thought that I was asking him. No, Jesus is the one asking. But he had given the good answer. "Martha said to him, `Yes, Lord; I believe.'" Believe what? That Jesus himself is the resurrection and the life? I don't think she had the foggiest notion what he was talking about. What he had just said was way beyond her. So she fell back on what she did believe: "I believe that you are the Christ: in other words, "the Son of God," and "he who is coming into the world." Actually Jesus is always coming into the little world of our own personal lives in ever new and surprising ways. Do we perceive him? I talked to a black man today whose throat had been slashed recently in a robbery. As he thought he was bleeding to death, he saw the face of Jesus momentarily, as he had seen him in the white woman who drove him to the hospital.

❦

THE TEACHER IS HERE

"**W**hen she had said this, she went and called her sister Mary, saying quietly, 'The teacher is here and is calling for you.'"

John 11:28

Martha whispered the information to Mary, trying to keep it a secret. "And when she heard it, she rose quickly and went to him. Now Jesus had not yet come to the village, but was still in the place where Martha had met him."

These verses illuminate for us the coming of Jesus for his bride the Church. The word "here" in the Greek is pronounced "parestin." It is the verbal form of the noun "parousia," used by Paul in I Thess. 4:15. "For this we declare to you by the word of the Lord, that we who are alive, who are left until the coming (parousia) of the Lord, shall not precede those who have fallen asleep." Then in verse 17 he writes, "we shall be caught up together in the clouds to meet the Lord in the air." Jesus' parousia refers to his presence in the clouds, where he will call his own, saying, "Come up here." Then will occur for believers the catching up (the quick violent grab, "faster than a speeding bullet?") They will meet the Lord in the atmosphere of earth. Then he will take them to their heavenly home, where they will be with the Lord forever.

"When Mary heard that Jesus was in the neighborhood of Bethany (for he had not yet come into the village), she rose quickly and went to him." She was thereby illustrating the catching up of the church. In his parousia Jesus comes to the air above the earth, where we meet him in the clouds. Subsequently he will return to the earth in what is called his second coming. This occurs in my persuasion some years after his coming to fetch away his bride. We look at this when we come to the Book of Revelation. Even so, are you ready to hear the archangel summons, "The teacher is here and is calling for you?" If not, you should prepare for martyrdom should you decide to resist Antichrist, and being sent to hell.

❦

JESUS WEPT

"**W**hen the Jews who were with her in the house, consoling her, saw Mary rise quickly and go out, they followed her, supposing that she was going to the tomb to weep there." John 11:31

Someone asked Mazie, "How does you take all the troubles you takes?" She said, "I've got a little secret." "What is it?" "Well, when I sits, I sits loose!" The person then asked, "Suppose you should fall on the ice and go to the hospital. Or suppose your son should lose his job or die. Or suppose your house should burn down." She said, "I never supposes." The Jews' supposing was in error. Mary went to be with Jesus, always a wise thing to do. "Then Mary, when she came where Jesus was and saw him, fell at his feet, saying to him, `Lord, if you had been here, my brother would not have died.'" "If" is a mighty big word. Armies have fallen through the crack it opens up.

"When Jesus saw her weeping, and the Jews who came with her also weeping, he was deeply moved in spirit and troubled." The expression "deeply moved" is literally became indignant. He became angry as a horse when it snorts; and he said, "Where have you laid him?" Why this outrage? I believe it was because he was about to confront the last enemy that is to be destroyed, even death, in all of its horror. Love incarnate hated death with perfect hatred. "They said to him, `Lord, come and see.' Jesus wept." But why? Lazarus had entered into Abraham's bosom among the blessed dead, and Jesus was about to call him back into the storms and strife of this mortal life. He would be obliged to pass through the door of death a second time.

It was reported to me that when my Seminary professor's wife died, his joy over her coronation was greater than his sorrow for himself. A woman I know told me that she heard the angels sing the Hallelujah Chorus at her father's burial. "Precious in the sight of the Lord is the death of his saints." Psalm 116:15

THE SHORTEST VERSE?

"Jesus wept." *John 11:35*

Everyone knows that the shortest verse in the Bible is, "Jesus wept." They are wrong. It is not the shortest, but one of the shortest. The other shortest verses put "Jesus wept" into context. "Rejoice always." I Thess. 5:16. "Pray constantly." I Thess. 5:17 "Rejoice with those who rejoice, weep with those who weep." Romans 12:15. Rejoice that you are among the weepers. Why is that? Because the "Weeping may tarry for the night, but joy comes with the morning." Psalm 30:5

When they saw Jesus weep, "the Jews said, `See how he loved him!'" God does not play favorites, neither does Jesus. He loves you as much as he loved Lazarus. "But some of them said, `Could not he who opened the eyes of the blind man have kept this man from dying?'" Of course he could, but not dying, for the time being, does not solve the problem of death. Dying apart from faith in Jesus Christ is an enormous problem. A famous theologian wrote, "For a person to face a Christless grave would be to go stark raving mad." "Then Jesus, deeply moved (indignant) again, came to the tomb; it was a cave, and a stone lay upon it." We are reminded of the scene at Jesus' own burial. It is a touching experience to visit the two tombs in Jerusalem, in one of which Jesus may well have been buried; one in the Church of the Holy Sepulcher, the other at Gordon's Calvary, outside the Damascus Gate. (Gordon is a Scottish name which means "a high cornered hill," reminding us of that hill upon which Jesus allowed himself to be cornered on a cross.)

"Jesus said, `Take away the stone.' Martha, the sister of the dead man, said to him, `Lord, by this time there will be an odor, for he has been dead four days.'" In other words, "Don't do it." Jesus said to her, `Did I not tell you that if you would believe you would see the glory of God.'" The first time the disciples saw the glory was at the wedding in Cana. History is about to repeat itself.

LAZARUS, COME OUT

"**S**o they took away the stone." *John 11:41*

They did exactly what he told them. So expect a miracle. But the proviso is that you obey him whether it makes sense or not. "And Jesus lifted up his eyes and said, 'Father, I thank thee that thou hast heard me. I know that thou hearest me always, but I have said this on account of the people standing by, that they may believe that thou hast sent me.'" The purpose of his mighty works was to engender faith in his heavenly Father whose plan and purpose he was executing. "When he had said this, he cried with a loud voice, "Lazarus, come out.'"

In John 5:25 Jesus had said, "Truly, truly, I say to you, the hour is coming, and now is, when the dead will hear the voice of the Son of God, and those who hear will live." He was speaking then of the spiritually dead. Even more wonderful is his power to raise the physically dead. "The dead man came out, his hands and feet bound with bandages, and his face wrapped with a cloth." It was enough to scare a person to death. "Jesus said to them, 'Unbind him, and let him go.'" To the present hour Jesus gives life to the spiritually dead, but he expects his servants to free them up from all that constrains the life of the Spirit within them. We are to minister freedom to those to whom the Lord imparts life.

In ch. 11 we have encountered for the second time the themes of faith and of life. Martha said, "Yes, Lord; I believe." "I kept my faith," said the Psalmist, "even when I said, I am greatly afflicted" - faith in long trousers, the faith of grown-ups. "The dead man came out" - alive. We are back at Cana, where Jesus restored life to the party, because he is life. Now there was more joy in Bethany than there had been at Cana. It is one thing to turn water into wine, something else to restore to life a man four days dead. Has he brought you to life as yet?

❦

UNBIND HIM AND LET HIM GO

"*The dead man came out, his hands and feet bound with bandages, and his face wrapped with a cloth. Jesus said to them, 'Unbind him, and let him go.'" John 11:44*

Lazarus had been restored to life by Jesus but he was still bound up. Those standing around were called upon to release him. Jesus is the only one who is able to give us spiritual life, but we are called upon to free one another from those impediments that hinder the operation of God's Spirit within us.

When I was in the Seminary, I became so discouraged that I was ready to drop out. So I went to my professor for counsel. After I had poured out my tale of woe, I was asked by him, "Do you believe that God exists?" I said, "Yes." Then, "Do you believe that God has expressed his attitude toward you through Jesus Christ?" Again I said, "Yes." Next he asked, "Do you believe that God's attitude toward you changes with your mood?" I answered, "No," thinking that, "God is the same yesterday, today and for ever." Then he asked me, "This conflict within you, is it caused by something without or within?" I said, "Oh it is just something subjective within me." He said to me, "That is where you are wrong. You are experiencing the devil, seeking to wrest you from the service of Christ, and the devil works the hardest on those whom the Lord can use the most." He said, "When God calls you into a certain situation, he gives you the ability to fulfill in that situation." Then he said, "Let's pray. You first." So I offered a short prayer. Then he offered a short prayer, and I went my way. I did not feel any better, but I had a different perspective. And it made all the difference. So my discouragement was not a negative after all but a positive. That half hour conversation saved me for the gospel ministry. The professor had done what Jesus had enjoined, when he said, "Unbind him and let him go." He had ministered to me in wisdom and in prayer. I felt no better, but I had an insight far more valuable than feelings.

❧

ARE YOU LIKE CEPHAS OR CAIAPHAS?

"**M**any of the Jews, therefore, who had come with Mary and had seen what he did believed in him." John 11:45

It is surprising that all of them who had seen Lazarus raised from the dead did not believe. It makes ludicrous the adage, "Seeing is believing." It ain't necessarily so. "But some of them went to the Pharisees and told them what Jesus had done." Surely this, the last of Jesus' signs, would persuade the religious authorities that he was the One who was to come. "So the chief priests and the Pharisees gathered the council, and said, `What are we to do? For this man performs many signs. If we let him go on thus, everyone will believe in him, and the Romans will come and destroy both our holy place and our nation.'" They were persuaded that if they did not stop Jesus in his tracks three evils would occur: 1) "Every one will believe in him." Eventually everyone will bend the knee to him, willingly or unwillingly. 2) "The Romans will come and destroy our temple." They did 40 years later. 3) "And our nation." This the Romans did also. Their nation did not exist from A.D. 70 until 1948, for 1878 years. In May, 1988 Israel celebrated her 40th birthday as a reconstituted nation.

Forty is the year when maturity blesses. It has been said that life begins at 40. It was my most blessed year. That was the year I received the empowering of the Holy Spirit, and all sorts of good things happened. "But one of them Caiaphas, who was high priest that year, said to them, `You know nothing at all.'" Caiaphas, like Cephas, means "a rock." It is also said to mean "depression." If we do not build our lives, as Cephas (Peter) did upon Jesus Christ, the only alternative is to become like Caiaphas, "the know it all." We are then heading for an enormous depression, when the universe will collapse around us, and all that we have held dear will be forfeited. Going the Cephas route will cause us to become in time stabilizers for those around us.

❦

A BRIGHT IDEA

"You know nothing at all; you do not understand that it is expedient for you that one man should die for the people, and that the whole nation should not perish." John 11:49,50

Caiaphas, the President of the Ruling Council, was a self-confident leader, who regarded the council members in the matter before them as a bunch of lunkheads. He just had a bright idea, to which we might retort, "Hold on to it; it's in a strange place." The solution to their problem was to him self-evident. Expediency (self-interest) demanded the sacrifice of Jesus. The whole nation would thereby be spared. "He did not say this of his own accord, but being high priest that year he prophesied that Jesus should die for the nation, and not for the nation only, but to gather into one the children of God who are scattered abroad."

His "bright idea" was self-serving to the core. We might call it brutal. But was not their priestly religion horrendously brutal? Animal lovers would protest this "needless slaughter of innocent creatures before the Temple as a hideous blood-bath unworthy of a civilized people." The priests were through the centuries though conditioned to accept the shedding of innocent blood. The sacrifice of Jesus may be regarded as the inevitable consequence of the Jewish religion colliding with the irresistible Roman power. The crucifixion of Jesus was built into the situation. It was humanly logical because it was divinely ordained.

Today there are those in every nation who have it in their hearts to do what is pleasing to their Creator. When they hear of Jesus' sacrificial love, they will say, "That's for me." Their recognition of Jesus as the unique expression of the God who fashioned this universe is gradually drawing them into a unity that is a delight to behold. "This is God's doing, and it is marvelous in our eyes."

❧

THE PASSOVER FORESHADOWED
BY THE EXODUS

"*So from that day on they took counsel how to put him to death.*"
John 11:53

It is extraordinary that because Jesus raised Lazarus from the dead, he must die. It was now settled. They did not yet realize that the "how" of it had been determined before the creation: that he must die by crucifixion, the death of the damned. See Deut. 21:22-23

"Jesus therefore no longer went about openly among the Jews, but went from there to the country near the wilderness, to a town called Ephraim; and there he stayed with the disciples." Ephraim, meaning fruitful, was about 15 miles northeast of Jerusalem. There Jesus was biding his time until the occasion of Passover, when by his death and resurrection he would become fruitful by repeating himself in others. This was the purpose of it all.

"Now the Passover of the Jews was at hand, and many went up from the country to Jerusalem before the Passover to purify themselves." All who seek to be pure before God inevitably look for Jesus, for he is the only one who is able to render us acceptable in the sight of God. So we read, "They were looking for Jesus and saying to one another as they stood in the Temple, `What do you think? That he will not come to the feast?'" They realized that for Jesus to come to this Passover would be to sign his own death warrant. "Now the chief priests and the Pharisees had given orders that if anyone knew where he was, he should let them know, so that they might arrest him," and, as we know, murder him. Needless to say, he would be coming to this particular Passover in the year of our Lord 30, because it was for this that he came into the world.

For what purpose did we come into the world? "That (we) may know him," said Paul, "and the power of his resurrection, and may share his suffering, becoming like him in his death, that if possible (we) may attain the resurrection from the dead." Phil. 3:10,11

151

THE HINGE

"*Six days before the Passover, Jesus came to Bethany.*"

John 12:1

We have come to the hinge in John's expression of the gospel, the half-way point. We have already encountered the seven themes twice over, and we shall encounter them twice again. We saw the seven themes in the first four chapters. (Actually in chapter 3:22-36 we heard the testimony of John the Baptist a second time). Then in chapters 5 to 11 the themes are reiterated. Chapter 5 - Healing. Chapter 6 - Nurture. Chapters 7 and 8 - Homecoming. Chapters 9 and 10 - New Birth. In chapter 11, concerning the death and raising of Lazarus, we encountered again the themes of Faith and Life. When Jesus told Martha that he was the resurrection and the life, and that he who believes in him though he die (like Lazarus) would live again, he then asked her, "Do you believe this?" She answered, "Yes, Lord, I believe." That is faith strong and sure. Then he came to the grave and said, "Lazarus, come out." And the dead Lazarus came out of the grave alive. Here we have the foreshadowing of Jesus' own resurrection. This was the seventh time in the gospel that Jesus displayed his life-giving power, by giving a sign. Each sign is greater than those that preceded.

In chapters 12-17 we will encounter the seven themes in the original order again. In chapter 12 - Testimony and Faith. Chapter 13 - Life. Chapter 14 - Homecoming. Chapter 15 - Fruitfulness. Chapter 16 - Nurture. Chapter 17 - Healing. Fasten your seat belt, for now we launch into the deep water. What we are about to see illuminates the Book of Revelation. In that Book (also by John) the sequence begins again in chapter 12. Apart from a deep understanding of this Gospel, we will find the Book of Revelation largely incomprehensible. We begin a survey of Revelation beginning on November 18. It is exciting to see how both books parallel one another, each throwing light on the other.

THE ANOINTED ONE

"*Six days before the Passover, Jesus came to Bethany, where Lazarus was, whom Jesus had raised from the dead.*" *John 12:1*

What day of the week was it when Jesus came to Bethany? John 19:14 tells us that Jesus' trial before Pilate and execution occurred on "the day of Preparation of the Passover." Since Jesus was crucified on Good Friday, Passover that year fell on Saturday, the seventh day of the week, or Sabbath. Six days before the seventh day of the week is the first day of the week, Sunday. So it was on Sunday, later known as the Lord's Day, that in Bethany "they made him a supper; Martha served, and Lazarus was one of those at table with him." In the gospel Lazarus never says a word. He doesn't have to. His living presence speaks volumes. When the Lord has brought us out of spiritual death by new birth, we don't have to say anything. People will recognize that we have been touched by Jesus. Someone said to a person come alive in Christ, "You are cracked," to which she responded, "Thank God. How do you suppose the light got in?"

"Mary took a pound of costly ointment of pure nard and anointed the feet of Jesus and wiped his feet with her hair; and the house was filled with the fragrance of the ointment." What is happening here? On the first day of Holy Week Mary of Bethany is doing silently what the Baptist did verbally on the first day of the gospel. She is bearing witness to the fact that Jesus is the Christ (the Anointed). We had hoped that the High Priest Caiaphas would have anointed Jesus as Messiah, but in the providence of God a woman did him this sacred honor, not upon his head but upon his feet, symbolic of Jesus' humility. Now he is entitled to be known as the Anointed One from the standpoint of man as well as of God, who had anointed him with the Holy Spirit at his baptism. We will miss the glory of this gospel if we seek to harmonize it with the others. Matthew, Mark and Luke view the Lord's ministry from the perspective of Peter.

❦

153

WHY DID JUDAS BLOW THE WHISTLE?

"*Mary took a pound of costly ointment of pure nard and anointed the feet of Jesus and wiped his feet with her hair.*" *John 12:3*

Why did she do that? Because she loved him so. I Corinthians 11:15 says, "If a woman has long hair, it is her glory." Having "Messiahed" him, she is now glorifying him, ministering to him with her hair, her glory and pride. The greatness of this occasion is underscored by the quantity and costliness of the perfume. It was fit for the anointing of the King. "And the house was filled with the fragrance of the ointment." The whole inhabited world will ultimately be filled with the loveliness and significance of what Mary did that day, because it was essential that Jesus be "confirmed" in his messianic office before he went to the cross. She had functioned as the Maid of Honor, the Baptist as the Best Man.

"But Judas Iscariot, one of his disciples (he who was to betray him), said, `Why was this ointment not sold for three hundred denarii and given to the poor.' This he said, not that he cared for the poor but because he was a thief, and as he had the money box he used to take what was put into it." Someone said that Judas was the first communist, because communists pretend they care for the poor, but actually they are thieves and steal from them. How extraordinary that Jesus should appoint the thief in the company to be the treasurer.

The retired missionary President of the Presbyterian College in Rawalpindi, Pakistan, was showing us a colored slide of the faculty. He pointed out the treasurer, and said, "That man is worth his weight in gold - an honest treasurer!" They were apparently hard to come by in Pakistan. But Jesus chose Judas as treasurer. God's ways are not our ways, are they? Where I am weak, there I may become strong. Recently I was feeling blue. Then it dawned on me that blue is the color of faith. When I am in the pink, I walk by feeling, but when I am blue, I must walk by faith.

ANOINTED FOR BURIAL

"**J**esus said, `Let her alone, let her keep it for the day of my burial.'" John 12:7

Jesus defends Mary's action, warding off the attack of Judas. He connects the anointing with the day of his death and burial. This means that Jesus functions as Messiah by means of his sacrificial death. He does something for us thereby that no one else can do. He rescues us from the evil consequences of our sin. His death as our representative is the universal death. As believers in him we acknowledge that our burial in the water of baptism is our acceptance of the fact that we have been crucified with Christ. Since our baptism, we are obliged to allow Jesus to live his resurrection life in us. It was for this that he died and was raised, that he might repeat himself in us. "You are not your own. You have been bought with a price:" the agonizing death of Jesus' crucifixion. He took what we had coming that we might receive what he had coming: eternal joy in the Father's bosom.

"The poor you always have with you." Whenever you will you can do good to them. "... but you do not always have me." We delight in the knowledge that Mary seized the opportune moment to lavish her love in a spontaneous demonstration of generosity upon the Saviour about to die. Throughout eternity the universe will applaud her necessary deed. We also take note of the fact that even Christianity will never eliminate poverty on earth. Whenever we are moved to do so, we may minister lovingly to the poor with whom Jesus identifies himself. "Foxes have holes, the birds of the air have nests, but the Son of man has no where to lay his head," he said. He lived the life of a wayfaring vagabond for three years. The growing number of street people in our society present us with an ever increasing opportunity to do something for those with whom Jesus felt right at home. "Whenever you do it to the least of these, you do it unto me," said Jesus.

THE PLOT THICKENS

"*When the great crowd of the Jews learned that he was there, they came, not only on account of Jesus but also to see Lazarus, whom he had raised from the dead." John 12:9*

On the first day of Holy Week we have experienced with Jesus what we may have anticipated: Testimony/Preparation. Mary of Bethany has borne her silent witness to Jesus, the Messiah. Actions speak louder than words. Indeed in the providence of God she was the human agent through whom he was anointed as Messiah, not upon his head, as David had been anointed by Samuel, but upon his feet, expressive of his humility. No wonder then that what she did would be heralded around the earth wherever the gospel would go, as a memorial of her. Her role was an essential one in holy history. Womankind has been forever dignified by her deed.

We might have supposed that the High Priest would have anointed him. Strangely the High Priest though had prophesied and decreed his sacrificial death. He was positioned by God to see to it. So all the actors are now on the stage fulfilling their divinely assigned roles. We are thankful that a woman was privileged to assume such a major part in this prophecied drama that is unfolding.

If we look at the parallel chapter in the book of Revelation (12:1-6), we see the sun- clothed woman standing on the moon about to give birth. The woman's adversary there looms larger than Judas. It is the great red dragon himself, whose role Judas fulfills in this miniature of the universal crisis there depicted. Be that as it may, in our verse today we see that "the chief priests planned to put Lazarus also to death, because on account of him many of the Jews were going away and believing in Jesus." The plot thickens. The beneficiaries of Jesus' life-giving power may anticipate from the professionally religious a fate similar to that of Jesus: if not death, then certainly persecution.

❧

THE DAY OF COURTSHIP

"The next day a great crowd who had come to the feast heard that Jesus was coming to Jerusalem." John 12:12

We have established that the anointing at Bethany occurred six days before the Passover (the Sabbath day), on the first day of Holy Week. "The next day" then is Monday, the second day of the week. This is the day of the so-called Triumphal Entry, which we associate with Palm Sunday. John surprises us by saying it really took place on Monday. Don't get angry with me. I didn't say it, John did. And he was there. So let us listen to what he has to say. The result will be depth perception. It happens when we look at reality through two eyes. We miss it when we attempt to harmonize John and the other three gospels.

The second day in this gospel is the day of faith/courtship. See 1:35-51 for the first occurrence. Sure enough on the second day of Holy Week Jesus enters Jerusalem, the City of David, in the way Zechariah 9:9 prophesied he would, "upon an ass's colt." Why did he do that? He was fulfilling the Scripture in an attempt to woo and win Jerusalem and official Judaism to himself.

On this occasion he master-minded a Messianic demonstration, claiming in an official way to be the long awaited Messiah. His public claim to be Messiah/Saviour meets with faith on the part of the great crowd who had come to the feast. Even some Greeks came to him, taking thereby the first steps toward faith. Above all the Heavenly Father thunders from heaven his endorsement of Jesus' sonship. Tragically, though, as we shall see, official Jerusalem rejects his overture of love. His courtship meets with failure. The religious establishment, hardened against him in their stony disbelief, will oversee the murder of their Messiah and the destruction of their nation for nearly 2000 years.

A BASIC PRINCIPLE

"*So they took branches of palm trees and went out to meet him, crying, 'Hosanna! Blessed is he who comes in the name of the Lord, even the King of Israel!'" John 12:13*

The rejoicing pilgrims had palm branches in their hands. So do we. We may wave the palms of our hands toward God in heaven in sacred praise anytime we feel like it. Prim and proper as we are, we are loath to do such an undignified thing. But those who came out to meet Jesus were not standing on their dignity; they were exulting in God's saving love. They were singing a portion of the Martyr's Song in Psalm 118: "Hosanna" (Save us now), verse 25. And then comes verse 26 in which they bless him who enters the Temple, identifying him as Israel's King. It is remarkable that several sentences earlier it is said concerning this King: "The stone which the builders rejected has become the head of the corner. This is the Lord's doing; it is marvelous in our eyes." He is always rejected by the religionists.

Here we encounter a basic principle. We are enjoined in the Bible to watch our dreams. See Acts 2:17. We find in our dream material a rejected, loathsome part (for example bodily wastes). What we deem hateful can become the cornerstone. If we can accept it, we will discover that God uses the very thing we detest to transform us into the new creatures he calls us to become. That which you most hate is the fulcrum God is using to raise you into a new and higher realm. Believe me. No, believe Jesus! He is the friendly enemy who is attacking you at your strongest point. Just there you must be broken. You will leave the encounter as Jacob left the Jabbok (Genesis 32:22-32), a broken man or woman. Ever after he had a limp, but he was limping in the presence and direction of his God. That which God uses he first breaks. It hurts like fury. That is why Jesus has many lovers of his glory, but few lovers of the cross.

DUMB BUT WISE

"And Jesus found a young ass and sat upon it." John 12:14

Why didn't he find a white horse? Since he is the King sent from heaven wouldn't it be more appropriate? Revelation 19:11 says, "Then I saw heaven opened, and behold a white horse. He who sat upon it is called Faithful and True, and in righteousness he judges and makes war." But that is his second coming. In his first coming he always fulfills what had been written about him. Now he fulfills Zechariah 9:9, "Fear not, daughter of Zion; (In his second coming he will scare the bejeebers out of everyone, with the exception of those who have longed for his appearing.) behold, your King coming, sitting on an ass's colt!" A king rode upon an ass when he came in peace, upon a horse when he came for war. We are told elsewhere that no one had ever ridden upon the colt before. How come it didn't buck? The unbroken colt knew its Master. Tragically it knew more than Jerusalem did. It doesn't know it's Master yet, to this very day.

"His disciples did not understand this at first; but when Jesus was glorified, then they remembered that this had been written of him and had been done to him." They didn't realize that Jesus was fulfilling Old Testament Scripture point by point, step by step. Jesus read the Jewish Bible to learn from God his job-description. It was all there in black and white.

Hopefully we are reading the New Testament to learn our job-description. As a young believer I read in Matthew 28:19, "Go, ye therefore, and teach all nations." I took the "ye" to be "me." That idea has taken me to a number of different countries to teach the gospel. Hence the motto: Have gospel, will travel (with apologies to Palladin). Have you found the verse, quickened by the Spirit, that illuminates your sacred task? "Living for Jesus, a life that is true. Striving to please him in all that I do." Good for starters.

❦

THE DEAD BORE WITNESS

"*The crowd that had been with him when he called Lazarus out of the tomb and raised him from the dead bore witness.*" *John 12:17*

The moment I surrendered myself totally to Jesus Christ, I experienced something of that electric energy that raised Lazarus from the dead. For several seconds I felt as though I was being electrocuted. I didn't see anything or hear anything as Saul of Tarsus did on the Damascus Road, but I sure felt something. And it is "better felt than telt." Then I had an enormous sense of peace.

For four months I had been agonizing over what I was to do with my life. What really got to me was the preacher saying, "A surgeon would never dare take up a scalpel to perform delicate brain surgery if that scalpel was not completely yielded to his hand." I hated public speaking. It scared me to death. But I reasoned that Jesus had died for me, therefore I must be willing to die for him. Dying of fright speaking to people in public about Jesus is as good a way to die as any. So Jesus, okay, I am all yours. If you want me to preach your gospel, I am willing to do it. I will step out in that direction. If you don't want me to be a minister, shut the door.

I said that inwardly at 9 p.m. on Passion Sunday evening, April 3, 1949, lying on my bed in the UCLA fraternity house at 612 Landfair, Westwood, California. The moment I did, the fire fell. I can say as John Wesley put it, "My heart was strangely warmed." From that moment on my greatest delight has been to tell others about Jesus Christ. Isn't that what "new birth" is all about? When the baby is born it produces sounds outside its mother's body. Prior to that it is as quiet as a church mouse. Don't be a mouse in the house, but a witness in the world. Before I was born from above I taught a Sunday School class of young boys, but that was safely within the walls of the church building. New birth requires us to take the gospel into the world. Have we? ❦

THE WORLD HAS GONE AFTER HIM

"*The reason why the crowd went to meet him was that they heard he had done this sign.*" *John 12:18*

I have seen my share of parades. I won't go far to see another. But if I hear that someone raised another from the dead, who had been four days in a tomb, I will go some distance to see and hear the two of them. "The Pharisees then said to one another `You see that you can do nothing; look, the world has gone after him.'"

I had a visit with Mel Tari, who tells in his book Like a Mighty Wind about the Indonesian revival that began in the Presbyterian Church on Timor in 1966. Mel was there. He and his associates sang hymns over a stinking corpse about to be buried, believing it would be raised from the dead. When the dead man sat up, it scared them half to death. The dead man said, "There really is a hell. I know. I was there." Thirty thousand became Christians as a result. When I asked Mel about the man going to hell, he said, "The man witnessed hell, but as a Christian he went to heaven." When I asked him about heaven, Mel said, "The more he told us, the more confused we got. It was like someone who had never seen an airplane asking what it was like. When told it was like a bird with stationary wings and that one goes in a door, where a stewardess serves meals, etc. - the more one hears, the more confused one gets." I asked if the man is now a preacher. Mel said, "If he was in the U.S., he would probably be a preacher. But the Lord did not call him to preach, but to farm. He is a farmer."

In his book Mel tells about other miracles the likes of which are recorded only in the Bible. Several years ago I asked the Professor of Evangelism of a leading Presbyterian Seminary if he had ever heard of Mel Tari. He never had. It is as though the Indonesian Revival happened in a corner. Most have never heard. If they heard, would they believe? Do you? Only if God enables you to.

THE SECRET OF ETERNAL LIFE

" *Now among those who went to worship at the feast were some Greeks.*" *John 12:20*

These Greeks were known as God-fearers, worshipers of the God of Israel. They stopped short of submitting to circumcision and becoming Jews. "So these came to Philip, who was from Bethsaida in Galilee, and said to him, `Sir, we wish to see Jesus.'" This motto is inscribed in the pulpit of a church to be seen by the preacher every time he enters it. Isn't that what every congregation desires - to see Jesus?

"Philip went and told Andrew; Andrew went with Philip and they told Jesus." What was now happening was so significant that Philip did not have the courage to bring the Greeks to Jesus by himself. He needed the bolstering of Andrew, who seems to have had the knack of introducing people to Jesus, as he had his brother and the lad with the sack lunch. The church could use more of his ilk. "And Jesus answered them, `The hour has come for the Son of man to be glorified.'" He speaks of his hour of departure, when he reveals his essential nature to be love incarnate.

"Truly, truly, I say to you, unless a grain of wheat falls into the earth and dies, it remains alone; but if it dies, it bears much fruit." If Jesus' first sign of turning water into wine is the key sign, this "truly, truly" statement is the key secret underlying eternal life. It lies in the mystery of the seed. It is able to reproduce itself only by forfeiting its own identity. The seed contains germinal life. That life is released only by burial in the ground. Once buried, its miraculous power to repeat itself is released, when water comes to it. The seed of God's word within us touched by the water of God's Spirit produces supernatural results. God has arranged that death is the source of life. Sacrifice of self and love of the other are the basis of reproducing after our kind.

❦

A QUESTION OF LOVING AND HATING

"*He who loves his life loses it, and he who hates his life in this world will keep it for eternal life.*" *John 12:25*

  The word "life" here is literally "soul," referring to one's individual human existence. The emotion of loving or hating is the important thing. What do you love? What do you hate? Our emotional aspect is perhaps the most powerful component of our personality. Some say, "A man must live. Survival is the most important thing." Jesus contradicts that assumption. Serving the divine purpose is more important than continuing on indefinitely as an individual. One must die eventually anyhow. Whether my life is long or short, what is the difference so long as I fulfill my task. If I regard my individual existence as the highest good, I have deified myself. But I am only a creature here, not God. On the other hand, Jesus does not tell me that I am to hate myself - far from it. In fact I am commanded to love myself, and others in the same measure. What I am to hate is my life "in this world." By that he means that I am to hate the kind of life this world seeks to impose upon me. The world says, in effect, "The devil take the hindermost." In the world it is dog eat dog, every man for himself. But Jesus says not so. It is man for others. We are to defy the world's system of values by laying our lives down for one another. We are saved to serve.

  "If anyone serves me, he must follow me; and where I am, there shall my servant be also." Where is Jesus as he says this? In the center of God's perfect will. He is totally yielded to his Father's plan for his life, facing the cross. His cross is, in a word, his job description. There is a cross in God's plan for each one of us. It is where God's will intersects my own. "If anyone serves me, the Father will honor him." How? He will do so by exalting that one to his right hand. Paul says that is exactly where we are already in Christ Jesus. In Ephesians 2:6 we are seated in Christ in heavenly places.

❧

SOME SAID IT THUNDERED

"*ow is my soul troubled. And what shall I say? 'Father, save me from this hour'?*" John 12:27

The coming of the Greeks was evidently the sign that Jesus was waiting for. It prophesied the coming of the heathen world into his Kingdom. He was delighted at the prospect. But it meant that the hour of his death was at hand. We have seen that the mystery of Christ's death is contained in the seed. By dying, we return the life we have received from God back to God. This life-style was adopted by the apostles as they "died daily," in the words of St. Paul. They regarded their daily lives as at the disposal of God, to do with as He saw fit. They allowed God to determine their daily agenda, accepting interruptions as divinely sanctioned interventions.

As Jesus contemplated the cross, his soul was troubled. He was a human as you and I. The temptation was to seek an alternative arrangement. Dying of cancer would have seemed a far lesser evil. Should he ask God to cancel his appointment with Calvary's cross? 'No, for this purpose I have come to this hour. Father, glorify thy name.' (Make your nature known.)

"Then a voice came from heaven, `I have glorified it, and I will glorify it again.' The crowd standing by heard it and said that it had thundered. Others said, `An angel has spoken to him.'" What is your opinion? Did God really speak to him? Was it important for God to say what he is reputed to have said on this occasion? Here we have a confirmation of the validity of Jesus' ministry up to this point, and the promise that the future would be equally substantive. The worshiping multitudes had expressed their faith in Jesus. The Greeks were coming to faith in Jesus. Now on the second day of Holy Week the Almighty himself in a voice like thunder said, I am with you, Son. That is more than a pat on the back. It is a mandate to keep his appointment with Calvary.

❧

TALK ABOUT ATTRACTING POWER

"**J**esus answered, 'This voice has come for your sake, not for mine.'" *John 12:30*

Jesus said earlier to the Jews, "His voice you have never heard, his form you have never seen." Now they had actually heard the Father's voice, though most could not understand the words uttered. Jesus continually heard the still, small voice of God in his heart of hearts. It has been called "the still small voice," the voiceless voice of God, the silence of a gentle whisper. He always followed the Father's counsel. As Christians, so should we. When we undertake some activity, it should be asked, "Was that your idea, or God's?"

"Now is the judgment of this world ("now" referring to his death upon the cross), now shall the ruler of this world be cast out." Cast out of where? He had already been cast out of God's presence (the third heaven or paradise). See Isaiah 14 and Ezekiel 28. He is about to be cast out of the church (ecclesia or called out ones). As he had no power over Jesus, so he would soon lose his power over the disciples of Jesus. His influence over them would be broken at the cross. When the Bride of Christ is dismissed from the scene, Satan will be cast from the heavenlies down to the earth. (Revelation 12:9). After the Battle of Armageddon, he will be cast into the bottomless pit for a thousand years of imprisonment. After his release to tempt the nations once more, he will be cast into the place prepared for him and his fallen angels, the lake of fire and sulphur, which is the second death. (Revelation 20:2) In all he is the victim of five "castings out", two in the past, three yet in the future.

"And I, when I am lifted up from the earth, will draw all men to myself." Ultimately the risen, exalted Christ will see the universe pass in review before himself. What an exciting thought! Followers of other religious leaders and systems, take note.

WHO IS THIS SON OF MAN?

"*He said this to show by what death he was to die.*" *John 12:33*

The Jewish mode of execution was by stoning. Jesus foretold that his manner of death would be by being lifted up the Roman way upon a wooden cross. Would you like to know your manner of death? If ignorance is bliss, it doubtless applies to the question just asked. The thought of how we will die, as well as the when of it, is seldom considered. It is too heavy a subject, but should it be, seeing as how "our birth is the wound from which we die." I talked long distance on the phone the other day to a high school classmate who is dying of cancer. We ended the conversation that he might go take another pain pill. I am not free to tell how he depicted the pain. It is a bit too earthy. But Jesus knows. He tasted it all. For you. For me.

"The crowd answered him, `We have heard from the law that the Christ remains forever. (David my servant shall be their prince forever. Ezekiel 37:25) How can you say that the Son of man must be lifted up? (Killed by crucifixion?) Who is this Son of man?'

"Jesus said to them, `The light is with you for a little longer. (In other words, I am, as I said before, the light of the world, the One who led your ancestors out of Egypt, through the wilderness, into the promised land.) Walk while you have the light (follow me while the opportunity remains), lest the darkness (the evil one) overtake you (he is surely gaining on you); he who walks in the darkness does not know where he goes.' If we persist in our rejection of Jesus and his guidance, we are going to step into outer darkness (a spiritual black hole?) when we breathe our last. `While you have the light, believe in the light, that you may become sons of light.'" The Son of man is able to make us like himself. He is the power for good released in the universe that is capable of restoring to us God's lost image.

❦

THE GOD WHO STILLS WORKS SIGNS

When Jesus had said this, he departed and hid himself from them." John 12:36

"Truly, thou art a God who hidest thyself, O God of Israel, the Savior." Isaiah 45:15. That is why we must seek him with all of our heart. We are privileged to make of our lives a pilgrimage in search of God; then we will surely find him, as he has promised.

"Though he had done so many signs before them, yet they did not believe in him." We have come to the end of Jesus' public ministry. We have seen seven of the signs, illustrations of the thousands, the tens of thousands that he did. "Jews demand signs," wrote St. Paul. They had them to their hearts' content, and still they rejected Jesus. A physicist went to the Carl Jung Institute in Switzerland to study his dreams. Those in the Jung school believe in God. Jung said, "If you do not believe in God there is no healing for you." This man was an atheist, so he ran a test. He filled a glass with water and set it almost teetering on the edge of a table. He said, "God, if you exist, prove it. Cause this glass of water to fall on the floor." He waited for an hour. Nothing happened, proving to his satisfaction that God does not exist. That night all he remembered of his dreaming was several letters and numbers, which he dutifully recorded. The next day his car collided with another. The license plate of the other car bore the numbers and letters he had dreamed.

A minister I told this story to expressed incredulity. He refused to believe that it actually happened. I have no problem with it, because God has spoken to me on occasion through dreams. To those who keep alert God is still willing to prove himself. But it is not for us to tell him how he must do it. He is a God of signs, but he does not do them on command. We are to recognize signs when they occur. I suggest that you watch your dreams. It is one of easiest ways for him to speak to us.

WHY DID THE JEWS REJECT JESUS?

"*It was that the word spoken by the prophet Isaiah might be fulfilled.*" *John 12:38*

Why was it that the Jews as a people did not believe in him, despite the many signs? It was because God had so decreed it. The Apostle Paul reveals the why of it in his letter to the Romans (Chapter 11) where he discloses the divine intent that Gentiles be permitted to become Christians without becoming Jews. Had the Jews as a nation accepted Jesus, we Gentiles would have been obliged to embrace their law as well as their Savior.

God loves diversity. Until the principle of diversity is firmly established in mankind, God will not lift the veil from the hearts of his covenant people, allowing them to believe in Jesus. Isaiah foretold their unbelief in 53:12, "LORD, who has believed our report, and to whom has the arm of the Lord been revealed?" The answer he anticipates is, "No one." Absolutely no one had forseen that the Messiah would be the Suffering Servant spoken of in Isaiah 53. Jesus himself was the only one who saw in that chapter his job description.

"Therefore they could not believe," said Jesus. God would not allow it. He had to die at the hands of his own people in order that he might become the Savior of all humanity. "For Isaiah again said, `He has blinded their eyes and hardened their heart, lest they should see with their eyes and perceive with their heart, and turn for me to heal them.'" Isaiah 6:10. The responsibility for Jewish unbelief rests with God, who alone is sovereign over the affairs of men. If you believe in Jesus, give God the glory. "Isaiah said this because he saw his (Christ's) glory and spoke of him." This means that in 740 B.C. when King Uzziah died, Isaiah saw the LORD Jesus "sitting upon a throne high and lifted up; and his train filled the temple." He was called into his prophetic ministry by the Word of God, just as you and I have been called into our humbler ministries.

WHO AM I SEEKING TO PLEASE?

"*Nevertheless many even of the authorities believed in him, but for fear of the Pharisees they did not confess it, lest they be put out of the synagogue.*" *John 12:42*

It is a sad thing to believe in Jesus and to keep it secret, sad but understandable. The churches are full of secret believers. They have not been born again. New birth means that our silence has been put to death. Before birth a baby is as quiet as a church mouse. After birth it is difficult for the parents to get a good night's sleep. Had the authorities who believed in Jesus spoken up in his behalf, they would have fared no better than the man born blind. They too would have been cast out of their mother's body (the synagogue), and followed Jesus into the Kingdom of God. But they would not. Do you know why? "For they loved the praise of men more than the praise of God." Whom are we seeking to please? "If I were still pleasing men, I would not be a servant of Christ," wrote St. Paul.

One of my memorable experiences was the evening I expressed the gospel after the evening meal to my fraternity brothers in the fraternity house. I had asked the fraternity president if I could say a few words to the brothers. Given permission, I explained the plan of salvation through six scripture verses I had learned from the Navigators. My roommate afterwards shook my hand and told me that he was surprised they did not laugh. "The message of the cross is foolishness to those who are perishing, but to us who are being saved it is the power of God." I Cor. 1:18.

A few months later I moved out of the fraternity house, perceiving myself to be "persona non grata" (a person not welcomed). I would rather be squeezed out of the fraternity and remain in the Kingdom than the reverse. When one fraternity "brother" learned that I had decided for the gospel ministry, he said to me, "That is a good racket." Tragically for some who have not been called, it might be.

SOME HAVE NO KNOWLEDGE OF GOD

"*And Jesus cried out and said, 'He who believes in me, believes not in me but in him who sent me.'" John 12:44*

If I said I would come to visit you this evening, and you believed in my word to you, you would be believing in me, that I was as good as my word. To believe in the Word of God (Jesus) is really to believe in God.

"And he who sees me sees him who sent me." Like Father, like Son. "I have come as light into the world, that whoever believes in me may not remain in darkness." Those who have not learned of Jesus are in the dark about God. They do not know what he is like. The scientist reputed to have the most powerful mind since Einstein said he believes there is a God but that He is not personal. In other words, He is not interested in communicating with man, a clear rejection of the gospel.

"If any one hears my sayings and does not keep them, I do not judge him; for I did not come to judge the world but to save the world." Isn't that good news? "He who rejects me and does not receive my sayings has a judge; the word that I have spoken will be his judge on the last day." I am not so sure that is good news. I am going to be judged by the word I have already heard. My knowledge will be held against me if I do not act upon it. "Some have no knowledge of God," wrote St. Paul. I say this to their shame! No. "I say this to your shame." We who have heard the gospel are under obligation to proclaim it. One of the simplest ways is to partake continually of the Lord's Supper. By doing so, "we proclaim the Lord's (sacrificial) death until he comes." I Corinthians 11:26 Another way is to gossip about Jesus. The gospel has been called the divine contagion. We spend too much time sneezing in the faces of other believers. Let us go out and sneeze in the faces of those who are in the world. The gospel is easier caught than taught.

❧

I SEE A PLAN HERE

"**F**or I have not spoken on my own authority; the Father who sent me has himself given me commandment what to say and what to speak." John 12:49

"And I know that his commandment is eternal life." Jesus came to us as One under orders. The God who created the universe is a God of order. Einstein regarded God as the Great Mathematician. "All things should be done decently and in order," wrote St. Paul. "With order and ardor," we might add. Every group has its battle cry. The Baptists come shouting, "Water, water." The Pentecostals shout, "Fire, fire." The Presbyterians come saying "Order, order. Order in the court. Here comes the Judge." Is our life in order? Are we undertaking what the Master Designer has laid out for us in our life?

A minister of the gospel told how he died while sleeping in the night. As he journeyed to heaven he became more and more anxious, because he knew he had not finished his work. Sure enough, Jesus told him that he had not, and sent him back into his body. The Lord told him to tell people that God has a perfect plan for every one's life, and that we should not settle for God's good will or acceptable will only, but that we should strive to achieve his perfect will for our lives before we get the upward call of God in Christ Jesus. Jesus proved by his resurrection that the fulfilling of God's commandment is eternal life. "What I say, therefore, I say as the Father has bidden me." To hear from Jesus is to hear from God.

But Jerusalem in the personalities of their leaders rejected Jesus. He had presented himself as their King on the tenth day of Nisan (Monday of Holy Week). Rejecting him as their King, they accepted him as their Passover Lamb. Thus they fulfilled Exodus 12:3. Read it for yourself. We can say with the Old Testament Professor at Seminary, "I see a plan here." May God grant us the grace to see his plan working itself out in our own lives.

❦

PERFECT LOVE

"*Now before the feast of the Passover, when Jesus knew that his hour had come to depart out of this world to the Father, having loved his own who were in the world, he loved them to the end.*"

John 13:1

We have come to the feast known as the Last Supper, celebrated on Maundy Thursday. Maundy means command. He commanded his disciples, saying "Do this in remembrance of me." In Matthew, Mark, and Luke (the Synoptic "seen together" gospels) the Last Supper is referred to as the Passover. See Matthew 26:17-19. John tells us that the Last Supper preceded the Jews' feast of the Passover, which was eaten that year on Friday night. This means that what was eaten on Thursday evening by Jesus' disciples was the Christian Passover. Christians are privileged to partake of the Sacrificial Lamb of God under the guise of bread and wine. Jews were obligated actually to eat lamb.

"When Jesus knew that his (long-awaited) hour had come." To what? "To depart." In the Greek text the verb is a form of "metabasis," which may be literally rendered "pass over." Pass over from where to where? "Out of this world to the Father." Here we have the profound fulfillment of the Passover recorded in Exodus. "Exodus" is a Greek word meaning "the way out," the departure from Egypt. Jesus himself is "the way out" of this world, under the dominion of the devil and death, to the Father, who is enthroned over the material universe. It is getting exciting, isn't it?

Knowing where he was going, Jesus, "having loved his own who were in the world, he loved them to the end." We have returned to the Great Love Story, the wedding at Cana, when Jesus said, "My hour has not yet come" to depart. So he didn't leave. He performed a sign. Now, because he is leaving, he will perform not one sign, but two. These will disclose his perfect love.

THE TROUBLE WITH SANDALED FEET

"*And* during the supper, when the devil had already put it into the heart of Judas Iscariot, Simon's son, to betray him." John 13:2

Here we have come to the very heart of this gospel, the story of God's redeeming love for his people, who were (still) in this world, as we saw in verse one. The disciples, though Jesus' companions for three years, were still part and parcel of this world system. Their attitudes and actions were grounded in the realm of "the prince of the power of the air, the spirit that is now at work in the sons of disobedience." Ephesians 2:2. Jesus' loyalty was elsewhere. His affection was toward his Father in heaven. Judas had already sold out to the devil.

Jesus, fully aware of Judas' treachery, and "knowing that the Father had given all things into his hands, and that he had come from God and was going to God, rose from supper, laid aside his garments, and girded himself with a towel." He had given his disciples full opportunity to undertake the demeaning task of foot washing. Not one of them seized the opportunity of engaging in the role of the servant. In a sense they had all flunked their final exam. The towel girded about the loins was the badge of the slave.

"Then he poured water into a basin, and began to wash the disciples' feet, and to wipe them with the towel with which he was girded." They accepted this ministry with embarrassed silence. "He came to Simon Peter, and Peter said to him, `LORD, do you wash my feet?' Jesus answered him, `What I am doing you do not know now, but afterward you will understand.'" Your feet put you in contact with the dirt and grime of this world. I, Jesus, am the only one who can cleanse you from the filth that comes upon you inevitably by reason of your association with this fallen world. I know your heart is right. It is your feet that require the daily cleansing. Lord Jesus, wash us. Purify us, as we place not only our feet, but all of our members into your loving care and keeping.

❧

LET JESUS WASH YOU

"Peter said to him, 'You shall never wash my feet.'" John 12:8

This was intolerable to Peter, and he probably drew his feet up under his mantle. He refused to allow his LORD and Master to do him the service of a footman. Little did he realize at the time that the hands of this One were involved in flinging the innumerable stars into space. He could have been sent into a state of shock. "Jesus answered him, 'If I do not wash you, you have no part in me.'" How beautiful upon the mountains of God are feet washed clean by the love of God. Only he can bring good tidings, and publish peace. "Simon Peter said to him, 'LORD, not my feet only but also my hands and my head!' Jesus said to him, 'He who has bathed does not need to wash, except for his feet, but he is clean all over.'"

In your baptism you received the divine bath. You were washed; head, hands, and torso. It is your feet, representing your point of contact with the world, that gives you trouble. There you must allow your Lord to cleanse you daily. Let us confess this moment wherein we know we have fallen short of the divine expectation, and ask Jesus to wash us and forgive us. "'And you are clean, but not every one of you.' For he knew who was to betray him, that was why he said, 'You are not all clean.'"

Jesus is in the midst of expressing love to the uttermost. His love is self-effacing, serving the humblest needs of others. Judas was one of those whose feet he washed. He washed his feet, but he could not wash his heart. Judas proffered Jesus his feet, but he refused to yield him his heart. Why? Only God and Judas have the answer to that. I say to Jesus just now, "Lord, wash my feet, and flood my heart with reciprocal love, that I may love you, as you already love me. Now give me a desire to tell one other person this day about you. For this you have singled me out. Amen."

THE EXAMPLE OF OUR EXEMPLAR

*"**W**hen he had washed their feet, and taken his garments, and resumed his place, he said to them, 'Do you know what I have done to you?'" John 13:12*

What had he done? He had given them a dress rehearsal of his coming death and resurrection. As freely as he had laid aside his garments, so freely would he on the morrow lay down his life. Why would he do so? That he might wash us of our filthy stains, purify us by faith in his precious blood. Having done so, he would then of his own volition take up his life, as he took up his garments, and resume his rightful place among us, now as our risen LORD and Savior.

"You call me Teacher and Lord; and you are right, for so I am. If I then, your Lord and Teacher, have washed your feet, you also ought to wash one another's feet. For I have given you an example, that you also should do as I have done to you." Some of us grew up without a father. Even so, we are not fatally handicapped, especially if we grew up hearing the story of Jesus. We have an example, a role model, in Jesus. As he gave himself in self-effacing, humble service to those around him, so are we summoned to do.

I met an elderly minister reported to have an apostolic ministry. He had established many churches in the South Pacific Islands. I watched him leave the outdoor worship under a tent, and walk back toward the camp. Fifteen minutes later he returned carrying a tall glass of water for the speaker on that hot summer afternoon. I don't remember a word that the famous evangelist said, but I will never forget the apostle bringing a glass of water to the preacher. He was the only one who saw what was desired in that situation. It was his nature to be helpful. He was following the example of our Exemplar. They said concerning Philips Brooks, "If you want a favor from Brooks, kick him." Has anyone kicked you lately?

❦

DON'T TELL ME, SHOW ME

"Truly, truly, I say to you, a servant is not greater than his master; nor is he who is sent greater than he who sent him."

John 13:16

No, "a slave is not greater than his LORD," literally. A servant can quit and change jobs, but a slave is not a free agent. He was regarded as "the living tool" of his owner, who had the power of life or death over his slave. As our LORD, Jesus is essentially superior to us, as a shepherd is superior to his sheep, towering over them. Similarly Jesus looks to the Father who sent him as greater than himself. To Him he always looked for instructions.

"If you know these things, blessed are you if you do them." The Greek thought with his mind, whereas the Hebrew thought with his body. "Don't tell me, show me, for actions speak louder than words." The Greek mentality produced the Apostles' Creed. Jesus, on the other hand, expressed the faith by the Sermon on the Mount. It has to do with action. Faith is not what you say; it is what you do. The Eternal Word fleshed himself out in a body and did something. He washed his disciples' feet, and then stretched out his arms upon a cross and died, saying, "I love you this much." Upon the cross Jesus did something that we could not do for ourselves: he forgave us. Now we are obliged to forgive one another and ourselves.

A child was naughty and asked her mother to forgive her. "I forgive you, child," said the mother. But the child persisted in begging for her mother's forgiveness. What has happened here? The mother has forgiven her child, but the child has not yet accepted her forgiveness. She therefore has not forgiven herself. If you have a spiritual problem, go to the clergy and learn of the forgiving love of God. If hearing, you still do not feel forgiven, you do not have a spiritual problem, but an emotional one. You are suffering from false guilt. Go to someone skilled in the area of the soul (the psyche).

THE DAY STAR, SON OF DAWN

"J *am not speaking of you all; I know whom I have chosen."*

John 13:18

"Many are called, but few are chosen," said Jesus. Matt. 22:14. Though Judas had responded to the call to follow Jesus, he had not been chosen to be a part of Jesus' bride. That was why he was not clean. He had evidently been baptized by the Baptist, but he had not truly repented by letting go of his god, Mammon. It is the evil spirit that possesses all who are in love with money.

"It is that the scripture may be fulfilled, `He who ate my bread has lifted his heel against me.'" The quotation from Ps. 41:9 begins with the expression, "Even my bosom friend in whom I trusted..." The implication is that Jesus had reposed his head in the bosom of Judas at the Last Supper. So Judas was on his left, as John was on his right, reposing his head in Jesus' bosom. Jesus allowed Judas the second place of honor, while John enjoyed the first place. Like his father Lucifer, Judas did not enjoy playing second fiddle. His ambition was such that the office of treasurer did not satisfy his egocentricity. He would ascend even higher as the Day Star (Satan) in Isa. 14:12-14. Therefore, "You are brought down to Sheol, to the depths of the Pit" (15). Why would he lift his heel against Jesus? To kick him, of course. Jesus might have said to Judas as he did to Saul on the Damascus Road, "It is hard for you to kick against the goads." Whoever kicks at Jesus only succeeds in inflicting injury upon himself. In vain do we fight against God. He always has the last word.

"I tell you this now, before it takes place, that when it does take place you may believe that I am he." Jesus' disclosure that there was a traitor in the midst would afford a gleam of light in the darkness that was about to descend. This revelation was the divinely given Day Star that would herald the coming of the Dawn on Easter Morning.

A GRACIOUS PROVIDENCE

"Truly, truly, I say to you, he who receives any one whom I send receives me; and he who receives me receives him who sent me."

John 13:20

This verse was a comfort to me when I went to California in my 40th year to get acquainted with my father, age 69. He had become an atheist when he was 18 because of an immense disappointment. When he asked me how I happened to become a minister, I responded, "When my father forsakes me, then the Lord takes me up." I discovered through our conversation that he was no longer an atheist, but a deist. A deist believes that God made the universe as a clock-maker a clock, and then wound it up, allowing it to tick on, until it runs down. He does not believe in divine intervention. At his wife's suggestion, he accompanied me to church on Sunday morning - the first time he had been to church in 50 years. By receiving me, he had, I believe, whether he knew it or not, received Jesus. A few months later he died. I returned to California to conduct a private memorial service.

Why had I become a minister of the gospel? For two reasons, I am persuaded. Because I was called by God (on the head side of the coin), and also because I am living out my father's shadow (on the tail side). He had turned his back on his religious upbringing, as an Episcopalian. So it fell to me to live out that which he had suppressed. Had he lived out that which had been inculcated within him, it is likely that the mantle to take Christianity so seriously might not have fallen on me. I understand experientially the truth stated in Jeremiah 31:29: "The fathers have eaten sour grapes, and the children's teeth are set on edge." The offspring are the victims of parental errors. It may not be fair, but it is true. Thank God, we are all privileged to benefit from Jesus bearing the rap for us all. I forgave my father for deserting us years before I went to see him. Have you forgiven those near and dear who have forsaken you?

❧

BETRAYED

"When Jesus had thus spoken, he was troubled in spirit, and testified, 'Truly, truly, I say to you, one of you will betray me.'"

John 13:21

He now made explicit that to which he had been alluding. The word "betray" is literally "hand me over." In this context it means hand me over to my enemies. In another setting it may refer to handing over the sacred deposit of the gospel to another, who in turn should do the same. We are called to do this without tampering with or diluting the message. It is not so easy. Human tradition has a way of watering down the gospel. Add a little water to your gasoline and suddenly you don't go anywhere; the power is gone.

I was told that Professor Otto Piper at Princeton Seminary, when asked what he thought of speaking in tongues, responded, "Would that we heard more speaking in tongues on the Princeton campus." His wish was fulfilled. In 1964 half the students were speaking in tongues; they had a prayer language.

On January 21, 1967 I heard Dr. Derek Prince, former Professor of Philosophy at Cambridge University, teach on this subject. I had seen that on the day of Pentecost the 120 spoke in tongues as the Spirit gave them utterrance. Acts 2:4. But I had not perceived that ten years later they all spoke in tongues in the house of Cornelius. Acts 10:46. Also it had to be pointed out to me that some 25 years after Pentecost the 12 disciples at Ephesus spoke in tongues when Paul ministered to them. Acts 19:6. How many Christians realize that praying in tongues was normative in the first century Church? Since Jesus never changes, he is baptizing in the power of the Holy Spirit now as he did then. Of this we may be sure. If we think otherwise, we are victims of a watered down gospel. Someone has betrayed the sacred trust. In all faith let us ask Jesus to baptize us, and then begin inhaling the Holy Spirit. When the overflow occurs, we will be free to speak a new language.

❧

THE JUDAS WITHIN

"*The disciples looked at each other, uncertain of whom he spoke.*"
John 13:22

In Mark 14:19 they say to him one after another, "Is it I?" "The heart is deceitful above all things, and desperately corrupt; who can understand it?" Jer. 17:9. If you have placed your unconscious under scrutiny by watching your dreams, you have seen something of the evil that lurks within. All of us are like the Scribes and Pharisees, "whitewashed tombs, which outwardly appear beautiful, but within are full of dead men's bones and all uncleanness." Mt. 22:27.

If you think your unconscious is not as so depicted, you are claiming a sinless nature that belongs alone to Jesus. "There is a little larceny in all of us." Judas resides within us all. If you recoil at the suggestion, you are not yet trusting in the grace and mercy of God. You are leaning upon your own righteousness. Isaiah 64:5 says, "All our righteousness is as filthy rags." Within the noblest saint resides the sinful tendency. But "those who belong to Christ Jesus have crucified the flesh with its passions and desires." Galatians 5:24.

How have we succeeded in doing so? By divine reckoning. Hear the good news: "For the love of Christ controls us, because we are convinced that <u>one has died for all</u>; therefore <u>all have died</u>." 2 Cor. 5:14. Are you convinced as yet that Christ died for you, and in your place? God has said so, by raising him from the dead. Believe it, by reckoning it so. Reckoning has to do with math, an exact science. It is either right or wrong. Agree with God's evaluation of Jesus' substitutionary death. Your sinful nature was crucified when Jesus was nailed to the cross. Your evil Judas-nature is still a part of you, but it has lost its power fully to express itself. Why? Because it is writhing in agony on the cross of Christ. The cross holds it fast. It will die and be gone forever when you breathe your last.

❧

THE PLACE OF INTIMACY AND LOVE

"*One of his disciples, whom Jesus loved, was lying thus close to the breast of Jesus.*" *John 13:23*

This was John, son of Zebedee. He could not get over the fact that Jesus loved him. Karl Barth, the famous German theologian, was asked if he could express his theology in terms so simple that a child could understand. He answered, "Jesus loves me; this I know, for the Bible tells me so. Little ones to him belong. They are weak, but he is strong. Yes, Jesus loves me. Yes, Jesus loves me. Yes, Jesus loves me. The Bible tells me so."

Something within us says you've got to be kidding. We don't feel lovable because we aren't. But God loves us in spite of ourselves, because He is love. Jesus had nick-named John and James "Sons of thunder," because they were so hot tempered. They wanted to call lightning down from heaven to consume the Samaritan town that would not receive them.

Jesus said, "You do not know what spirit you are of." They were motivated by a spirit of murder, not by God. Jesus came to us from the bosom of his Father, the place of intimacy and love. John comes to us from near the heart of Jesus. Remember the words of the hymn, "There is a place of quiet rest, near to the heart of God. A place where sin cannot molest, near to the heart of God. O Jesus, blest Redeemer, sent from the heart of God, hold us who wait before thee, near to the heart of God." What a delightful place to be. And that is where we are, "seated in Christ Jesus in the heavenly places at the right hand of God." Eph. 2:6. We perceive our glorious position by faith, not by sight. People will say, "I feel miserable, down in the dumps. My life is horrible." To this we say, "Do you believe in Jesus? If so, wrap your feelings up in praise, and hand them over to Jesus. You are, as a matter of fact, more than a conqueror through Jesus Christ, who has proved his love by dying for you."

THE KING OF PRIDE

"*So Simon Peter beckoned to him and said, 'Tell us who it is of whom he speaks.'" John 13:24*

Peter wanted to know so that he might plunge his sword through the traitor's heart. What follows happens so quickly that Peter had no time to act. Jesus would literally save Judas' life.

"So, lying thus, close to the breast of Jesus, he said to him, `Lord, who is it?' Jesus answered, `It is he to whom I shall give this morsel when I have dipped it.'" The dipped morsel was given by the host to the guest of honor. Who ever received the morsel would thus be regarded as above suspicion. "So, when he had dipped the morsel, he gave it to Judas, the Son of Simon Iscariot." This was the sign to John that Judas was the traitor. Simultaneously he covered up for Judas, protecting him from the animosity of Peter and the rest. Judas had to be allowed the freedom to fulfill his dastardly mission. It was a divine necessity. The giving of the dipped morsel was not only a sign of Jesus' love for Judas, but also expressive of his self-giving. In a sense Judas was being offered holy communion beforehand. The Lord's Supper would not be instituted until after his departure. What happened when Jesus proffered love's last overture?

"Then after the morsel, Satan entered into him." What does that mean? He resolved just then that he was going to go through with it. He would betray Jesus. Nature abhors a vacuum. Rejecting Jesus Christ, he allowed himself to be devil-possessed. He became Satan's agent, foreshadowing Mr. 666, the beast of Rev. 13, that comes out of the deep. The beast is filled with yeast, the leaven that puffs up. He is the King of pride. He will rule over the nations after the Prophetic Church, symbolized by the Church of Philadelphia, has been dismissed from the earth. God grant that none of us will be here to experience his rage.

LOVE HIM OR LEAVE HIM

"Jesus said to him, 'What you are going to do, do quickly.'"

John 13:27

"Use your freedom" is an expression we have heard with appreciation. This is what Jesus had said to Judas. Get on with it. Your task is urgent. If you delay, you will be struck down before you reach the door. Peter will see to that with his sword. Jesus is Master of the situation. He gives orders for the devil's man, and he obeys him.

"Now no one at the table knew why he said this to him. Some thought that, because Judas had the money box, Jesus was telling him, `Buy what we need for the feast; or, that he should give something to the poor!'" Buy for what feast? Why for the Jewish Passover Feast, of course, which was to be eaten the next night on Friday. This was Thursday evening, when the Christian Passover Feast was to be instituted, after Judas had been dismissed. It was the Jewish custom on this particular evening to light a lamp and search the house for leaven. All the leaven was to be expelled from the house in observation of the Feast of Unleavened Bread, which coincided with the Passover. Love him or leave him. Since Judas had not come to love Jesus, it was time for him to leave him. By his leaving, he proved himself to be the leaven among the twelve - the odd man out. "Drive out the wicked person from among you," wrote Paul in I Corinthians 5:13. Jesus, on the other hand, never drives anyone from himself. He allows us to leave of our own volition, and so prove ourselves to be leaven (evil).

"So, after receiving the morsel, he immediately went out and it was night." Leaving the presence of the Light of this world, Judas found himself in the outer darkness, where he would come to grind and gnash his teeth. "There is no peace, says the Lord, for the wicked." In the dark they stumble and fall to their ruin. "If the light in you is darkness (Satan's counterfeit), how great is the darkness!" Matthew 6.23

THANK GOD, HE'S GONE

"**W**hen he had gone out, Jesus said, 'Now is the Son of man glorified, and in him God is glorified.'" John 13:31

With Judas gone, they could heave a collective sigh of relief. The devil had been dismissed. Satan's man was on his providentially designed mission. The goat had been separated out. Now, at last, Jesus could open up his heart. He could disclose the deeper things without experiencing overt opposition. John noticed that when Judas had opened the door to leave, it was night. Since the Biblical day begins at sundown, it was now the fourteenth of Nisan (Friday), the day the Passover Lamb was to be sacrificed. The divine plan and purpose from before creation was on track and on time, just as the trains operate still in Switzerland. Jesus had covered up nicely for Judas, since "love covers a multitude of sins." He had been his Savior, if not from sin, at least of his life. Simon the Zealot (the other sword-bearer) or Simon Peter would surely have separated his head from his body before he reached the door had they discerned his nefarious design.

Jesus had done two deeds, as recorded in this chapter, that were so humble they were not deemed worthy of mention in the synoptic tradition (the first three gospels). Yet the washing of the disciples' feet and the giving of the dipped morsel to Judas (which he received but probably refused to eat - it would have gagged him) were the Lord's way of expressing his love to the uttermost extent. His love found a practical expression and was all-inclusive.

Jesus knew failure just as we do. He had failed in breaking through to Judas. He could not penetrate the invisible shield that Judas had about him. Now Judas' departure had set the wheels in motion that would eventuate in Jesus mounting his glorious, yet ignominious throne - the Cross of Calvary. We must wait for Revelation 19 to see his heavenly coronation.

GLORY, GLORY, GLORY

"*If God is glorified in him, God will also glorify him in himself, and glorify him at once.*" *John 13:32*

Five times the word "glory" occurs in one sentence. Verses 31 and 32 comprise the most glory-filled sentence ever uttered, and all because Judas is on his way. He will see to it that Jesus is sent on his way back to heaven - a consummation devoutly desired by Jesus. Do you remember what glory means? It is pronounced "kavoth" in Hebrew, "doxa" in the Greek, and its basic meaning is heaviness, weightiness. It's secondary meaning is splendor, brightness. "The earth is the Lord's and the fulness thereof, the world and those who dwell therein." Psalm 24:1 "The fulness" is the multitudinous plants and creatures, displaying the divine glory in the form of his infinite creativity. At one of our small group meetings I tried to impress upon a young man the meaning of glory, so I walked across the room and sat on his lap, saying "Now you feel my glory." If Jesus should come into the room in his full glory, he would crush us. He would be more than we could bear.

When Jesus first made himself known to me I thought I was being electrocuted. A month later the glory fell as I was driving my car. I experienced such joy for a brief interval that I could scarcely bear it. It almost blew all my circuits. I was obliged to say, "Praise God! Praise God!" Experiencing God's glory involves one in reciprocity. One is obliged to return the blessing to God in some way. One can't keep it to oneself. It would overload the wiring and blow a fuse.

Someone said, "If Jesus should suddenly come into the room, we would all stand." Another said, "No, we would all fall on our faces." He is with you. Now! "Lo, I am with you always," he said after his resurrection. A young man from China was thrilled to read this. His name was Lo. You can put your name there.

❧

LITTLE CHILDREN?

*"**L**ittle children, yet a little while I am with you." John 13:33*

How can he get away with calling these grown men
"little children?" You call a bunch of fishermen and taxi drivers
little children and watch out that they don't blacken your eye.
I called in New Jersey upon a man who had sold his fishing boat,
retired and moved to Farmingdale. He said he thought his Tom
cat was tough, until it came home one night with an eyeball
hanging out. Farmingdale was so tough that if you saw a cat
going by with a tail you knew it was a tourist.

Well, Peter, John and the rest accepted the designation
"little children" because they were so little that they hadn't been
born yet. They were alive but still in the womb. Never forget,
there is life before birth in the natural and the spiritual. I
weighed four pounds, four ounces when I was born in the
natural. I weighed about 155 pounds when I was born into the
spiritual. I had been in the church (my spiritual mother's body)
for 18 years before I was thrust out of it into the world producing
a few strange sounds for Jesus. I saw Verne Zuck, who had been
a Captain in the Air Force in WW II, wearing a "?" (question
mark) on his lapel. I asked, "What does that mean?" He
answered, "That means, where are you going to spend eternity?"
Born again people are fools for Christ. They are audacious.
They do what they can to get the gospel out.

After the Sunday evening service several of us went to
a restaurant for a bite to eat. Verne let it be known that he was
fasting. On the 33rd day of his fast, he enjoyed a visit from the
Lord that profoundly altered his life. Years later in New Jersey
I was listening to the news on the radio, when the announcer
told of a man who had opened a restaurant in San Francisco.
This man employed only street people, who could not find work.
His name was Verne Zook. To God be the praise.

AN ALTAR CALL

"𝔜*ou will seek me; and as I said to the Jews so now I say to you,
'Where I am going you cannot come.'" John 13:33*

Now that Judas had left, and the leaven (the corrupting influence) had been expelled, things were going to move very quickly to their divinely ordained climax. Jesus' death by sacrifice was imminent. He had to give them his last will and testament before offering himself up. They were to be his beneficiaries. To benefit from his self-giving a specific response was called for. That response was mandated in a new requirement. Come up a little higher, friend.

Are you ready for the next rung in the ladder? Here it is: "A new commandment I give to you, that you love one another; even as I have loved you, that you also love one another." This rung turns out to be one giant leap for mankind, comparable to Armstrong's step on to the moon. This new commandment is bestowed upon the newly weds at the conclusion of every wedding we officiate. To love as Jesus loved? It sounds simple, until you consider the implications. It points us to the cross. It means there is a cross waiting for each of us.

Rev. Richard Wurmbrand told of hearing a young minister "laughingly give an altar call." He said, "Do you know what an altar is? An altar is the place where the victim dies, and all the blood flows out." An altar call is no laughing matter. I am sorry that Jesus gave his followers a new commandment as the first point of his commencement address on that holy night. To love others is one thing, but to love them as Jesus loved is a horse of a completely different color. It seems to me that he just succeeded in closing the door in my face. I remember Jack Parr's expression, "I kid you not." I hope Jesus was only kidding, but I fear he was not. To follow Jesus to the cross is the call for a new kid on the block. It is not one of my natural inclinations.

THE REWARD OF SELF-ESTEEM

"*By this all men will know that you are my disciples, if you have love for one another." John 13:35*

The world said concerning the primitive Church, "See how the Christians love one another." Today the world says concerning the Church, "See how they argue with one another." I say, "Let us endure our differences for Jesus' sake." That is no small step toward loving one another.

"Simon Peter said to him, `Lord, where are you going?'" If you are going to Borneo, I will go with you. "Jesus answered, `Where I am going you cannot follow me now; but you shall follow me afterward.'" I am going the way of the cross. You are incapable of accompanying me, because you are merely human. No one merely human can do what I am about to do. Afterward (after my death and resurrection) I will breathe my divine breath into you, and you will become a new creature altogether. Then you will follow me to a cross with your name on it. "Peter said, `Lord why cannot I follow you now? I will lay down my life for you.'" The philosophers said, "Know yourself." Peter had too little self-knowledge and too much self-esteem, exactly what the world says we don't have enough of. What does the world know?

"Jesus answered, `Will you lay down your life for me? (You have it completely reversed. I am the one who will and must lay down my life for you. Otherwise you will never enter into eternal life.) Truly, truly, I say to you, the cock will not crow, till you have denied me three times.'" This prophetic word would disclose to Peter and the rest how precise was Jesus' knowledge of all that was to befall him. Peter is well on his way to his collision with the brick wall. "Pride goes before destruction and a haughty spirit before a fall." Proverbs 16:18 European churches are seen with crowing cocks instead of crosses on their spires - reminders of how easy it is to deny the Lord.

❧

I SHALL RETURN

"Let not your hearts be troubled; believe in God, believe also in me.'
John 14:1

Chapter 13 developed the theme of the third day of this gospel, the day of the marriage. Marriage is the love relationship. We saw in that chapter the infinite dimensions of Jesus' love and the wisdom of it. He foresaw the frailty of Peter's loyalty. In chapter 14 the fourth theme of homecoming comes again into view. Jesus is on his way back to his Heavenly Father's house, where there is room for all. In chapters 14 to 17 Jesus will bring out the significance of his death.

We can't imagine how confused and devastated the disciples were over the news of Jesus' immanent departure. That one would betray him, and that Peter would deny him seemed to them incredible. The antidote to the despondency that threatened to overwhelm them was trust in God and in Jesus. No matter how evil the circumstances are the universe is going to hold together. God and Jesus will see to that. "In my Father's house (universe) are many rooms (dwelling places)." He didn't say how many. It would have blown their minds. They are more numerous than the grains of sand on the seashores of earth.

"If it were not so, would I have told you that I go to prepare a place for you?" Since this place has been under construction for 2000 years, we may be sure that the accommodations are beyond our fondest imagining. It took only six days to fashion creation in the beginning. "And when I go and prepare a place for you, I will come again and will take you to myself, that where I am you may be also." "I shall return," said General Douglas MacArthur to those living in the Philippines. And he did, though it was a battle. We may be infinitely more certain that Jesus is going to keep his promise to return in an hour that we do not expect. Before he can come again, though, this good news of the Kingdom must be carried to all the nations.

❧

A MIGHTY BIG WORD

"*And you know the way where I am going.*" John 14:4

"Thomas said to him, `Lord, we do not know where you are going; how can we know the way?'" A good question. If I told you I was going to my old home town, and that I would like you to meet me half way next week when I return, I would have you totally confused, if you did not know the name of my home town. "Jesus said to him, `I am the way, and the truth, and the life; no one comes to the Father but by me.'" Jesus' home, it turns out, is not a place but a person - the Father. And Jesus is the only road that takes us to him. Some pretend that God is like the hub of a wheel and that the various religions are like spokes that enable us to make contact with him, her or it (whatever). Someone said, "I met God, and she is black." Jesus claimed that he is the only path to God.

Furthermore he is the pattern. If anyone wants to emulate God, to become like him, let that one examine with care what Jesus said and did. Then go and do likewise. He is the Good Samaritan, and you and I are the man who fell among the thieves. The devil had robbed us of our faith, killed our spirits, and has planned to destroy us in hell with himself. Then along came Jesus to pour upon us the wine of his blood and the oil of his Spirit.

Jesus is also the very life of God. This gospel, you will remember, defines life as toGodwardness. Until we get something of Jesus in us, we are spinning our wheels, marking time, loitering, while we ought to be living. "If you had known me, you would have known my Father also; henceforth you know him and have seen him." The word "seen" here is "horao", and it means experienced. In your experience of Jesus, you have encountered the Creator of the universe. Such a statement is enough to make you jump out of your skin. Note, though, the "if." "If you had known me." Little "if" is a mighty big word. It is as vast as eternity itself.

WHAT THE WORLD NEEDS NOW

"*Philip said to him, 'Lord, show us the Father, and we shall be satisfied.'" John 14:8*

When I was a youngster I remember the radio commercial, "What the world needs now is a good five cent cigar." More recently we have heard the song, "What the world needs now is love, sweet love." That is nearer to the target. Philip was of the opinion that a vision of God was the great requirement. Let the heavenly veil be momentarily lifted and everything will be okay.

"Jesus said to him, `Have I been with you so long, and yet you do not know me, Philip? He who has seen me has seen the Father; how can you say, "Show us the Father"? What immense frustration Jesus must have experienced. It was like the frustration of the minister who waxed eloquent on the coming day of the Lord's wrath, to whom the parishioner said in parting, "That was a nice sermon." Some people never get the picture.

"Do you not believe that I am in the Father and the Father in me?" "God was in Christ," wrote Paul, "reconciling the world to himself." 2 Cor. 5:19 When he encountered Jesus on the Damascus Road, he asked, "Who are you, Lord?" He knew Jesus was divine. He just didn't know how to address him. "The words that I say to you I do not speak on my own authority; but the Father who dwells in me does his works." There is a depth within Jesus that no one can fathom. Strangely enough there is within every human being an incomprehensible dimension. Look within and you find mystery. Einstein said that we are using only one-tenth of our minds. I didn't believe it until I learned that the human personality is like an iceberg with only about one-ninth above the surface, comprising what is called our conscious awareness. The more significant portion of us is our spirit (collective unconscious) and our soul (personal unconscious). The latter retains all that has happened to us from conception on. Truly we have been fashioned in the image of God.

❧

TAP INTO YOUR CREATIVITY

"*Believe me that I am in the Father and the Father in me; or else believe me for the sake of the works themselves.*" John 14:11

The Father within Jesus was the Creator. So Jesus had creativity within him. That was why he could do the seven sign/works recorded previously. As a believer in Jesus, you have the creative Spirit within you. You are called to express something of God toward others in new and creative ways. "Be subject to the Father of spirits and live." Heb. 12:9 That is the secret. You can't be subject to the Father Creator of your spirit/ inner man without keeping in touch with the depths of yourself where the Holy Spirit resides. Learn the language of your unconscious depths by recording and comprehending your dreams.

We have identified this as The Homecoming chapter because Jesus is homesick for God, whom he refers to as his Father 22 times in thirty-one verses. The Holy Spirit is drawing him back to the Father. He does the same with us. That is why the human heart is restless until it finds its rest in God. There is a God-shaped vacuum in every human heart which only Christ can fill. We are aspiring after the Sabbath rest of the people of God, which we cannot enjoy until our work on earth is done.

"Truly, truly, I say to you, he who believes in me will also do the works that I do; and greater works than these will he do, because I go to the Father." What greater work than Jesus did can we do? He never led another into new birth during his earthly days, because the Spirit was not given until after he was glorified. This we can do, if we approach others creatively as the Holy Spirit leads, prepared to sow the gospel seed.

As a youth Dawson Trotman led another youth to Jesus Christ. A friend said, "I would give my right arm to be able to do what you just did." Dawson said, "It will cost you more than your right arm. It will require the memorization of much scripture and deep dedication to God."

❦

I WILL DO IT

"**W**hatever you ask in my name, I will do it, that the Father may be glorified in the Son." *John 14:13*

Whatever you ask whom? The Father, of course. "If you ask (the Father) anything in my name, I will do it." Now we can understand why we are able to do greater works than Jesus did. Jesus does his greater works in answer to our asking the Father in his name for whatever we need in his service. It is not really we who do the greater works, but Jesus who does them through us.

Years ago a lady who had suffered a serious spine injury in an automobile accident came for prayer. Her bone graft had deteriorated and the pain had returned. She had phoned her surgeon at Stanford Medical Center about what had happened. He had performed three different bone-graft operations, each in turn having deteriorated. He told her to reconcile herself to life in a wheelchair. She was a young mother with two small children. She could not reconcile herself. So she came for prayer. Jack and I spent two hours encouraging her faith, before the three of us in turn offered prayer. We had evidently agreed in our spirits according to Matthew 18:19, because an hour later she discovered that the pain was gone. That afternoon she felt good enough to give her house the first thorough house-cleaning it had enjoyed since she lived there. Sure enough her local physician confirmed that her back had been restored to normal.

Fifteen years later she flew to the Far East where she ministered for several years among the Karen people who live on the border between Burma and Thailand. She saw the Lord work many miracles while there. We are living in the time when the Lord is undertaking his supernatural ministry to confirm the gospel that is going forth, especially in the third world. "If we believed what the first century Christians believed, we would achieve what they achieved." - J. B. Philips.

THE JONAH COME FROM HEAVEN

"*If you love me, you will keep my commandments.*" John 14:12

Love is not an emotion. Agape/love is something you do. Love never sits on its hands. It goes about doing what Jesus instructs us to do. On Ascension Day Jesus told his disciples to stay in Jerusalem until they were clothed with power from on high. One hundred and twenty did as they were told. Ten days later they were all clothed with the Spirit's power. Those who did not stay, but went about their own affairs, missed out on the baptism of fire.

"And I will pray the Father, and he will give you another Counselor to be with you forever." This other "Called Alongside One" (literally) Jesus then identifies as "the Spirit of truth, whom the world cannot receive because it neither sees him nor knows him." The Spirit is the invisible Person who came upon Jesus at his baptism in the likeness of a Dove. The first mention of a dove is in Genesis 8:11, where it says she came back to Noah in the ark with a freshly plucked olive leaf in her mouth. Dove in the Hebrew is pronounced Jonah. The Book of Dove/Jonah is the story of Ninevah repenting, thanks to the message of Dove/Jonah. Jonah himself was unlikeable because of his fierce prejudice, but his message was effective in the extreme. Jonah's message brought life to Ninevah out of imminent disaster, as the dove brought life in the form of an olive leaf to Noah from the flood devastated earth.

We may rejoice in the fact that once we have been inhabited and empowered by the Heavenly Dove, we too shall have a message and ministry to our generation every bit as effective as the prophet had toward those Ninevites to whom he was sent. "You know him, for he dwells with you (in the person of Jesus) and will be in you" (when you have experienced the truth of Jesus' resurrection from the dead, and he has breathed his divine breath into you).

❦

INAPPROPRIATE BUT MEMORABLE

"**I** *will not leave you desolate; I will come to you."* John 14:18

The word desolate is literally "orphans." The day after Jesus' crucifixion, Jesus' disciples were singing that old spiritual, "Sometimes I Feel Like a Motherless Child." But on Easter evening something happened that gave them great joy.

"Yet a little while, and the world will see me no more, but you will see me." On the third day Jesus, in the realm of the dead, utilized the words of Isaiah 33:10 - "Now I will arise," says the Lord. "Now I will lift myself up; now I will be exalted." "Because I live, you will live also." Why? Because I will breathe my resurrection life into you. After you have gone flat like a tire, you will have my divine life imparted to you, and you will soar like the eagles. Did you see the bumper sticker, "How can I soar with the eagles, surrounded by all these turkeys?" You will say to those who think their goose is cooked, "Get out of the oven, Shadrach, Meshach and To-bed-we-go, you have got work to do. Go tell it on the mountains that Jesus Christ is LORD!"

It kind of stirs you up doesn't it? "In that day you will know that I am in my Father, and you in me, and I in you." We are all bound up in one another - you, God, and me, like Siamese triplets, only we can't be separated. Please forgive the grotesque imagery. But Jesus used grotesque imagery when he compared the Kingdom of heaven with a woman mixing leaven (a symbol of evil) with her dough. A seminary student leading a chapel service, asked God to "make his church one like a great popcorn ball." The concept may be inappropriate but it is memorable. Another preacher took extreme liberties by saying that if we would get around to doing what Jesus told us by praying, seeking his face, and getting the gospel out, "then the kingdom of God would come faster than a rat could eat its way through a head of cheese."

❦

THE HOMECOMING QUESTION

"**H**e who has my commandments and keeps them, he it is who loves me; and he who loves me will be loved by my Father, and I will love him and manifest myself to him." John 14:21

The word "love" occurs four times in this verse. The reciprocal nature of love is here expressed. There is nothing more sad than unrequited love. The way in which we are privileged to affirm our love for Jesus is by doing what he has told us to do. "Why do you call me 'Lord, Lord,' and do not do what I say?'" As soon as we put Jesus first in our lives, we find that he becomes real to us, but not until we do.

"Judas (not Iscariot) said to him, 'Lord, how is it that you will manifest yourself to us, and not to the world?'" Judas Iscariot had departed. He was, so to speak, the conductor, who punched Jesus' ticket to send him home to the Father. God is never left in the lurch. He has another Judas in the company, identified in Luke 6:16 as the son of James. This other Judas is also identified with the theme of this chapter, which is homecoming. In fact he has asked what turns out to be the homecoming question, for Jesus answered him, "If a man loves me, he will keep my word, and my Father will love him, and we will come to him and make our home with him." The ultimate way in which this will happen is expressed in Rev. 21:2, "And I saw the holy city, new Jerusalem, coming down out of heaven from God, prepared as a bride adorned for her husband." The universe will in that day be healed. Heaven and earth will have become one.

A question worth considering: Is the heavenly Jerusalem here depicted a reflection of the perfected Church, which is also referred to as the bride? The most important question for me to answer is this: Am I aware of the fact that the Eternal God has taken up his residence within me? If God is within me, then I cannot be defeated. If he is not within, then I am of all people most forlorn.

❧

THE REMEMBERER

"*He who does not love me does not keep my words; and the word which you hear is not mine but the Father's who sent me.*"

John 14:24

She was a member of the church. He was a stranger to me. As they had asked me to officiate their coming wedding, they were obliged to learn from me what the Bible says about holy marriage. After I had spent an hour opening the scriptures to their understanding, I heard him say, "And I drove 70 miles to listen to this foolishness." He took her by the hand and walked her out of the church, slamming the door behind them. I shouted after them, "Peace be with you." Thank God, that was one wedding I did not perform. The world hates Jesus' words, because they are in rebellion against his Father, their Creator. Afterward I warned the bride-to-be that she was putting her neck in a noose, but she married him even so. I fear they had the devil for their roommate.

"These things I have spoken to you, while I am still with you. But the Counselor, the Holy Spirit, whom the Father will send in my name, he will teach you all things and bring to your remembrance all that I have said to you." Jesus, the King, has a Secretary of State who represented him in all of his negotiations. In Israel the Hebrew word for secretary is rememberer. The pure Spirit not only reminds us of our King's words, but teaches us the implications of them in our daily rounds. Our life is an ongoing dialogue between our minds, our spirits, and the Holy Spirit. Blessed are those who are attentive to the counsel of the friendly Presence within.

A man going to Africa as a missionary was inwardly obliged, he knew not why, to take with him at great expense a red jeep. When he arrived, he met in his travels a tribe in which a woman had dreamed that a stranger would come to them with the truth they needed. They would recognize him by his vehical, that would be the the exact color of their native red beetle. It was.

❧

FEARFUL OR FAITHFUL

"**P**eace I leave with you; my peace I give to you; not as the world gives do I give to you."   John 14:27

As a child I was told that my grandfather wanted me to have his gold pocket watch after he died. But it didn't happen. What would I do with a gold pocket watch anyway? It would be just a keepsake. Jesus has willed us something infinitely more valuable than a keepsake - his peace. The peaceful relationship that he enjoyed with his Father he would impart to his disciples after his death and resurrection. Actually he purchased our peace with God by dying for us upon the cross. Not as the world gives does he give to us. The world is "an Indian giver." It gives only to take it back again. All of the world's gifts are transient, temporary - here today, gone tomorrow.

"Let not your hearts be troubled, neither let them be afraid." Our heart is the seat of our emotions. Our emotions have been compared to a horse. A horse is more powerful than its rider, but it may be trained to obey the dictates of the one who holds the reins. When Jesus was arrested his disciples gave way to fear and ran off in all directions. As broken men they deserted him, but the day would come when the Holy Spirit would commandeer their lives. With supernatural boldness they would then march off the map taking their witness for Christ to the four winds.

Similarly empowered we may get the upper hand over our emotions. It is the labor of a lifetime, but certainly worth the effort. It is important for us to master our fears. "For the thing that I fear comes upon me, and what I dread befalls me." Job 3:25. Faith is the opposite of fear. Fear draws to us the thing we dread, whereas faith is the magnet that attracts to us the good things we hope for. See Hebrews 11:1. Ultimately we will be fearful or faithful. "The fear of man is a snare." The fear of God liberates from that.

❦

THE HEAVENLY VIEW

"*You have heard me say to you, 'I go away, and I will come to you'. If you loved me, you would have rejoiced, because I go to the Father; for the Father is greater than I." John 14:28*

On Sunday, April 8, 1945 Pastor Dietrich Bonhoeffer, imprisoned by Hitler, had just finished conducting a worship service for his fellow prisoners, when the door opened and two evil-looking men in civilian clothes came in and said, "Prisoner Bonhoeffer, get ready to come with us." Those words "come with us" - had come to mean one thing only - the scaffold. He drew his fellow prisoners aside, and said, "This is the end; for me the beginning of life." The next day he was hanged. The end of life for Bonhoeffer was the beginning, because of Jesus - "the pioneer and perfecter of our faith, who for the joy that was set before him endured the cross, despising the shame, and is seated at the right hand of the throne of God." Hebrews 12:2

If we truly loved our dear ones, we would rejoice at their death. Dr. Percy Collette, for 50 years a medical missionary among the Amazon River natives, tells how he was five years of age when his mother lay dying. She had the children come into her room to pray for them. Then through the open window a white dove flew in, circled her head, and flew out. Just then she died. That night an angel appeared to him at the foot of his bed.

When he was 80, he had the experience of going to heaven, where he danced with his mother on the sea of glass before God's throne. He talked to the Lord's mother, who said that she had other children after Jesus. An angel took him to his room in the foursquare city, which is 1,500 miles in every direction. His accommodation is 700 miles up. From there he had a good view of the mansions being constructed outside the heavenly Jerusalem, our city of refuge. If this seems to you fantastic, read again Revelation 21. Spiritual experiences that do not agree with scripture are to be discarded.

THE SON GOES TO THE FATHER

"*And now I have told you before it takes place, so that when it does take place you may believe.*" *John 14:29*

Their hearts were filled with sorrow instead of joy at the thought of Jesus' departure, because they were egocentric and not yet Christocentric. Until Copernicus, everyone thought the sun revolved around the earth. No, it is the other way around. Don't judge by appearances. Jesus' life revolved around the Father, "for the Father is greater than I," he said. Jesus is on his way back to him to prepare the way for his followers, and then he shall return. Since he was right about his going back to the Father via death, burial, resurrection, and ascension, he is for sure going to return for us "in an hour that we think not."

A gospel minister did not believe in higher education, because Jesus said he would return in an hour that we think not. If we could get people to stop thinking, he reasoned, Jesus would come again. Quite the contrary, we are to love God with all of our minds. Let us think as deeply as we can, and then act on what we have discovered.

My father left us when I was three. I felt it was his responsibility to come back to me. Finally I concluded that the son goes to the father. Jesus went to his Father. The prodigal son returned to his father. When I finally flew from the middle west to California to see him, my first words were, "I'm sorry it has taken so long." I was 40, he was 69. But better late than never. Don't you agree? He had grown up Episcopalian, but had become an atheist when he was 18. I was pleased to learn that he was no longer an atheist. When I conducted his private memorial service five months later, I was comforted by Jesus' words, "Whoever receives you receives me, and he who receives me receives him who sent me." Perhaps there is someone whom you should go see, before it is too late.

❦

THE RULER OF THIS WORLD

"I *will no longer talk much with you, for the ruler of this world is coming."* John 14:30

Jesus keeps telling his disciples what is about to happen so that they may believe that he knows what he is talking about. He is human for sure, but also more than human. He has information that comes from God. He realizes that Judas by now has contacted the authorities, who are on their way. Behind the ruling circles is the ruler of this world, says Jesus. "He has no power over me." The devil never found a chink in Jesus' armor, so he could not get a hook in him. All the rest of us have taken the devil's bait, so we have his hook in our flesh (our lower nature). We must struggle continually to keep out of his net. But it was not so with Jesus. Many of us are troubled about the existence of the devil. As children of the 20th century, we are scientifically minded. The concept of the devil smacks us as superstition.

Dr. C.E.M. Joad, Professor of Philosphy at London University, had a monistic view of reality. He did not believe in the created dualism taught in the Bible. His philosophy, however, could not account for the radical evil he saw in Hitler's Germany. So at length he turned to Jesus Christ and became a Christian. But he came into the faith through the back door. He was obliged to accept the Biblical teaching about the devil as the source of radical evil. Since the Bible was right about the devil, he reasoned, it must also be right about Jesus as the Son of God. We have the victory over the enemy through the blood of the Lamb and the word of our testimony. Revelation 12:11

I had inadvertently offended a patient in the hospital. He came at me flourishing a metal footstool over his head to strike me a blow. I responded by saying, "In the name of the Lord Jesus Christ." Before I could finish the sentence, to my utter astonishment, he had retreated and began cowering in the corner.

❧

HOMESICK FOR HEAVEN

But I do as the Father has commanded me, so that the world may know that I love the Father. Rise, let us go hence."

John 14:31

The upper room is no longer a resting place. It is time to move on. We too cannot accept the teaching of this chapter with a "let us take it easy" attitude. We are pilgrims on a journey. We partake of Jesus, our Passover meal, with a staff in our hand, and ready to hit the road. In Exodus the people ate the Passover lamb and then struck out for the Red Sea which they crossed supernaturally. Following Jesus, the disciples would cross with him their Red Sea. The Red was his precious blood which flowed so lavishly from thorn crowned brow, scourged back, pierced hands and feet, that it seemed a veritable Sea that would inundate them. And it would have, were it not for the presence of his steadying hand on the third day, and the resurrection life breathed into them.

In chapter 13 we heard the theme of the third day - the wedding at Cana. At Cana we learned of the love that turned water into wine. The same "love to the uttermost" washed the disciples' feet and gave the dipped morsel to Iscariot. Such serving love will eventually wipe away all of our fears and present us before God with shouts of joy.

In chapter 14 we encountered again the theme of the fourth day, when he conducted his disciples to his Father's house in Jerusalem where he cleaned house. In ch. 14 the scene shifts to the heavenly Jerusalem and the house of many mansions to which he is taking us. Here we have no lasting city. We seek the city that has foundations (in eternity) whose maker and builder is God. "This world is not my home. I'm just a passing through. If heaven's not my home, good Lord, what will I do. The angels beckon me from heaven's open door, and I can't feel at home in this world anymore." The older we are, the more homesick for heaven we become.

❦

JESUS' PHILOSOPHY OF HISTORY

"**I** *am the true vine, and my Father is the vine-dresser.*"

John 15:1

In Psalm 80:8 Asaph wrote, "Thou didst bring a vine out of Egypt; thou didst drive out the nations and plant it." Asaph and other Old Testament writers called the nation of Israel a vine. Jesus says that Israel foreshadowed him, the True Vine. Israel was the type of which he is the reality. Then Jesus called his Father the vine-dresser or gardener (pronounced georgos in the Greek from which George is derived).

"Every branch of mine that bears no fruit, he takes away, and every branch that does bear fruit he prunes, that it may bear more fruit." The vinedresser is concerned that the branches bear fruit, not foliage; grapes, not leaves. Underlying this teaching is a philosophy of history. It explains what has been going on within the Church through the centuries. At one time Christianity seemingly flourished in North Africa, but evidently it was not producing adequate fruit. So what did the Vinedresser do? In the seventh century A.D. he pruned it off through the Sword of Islam. Centuries later the religion of Jesus Christ was well established in Russia, but in the judgment of God the grapes were scanty and bitter. So he used Marxist atheism to cut back that significant branch of the Church. The Church was driven underground where it flourishes as never before.

I heard a Catholic bishop say on television, "As the Bible says, 'The blood of the martyrs is the seed of the Church.'" I wished I could have asked him for chapter and verse. The expression is not in the Bible, but it is nevertheless true. "God makes evil to bless him," says the Bible. His plan and purpose cannot be thwarted. The truth will win out in the long run. We live out our lives in the short run. If we do not develop the long view, we will fall on our faces. We run a marathon. The important thing is that we hold to our faith until the very end.

❦

THE LAW OF OBLIVION

"**ᴅ**ou are already made clean by the word which I have spoken to you." John 15:3

The word "clean" is the same as the expression for pruned. What Jesus had said and done at the last supper had already diminished the foliage of their pride. He had told them that they would be offended because of him and fall away. He was like a football coach telling his team before the big game that they were bound to lose. It would be depressing. Listening to the gospel and reading the Bible does have a cleansing effect upon us. "Abide in me and I in you." Jesus wants us to stick close to him. I am reminded of the time I heard the composer Sigmund Romberg play on the piano his song: "We'll Be Close As Pages In A Book." That is what Jesus is looking for from us.

"As the branch cannot bear fruit by itself, unless it abides in the vine, neither can you, unless you abide in me." The husband and wife cannot have children if they do not cling together. Jesus is the husband and together we are his wife. His words are the seed that germinates in us producing new life.

"I am the vine, you are the branches. He who abides in me, and I in him, he it is that bears much fruit, for apart from me you can do nothing." It is the secret of mutual indwelling. He did not say, "apart from me you can do precious little." No, separated from Jesus we can do absolutely nothing of lasting significance. Unless we cling passionately to Jesus, we shall be wiped off the face of the earth, and our place will remember us no more. The law of oblivion is at work. I can go back to my grade school or high school and they will say, "Who are you?" That was the favorite expression of a man in the army. The expected response was "No one at all." We are learning again about Fruitfulness/New Birth from the standpoint of how we become a spiritual parent. Ch. 3:1-21 deals with the same theme from the perspective of passing through the birth canal.

❦

A FRIGHTENING THOUGHT

"**I**f *a man does not abide in me, he is cast forth as a branch and withers; and the branches are gathered, thrown into the fire and burned.*" *John 15:6*

As a youngster I read this and was frightened. It frightens me still, since Christians are nothing more or less than grape vines. The only function of the vine is the production of grapes. The wood is so soft that it has no other value. If it fails to produce the intended fruit, it is good for nothing. Its destination then is the bonfire. "Our God is a consuming fire," we read in Hebrews 12:29. He is, though, a holy fire. Holy means "different," set apart from ordinary fire. The closer we get to an ordinary fire, the more we are burned. It is just the opposite with God. The farther away we are from him, the greater the pain. To escape the pain altogether, we must leap into the very center of the consuming fire. At the heart of the fire there is love, for "God is love."

In the parable of the vine and the branches, our flesh (that is to say, our souls and our bodies) are likened to the wood of the vine which is soft and weak. "The spirit is willing," said Jesus, "but the flesh is weak" - so weak that we cannot even keep our eyes open when deprived of sleep. Our eyelids become like hundred pound weights. The Lord's "eyes behold, his eyelids test, the children of men." Psalms 12:4 But how? When his eyes are open toward us, he is guiding and guarding us, and we feel secure. But when his eyelids close, he has withdrawn his self-evident presence from us. We feel forsaken. At such a time he is testing us to see whether or not we believe his promise, "I will never leave you nor forsake you."

In the dark night of the soul, we are obliged to walk by faith, not by sight or sense experience. One time when I was depressed I asked the brothers to pray for me. After they prayed, I felt no different, but I later discovered that the depression was gone. ❧

BORN AGAIN TO REPRODUCE

"*If you abide in me, and my words abide in you, ask whatever you will, and it will be done for you.*" *John 15:7*

The condition attached to getting our prayers answered is to remain in intimate contact with Jesus. We do this by hiding the words of the Bible in our hearts. They are the containers of the Holy Spirit. "Man shall not live by bread alone, but by every word that proceeds from the mouth of God." Matthew 4:4. A week without church makes one weak. Even more so, a day without reading the Bible starves one's faith, for the Bible is faith food.

"By this my Father is glorified, that you bear much fruit, and so prove to be my disciples." The grape is the reproductive organ of the vine. It is the receptacle of the seeds. God's words are seeds that may be sown abroad into human hearts. Some people say they do not believe that the words of the Bible are God breathed (inspired). It makes no difference. If I stick you with a knife, I make you bleed whether or not you believe I hold a knife. And the word of God is more penetrating than a knife. It is the sword of the Holy Spirit, and it accomplishes the purpose for which it was given, whether we believe it or not. Johnny Appleseed succeeded in planting apple trees wherever he went just by scattering seeds. Don't be a name dropper; be a scripture verse dispenser. If you must gossip, gossip about Jesus. Christians should stop sneezing in each other's faces. Let's go out and share the divine contagion with the world. In this way we can prove to ourselves even that we really are Jesus' disciples. There is a world waiting to be won.

D. L. Moody heard, "It is yet to be seen what God can do with one human life totally sold out to God." He responded, "I propose to be that man." He was the Billy Graham of the nineteen century. I met Billy Graham in L.A. in 1949. A few weeks later I heard him preach in a tent on five occasions.

AS EASY AS FALLING OFF A LOG?

"*A s the Father has loved me, so have I loved you; abide in my love.*" *John 15:9*

The Father loved Jesus so much that he raised him from the dead. Jesus loves us so much that he is going to raise us also. All he asks is that we remain in his love. But how you may ask? He tells us. "If you keep my commandments, you will abide in my love, just as I have kept my Father's commandments and abide in his love." It is just as simple as doing what Jesus tells you.

"These things I have spoken to you, that my joy may be in you, and that your joy may be full." Does it strike you as remarkable that Jesus could talk about his joy on the same occasion as he talks about his crucifixion? Joy is deeper than happiness. Happiness rests on what happens to us. Both words are derived from "hap", which means chance or good luck. Joy, on the other hand, comes from the assurance that God is faithful, and will not fail to keep his word. "Let God be true (reliable), though every man be found a liar." Jesus has told us to keep his commandments.

Under the Old Testament there were 613 commandments to be kept. You have to know them (no small task in itself) before you can keep them. Simplicity is a virtue, so Jesus makes it simple. All the commandments he boils down to one. "This is my commandment, that you love one another as I have loved you." Love one another. It sounds easy. I heard a preacher say, "Why that is just as easy as loving your wife, just as easy as falling off a log." But it is not so easy when the log is the cross, and you are nailed to it. Do you realize that Jesus has just fastened us to the cross by his words, "as I have loved you?" There is a measure for love. How much is the lover willing to endure for the sake of the beloved? Jesus endured the cross, despising the shame, out of his love for you and me. How much do you love us, Jesus? "This much," he said. And he stretched out his arms and died. ❧

THE CHOSEN FEW

"*Greater love has no man than this, that a man lay down his life for his friends." John 15:13*

Yes, that is the limit of human love, "but God shows his love for us in that while we were yet sinners Christ died for us.... While we were enemies we were reconciled to God by the death of his Son." Romans 5:8,10 This explains the assertion that "God is love." He loves, because it is his nature to do so, not because of any admirable quality in the objects of his love.

"You are my friends if you do what I command you." Here his disciples are being elevated to the status of Abraham, who was called "the friend of God." It was contingent, as with Abraham, upon obedience to the Word of God. "No longer do I call you slaves, for the slave does not know what his master is doing." The master orders his slave around without explaining the whys and wherefores. Jesus then explains why "I have called you friends: for all that I have heard from my Father I have made known to you." Jesus did not live in an ivory tower, above and beyond his followers. He told the inner circle all that was in his heart. He was careful though not to cast his pearls before swine. He conveyed the revelations he received from his Father only to those who were prepared to receive them. Judas had to be dismissed before he could impart the truths we are now learning. They did not pertain to the wolf in sheep's clothing.

"You did not choose me, but I chose you." Some people still refer to the Jewish community as the chosen people. Not so. They are "a peculiar people" whom the Lord has not abandoned, though they have rejected him. The New Covenant community is the chosen people. "Many are called, but few are chosen" - only those who respond affirmatively to the call. Every time we attend a wedding or a funeral we are exposed to some expression of the gospel - enough, it seems to me, so that precious few in our society can say that they have never heard.

A RICOCHET ROMANCE

"You did not chose me, but I chose you and appointed you that you should go and bear fruit and that your fruit should abide."

John 15:16

It used to be that the young man chose the maid that he would marry, and then he proposed. I am not so sure anymore who does the choosing. But of this we may be sure: that Jesus chose us and not vice versa. He initiated the relationship. He said to us, "I want you." He, who is altogether desirable, desired us long before we desired him. This is why our evangelist always refers to himself as "the disciple whom Jesus loved." He could never get over the fact that Jesus loved him, a "son of thunder", who lost his temper at the drop of a hat. He and his brother were eager to incinerate the Samaritan town that would not receive them.

It blew the mind of the Apostle Paul that Jesus could love and choose him. He refers to himself in I Cor. 15:8 as the extroma - the abortion. The other disciples experienced a normal spiritual birth, but his was abnormal in the extreme.

The early Church never dreamed that the prayer of dying Stephen, "Lord, do not hold this sin against them," would light a fuse within Saul of Tarsus. Sometime later the explosion occurred on the Damascus Road. And Saul, like their first king, a giant among his contemporaries, would be reduced to a little child, and begin his life all over again as a babe in Christ. When he went into the synagogues to tell his people that Jesus is the Son of God, they called him "the abortion." He had aborted his former religion for a personal relationship with Jesus. He was not disobedient to the heavenly vision, but worked harder than any of the other apostles, and bore more abiding fruit than all of them put together. Do you know why? Because he who is forgiven much loves much. He ricocheted around the Roman world saying, "Jesus is Lord", and "just call me Paul" (the little one) - in our nomenclature "Shorty."

❧

THE ONE SACRED OBLIGATION

"**I** *chose you and appointed you that you should go and bear fruit and that your fruit should abide; so that whatever you ask the Father in my name, he may give it to you." John 15:16*

Is it possible that those who have been Christians for a long time do not get their prayers answered for this very reason - they are not reproducing after their kind. If my Christian life is not winsome - if I never win some for Jesus - why should God bother himself to answer my prayers? I am stone-cold dead in the market and do not know it.

As a youngster I read this chapter and it frightened me. I perceived that if my life was not productive for God, I would be a castaway. What is the use of being good, if I am good for nothing? God means business. If I am not in his Kingdom business, I may amass a fortune, but to what purpose? I have never seen a U-Haul trailer behind a hearse. It is reported that a Chicago mobster had been gunned down, and his request to be buried in his gold Cadillac was honored. The grave diggers looked down at his corpse propped up in the back seat of his Cadillac. One said to the other, "Man, that's living." Don't you believe it. The man was dead even while alive.

Jesus said to a young man, "Follow me." But he said, "Lord, let me first go and bury my Father." But he said to him, "Leave the dead to bury their own dead; but as for you, go and proclaim the kingdom of God." I heard a rabbi say that Jesus could not have said that, because to bury one's father is the most sacred obligation in their religion. I suggest that the rabbi does not know who Jesus is. To obey Jesus by going out in his name to reproduce his life in others is the one sacred obligation that falls on every one. I am going to ask you a rather impudent question. Whom have you led to Jesus Christ recently? In the past year? In the last ten years? Ever? If you are beginning to squirm, perhaps the Holy Spirit is convicting.

❦

THE TRUTH THAT HURTS

*"**T**his I command you, to love one another."* John 15:17

Last evening I encountered in the skid row mission a man whom we have frequently sought to help financially and spiritually. I could detect alcohol on his breath. He told me that since we last met he had stolen a car while in a drunken condition, had spent ten days in jail, and was out on bond awaiting his trial. Then he asked if I could help him. I said, "I will not give you money, but I will talk to you." I told him that all of us are addicts, if not to the bottle, then to sex, or drugs, or money, etc. We joined hands and he prayed as he has before, that the Lord would save him. I told him about plucking out the offending eye or cutting off the offending hand, and that it speaks symbolically of our maiming ourselves, if need be, to get the victory over our besetting sin.

Do not get drunk with wine, which is debauchery, but get drunk on the Holy Spirit. There is an alternative to the bottle. Some of us got addicted to the Bible and its message years ago. It is the divine addiction, the alternative to futility.

Before the evening was over a Pentecostal preacher told me that as a teenager he was in a gathering of Mennonites, who considered themselves spirit-filled. A young Presbyterian lad was also there. The Spirit told Terry that the Lord was going to baptize the Presbyterian in the Holy Spirit, and to get close to him. When it happened the young man began praying fluently in a strange language and became drunk in the Spirit. The Mennonites were astonished, saying that this had ceased with the first century Church. But there it was, big as life. Terry expressed his love for the Mennonites by telling them the truth, which they preferred not to hear or believe. "You will know the truth, and the truth will set you free," said Jesus. But you have got to hear it, like it or not.

❧

LET IT ALL HANG OUT

"If the world hates you, know that it has hated me before it hated you." John 15:18

A Communist jailor in Rumania, as he tortured Christians, was heard to say, "I thank the God in whom I do not believe that I have the privilege this day of expressing all the hatred that fills my heart."

We are living in a permissive age, when we are privileged to let it all hang out. Every one is coming out of the closet: sodomites, both masculine and feminine. I refuse to call the men "gays". There is nothing gay about them. Gray, yes. Gay, no. Call it "an alternate life style" if you want. It is actually the style of spiritual and moral death. The wheat and the tares are coming to fruition simultaneously. If we refuse to become saints we will become devils. Count on it. I have heard the deceased eulogized, "Every one loved him." They are saying that he stood for nothing. He was swayed by every breeze. You know a person by her enemies. The hostility directed against Jesus will be visited upon his followers.

Once I received an anonymous hate letter from a church member. At the time it shivered my timbers. Today I count it a compliment. Beware when all speak well of you. "If you were of the world, the world would love its own; but because you are not of the world, but I chose you out of the world, therefore the world hates you." In the army we all marched in step. The soldier that fell out of step was severely castigated. When a person surrenders to Jesus Christ, that one falls out of step with the world and into step with God. All sorts of evil percussions result. I have been called worse than "a pious Psalm singer." One will be shunned by the "church world," because it is part of the world. As a first-year student in Seminary I was singing a gospel song in the shower. An upper classman said, "Do you still sing gospel songs?" I stopped doing so in Seminary, but I am back to doing so now. Christianity is a singing faith.

❦

THEY PERSECUTE A PERSON

"**R**emember the word that I said to you, 'A slave is not greater than his master.'" John 15:20

The world loves its own, but the word Jesus used means "likes." The world knows nothing about agape-love, which is depicted in detail by St. Paul in I Cor. 13. Agape-love is patient and kind toward those who differ with it. It bears all things. It covers, protects and shields. It covers a multitude of sins! The world on the other hand is critical of those who do not conform. It is touchy, and deplores all criticism. It delights in the status quo.

"If they persecute me, they will persecute you; if they kept my word, they will keep yours also." Believers are an extension of Jesus himself. They have not only adopted in a measure Jesus' life-style; they have Jesus' life within them. That was why Jesus accused Saul of Tarsus of persecuting him when he persecuted Christians. A believer was afraid that she might fall out of Jesus' hand, until she learned that she was his hand.

"But all this they will do to you on my account, because they do not know him who sent me." Ignorance of the Creator is the core of all hostility directed against Christians. Einstein was deeply religious. He regarded God as the "Great Mathematician," which he is. Tragically, from our perspective, he felt that belief in a personal God was too specific a concept to be applicable to the Being at work in this universe. He was brilliant but blind. Had he accepted Jesus as his Savior, he would have recognized the astonishing fact that it is possible to be personally related to the Creator of all worlds. The transcendent God is simultaneously imminent, closer than breathing, nearer than hands or feet, or than our right elbow. Speak to him. He listens. On the train back to Princeton I sat next to a personal friend of Einstein. He sent me a copy of the letter he wrote the good professor, asking him to grant me an interview. I am still waiting.

❧

NO EXCUSE

"*If I had not come and spoken to them, they would not have sin, but now they have no excuse for their sin.*" *John 15:22*

Jesus did not say that they would not be sinners had he not spoken to them. To be sure they were sinners before he spoke to them, in the sense that they were violators of God's law, as we all are. But after he revealed the Father's love to them, by rejecting that revelation they became guilty of the sin of unbelief. Now their unbelief (sin) held them fast.

Furthermore they now have "no excuse for their sin." The word "excuse" is literally cloak. Their unbelief in God is now without a cloak; it is exposed for all to see. They cannot say they never had a chance to know God personally and intimately. The opportunity was presented to them, but in refusing to become students of Jesus, they turned it down. The same may be said of all who have heard the gospel of Jesus Christ, but decided not to believe it. Once we have heard, we decide whether to believe it or not, and so we determine our own destiny.

Years ago I called upon a man who managed a large plant. I presented this gospel to him with visual aids, showing how it was structured in the form of a cross. It was the first time I had so presented the gospel, taking him all the way through it. I assumed that "seeing is believing." He acknowledged that he perceived the logic of it, and understood the message. Praise God, I thought, we are home free. Then he said to my amazement, "But I do not believe it!" It turned out that he was a Unitarian. Unitarians reject the deity of Christ, pretending that Jesus was only a great teacher, a marvelous human being, but nothing more. They joined forces some years ago with the Univeralists, who pretend that ultimately every one will be saved. I never called upon him again. He taught me a big lesson: seeing is not believing, but believing is seeing.

❦

A BARE BONES GOSPEL WILL NOT DO

"*He who hates me hates my Father also.*"   *John 15:23*

Whom do you love and whom do you hate? If you love Jesus, you love the Father also. If you hate Jesus, then inevitably you hate the Father also. The Lord loves those who hate evil. Ps. 97:10. A young missionary by the name of Jim Kooiman was asked by his friend if he hated the devil. "Yes, of course," he replied. "Then tell him you do." "Devil, I hate you," he said. "You don't sound like you do," exclaimed his friend. Before they were through he shouted, "Devil, I hate you!" and really meant it. All of us love and all of us hate. We are entitled to ventilate our hatred toward the devil, and get it out of our system. It is spiritually and emotionally a wise thing to do. Some people do not hate evil with perfect hatred, so they cannot love God with perfect love.

"If I had not done among them the works which no one else did, they would not have sin; but now they have no excuse for their sin." First it was the words of Jesus, but now it is his supernatural deeds that laid bare their sin of rebellion against God. We are living in a time when the gospel of the kingdom is going forth among all the nations. It is no longer a bare bones gospel, but a gospel fleshed out with signs and wonders attesting to the truth of it.

Several years ago in Mexico we prayed for a girl about eleven years of age. My companion and I did not know what her need was. Suddenly she shouted, "Gloria Christo," and again, "Gloria Christo" (Glory to Christ). We didn't know why the people were weeping, until we were told that she was dumb and had never before spoken. For the message of Christ to progress in the third world miracles are mandated, and we rejoice to see them taking place. The arm of the One we serve is not shortened. It is still reaching out with supernatural power to those who are hungering and thirsting for God.

❧

RELIGION'S FAILURE

"But now they have seen and hated both me and my Father."
John 15:24

How was it possible for them to hate the very God whom they thought they served? "It is to fulfill the word that is written in their law, 'They hated me without a cause.'" Without a cause is literally "freely." It was their free choice, there being no reason or motivation for doing so. But they were fulfilling Psalm 69:4, a Psalm fortelling the sufferings of Jesus, their Savior.

In a profound sense they were bound to resist the love of God, because they were slaves of the devil, whose nature it is to fight against the saving activity of God. All religion is hostile to God, because it is man's attempt to justify himself, to make life meaningful on the basis of his own activity. On the contrary, the Bible is the story of God involving himself in the life of humanity. He rescues us from our futility as we are in the very act of fighting him hammer and tong. He wants us to let go and allow him do for us that which we cannot do for ourselves. What he is looking for from us is absolute surrender. That is the very last thing we are inclined to do. "Nothing in my hand I bring, simply to thy cross I cling." That is the response which rings the bells of heaven with exultant joy.

"But when the Counselor comes, whom I shall send to you from the Father, even the Spirit of truth, who proceeds from the Father, he will bear witness to me." The Counselor just mentioned testified to Jesus' innocence and Judaism's guilt in rejecting him. The Spirit of truth that fell on the occasion of Pentecost would persist in bearing witness to Jesus. The Spirit would perpetuate the ministry which Jesus had undertaken during his days in the flesh, and even multiply its effectiveness. Through one cast of the gospel net, Peter added three thousand to the company of believers in one day. Jesus had never enjoyed such immense success prior to his death and resurrection.

PLEAD YOUR CASE

"*And you also are witnesses, because you have been with me from the beginning.*" *John 15:27.*

They had witnessed all that had transpired over the three years of Jesus' ministry. They were not yet bold enough to take the witness stand in Jesus' behalf, but their day would come. It does for all of us.

I wrote these words in the Civil Courts Building in Small Claims Court. The defendant did not show up, so the judge told us that we had won by default. Since he had no case, he did not plead it. As Christians we are privileged to plead our case and to bear our witness in the courtroom situation, where the claim of Christ to Lordship is being contested. We are speaking of the world, which is by nature hostile to God and the gospel.

So ends John chapter 15, which is concerned with bearing fruit for Jesus - reproducing after our kind. Now we have come to chapter 16, which has to do with nurturing the life of God within us by means of the Holy Spirit.

"I have said all this to you to keep you from falling away." Fall away they would in the short run, but not in the long run. To be forewarned is to be forearmed. "They will put you out of the synagogues; indeed, the hour is coming when whoever kills you will think he is offering service to God." That which happened to the man born blind, when he was cast out of the community, will be the normal experience. Indeed, it will get even worse than that. Jesus had in mind what happened to Stephen as recorded in Acts 7, when they stoned him to death. On that occasion he experienced what Jesus had told Nathanael would happen in 1:57, "He saw heaven opened," and something more welcome than angels ascending and descending. He saw Jesus, "standing at the right hand of God," waiting to receive him into glory. If we testify for Jesus here, he will testify in our behalf before his Father in heaven. If we deny him here, he will be obliged to deny us there. ❧

ONLY TWO RELIGIONS

"*And they will do this because they have not known the Father, nor me.*" *John 16:3*

When all is said and done there are only two religions: the religion of Cain and the religion of Abel. Cain offered to God the fruit of the ground cursed by God. His offering was not accepted, bearing as it did the taint of the curse. Abel offered to God of the firstlings of his flock and of their fat portions. His offering was accepted by God. Doubtless the fire fell and consumed it. It was accepted because it expressed the principle "without the shedding of blood there is no forgiveness of sins." Hebrews 9:22

Abel's offering pointed beyond itself to the sacrifice of the Lamb of God upon the cross. Cain's religion came to be known as "works righteousness": "God, I'm doing it, and you have got to accept it." But God alone determines what is acceptable to him. Cain was jealous of his brother and became a murderer. Abel became a martyr. Followers of Jesus are on the road to martyrdom. Followers of "works righteousness" persecute those who do not share their views, and are on the way to becoming murderers.

In the Book of Revelation the religion of Abel is that of the Bride. "She has washed her robes and made them white in the blood of the Lamb." All she has is faith in Jesus and his perfect sacrifice. "Without faith, it is impossible to please God. To please him one must believe that he is, and that he is a rewarder of those who diligently seek him." Hebrews 11:6. The religion of Cain is that of the Harlot. She is clothed in three of the four colors found in the Old Testament temple: gold, purple and scarlet. She is missing the blue, the color of the sky and of faith. She has all the pageantry and ritual that pleases men. But without faith she displeases God and is drunk on the blood of the saints. I would far rather be persecuted than persecute, wouldn't you?

❦

HEADING HOME

"But I have said these things to you, that when their hour comes you may remember that I told you of them." John 16:4

When would their hour come? It would come before the night was over. Jesus said just before they seized him at his arrest, "But this is your hour, and the power of darkness." Luke 22:53. Light and darkness continually battle; but there was an hour when darkness gained the upper hand and reigned. A similar hour is approaching again. It is called "Jacob's trouble," when all hell breaks loose. I hope not to be here when it happens.

We experience trials and troubles continually. Paul exhorts us "that no one be moved by these afflictions. You yourselves know that this is to be our lot." I Thess. 3:3. I would much prefer having my lot in afflictions here than to have my lot in the lake of fire and brimstone in the hereafter. Life was not meant to be easy, but heroic. And heroes are made by circumstances; they are not born heroic. Do you remember the Scottish song that goes, "You take the high road, and I'll take the low road, but I'll get to Scotland before ye." It refers to two men in an English prison. One was to be released the next morning, while the other was to be executed. The one to be executed was saying that he would be taking the low road via death, but would precede his companion back to his native land.

A woman overheard another woman speaking in tongues, and asked, "What language were you speaking?" She answered, "I was speaking the language of my homeland." It was her heavenly language. Speaking in a language taught by the Holy Spirit is a sure sign that he has conquered our affections. Eventually the defeated speak the language of the conquistadors (the conquerors) as the Indians do in Mexico. They speak the language of Spain. Have you learned as yet your heavenly language? If not, isn't it time that you sought it out?

❦

A BLESSING THAT BOGGLES THE MIND

"I *did not say these things to you from the beginning, because I was with you. But now I am going to him who sent me, yet none of you asks me, 'Where are you going?'" John 16:4,5*

Why didn't they ask this seemingly inevitable question? Jesus answered the why of it in his next expression, "But because I have said these things to you, sorrow has filled your hearts." Their lives were about to come apart at the seams. They couldn't face the pain of separation heading their way. Can you blame them for attempting to put their heads in the sand?

Two girl ostriches looked back and saw two boy ostriches that appeared to be following them. One said to the other, "Let's run." So they began running. Sure enough, the boy ostriches ran too. A girl ostrich said, "Now let's walk." The boy ostriches fell to walking too. One girl ostrich said, "Let's put our heads in the sand." So they did. Then one boy ostrich said to the other, "Just where did those girls go?" Jesus would not let his disciples play ostrich, and hide their heads in the sand. He demanded that they face the facts, horrible though they be. The way out of an ordeal is to go through it, not to back off from it, or to close one's eyes.

Jesus' next statement is the key expression in this chapter. He tells them why it is so essential that he go away. "Nevertheless I tell you the truth: it is to your advantage that I go away, for if I do not go away, the Counselor will not come to you; but if I go, I will send him to you." It is one thing to have Immanuel, God with us, in the person of Jesus Christ. It is even more wonderful to have the Counselor, God in us. He is the wonderful Counselor spoken of in Isaiah 9:6. In many counselors there is wisdom, but having the Holy Spirit as our Counselor is having Christ in us. That is having in us, at least potentially, all the treasures of wisdom and knowledge, a blessing that boggles the mind.

❦

GOD'S PROSECUTING ATTORNEY

"*And when he comes, he will convince the world concerning sin and righteousness and judgment.*" *John 16:8*

This verse tells of the work of the Holy Spirit in the world. The word "convince" may also be rendered convict, or prove wrong. The third Person of the godhead is the defense counsel of the Church, but he is the prosecutor of the world. The same gospel by which he encourages and builds up the church, he uses to convict the world in three particulars. First "concerning sin, because they do not believe in me." The root sin is the rejection of Jesus. Jesus is God's offer to us of pardon. If I reject the pardon, I remain in the prisonhouse of sin and death. I continue in the circle of the unforgiven. The story is told of Frederick the Great of Prussia who questioned prisoners about their crimes. One after another said he fell victim to a trumped-up charge. Finally he encountered a man who acknowledged that he was guilty of the crime for which he had been sentenced. Frederick shouted, "Jailer, come quick. Release this guilty man before he corrupts all these innocent inmates."

Second, he convicts "concerning righteousness, because I go to the Father, and you will see me no more." God's righteousness is expressed by his raising Jesus from the dead, and that now the world cannot touch him nor get their filthy hands upon him ever again.

Third, "concerning judgment, because the ruler of this world is judged," and found wanting in that the devil failed to entice Jesus to stray from the perfect will of his Heavenly Father. The devil has already been judged. It is just a matter of time until he and his fallen angels are cast into the jail that has been prepared for them, "the eternal fire." See Matthew 25:41. If I say "yes" to Jesus, I spend eternity with him. If I persist in saying "no," I will be rewarded by spending eternity with him who is my god. Fair enough!

❧

THE REVERSAL INTO OPPOSITES

"*A little while, and you will see me no more; again a little while and you will see me.*" *John 16:16*

Here we learn how the disciples' grief will turn to joy. In the verse just cited it is important to note that Jesus uses two different words for "see". The first is a form of theoreo, which means to theorize or ponder. I once officiated the wedding of a man who had the surname Ponder. I assumed that his ancestors in England worked at a nobleman's pond, where they had opportunity to reflect upon the images that appeared before them. They had occasion to contemplate all that they saw in and about the pond. Jesus is here telling his disciples that the time for them to enjoy the leisure of reflecting upon him and his teaching is coming to an end.

In a very short interval a drastic change would take place, after which they would see in an altogether new way: they would "horao" him. The word is meant to express the fact that they would experience him in his resurrection body. A profound realization would dawn upon them that would transport them into a new domain. Their conception of reality would be altered in such a way that they would never be the same again. Old things would pass away; all would become new. The Greeks had a name for it - enantiodromia - the reversal into opposites. It is illustrated by what happened to Saul of Tarsus on the Damascus Road. He came to that experience a fire breathing dragon, full of threats and murder against the followers of Jesus. He was turned inside out, and instantly became a little child being led by the hand to learn what he must do in the service of this Jesus whom he had so hated.

Life changing experiences are in store for all who continue in the way of him who is the Way, the Truth, and the Life. Perhaps it will happen gradually, but happen it will. Inch by inch, it's a cinch. Yard by yard, it's very hard.

❦

TO THE DESPERATE IT MAKES SENSE

"*Some of his disciples said to one another, 'What is this that he says to us, "A little while, and you will not see me, and again a little while, and you will see me."'* John 16:17

What Jesus had just said left them totally confused. Indeed everything he had said going back to chapter 14:12, "because I go to the Father," was a dark saying to them. "They said, 'What does he mean by "a little while?" We do not know what he means.'" Here is illustrated what Paul talks about in I Cor. 2:11, "No one comprehends the thoughts of God, except the Spirit of God.... The unspiritual man does not receive the gifts of the Spirit of God, for they are folly to him, and he is not able to understand them because they are spiritually discerned." Jesus' disciples were still unspiritual, natural men. They were behaving like ordinary men, who could not comprehend the things of God.

Just now I returned from an Alcoholics Anonymous meeting where we celebrated a friend's 28th anniversary of sobriety. God's Spirit was there. Individuals introduced themselves, saying for example, "I am Ray. I am an alcoholic." Then the individual was privileged to testify as to how he experienced rescue from the bottle through following the twelve steps, which are derived from the Bible. A person has to admit that she had lost control over her life, and was willing to seek help from the higher power who is God. There is no room for pride. A person must admit that he is a failure, just as all the apostles did. There is no human possibility of victory over the addiction of alcohol.

All of us are addicted to sinful behavior in some form. We cannot understand the religion of the Bible and be helped by it until we become desperate for God. Prior to our divinely designed desperation, our religion is nothing more than a theory, an intellectual attempt to walk the high wire.

THE BLESSED REVOLUTIONS

"They said, 'What does he mean by "a little while?" We do not know what he means.'" John 16:18

"A little while" means something different to different people. It is always relative. Seat a young man on a park bench with his favorite girl, and two hours seems like two minutes. Seat that same young man on a hot-plate for two seconds and it seems like two hours. What is a little while? Man's days are as a handbreadth, says Psalm 30:5. Yet it seems to me as though I have been around forever. Even so life has been characterized by a little boy pulling his wagon up a hill. He pulls it up the hill until he is 27, then he gets in the wagon and coasts down the other side. And the fatter the body, the faster the roll.

"Jesus knew that they wanted to ask him; so he said to them, 'Is this what you are asking yourselves, what I meant by saying, "A little while, and you will not see me, and again a little while, and you will see me?" Truly, truly, I say to you, you will weep and lament, but the world will rejoice.'" The world will rejoice again over the death of the two prophets, as recorded in Rev. 11:10. As a matter of fact, they will celebrate an anti-Christmas by making merry and exchanging presents. Won't they be astonished when over worldwide color TV, they will see the unburied bodies after three and a half days stand up and ascend into heaven.

God still has some surprises up his sleeve. Happily those of us who study the Bible will not be taken by surprise. A little girl said, "The Bible begins in Genesis and ends in Revolutions." May we experience the two blessed revolutions that will head off our participation in the dreadful ones: the tribulation period depicted in Rev. chapter 6, and the day of wrath described in Rev. chapters 8 to 11. The blessed revolutions are our new birth (3:1-21) and our baptism in the Holy Spirit (Acts 2, 10, & 19).

❦

SORROW NOW, JOY HEREAFTER

"𝔜ou will be sorrowful, but your sorrow will turn into joy."

John 16:20

It reminds us of the beatitude, "Blessed are you that weep now, for you shall laugh," and its companion woe, "Woe to you that laugh now, for you shall mourn and weep." Luke 6:21,25. I would rather have tails here and heads hereafter, than the reverse, wouldn't you?

Jesus now illustrates the principle just stated. "When a woman is in travail she has sorrow, because her hour has come, but when she is delivered of the child, she no longer remembers the anguish, for joy that a man is born into the world." The woman's hour is her time of going into labor, which she must endure to give birth to an anthropos (not a baby, but a human being). No one ever hangs upon a cross. The victim writhes upon a cross, always seeking a less painful position, but each new position is worse than the one before. Jesus, as the crucified, writhed as a woman in labor. He saw the fruit of his travail and was satisfied, for he produced the new humanity, recreated after the likeness of its Creator.

"So you have sorrow now, but I will see you again and your hearts will rejoice, and no one will take your joy from you." They were in the process of sharing his sorrow, but it would not last. Nothing lasts forever; it just seems like it. St. Paul aspired to share Jesus' sufferings, "becoming like him in his death, that if possible I may attain the resurrection from the dead." Philippians 3:10,11 Only those who participate in Christ's passion are productive for God, and are assured of being part of that company represented by the five wise maidens who are invited into the marriage supper of the Lamb. Matthew 25:1-12 They will see the exalted Christ face to face, and no one will take their joy from them, not for countless ages. We regard the Church of Philadelphia in Rev. 3:7 as the five wise maidens, and aspire to be in that company.

❦

FATHER KNOWS BEST

"**I**n *that day you will ask nothing of me. Truly, truly, I say to you, if you ask anything of the Father, he will give it to you in my name.*" *John 16:23*

During his days in the flesh, Jesus did all the praying. His disciples came to him with their requests and needs. After his resurrection it would be different. His followers would then turn to God the Father, even as he taught them to do in the Lord's Prayer. The petition for daily bread speaks of asking for our necessities. They will be met, if we petition in his name. This has reference to our chief concern being the advancement of his Kingdom. His name as King of Kings and Lord of Lords must be made known world wide.

"Hitherto you will have asked nothing in my name; ask, and you will receive, that your joy may be full." The emphasis upon joy is remarkable on this night of foreboding and betrayal. The same note of joy resounds through St. Paul's letter to the Philippians, written from prison when his life was in the balance. Happiness is ephemeral and depends upon circumstances. A bumper sticker read, "Are you having fun yet?" Life is not a cabaret, as the old song has it. Life is meant to be a labor of love. And the fruit of love is joy.

A little girl had two older brothers who picked on her. A neighbor said to her, "I understand that your mother is going to have a baby. Would you like to have a baby brother or a baby sister?" She answered, "I pray to God it is a baby sister." The neighbor responded, "Suppose it should be a baby boy." Her face grew serious as she said, "God wouldn't do that to me." But it is not what we like that counts with God. It is what his love decrees. And Father knows best. When the fiery ordeal comes, we are called to "rejoice in so far as we share Christ's sufferings, that we may rejoice and be glad when his glory is revealed." I Peter 4:13. Paul and Silas rejoiced over their pain in a Philippian prison. Suddenly his glory was revealed in the earthquake that freed them.   ❦

TOO GOOD TO BE TRUE?

"**I** *have said this to you in figures; the hour is coming when I shall no longer speak to you in figures but tell you plainly of the Father." John 16:25*

Jesus was the greatest story teller of all time. His stories were all true stories, not in the sense that they really happened, but in that they told us something about God and his ways. When he told the story of the Prodigal Son, was he telling of something that had happened historically? What earthly father would allow his son to say in effect, "Drop dead, Dad. I want to bail out and get my share now." He would see the back side of the moon. Only our heavenly Father is as wise and loving as the father in Jesus' parable. Jesus used earthly figures to present heavenly realities. After his resurrection, though, he would be able to reveal his heavenly Father with crystal clear clarity. How? By pouring into us something of the Father's essential nature, which is love. Peter, after the resurrection, was a different man from Peter before that triumphal event. Before he was as instable as water. Afterward he enjoyed a good night's sleep before his scheduled execution. See Acts 12:6. The explanation? He was inhabited by God. Perfect love had cast out fear.

"In that day (after the resurrection) you will ask in my name; and I do not say to you that I shall pray the Father for you; for the Father himself loves you, because you have loved me and have believed that I came from the Father." The Father loves his whole creation, no doubt about it. But only those who love Jesus and receive him as the Father's gift are able to receive his second gift. That gift is in the indwelling presence and empowering of the Holy Spirit. The greatest discovery a person can make is that he or she is the dwelling place of God, the habitation of the Most High. It is almost too good to be true. But it isn't. As believers we are never alone. Always we have a friendly, encouraging Presence within us.

❧

GOING HOME

"**I** *came from the Father and have come into the world; again, I am leaving the world and going to the Father." John 16:28*
Literally, "I came forth out of the Father" - out of his bosom. A dear man who nearly died when he was 18 miraculously survived. So he dedicated his life to God and endured innumerable hospitalizations with the fortitude of a saint. As an old man, he was asked his secret. At first he didn't think he had one. Then, after reflecting, he said, "I think of myself as always in the position of St. John at the last supper." He lived his life as though he was in the bosom of Jesus. Jesus had lived his life as though he was in the bosom of his heavenly Father. He actually was in the center of his Father's love, was he not?

I had ministered for a week and a half in Tima, Upper Egypt. Pastor Samir and I went to the Railroad Station for the eight hour train ride to Cairo, for the first leg of my journey home to the USA. I was in a happy frame of mind. St. Louis, here I come. To my grateful astonishment more than a dozen men of the church were at the station to see me off. It was a touching thing.

Jesus was on the verge of returning home to the Father. It would not be a pleasant train ride down the Nile Valley. It would begin in the middle of the night and would last through most of that horrendous Friday. But that was just the first leg of the journey. Instead of returning to his Father when he breathed his last, he descended into the region of the damned, where he preached the gospel to the most wicked people who had ever lived, "that though judged in the flesh like men, they might (repent and believe and so) live in the spirit like God." See I Peter 3:18-20, 4:6. The twelve did not gather around the cross to see him off. They watched the proceedings from a safe distance, lest they too be caught up in the violence against God that was unleashed that day.

PLAIN TALK

"**H**is disciples said, 'Ah, now you are speaking plainly, not in any figure.'" *John 16:29*

Now we understand. Now everything is clear. "Now we know that you know all things, and need none to question you; by this we believe that you came from God." They believe everything he had said with the top of their minds, but their hearts (their unconscious) were still unpersuaded. How deep down has the gospel penetrated within us? Only God knows for sure.

As an eighteen year old, I was inducted into the U.S. Army, and took basic training in the infantry. During the fourteenth week of training, our unit was on the mortar range, firing live ammunition for the first time. A corporal cadreman, overseeing our position, said to me, "Let's pull the safety pins on a dozen shells, and see how many rounds we can get into the air before the first one lands on target." I heard, but I didn't hear. He had said "us" and "we". As the assistant gunner, I was to load the 30 mm shells. We pulled the pins, and I took two rounds and dropped them into the mortar tube as fast as I could. Behind my back he was loading too. I tried to slip my third round in while a round he had dropped in was coming out. My shell cartwheeled out of my hand, went up into the air and exploded on the side of the bunker facing out toward the range. We were very nearly killed, and I spent eight months in the hospital undergoing hand surgery.

I reflected as to why this had happened. It dawned on me that I had made the same mistake Germany had made before World War II. I had paid attention to a two-bit corporal who had violated the rules. Ever after I have been wary of authorities who may tell me to do something. It is perfectly all right to make a mistake, just so it is always a different one. When we hear something, before we act, let us make sure it passes muster within our hearts as well as our minds.

❦

DESERTED, BUT NOT UTTERLY FORSAKEN

*"**J**esus answered them, 'Do you now believe?'" John 16:31*

When someone says, "Trust me," I lean the other way. The fact that they now say that they believe Jesus does not make them worthy of trust. Jesus does not congratulate them for their conviction. On the contrary, he says, "Behold, the hour is coming, indeed it has come, when you will be scattered, everyone to his own home, and leave me alone." They would all be deserters. In time of war deserters are lined up and shot. That is how the world treats deserters, but not so God. He is merciful. When I am stopped by a police officer for some traffic violation, I do not ask for justice, I plead for mercy. On one occasion my request was granted, when I pleaded ignorance. I wonder about those who are always crying for justice, if they know what they ask.

"You will leave me alone. Yet I am not alone, for my Father is with me." The Apostle Paul, as one sold out to Jesus Christ, made the same assertion. He wrote, "At my first defense no one took my part, all deserted me. May it not be charged against them! But the Lord stood by me and gave me strength to proclaim the message fully, that all the Gentiles might hear it. So I was rescued from the lion's mouth." 2 Tim. 4:16,17. Paul did not hold it against his deserters. He followed the example of Stephen, who, when he was stoned, forgave Paul and the rest for their crime against him. Acts 7 "To err is human, to forgive divine." It must be human also. As the Father stood by Jesus at his arrest, so Jesus stood by Paul in his ordeal.

Tragically, though, even the Father had to forsake Jesus when he was nailed to the cross. He became thereby the sin-offering for us all. Jesus took what we had coming that we might receive what he had coming - a place in glory by the Father's side. Say now with me, "I thank you, Jesus, for dying in my place and stead, and for living within me now by faith."

❦

THANK GOD FOR LITTLE TOES

*"**I** have said this to you, that in me you may have peace."*
John 16:33

Jesus had revealed that his disciples would all fail him. Even so, they would not prove to be failures because he would not fail them. Far from it, his contact with them would become infinitely closer. Before long they would actually be in him. Now they were with him, but after his resurrection and ascension, he would become their head enroute to his becoming head over the universe.

As our head and body are intimately connected, so would he be bound up with them. When I stub my toe, my head says, "Ouch!" Saul of Tarsus persecuted Jesus' followers, but Jesus said to him, "Why do you persecute me?" What we feel, Jesus feels. Jesus' first word to them on Easter evening was, "Peace be with you." Thanks to his sacrificial death, they now enjoyed peace with God. But that would be only half the story. "In the world you have tribulation." Why is that? Because the world is society organizing itself in opposition to God. Today it goes by the name of secular humanism. This outlook leaves God out of the picture and pretends that he does not exist. It places man on the throne over the universe. This philosophy is the Western counterpart of Marxism. They are fraternal twins.

Despite the miserable time the world gives you, "Be of good cheer." Don't let them get you down, for "I have overcome the world." There are two ways of viewing life. The tails side of the coin says that I am a survivor. I feel as though I have barely survived the slings and arrows of outrageous fortune. But, turning the coin over, I recognize Jesus as head, and say, "I am more than a conqueror." His love will never let me go. I sure don't feel lovable, but as a believer, I don't go by my feelings. I trust what Jesus said, "I have overcome the world." If I am only a little toe in his body, I will be used to crush Satan under his feet.

❦

LIFT UP YOUR EYES TO HEAVEN

"*When Jesus had spoken these words, he lifted up his eyes to heaven and said, 'Father, the hour has come.'*" *John 17:1*

Chapter 16 developed the sixth theme: nurture through the Holy Spirit. The Holy Spirit would come to empower the disciples to bear witness in the world. As they did so, they would stake their all on the truth of Jesus Christ, and thereby eat solid spiritual food. Milk Christians stay spiritual babes. They drink the sincere milk of God's Word, but fail to take the witness stand for Jesus where his claims are being contested, in society.

Chapter 17 takes up again the seventh gospel theme, which is healing in answer to prayer. Having said all that needed to be said to the disciples, Jesus now turned his attention heavenward, that he might bare his heart to God. In his prayer he discloses the full secret of a truly human life. A human is a heavenly oriented man or woman. Only so may one become humane. There is power in a spiritual approach. Looking at life from the perspective of the eternal, one can see meaning in the smallest things.

A little boy asked his mother, "Can Daddy go to heaven?" "Why of course," she responded. "Why do you ask?" He said, "But he won't leave the store." A sick business man said to his partner, "We didn't have time to go to church, but we made money, didn't we, Harry? We didn't have time for family or the great outdoors, but we made money, didn't we, Harry?" Harry said, "Yes, we made money." The partner then asked Harry to have inscribed on his tombstone the following: "Born, July 3, 1925, a man with a soul. Died ____ (you fill it in) a wholesale grocer." Money had kicked his soul to death! With no appreciation for the vertical, we become flat, stale, insipid. Take a sip of the water of life right now. "The hour has come" to do so. Father, we love you. We worship and adore! Now and forevermore.

THE GREATNESS OF THE HUMAN SOUL

"*Father, the hour has come, glorify thy Son that the Son may glorify thee.*" *John 17:1*

Having "lifted up his eyes to heaven" foretells what must happen now that "the hour has come." His body must be lifted up in crucifixion. Only then could the Father glorify Jesus, first by raising him from the dead, and then by exalting him to his right hand.

The question as to how the Son would glorify the Father is answered in verse two: "Since thou hast given him power over all flesh, to give eternal life to all whom thou hast given me." The Son glorifies the Father by giving eternal life to others. Since God is love he delights in sharing his life with all who are willing to receive it. But what actually is eternal life? Answer: "And this is eternal life, that they know thee the only true God, and Jesus Christ whom thou hast sent." An ongoing experiental knowledge of God as he really is is the basis of life. The alternative is merely existing.

It happened to Blaise Pascal in the 17th century as he was reading this very scripture. He had an experience of God that lasted for two hours. As it went on he made notations: "God of Abraham, God of Isaac, God of Jacob, not the God of the philosophers and scholars. Jesus Christ, Jesus Christ, Jesus Christ. Joy, joy, joy. Tears of joy. I have crucified him..." He told no one of his experience, the record of which was discovered only after his death by his sister. She said that he all at once became as humble as a little child, gave away nearly all of his possessions, and devoted the rest of his life (four years) to writing a vindication of the religion of Jesus Christ - his Pensee (Thoughts). One of his thoughts concerns the greatness of the human soul. "The universe can crush me without knowing it, whereas I know I am being crushed. So one human soul has more value than the entire material universe." A thought worth contemplating.

❧

FRAMED IN ETERNITY

"**J** *glorified thee on earth, having accomplished the work which thou gavest me to do.*" *John 17:4*

"Man's chief end is to glorify God, and to enjoy him forever." (The Westminister Shorter Catechism) Jesus has accomplished the first in his life heretofore, and is about to launch into the second. "And now, Father, glorify thou me in thy own presence with the glory which I had with thee before the world was made." Jesus had come to the earth trailing the glory of heaven. Something of the aroma of God persisted with him. God created man out of the elements of earth, but Jesus was not created. He was begotten out of God himself in eternity. The Jehovah Witnesses pretend he is "a spirit creature," the "Archangel Michael" come to earth. Such teaching is earthly, psychic, demonic. They have a zeal that is unenlightened. May we capture their zeal for evangelism, but hold fast the truth about Jesus' human yet divine nature.

"I have manifested thy name to the men whom thou gavest me out of the world." That in a word was the work which Jesus had accomplished. "Thine they were, and thou gavest them to me, and they have kept thy word." God himself had transplanted the disciples out of the world into the Kingdom, the proof of which is contained in Jesus' next statement, "Now they know that everything that thou hast given me is from thee; for I have given them the words which thou gavest me, and they have received them and know in truth that I came from thee; and believe that thou didst send me." Jesus himself is the Word of God. Therefore it follows that all the words he spoke as Teacher came from God.

A little boy's father had been killed in the war. All he had of his father was a framed photograph of him. He said, "I wish my father could step out of that frame." That is exactly what God has done through Jesus Christ. He has made himself visible in a human life, and now the disciples knew it. Do you?

❧

THE GREAT DIVIDE

"**I** *am praying for them; I am not praying for the world but for those whom thou hast given me, for they are thine."* John 17:9

There is a world of difference between selfishness and enlightened self-interest. The selfish person is concerned only about his own welfare. Jesus was concerned about his own ultimate welfare and that of others as well. Chapter 17 verses 1-5 reveal Jesus praying for himself. In verses 6-19 he prays for the eleven, then in 20-26 for all believers through the centuries.

In this Great High Priestly Prayer we enter into the Holy of Holies, and encounter thoughts that go deeper than the human mind. It is frightening to perceive that Jesus does not pray here for the world, but only for those who respond to the gospel. This means that the world system is headed for disaster both in the East (Communism) and in the West (Secular Humanism). We are obliged to save ourselves from this crooked generation by turning to Jesus. The world is unrepentant humanity. It consists of all who refuse to fix their eyes upon Jesus and to invoke his name. Jesus, you see, is the only adequate symbol and expression of God, because he actually came from God.

"All mine are thine, and thine are mine, and I am glorified in them." Jesus was already glorified in them, because he was the center of their lives and the object of their affection. "And now I am no more in the world, but they are in the world." A few days ago we were vacationing on the Gulf Coast. One morning we woke up and decided we would rather be home. From that moment we were heading home. Our body was still in Mississippi, but our heart was in Missouri. For Jesus the center of gravity had shifted from earth to heaven. His disciples, despite their seeming loyalty to him, were still grounded in this passing scene. They had yet to make the crossing of the great divide - from the secular to the eternal.

❦

THE DRAGON SLAYER

"**J** *am coming to thee."   John 17:13*

In Seminary the newly arrived students were called "erchomai", which is the Greek for "I am coming/I am going." Half the time we didn't know whether we were coming or going. If we are honest, we will admit that we have a love/hate relationship with Jesus Christ. Part of us loves him. Part of us hates him. He is too deep for us. And he keeps calling us into the deeper waters where we do not want to go. The way of the cross leads home. The cross makes us cross, because it says "no" to that within us which is self-indulgent and willing to settle for the mediocre. The message of the cross says "Only one life, 'twill soon be past. Only what's done for Christ will last. He will be Lord of all, or not Lord at all." To this a part of us says, You've got to be kidding.

"Holy Father, keep them in thy name, which thou hast given me, that they may be one, even as we are one." Jesus' first request for his disciples is that God be Father to them as He was to himself. The two primal screams are: Mama, Mama, protect me; Daddy, Daddy, direct me. Though God's name is Father, he transcends sexuality, having both masculine and feminine characteristics. This fact is explicit in Genesis 1:27, where it says God created man in his own image, male and female.

James Bishop in his book, <u>The Day Christ Died</u>, puts these words in Jesus' mouth, when his mother said to him, "They have no wine." "What would you have me do now, Mother?" He would turn Jesus into a mama's boy. Not so. Jesus sought to please his Father. Had his goal been to please his mother he never would have gone to the cross. St. George slew the dragon, as every young man must if he would fulfill his destiny: the dragon of "smother love." The mother's instinct is to spare her offspring the agony of conflict and death by keeping him safely tied to her apron strings. God pity the man who fails to make the break, as Jesus did.

ONCE SAVED, ALWAYS SAVED?

"That they may be one, even as we are one." John 17:11

"The Fatherhood of God and the brotherhood of man," is a dictum that is untrue. It would be correct to say, "the holy Fatherhood of God and the believing brotherhood of man." Holy means "set apart" from all that is common and unclean. Our faith in the Holy Father sets us apart from the unforgiven, who are unforgiving. As believers we are obliged to tear up all the IOU's we hold against others, as The Lord's Prayer enjoins. Our free forgiveness of others enables us to become one. It breaks down all the barriers and so satisfies the desire of Jesus' heart.

"While I was with them, I kept them in thy name which thou hast given me!" How had he done that? He explains: "I have guarded them." "The angel of the Lord encamps around those who fear him." So did Jesus protect his own ones from the enemy's attack. "And none of them is lost but the son of perdition, that the scripture might be fulfilled." Judas is here referred to as the child of hell. From the human point of view Jesus could not defend Judas from the devil's machinations, because Judas had no fear of God, which is the first step toward wisdom. From the divine perspective, Scripture mandated in Psalm 41:9 that one of the twelve "enlarge his heel against him." (Hebrew).

Some say, "Once saved, always saved." This is dangerous doctrine. It is true that no one can snatch us from Jesus' hand, but "for freedom Christ has set us free." We are always free (God forbid) to walk out of his loving embrace. Judas did. And Jesus loved Judas as much as he did anyone, for God is no respecter of persons. He does not play favorites. The Christian life is likened to a marathon in Hebrews 12:1. It is not he who begins the race, but he who finishes who wins the prize. The believers who have died are crowding the grandstands to cheer us on. "We feebly struggle; they in glory shine."

❦

EVERYONE LOVED HIM?

"But now I am coming to thee; and these things I speak in the world that they may have my joy fulfilled in themselves.'

John 17:13

Nathan Sharansky, asked how he felt when after nine years in prison as a refusnik, he was allowed by the Russians to make the crossing from East to West Berlin, said, "I had to be careful that my pants did not slide down, as they did not give me a belt." Even so his face was wreathed with a smile as he crossed the border. Jesus faced an infinitely greater indignity in "crossing over" (the meaning of "Hebrew") from this world to the next. The joy of Sharansky in making it to freedom was a pale reflection of the joy Jesus felt at the prospect of his homecoming to heaven. His joy would be fulfilled in them on Easter evening. He greeted the women as they left the empty tomb on Easter morning with the word "Hail!" The expression in Matthew 28:9 means literally "Rejoice." Don't you know they did.

"I have given them thy word; and the world has hated them because they are not of the world, even as I am not of the world." Standing near the coffin of the deceased, I have heard on more than one occasion someone say, "Every one loved him." What an insult! If everyone loves you, it means you haven't stood for anything. Jesus had more enemies when he died than you could shake a stick at. "Beware when all speak well of you."

I was speaking in the skid row mission and had barely gotten started, when several men got up and stomped out saying some uncomplimentary things. Inwardly I rejoiced. In Seminary we were taught to speak about two things: about Jesus Christ and about 20 minutes. No souls are saved after 20 minutes, we were told. At the same mission a man responded to the message. When I asked him what was said that rang his bell, he answered, "About 5 minutes before you finished you said thus and so." I had preached for 45 minutes. Another cliche bites the dust. ❦

THE DIVINE CONTAGION

"**I** do not pray that thou shouldst take them out of the world, but that thou shouldst keep them from the evil one." *John 17:15*

Jesus' first request for the disciples was that the Father keep them in his name. One of the ways he does this is by disciplining us by means of our fiery trials. Through them we get our dross expurgated that we may come to share his holiness. Now Jesus' second request is that his Father keep them out of the grasp of the evil one, though not out of his realm - the world.

A missionary was asked if he enjoyed the mission field. He said, "Of course I don't enjoy it. I am not called to enjoy it, but to work in it." A young man told his pastor that he believed God was calling him into the gospel ministry. "What makes you think God is calling you into the ministry?" his pastor asked. "Because I like people so," he responded. To this his pastor retorted, "Yes, but do you like disagreeable people?" We are kept out of the grasp of the slanderer by allowing people to differ with us without rejecting them for it. Also we are called to give others the benefit of the doubt, and to bite our tongue rather than let it engage in idle gossip. Too many people have an overly developed sense of rumor.

"They are not of the world, even as I am not of the world." Having spent three years with Jesus, they could not feel at home in this world anymore. They had rubbed elbows with the divine too long for that. Christianity is the divine contagion. It is more easily caught than taught. We should not spend all of our time with other believers. Let us go out and sneeze in unbelievers' faces. It has been said, "You can lead a horse to water, but you can't make him drink." Someone said, "I can. I will force so much salt down his throat that he will get so thirsty that he will have to take a drink." As the salt of the earth, Christians have the function of making their neighbors thirsty for God.

❧

A KEY CHAPTER AND VERSE

"*Sanctify them in the truth; thy word is truth.*" *John 17:17*

This is Jesus' third request in behalf of his disciples. He asks God to set them apart for sacred use by allowing them to continue in the truth. He then identifies the Logos as the truth. The Logos is first himself, and then the Bible. What keeps the tree alive is the little edge of green under the bark. What keeps me alive is the food I eat, one bite at a time. I keep alive spiritually by the little bit of truth I gain day by day: a new insight here, a revelation there. Each one taken by itself doesn't amount to much, but accumulatively they add up to a great deal. "The sum of thy world is truth." Ps.119:160. Add together the information contained in the 66 books of the Bible and you have a word picture of the person and work of Jesus Christ. So we can say, "I get my kicks on route 66."

We have come to John 17:17 - a key chapter and verse. On the basis of the law of first mention, seventeen means deliverance out of tribulation. Gen. 7:11 tells that it was on the 17th day of the second month when the flood began. Then in Gen. 8:4, "In the seventh month, on the 17th day of the month the ark came to rest upon the mountains of Ararat." We must be delivered out of tribulation (symbolized by 17) to come into life. "Life" in the Hebrew is also the number 18. When I was 17 I could hardly wait until I was 18, which to me represented graduation from high school and becoming an adult.

Having said this, let us apply it to our verse. Do you want to be delivered out of your present tribulation and arrive into a larger, fuller life? Then continue in the word of truth, the message of the Bible. Not only will you grow in Christlikeness, which is sanctification, but also you will be kept out of sin. The Bible will keep you from sin, or sin will keep you from the Bible. I have never known a Christian worth his salt, who was not a student of scripture. Reading this book, you have become one.

❦

JESUS' PRAYER FOR YOU

"**A**s *thou didst send me into the world, so I have sent them into the world.*" *John 17:18*

Matthew 10 tells of Jesus sending the twelve apostles out on a mission into the world. Their message: The Kingdom of heaven is at hand. Their ministry: Heal the sick, raise the dead, cleanse lepers, cast out demons. Their ministry demonstrated the truth of their message. "And for their sake I consecrate myself, that they may be consecrated in truth." To what did Jesus consecrate himself, or set himself apart? To the perfect will of God for his life, which meant for him his dying upon the cross as the Lamb of God, slain from before the foundation of the world. The goal was that we might live as courageously and authentically as he. This means that time and again we must do the thing we dread, as Jesus did.

Hebrews 5:8 says, "Although he was a Son, he learned obedience through what he suffered." Question: Since Jesus was sinless, why did he have to learn obedience? Wasn't he by nature obedient? The answer is found in Phil. 1:8, "And being found in human form, he humbled himself and became obedient unto death, even death on a cross." Jesus was by nature obedient to God, who is life. To do an about-face and become obedient unto death, even the death of the damned, was something he had to learn. It did not come naturally. He had to school himself to come to the place where he could say "yes" to the cross. Are we schooling ourselves to take on the last enemy that is to be destroyed, death? We are if we are dying daily, saying, "Father, into your hands I surrender myself."

"I do not pray for these only, but also for those who believe in me through their word." That is you and me. What was his prayer for us? "That they may all be one." Are we able to reach out to Christians of other denominations, other traditions, and say, "Dear brother, dear sister, I accept you just as you are? God loves you and so do I." As a matter of fact, I can learn more from Christians of other persuasions than I can from those of my own background. I know what Presbyterians are going to say before they say it.

❦

241

BECOMING ONE IS NO SMALL ORDER

"That they all may be one; even as thou, Father, art in me, and I in thee, that they also may be in us, so that the world may believe that thou hast sent me." John 17:21

For 19 centuries the Church has been seeking to fulfill the Great Commission. It is estimated that there are currently one and a half billion Christians, so some success has been achieved in this matter. But in regard to the Great High Priestly Prayer, the Church has been largely delinquent. If we violently disagree with another Christian, we just up and move to another congregation. Instead of working through our difficulties, we prefer to avoid those who bring them to us.

We have learned that those whom we cannot tolerate are victims of the projections of the parts of ourselves which we cannot stand. What I cannot endure about you is what I hate about myself. C. S. Lewis in his book The Great Divorce depicts hell as a place where people move farther and farther into the suburbs, because they cannot abide their neighbors. It is nothing more than running away from reality. Accepting Christians who see life from another perspective is going the way of the cross. If you have the notion that other Christians are putty in your hands, you are going to be startled to find that there are thorns in the putty. It is possible to elevate our pain threshold by dying to self more and more. If we once died unto self with a great mortification, we would not be so irritated by all the hat-pin pricks that people give us.

A man went to the preacher to ask if there was a place where he could go when he died which would not be heaven, but still not be hell. When asked why he wanted to know, he looked at his wife, and said, "I can't stomach the notion of spending eternity with her." When we are with other Christians who rub us the wrong way, we should consider the possibility that God is using them to smooth off our rough edges. I fear we all still have them. After all, we aren't in heaven yet.

❧

A FAR FETCHED NOTION

"*The glory which thou hast given me I have given to them, that they may be one even as we are one." John 17:22*

What is that glory? Is it not the revelation of God's love! God's love is so immense that should we experience it all at once the weight of it would obliterate us. God's love on the other hand is the adhesive that keeps the universe from flying to pieces. It is the essence of that which Jesus came to make known. There is a centrifugal tendency in the universe. Heaven and earth are fleeing from the presence of God because of his holiness. It is the love of God that will succeed in reversing this activity. It is expressed most nobly in the parable of the Prodigal Son, who received a welcome home fit for a king.

"That they may be one even as we are one, I in them and thou in me, that they may become perfectly one, so that the world may know that thou hast sent me and hast loved them even as thou hast loved me." God wants the universe to know that he loves you just as much as he loves Jesus. Let there be a half-an-hour of silence for that to sink in. You say, "God doesn't love me as much as he loves Jesus. Jesus was sinless; I am sinful. Jesus helped people; I hurt people. Jesus never had an evil thought, but I don't want you peering into my thought life. I am basically prayerless, careless, Godless. How can God love me as much as he loves Jesus? An impossible possibility. It is the most farfetched notion I have ever contemplated!"

But wait a minute. If I reject this idea, I am calling God a liar. And God cannot lie. So I am stuck with it. God loves you and me with the same identical love with which he loves Jesus. I will admit that I have got to work on it. It will probably take me an aeon or two for it sink in, because I am a slow learner. I am thankful that "love is patient." Be patient with me, Lord. I have a lot to learn, and my head is hard. When someone calls me a nut, I am prepared to say, "thank God, at least I am tightened to the right bolt."

JESUS' FERVENT DESIRE

"*Father, I desire that they also, whom thou hast given me, may be with me where I am, to behold my glory which thou hast given me in thy love for me before the foundation of the world." John 17:24*

I heard Robert Frost recite his poem, "Good Fences Make Good Neighbors" while in Seminary. But I wonder if they really do. The heaven where God resides is fenced off, so to speak, from earth by the barrier of sin. We cannot see God and survive the experience because our flesh is too weak to bear up under it.

Jesus now expresses his most fervent desire for us. He yearns for us to behold him as he was before he descended into this fallen condition. In becoming man, he emptied himself of his divine appearance, taking off his robe of glory that he might don the garment of flesh. Nowhere in the Biblical narrative is mention made of his stature, the color of his eyes, or the shape of his nose. Why is that? St Paul writes: "Though we have known Christ according to the flesh, we do so no longer." II Cor. 5:16. His appearance as a man the apostles regarded as inconsequential. It would be interesting to see your baby pictures, but they bear no resemblance to how you are now. You are the same person, yet totally different. So the heavenly, glorified Christ is the very individual who walked upon the earth as the carpenter from Nazareth, only now he appears as he really is.

In Rev. 5:6 John writes, "I saw a Lamb (Jesus) standing, as though it had been slain (with the marks of slaughter), with seven horns (expressive of all-power), and with seven eyes (representing all-knowledge)." When he first saw him, (Rev. 1:17) he "fell at his feet as though dead." He could not endure his overwhelming presence. Jesus has prayed that we be privileged ultimately to see him as he actually is. When we do, it will be as though we are looking in a mirror, for we shall have been transformed into his likeness. What a glorious shock that will be!

❦

WHO IS RIGHT?

"**O** *righteous Father, the world has not known thee, but I have known thee; and these know that thou hast sent me." John 17:25*

God always acts in the right way. At the end of the age no one will say, "God, you did the wrong thing." We will all say, "God was right, and I was wrong." That is one of the things Jesus meant by saying, "O righteous Father." The world is identified as that portion of humanity which is ignorant of God. Some call themselves atheists, because they contest God's existence. "The fool says in his heart `There is no God.'" Psalm 14:1 Only the damn fool will say it with his lips. He is making public the fact that he has an evil unbelieving heart.

The agnostic declares that he does not know whether there is a God or not. The Latin word for agnostic is pronounced ignoramus. It is nothing to boast about. Agnostics and atheists have one thing in common: they never bow their heads to say thanks before eating. A little girl, witnessing this, said to her parents, "They are just like our puppy-dog. They dig right in, don't they?"

Believers have a reverent attitude toward life. Everything is so beautiful, so orderly. How did it get that way? Certainly not by chance. To assume that all we see around us occurred just by chance involves a staggering leap of faith, a leap dwarfing that of the believer. Unbelief in God is so astonishing that it must have, as the Bible makes clear, a supernaturally induced origin. In a word, it is the work of the father of lies, the devil. The life and teaching of Jesus makes even more reprehensible the posture of the world, which says, "My head may be bloodied, but unbowed. I am the master of my fate, I am the captain of my soul." All the while, we are so weak that we cannot even keep ourselves from dying. For God's sake and our own, let us at least be honest. Let us confess that we have missed the mark.

❦

TOO GOOD TO BE TRUE?

*"**I** have made known to them thy name, and I will make it known, that the love with which thou hast loved me may be in them, and I in them." John 17:26*

The greatest thought that will ever occupy your mind is that God is your Father. Do you know why he is? Because Jesus has included you in his last will and testament. This means that because of your faith in Jesus you are a member of the family of God. You can sing, "I have a heavenly Father, who hears and answers prayer." You are rich beyond imagining.

Some years ago in a Chicago newspaper two pages of names appeared for several days of those who had inherited unclaimed money which was accumulating in Chicago area banks. A man told a welfare recipient friend, "I found your name among those listed. You have inherited $5,000,000." The man said he did't know anyone who could have left him $5,000,000, and he refused to believe it. So his friend had the editor of the newspaper come and tell him he had inherited this vast fortune. He still refused to believe it. Finally his friend informed Mayor Daley, who came to the heir's house, picked him up in his own car and took him to the bank to claim the money. The mayor obliged him to repay Chicago all the money he had received in welfare checks. Thirty years before, he had helped the man who left him his entire estate.

A reporter researched all the banks in the Chicago area, and determined that the amount of unclaimed inheritance money could have paid off what was then the national debt. Are we not like this welfare recipient, living in poverty because we refuse to believe the immensity of our heavenly Father's love for us? Jesus must continually impress upon us the name of God as our Father, and the love he has for us which surpasses knowledge. In this world marred by broken hopes and piled high with dispair, it seems to us too good to be true. Let's believe our faith, and doubt our doubts.

❦

TALK ABOUT COURAGE!

"**W**hen Jesus had spoken these words, he went forth with his disciples across the Kidron valley, where there was a garden, which he and his disciples entered." *John 18:1*

"These words" in chapter 17 contained the full secret of a truly human life. They centered in the word "agape" (love), which means for us "always give a pardon everywhere" (seen as an acrostic). Since God in Christ has forgiven us, now we are obliged to pass the pardon on.

We have seen the seven themes in chapters 12 to 17. We shall see them again in chapters 18 to 20. Chapters 18 and 19 tell of Jesus' tribulation. Chapter 20 speaks of his triumph. All that occurs in chapters 18 and 19 in what is called the Passion Story happens on Friday, the sixth day of Holy Week. The sixth day in this gospel is the day of nurture. The narration of what Jesus endured on this day is used by the Holy Spirit to nourish the life of faith within us. Actually wherever the apostles went to proclaim the gospel, they began by telling the story of Jesus' sufferings. This was the two-by-four that got the listeners' attention - the injustice of it all. Why must an innocent man endure so much? Key question!

Chapter 18 takes us to a garden, reminding us of the garden of Eden where the Biblical narrative begins. On that occasion Adam failed to protect Eve from the beguiling serpent. On this occasion the last Adam defends his own ones from the devil's attack. The Passion Story in John is a streamlined expression of what took place. There are three main themes. First, Jesus is King. Second, the beginning of true faith. Third, the wickedness of unbelief. The story of what happened in Gethsemane (oil-press), when his sweat became as blood, is omitted. Every cell in his body screamed "no" to all that was about to happen, as the Holy Spirit was being pressed out of him. Yet he himself said "yes." Talk about courage!

NOT WHAT, BUT WHO

"*ow Judas, who betrayed him, also knew the place; for Jesus often met there with his disciples.*" John 18:2

As with the woman at the well, Jesus had an appointment with Judas and his entourage. Judas' knowledge here stated reminds us of the legendary apple that our first parents ate. Our moral awareness thereby expressed has gotten us into this vale of woe. Only by faith in Jesus are we delivered from our moral dilemma of knowing what should be done without having the power to do it. He not only pardons us, but also empowers us.

"So Judas, procuring a band of soldiers and some officers from the chief priests and Pharisees, went there with lanterns and torches and weapons." The soldiers came from the Roman world, the officers from the religious realm. Both the secular and the sacred were arrayed against Jesus, as today. The secularists hate him, because his emphasis on the vertical dimension exposes their superficiality. The religionists decry him, because they are persuaded that they are rightly related to God without him. Their approach with so many lanterns and torches expresses the fact that they are content to live in the light of nature, which they already enjoy. They can do without the light of revelation which Jesus brings from heaven. Furthermore they think that they are going to have to search for him, and drag him out of some hiding place. The many weapons reveal their hope that there will be a skirmish. They are prepared to elmininate Jesus and his followers. Then the matter will be settled once and for all.

"Then Jesus, knowing all that was to befall him, came forward and said to them, `Whom do you seek?' His first word was `What do you seek?' More important than `what' is `whom.' Science is able to go no farther than `what?' But behind the `what', says the Bible, looms the `whom.' Ultimately it is not what you know, but who.

REVERENCE FOR LIFE

"*They answered him, 'Jesus of Nazareth.'*" *John 18:5*

Jesus had displayed supernatural courage. Here they came, armed to the teeth, licking for a fight. They anticipated that they would find him cowering in some dark corner, when suddenly out of nowhere he appears and challenges them with the question, "Whom do you seek?" They, the shock troops, were about to get the shock of their lives. They heard themselves say, "Jesus of Nazareth." We are seeking a carpenter turned preacher from the non-descript town of Nazareth in the north. On the basis of what follows, we may know they were lying.

Early in this century Albert Schweitzer wrote a momentous book entitled <u>In Quest of the Historical Jesus</u>. He theorized that it is impossible to find the Jesus of history by seeking him in the four gospels, because they are embellished by the Christ of faith. He pretended that the Christ of faith and Jesus of Nazareth are totally different individuals. His philosophy was "reverence for life." This attitude made him so over-scrupulous that he was cautious about killing an insect. Our ethics professor at Seminary had a more balanced position, expressed in the statement, "It is perfectly alright to kill a fly, just so you don't kill him as though you were God Almighty." The Bible does not hold reverence for life as an ultimate, but reverence for personalilty.

Those who came to arrest Jesus had such a reverent awe for who he was that they were scared spitless when they found him suddenly confronting them. They were seeking God. And in the depths of themselves they knew it. Jesus said to them, "I am he." In the Greek text the "he" is missing. So in reality Jesus said, in effect, "I am the Eternal One." God has planted the desire for eternity within the heart of man. That desire finds satisfaction in coming to Jesus. "Draw near to God, and he will draw near to you."

SOMETHING GOOD TO KNOW

"Judas, who betrayed him, was standing with them." John 18:5

Faith in this gospel is defined as motion toward Jesus. Here Judas' motion toward Jesus has long since ceased. He is now standing with the enemies of Jesus. It is as though he were paralyzed. His name has gone down in history as the original Aaron Burr, the father of all traitors. Having walked in the counsel of the wicked, he is now standing in the way of sinners. He has become like chaff which the wind drives away. This is our last look at him.

"When he said to them, `I am he,' they drew back and fell to the ground," demonstrating that they were lying when they claimed they sought only a man named Jesus. Instead of pouncing upon him, they fell over one another in their panic to get out of there. At this point we are ready for a little comic relief. It is better to laugh rather than cry. In spite of themselves they assume the posture of utmost reverence and worship; they prostrate themselves before him. When Abraham Lincoln was near desperation during the tragic years of the Civil War, on more than one occasion he prostrated himself before God, as there was no place else to go.

"Again he asked them, `Whom do you seek?'" giving them another opportunity to tell the truth. But again they lied, `Jesus of Nazareth,' sounding like a broken record. Their action spoke louder than their words. Even so, they were stuck in their lying, as though it were quicksand. "Jesus answered them, `I told you that I am he; so if you seek me, let these men go.' This was to fulfill the word which he had spoken, `Of those whom thou gavest me I lost not one.'" The Good Shepherd allows the wolf to take him by the throat, that the sheep might be scattered but spared. He, as Lord of the situation, is now giving orders to the pawns of the enemy, and they obey him. When the chips are down, it is good to know who is really in charge.

❦

THE KING OF HEARTS

"*Then Simon Peter, having a sword, drew it and struck the high priest's slave and cut off his right ear.*"   *John 18:10*

Don't just stand there, Peter, do something, even if it is the wrong thing. So it is Peter like John Wayne to the rescue. Remember how Jesus counseled his disciples at the last supper that the time had come for them to sell their mantle to buy a sword. He was told they already had two swords, to which he responded, "It is enough." For he had to be numbered among transgressors, as prophecied in Isaiah 53:12. He had to have in his number a man of violence, who would swing his sword in reckless abandon, in flagrant disregard of all law and order.

It turns out that the victim of Peter's attack was a slave named Malchus. This bit of information happens to be the key to the whole episode. Malchus is the Latin form of the Hebrew melek, which means king. The question thereby raised is this: who is the king in this situation? Is it the slave of the high priest, who is the devil's agent? No, the King is Jesus, who is the King of Malchus, the King of kings, wherever they may be. The root meaning of melek is "the one who is able." Jesus, as we know from Luke 22:51, "touched his ear and healed him." He alone was able to meet the urgent need of Malchus and of the situation. He surely saved the life of Peter, who was in danger of immediate decapitation. He had lost his head in trying to decapitate Malchus. Thank God he missed or Jesus would have had to replace several heads and not just the right ear of the slave of sin.

We are called upon to use the sword of the Spirit, even the word of God, to prick the hearts of God's enemies. We are not called to deprive them of the organ by which faith comes - the ear that hears. "Faith comes through hearing, and hearing through the word of God." Romans 10:17 Let us express the gospel whenever the opportunity presents itself. Go for their hearts, not their ears.

❧

THE BITTER CUP

"Jesus said to Peter, 'Put your sword into its sheath, shall I not drink the cup which the Father has given me?'"
John 18:11

As recorded in the synoptic gospels, Jesus had prayed, "Let this cup pass away from me. Nevertheless, not my will, but thine be done." It was obviously not the Father's will, so Jesus would accept the bitter cup of divine displeasure and drain it to the dregs. In drawing his sword, Peter had done what came naturally to him. But doing what comes naturally does not advance the Kingdom, only what comes supernaturally does. The law of the sword belongs to the nations for the attaining of their ends. It is the law of love that operates in God's kingdom. Any action not motivated by love is out of step with the divine activity. The end never justifies the means. Pollute the stream feeding the lake, and the lake is also eventually polluted.

"So the band of soldiers and their captain and the officers of the Jews seized Jesus and bound him." It appears that together they pounced upon him, that they might overcome him by the force of their numbers. "One will put a thousand to flight, two ten thousand." If that holds true of genuine believers, how much more of the Son of God. They were obviously terrifed of him. He who had the power to raise the dead effortlessly with a word, would be able even more effortlessly to blast them into kingdom come should he so desire. He was the Eternal I Am, and they somehow knew it.

The last parable Jesus taught as recorded in Mark 12:1-11 indicates that his enemies rejected him not because they did not know who he was, but because they knew exactly who he was: "This is the heir; come, let us kill him, and the inheritance will be ours." When Jesus prayed, "Father forgive them, for they know not what they do," he was obviously referring to the Roman soldiers, not the Jewish leaders. Is it possible that some of them know to this day?

❦

252

A JUDICIAL MURDER

"*First they led him to Annas; for he was the father-in-law of Caiaphas, who was high priest that year.*" John 18:13

They led him; they didn't have to drag him. "Like a lamb that is led to the slaughter," we read of him in Isaiah 53:7. My first job as a sixteen year old was in a meat packing plant in Omaha. The pigs go to their death screaming bloody murder. A farmer told me that the pig is the smartest animal in the barnyard. They fear their approaching demise. The sheep-kill is a totally different scene. The "Judas goat" leads them from the stockyard to the packing house, where they are strung from the low ceiling by a rear leg. With scarcely a sound coming from them, their throats are cut that they might bleed to death. An Omaha barber told me that as a young person he saw the sheep-kill. He could never eat lamb again. He thought of sheep as innocent babies being slaughtered.

Why did they lead him to Annas? He had been the high priest years before, but had been deposed by the Romans for his unprincipled behaviour. The money changing and selling of sheep, oxen, pigeons and doves in the temple was from stalls called the bazaars of Annas. He and his family were getting as rich as the mafia as the result. No wonder he hated Jesus so.

Jesus' first and last public deeds had been the attacking of Annas' money-making operation. So Annas was the power behind the throne. He was the godfather, so to speak, who had master-minded the arrest and all that followed. What was about to transpire before Caiaphas and the ruling council was merely window dressing. The issue of Jesus' guilt or innocence had already been decided. Jesus would be the victim of judicial murder, in fulfillment of Isaiah 53:8, "By an oppressive judgment he was taken away" (killed). It had actually been decreed before the foundation of the world that he would die as the Lamb of God.

❦

NOT YET A DISCIPLE?

"**J**t *was Caiaphas who had given counsel to the Jews that it was expedient that one man should die for the people.*" *John 18:14*

Like father-in-law, like son-in-law: two totally unprincipled men. The spiritual leadership of the Jewish nation had sunk to a new low. So Psalm 119:126 comes into view, "It is time for the LORD to act, for thy law has been broken." When things get so bad that they cannot get any worse, look for divine intervention. This is most enouraging at the present time in view of things like the AID's epidemic, the drug-related violence in our schools and on our streets, etc. ad nauseum. Our verse reminds us again of Jesus' substitutionary death, which is about to take place.

"Simon Peter followed Jesus, and so did another disciple (even John our evangelist). As this disciple was known to the high priest (tradition says he provided fish to the high priest's household), he entered the court of the high priest along with Jesus, while Peter stood outside at the door. Peter had followed the LORD from a distance." "The LORD is our shield." Allow too much distance to intrude between you and your shield, and it cannot ward off the fiery darts of the enemy, as Peter is about to discover to his sorrow.

"So the other disciple, who was known to the high priest, went out and spoke to the maid who kept the door, and brought Peter in. (Peter is now in a precarious place, as are we all. "Let him who thinks he stands take heed lest he fall.") The maid who kept the door said to Peter, `Are you also one of his disciples?' (A harmless enough question.) He said, `I am not.'" Why did he say that? He was taken by surprise, and was instinctively ashamed of Jesus. After all, Jesus was regarded by many as a criminal, aiding and abetting the Romans. Was Peter a disciple? By his own admission, he was not. After more than three years with Jesus, not yet a disciple? He is on the road to becoming one.

A KANGAROO COURT

"*𝕹ow the servants and officers had made a charcoal fire, because it was cold, and they were standing and warming themselves; Peter also was with them, standing and warming himself.*" *John 18:18*

Birds of a feather flock together. Watch out, Peter. You have already disowned Jesus once. Two more strikes, and you are out.

"The high priest then questioned Jesus about his disciples and his teaching." Annas was interested first of all in his disciples. Without disciples to carry on Jesus' ministry, his teaching would die on the vine. True disciples convey to others what they have been taught. If they fail to do so, they are so many dead seas. "Jesus answered him, `I have spoken openly to the world; I have said nothing secretly.'" Notice that Jesus says not a word about his disciples. Instead he goes immediately to the matter of his teaching. He instinctively protects his disciples, drawing the attention instead to himself and his teaching, like the female bird that distracts the predators from her young by flourishing herself before their eyes.

"Why do you ask me? Ask those who have heard me what I said to them; they know what I said." Jesus refused to dignify this illegal procedure with an answer. He expressed his disdain of Annas and all that he stood for. How outrageous of Annas to interrogate the defendent in an attempt to have him bear witness against himself, in defiance of Jewish legal procedure. "When he had said this, one of the officers standing by struck Jesus with his hand, saying, `Is that how you answer the high priest?'" This was the first of many blows that Jesus would receive. The officer believed it was his role to defend the dignity of Annas. That Annas would allow Jesus to be struck in this way demonstrates that what transpired here was a kangaroo court. It looked like a fraternity hazing gone berserk. A frightening beginning to the longest day.

❦

THE KING AND THE COWARD

"**J**esus answered him, 'If I have spoken wrongly, bear witness to the wrong; but if I have spoken rightly, why do you strike me?'"

John 18:23

The officer did not answer, but he took that question with him to his grave. "Why did you strike me?" Jesus asks you and me. What is the source of that anger within you that would cause you to lash out at the Innocent One who only spoke the truth? The truth evidently angers us because it hurts. The truth always hurts. Quite possibly Jesus' question brought him to his knees. If we will not bend before God, we will break. Possibly he is the source of information as to what occurred before Annas, or could John have been there himself? "Annas then sent him bound to Caiaphas the high priest." Jesus had conducted himself as King before Annas. He had spoken the truth in love. Until we are free like Jesus in our inner, we cannot be a winner. Though bound externally, he was the only free one there.

Meanwhile down in the courtyard, "Simon Peter was standing and warming himself. They said to him, 'Are you not also one of his disciples?' He denied it and said, 'I am not.'"

What motivated this second denial? He was concerned lest he be pushed away from the fire. He might lose out on his creaturely comfort if he stood up for Jesus. Might not we all? Jesus had confessed twice at his arrest, "I am." Now for the second time Peter had affirmed, "I am not." Denying Jesus, Peter had cut the ground from beneath his feet. He had lost his foundation and is experiencing anomy, free fall. Unrooted in reality, he is on his way to disaster. By his own admission again he is not yet a disciple. But he is on his way to becoming one. After losing all confidence in himself, in his own strength and ability, he will put himself in the place where he can trust in Jesus, who had foreseen his tragic failure. After all, Jesus can only use failures, who will admit they are failures.

❦

256

THE STONE WITH A BROKEN HEART

"*One of the servants of the high priest, a kinsman of the man whose ear Peter had cut off, asked, 'Did I not see you in the garden with him?'" John 18:26*

The word "servants" is actually slaves. The high priest had slaves. Religion makes people slaves of the system to which they hold. Jesus sets his devotees free. If I would ascertain how far I have come in the kingdom of God, I should ask myself how free I am to be my best self, to be uniquely me. "Peter again denied it; and at once the cock crowed."

Why this third denial? This time it was craven fear. Should Peter confess, "I am the man," he would endanger his life. The kinsman would likely retaliate against him with the sword. "He who takes the sword will perish by the sword," said Jesus. Now it is evident that Peter had merely lost his temper in the garden. He had gotten hot under the collar, but he had by now cooled off and seen the danger of his situation. In a foolhardy way, he had strayed into the enemy camp. Now he felt obliged to extricate himself, in one piece, if possible. The law of self-preservation had come into play. He had eaten crow, swallowed his pride, and lost his integrity in one fell swoop.

Just then "the cock crowed." He went out and wept bitterly. Actually he is in the process of new birth. He ejected himself from the courtyard that was no longer congenial, just as the baby ejects from the womb, crying. As a horse cannot be ridden until it is broken, so a man (male or female) cannot be used by God until he or she is broken. The stone of India is the opal. The reason the opal flashes fire is because it is the stone with a broken heart. Simon is about to become Peter, the stone with the broken heart. And he will flash fire come the day of Pentecost. The denials of Peter are an essential part of the gospel. They warn us of how easy it is for us to disown the Lord. Possibly in little ways we do so every day.

HARDBALL

"**T**hen they led Jesus from the house of Caiaphas to the praetorium." John 18:28

The praetorium referred originally to the general's tent. It came to mean the palacial residence of the Roman governor. "It was early." This expression "early" was used in regard to the fourth watch of the night, from about 3 to 6 a.m. Since Jesus was sentenced to the cross at the sixth hour (Roman reckoning), which would be six in the morning, it was doubtless about three in the morning when Jesus was led to the dwelling of Pontius Pilate.

"They themselves did not enter the praetorium, so that they might not be defiled, but might eat the passover." Straining out the gnats, but swallowing the camels, they were meticulous about the little details of their religion, but blind as bats when it came to the major matters of love and justice. It was essential that they partake of their passover feast after sundown that Good Friday evening. In their zeal to do so, they would dispose of the true Lamb of God as quickly as possible, at the same time not contaminating themselves by entering a heathen household.

"So Pilate went out to them and said, `What accusation do you bring against this man?'" The Roman law required that a specific charge be brought against the defendent. "They answered him, `If this man were not an evildoer, we would not have handed him over.'" Astonishingly they did not specify a crime, but put forth a platitude. They endeavored to stonewall Pilate. It reminds us of a pitcher who would throw a beanball at the batter to brush him away from the plate. Take our word for it, Governor, this fellow is a bad egg. We expect you to dispose of him without further ado. "Pilate said to them, `Take him yourselves and judge him by your own law.'" Look, guys, I can play hardball too. If you won't play according to Roman rules, deal with him in your own ballpark.

❧

CAPITAL PUNISHMENT, RIGHT OR WRONG?

*"**T**he Jews said to him, `It is not lawful for us to put any man to death.'" John 18:31*

Where in their Old Testament did it say such a thing? Quite the contrary, capital punishment is mandated on countless occasions. For example, Leviticus 24:16,17 says: "He who blasphemes the name of the LORD shall be put to death; all the congregation shall stone him; the sojourner as well as the native, when he blasphemes the Name, shall be put to death. He who kills a man shall be put to death." Those who fight against capital punishment are not standing on Biblical ground, though in many instances they pretend to do so.

Why then did the Jews say such a thing? The answer is found in verse 32: "This was to fulfill the word which Jesus had spoken to show by what death he was to die." He was not to die the Jewish way, by stoning. He was to die the Roman way, by crucifixion. He had to be lifted up, made prominent, that he might draw all humanity to himself. The Jewish rulers were very cunning just like their god, the ancient serpent, who "was more subtle than any other wild creature that the LORD God had made." Genesis 3:1

The Romans had taken from them the right to execute criminals, allowing that privilege to themselves alone. In saying, "It is not lawful for us to put any man to death," they presented themselves to Pilate as law abiding citizens of Roman rule. They were hypocrites to the core, despising the Roman yoke, seeking to throw it off. When it suited their purpose, they snuffed out people's lives without a quibble. They would have stoned the adulterous woman had not Jesus prevented them from doing so. They actually did stone Stephen to death without seeking Roman permission. Acts 7:58. No, they contrived that the Romans crucify Jesus to prove that Jesus was not Messiah. God would never allow his Son to die the death of the damned they reasoned. Little did they know the depth of the divine love.

❧

WRONG QUESTION

"**P**ilate entered the praetorium again and called Jesus, and said to him, `Are you the king of the Jews?'" John 18:33

Already we have encountered the three main intertwining themes. Here again the question is raised concerning Jesus' kingship. We have seen in the story of Peter's denials the breakdown of human faith. The grain of wheat had to die, the egocentricity broken, that God's kind of faith might emerge on the third day. The wickedness of Jewish unbelief has come out in the fact that, "It is not lawful for us to put any (innocent) man to death." The upholders of the Law of Moses are in the midst of breaking the sixth commandment: "You shall not kill." Deut. 5:17. They are overseeing the murder of the one innocent man who ever lived. Outwardly they appear righteous, but within they are villains. Their disbelief in Jesus has gotten them into the most wicked deed ever to defile the earth.

It is the story of Cain and Abel all over again. Cain rose up and slew his brother, because his brother's offering to God was accepted and his was not. "Without the shedding of blood there is no forgiveness of sins." The shedding of Jesus' innocent blood was about to atone for the sins of the world. Through faith in Jesus' self-sacrifice, we are at one with God our Father.

"Well, Jesus, are you the king of the Jews? Yes, or no?" "Jesus answered, `Do you say this of your own accord, or did others say it to you about me?'" In other words, "What's it to you? Does it really make any difference whether I am or not? The important thing for you to determine, Pilate, is whether or not I am your king. It is for the Jews to decide whether or not I am their king. That is their problem, not yours." It reminds us of Jesus' mother saying to him, "They have no wine." To which Jesus answered in effect, "Wrong observation. Do you have wine?" (and all it signifies.)

A MORTICIAN'S NIGHTMARE

"**P**ilate answered, `Am I a Jew? Your own nation and the chief priests have handed you over to me; what have you done?'"

John 18:35

Pilate is about to discover that Jesus is "the tar baby." As a matter of fact, he is everyone's tar baby . Once I encounter him, or even hear of him, I am stuck with the question of who he is. He never goes away. He becomes "the hound of heaven," pursuing me down the corridors of time. "Am I a Jew, a member of this despicable race? What a disgusting thought! It is no personal concern of mine as to whether or not you are king. Don't think you can get me involved in this. I can see a hurricane brewing here. I am going to fly above it or around it. Be sure of that. I have just one question. What have you done to turn your own people and their leaders against you?" Jesus might have said, "I raised a man four days dead to life again."

A mortician dreamed that he and his assistant were looking at a corpse reposing peacefully in a casket, when suddenly it sat up. He and his companion immediately wrestled with it, trying to get it to lie down and close its eyes. The church may be likened to this corpse. All is well, until it starts to sit up to climb out of the coffin. Then all hell breaks loose.

Early in his ministry, Billy Graham was filling the high box-like pulpit in a church with arm-waving enthusiasm. A little boy in the last pew looked up with fear-filled eyes and said, "But, Daddy, what will we do if he gets loose?" What, indeed, will the clergy do, what will the world do, if the dead, lukewarm church should suddenly come alive and sit up like Gulliver among the Lilliputians? There will be heart attacks, nervous breakdowns, and strokes all over the landscape. Jesus raised up Lazarus. We can hardly wait for him to raise up his victorious Church. Let us pray to God that we will be a part of it. We can be, if we will settle for nothing less than his perfect will.

❧

OUR GREATEST NEED

"**J**esus answered, 'My kingship is not of this world; if my kingship were of this world, my servants would fight, that I might not be handed over to the Jews; but my kingship is not from the world.'"

John 18:36

The "evil" that Jesus had done was to bring the kingship of heaven to earth. That is the one thing humanity cannot tolerate, because it would overthrow the thralldom to Satan. Our first parents were given dominion over the earth. Then they believed the devil's lie, and disbelieved God, who said that in the day they ate the forbidden fruit, dying they would die. Sure enough, the Holy Spirit left them. They had been clothed in the glory of God. Suddenly they were naked, bereft of their former innocence.

They had to cover up. Having committed high treason in the garden of Eden, they allowed the ancient serpent to gain jurisdiction. The accuser of the brethren became the god of this world. He is the spirit that is now at work in the sons of disobedience. God said to the serpent, "I will put enmity between you and the woman, and between your seed and the woman's seed." Here is prophecied the virgin birth, as the woman has by nature an egg, not a seed. Also God foretold that the Saviour would be a male, who would deal the devil a mortal head wound, and deprive him of his crown.

"If our greatest need had been information, God would have sent us an educator. If it had been technology, he would have sent us a scientist. Had it been money, he would have sent an economist. If our great need had been pleasure, God would have sent us an entertainer. But our greatest need was forgiveness, so God sent us a Savior." But we must accept him. Jesus is the net that catches those falling toward hell. Only those who willfully stear clear of him will spend eternity with the god of this world in hell. It was never fashioned for humans, but for the devil and his angels. Matthew 25:41

❦

A BOOK FIT FOR A KING

"**P**ilate said to him, 'So you are a king?'" John 18:37

Pilate regarded Jesus as a man of mystery. He was trying to put him into some slot, to categorize him. But Jesus cannot be fit into any cubby hole. What is true of Jesus is true as well of the Book about him.

Dr. Derek Prince was Professor of Philosophy at Cambridge University prior to World War II. When he went to war, he took a Bible along that he might "acquaint himself with this literature." As a logician, he found the Bible an exeedingly difficult book to comprehend. After nine months, he made it only as far as Job. The Bible defied his ambition. Try as he might he could not fit it into any of his categories. It is like no other literature. To the serious student it demonstrates itself to be divinely inspired. The work of many hands, it enjoys a continuity from Genesis to Revelation. Were it merely the composition of mortals it would be filled with contradictions. But not so. There is a development from beginning to end of every conceivable subject without contradiction. It is the record of a divinely guided history, culminating ultimately in the return of Jesus as King of kings and Lord of lords. Yet as Jesus was human, so the Bible has a humanity about it.

When I was a college student, I visited with a clergyman who sought to undermine my confidence in the Biblical narrative. He told me that in a Psalm God instructed his people to dash their enemies' babies against the rocks. (God did not.) He asked, "How could that be an inspired word of God?" I didn't have an answer. The Canaanites, though, were so evil that they could be regarded as a cancerous tumor that had to be excised in order that God's people might survive. Abe Lincoln said to the artist painting his portrait, "Paint me warts and all." The Bible does. Every one but Jesus is found to be tainted with sin.

❦

WHAT IS TRUTH?

"**J**esus *answered, 'You say that I am a king.'"* John 18:37

Jesus knows who he is. The question is, does Pilate? A man is satisfied by the words of his mouth. It is not what Jesus says but what Pilate says that will determine his destiny. "The purpose in a man's mind is like deep water, but a man of understanding will draw it out." Proverbs 20:5 Jesus is truly the man of understanding. He is capable of drawing out of us all that resides within the depths of ourselves, that we may actualize our potential. In saying that Jesus is a king, Pilate is on the right track, but will he proceed down that track? It is not he who starts the race, but he who finishes who wins the prize.

"For this I was born, and for this I have come into the world, to bear witness to the truth." At his birth Jesus came into the world from the heavenly realm. In our birth, we had our origin. Some pretend that souls are prexistent, waiting to be born (the Mormons). Others maintain that we come many times to earth as insects, animals, humans, to work out our salvation enroute to divinity (Hindu reincarnation). The Biblical teaching is that Jesus is the only preexistant One, and that he came as a witness to the truth. "Every one who is of the truth hears my voice." Pilate said to him, "What is truth?"

Before Pilate's day the philosophers spent much of their time trying to ascertain the truth. Pilate lost interest in Jesus just then. To him "the truth" was a head-trip. He was too practical a man to bother himself with such discussions. A woman was driving a car that had a personalized license plate bearing the word "CYNIC." Another license plate says, "PHOOEY." Still another, "KO USSR." The individuals driving are of the same stripe as Pilate - hard headed realists. Or is their reality falsehood? When I saw a plate saying, "PSALM 4," I read the psalm and was blessed.

❧

BUT HE MEANT WELL

"**A**fter *he had said this, he went out to the Jews again, and told them, 'I find no crime in him.'* " John 18:38

To Pilate, "What is truth?" was merely a rhetorical question. He didn't wait for an answer, but turned on his heel to proclaim the innocence of Jesus. If there was literally no crime whatsoever in Jesus then he himself is the truth. The truth is not a "what" but a "who" - a person. The Christian faith is basically simple. All we need do is stay in contact with Jesus. He is able to conduct us through this vale of tears into the place where we most want to be. He can guide us through the heresies which abound. We have a way of wandering into the wilderness, but we don't have to stay there or die there.

"But you have a custom that I should release one man for you at the Passover; will you have me release for you the king of the Jews?" Pilate was an atheist. He had no interest in philosophical or religious matters. Even so he was not all bad. There is goodness in the worst of us.

After the fall, Eve credited God with the privilege of motherhood, calling her first-born "Cain", "gotten" with the help of the Lord. The Bible does not teach total depravity. There is goodness and evil within us all. "Good" in the Hebrew means having potential. Hitler and Stalin had the potential of responding to God, had they the desire of doing so. The Geresene demoniac could turn to Jesus. If he could, anyone can. Pilate meant well in seeking an out to release Jesus. He possibly thought it a touch of genius to give the Jews an alternative arrangement. Jesus or Barabbas? Surely they would call for the release of the innocent. We have heard the expression "the road to hell is paved with good intentions." It is not necessarily so, because God looks at the thoughts and intentions of the heart. If we meant well, we may find that our good intentions are recorded to our credit.

❧

JESUS OR BARABBAS?

*"**T**hey cried out, 'Not this man, but Barabbas!'"*

John 18:40

In the original Greek text the word "man" does not occur. We are reminded of the passage in Psalm 22:6, "But I am a worm, and no man; scorned by men, and dispised by the people." Jesus here was demeaned in the extreme. Far from hailing him as their king the Jews hardly regarded him as a man. They treated him as though he were a thing, an it.

"Now Barabbas was a robber." People frequently say, "I was robbed," when they mean, "My house was burglerized." A robber is someone who holds you up for all that is on you. He threatens your very life. The story is told of a robber who stepped out of the shadows, and held a gun to a man's head, saying, "Give me your money, or I'll blow your brains out!" To which the victim retorted, "Shoot! I can live without brains, but I've got to have money."

Barabbas was a "give me" guy. Today he would be called a terrorist. He sought to rid his nation of the Roman army through violence. He would feel right at home in the Middle East today, torn by strife. He had actually committed murder in the insurrection. The astonishing thing is that the people in Jesus' day would rather have an impenitent murderer walking their streets than the One who gives life. Here we have a forecast of the future. Before the end of the age, the Jews will be given again a choice. They will be privileged to decide whether they want Jesus their Messiah to rule over them or the one whom Barabbas prefigures - Mr. 666, the antichrist. Barabbas means literally "son of a father." He was a son of his father, the devil, and he did what he saw his father doing - lying, robbing, murdering. "I have set before you this day life or death," said the Lord. Which will it be? If you allow Jesus to rule over you, you accept life. If you go with Barabbas, you have opted for disaster and death. Jesus, be my Lord, my life today.

ALL OR NOTHING AT ALL

*"**T**hen Pilate took Jesus and scourged him." John 19:1*

Since the Jews refused to take Jesus as their king, Pilate was obliged to take him as a criminal. We are all in this dual position. If we reject Jesus as our King, we must treat him as a criminal. Once we have learned of him, we are obliged to decide. He is either king or criminal. If he is not the Son of God as he claimed to be, he is the perpetrator of the greatest hoax ever foisted upon mankind. The rich young ruler came to him, and said, "Good teacher." Jesus stopped him in his tracks, and said, "Why do you call me good? Only one is good, and that is God." In other words, don't call me good, unless you are willing to call me God. If Jesus be not God, he is the most evil man who ever lived, and the biggest fraud. Today some Jews are claiming Jesus to be one of their greatest rabbis. But Jesus rejects this designation. With him it is all or nothing at all.

It says, "Pilate took Jesus and scourged him," as though he did it himself. Actually he had him scourged. Even so, it was as though Pilate did it himself. If I reject Jesus as my King, I am as responsible as Pilate for what Jesus went through.

The Roman scourging was called the half-way death. Each leather thong was loaded with sharp bits of metal or jagged bone. The back of the scourged one was laid open by the blows. The victim would pass out from the pain, go stark raving mad, or on occasion die. It was a day in which sophisticated culture and barbarity went hand in hand, much as at the present time. Homosexuality was rife along with ruthlessness just as it is now. Sixteen of the first seventeen Roman emperors practiced homosexuality. This knocks in the head the notion that it is a biologically inherited condition. It is, on the contrary, a sign that one is existing under the wrath of God. You can't call it living.

❧

THE RECIPIENT OF THE CURSE

"*And the soldiers plaited a crown of thorns, and put it on his head, and arrayed him in a purple robe.*" *John 19:2*

Because Adam listened to the voice of his wife instead of to God, and ate the forbidden fruit, he was sentenced to eek out his existence upon cursed ground that brought forth thorns and thistles. Now Jesus, as the last Adam, the universal man, is bearing the consequences of nature's curse. He is crowned with thorns. One source of purple dye is thistle, which he takes upon himself in the form of the robe. God has consigned the fallen race to live in an environment that is inhospitable.

We can pursue happiness, but find it diabolically ellusive. Lord Bertrand Russell wrote a book entitled The Conquest of Happiness. Would that it were possible. Faust, in the very act of satisfying his desire with Gretchen, says, "I die of desire." We are never satisfied. Accumulate a million dollars, only to discover it is not enough. One must then have two million. Money is like sea water. The more one drinks, the thirstier one gets. This is the nature of the world in which we live by divine design.

"They came up to him, saying, `Hail, King of the Jews!' and struck him with their hands." This brutal horseplay enabled the Roman soldiers, some of whom were Syrian, to get their anger toward the Jews out of their system. An American citizen told of a Syrian cab driver taking him from Syria to Amman, Jordan. The driver pulled over when Israel came into view and spent a minute in silence. When asked what he was doing, he said, "I always stop here to observe a minute of hatred when I look out over Israel." Talk about perfect hatred! Jesus was the recipient of all of humanity's anger and hatred directed against God. Simultaneously he experienced God's holy reaction toward sin. Jesus bore the curse of the law for you and me. Because of the cross, we may be blessed by God.

❦

BEHOLD THE MAN!

"**𝔓**ilate *went out again, and said to them 'See, I am bringing him out to you, that you may know I find no crime in him.'*" *John 19:4*

For the second time Pilate as the judge declares Jesus' innocence. If he considered Jesus guiltless, why did he have him treated with such brutality? He hoped in this way to save Jesus from the cross. Surely, he felt, when they see Jesus in his blood drenched garment, they will say, "Enough! He has suffered enough. Let him go." This he surmised.

"So Jesus came out, wearing the crown of thorns and the purple robe. Pilate said to them, 'Behold the man.'" Look carefully at him. This is the beginning of Biblical anthropology. If you want to get an idea of true humanity, don't look to Adam and Eve, the procreators of the fallen race. Look to Jesus. He is the beginning of the new race of mankind. At the same time he discloses suffering without lament or complaint, and also the wickedness of this evil age that hates him so. The mask is ripped from the face of "mankind." Man is basically "unkind." Little boys pull the wings off of flies without being taught. Little girls stick out their tongues at children less fortunate than they.

How did we get this mean streak? "In sin did my mother conceive me," confessed David. We did not have to be taught to do wrong. We came by it doing what comes naturally. Our problem is not that we sin. Our problem is that we are sinners. Before we misbehaved, we were misbegotten. We do not need a higher ethic. We need a new and higher nature. This is imparted to us when we behold, and continue beholding, the man Christ Jesus. We become like the God we serve. Follow after bubbles, and bubbles (hollow people) we become. Follow after Jesus, and we become like him. Actually we are being transformed from one degree of glory into another, as we look to Jesus, the Author and Finisher of our faith. Praise God!

❧

CRUCIFY HIM

"*When the chief priests and the officers saw him, they cried out.*" *John 19:6*

Pilate anticipated that they would cry out, "Have mercy upon him." He could hardly believe his ears when he heard them shout in unison, "Crucify him, crucify him!" It seemed to him incredible. He could not comprehend such hatred for one of their own. The Jews had a reputation for standing behind their own. Blood is thicker than water, especially when it is Jewish blood.

As a young minister I had the opportunity of addressing the congregation of Temple Beth Am (House of the People) in Lakewood, N.J. on Brotherhood Sabbath. I taught on the subject *What Jews and Christians Can Teach Each Other*. Among the things the Jews can teach us is the sacredness of family life. What we can teach them is that Jesus is their Messiah. The next day I phoned Rabbi Leonard Zion, who told me that as the result of my message he had a better understanding of his congregation. He said that there were two diverse reactions to what I had said. "The hearts of some were warmed, whereas others said, `What is he trying to do, convert us?'" I am not sure which response was the more appropriate. Probably the latter. We do not do our Jewish neighbors a favor by simply congratulating them for their strengths, or for the fact that they have survived as a people. In a sensative and gracious way, we must tell them that their religion is on the wrong track, because it persists in the rejection of Jesus, and does not repudiate the hatred of those who cried, "Crucify him." They must be told to repent and turn to Jesus while there is yet time.

Esther, a rabbi's daughter, became a Christian through learning at the age of 13 that Jesus is the Suffering Servant of Isaiah 53. As a Christian she went from door to door bearing witness to her Savior. I never knew a more joyous believer, despite the fact she became arthritic and blind. What an example!

THE RELIGION OF SELF-REALIZATION

*"**P**ilate said to them, 'Take him yourselves and crucify him, for I find no crime in him.'" John 19:6*

Pilate was determined that he was not going to crucify Jesus. He would sooner eat his hat. For the third time he pronounced Jesus innocent. He had violated his conscience in even having him scourged. He was no beast. He could not, he would not crucify an innocent man. After all the Roman law demanded justice. He would not repudiate all that Rome stood for. To do so would be to introduce anarchy. Do your own dirty work, O Jews. Don't ask me to do it for you.

"The Jews answered him, 'We have a law, and by that law he ought to die, because he has made himself the Son of God.'" The law of Moses was clear about one thing: that God is God and man is man, and that no one dare seize for himself the divine prerogatives. In the beginning God created man out of nothing. There is therefore an infinite chasm separating God from man.

The alternative religion is Hinduism, which teaches pantheism, the persuasion that God is identical with creation. It is the religion of self-realization. Gautama Buddha was a Hindu who contemplated his navel for ten years. Finally his "eyes were opened" (the meaning of Buddha). It dawned on him that he was divine, and that "in reality there is nothing." The goal of humanity is therefore to experience nothingness (Nirvana), to merge with the infinite. One can believe this if one sees fit to do so. But the price paid is the rejection of the religion of the Bible and Jesus Christ, who said, "I am the way, the truth and the life. No one comes to the Father but by me." Once I sat on a plane next to an Air Force officer who identified himself as a Buddhist. I said, "Wonderful. What do you believe?" He said, "I am just a nominal Buddhist. I don't know." So I told him about Buddhism and Jesus Christ. I sowed some seed.

❦

TOO BIG FOR HIS BRITCHES?

"When Pilate heard these words, he was the more afraid."
John 19:8

When Pilate heard that Jesus had made himself out to be the Son of God, he was even more afraid than he had been before. Strangely enough atheists are frequently superstitious. Pilate has become a principle character in the Biblical narrative. A youngster was asked by her father what she had learned in Sunday School. She said, "I learned about the baby Jesus' flight to Egypt with three grown-ups." When asked to identify the three grown-ups, she said, "Mary, Joseph, and Pontius the pilot." Pilate would have loved to board a plane and fly Jesus and himself out of this perplexing situation.

"He entered the praetorium again and said to Jesus, `Where are you from?' But Jesus gave no answer." Why should he? He had already indicated to Pilate that his kingship was from heaven. If Pilate had not believed what he said the first time, why rub it in. It would only enhance his guilt. "Pilate therefore said to him, `You will not speak to me? Do you not realize that I have power to release you, and power to crucify you?'" We know that he had the power to crucify Jesus, because he did just that, but did he have the power to release Jesus? Only if he was willing to forfeit his successful career and his place in the sun. He had enjoyed by human standards a successful career. The price was too high. He was too concerned for his own welfare to take that course of action.

"Jesus answered him, `You would have no power over me unless it had been given you from above.'" You enjoy the highest political office in the land. Don't make the mistake of looking to Caesar who appointed you governor. In the final analysis you are answerable not to Caesar but to God above for approval or disapproval. God is the one who has raised you up, but only for an hour. Fame, wealth and health are fleeting. Don't get too big for your britches.

❦

A NO-WIN SITUATION

*"**T**herefore he who delivered me to you has the greater sin.'"*
                                                    John 19:11

"To whom much is given, from him is much required." The one given the most knowledge of Jesus was Judas Iscariot, so his sin was the most reprehensible. The most guilty after him was Annas, who had the longest history as high priest of God. Then the most culpable was Caiaphas, high priest that year. Pilate had little or no information about Jesus prior to this immediate encounter. As recorded in Matthew 27:19, "His wife sent word to him, `Have nothing to do with that righteous man, for I have suffered much over him today in a dream.'" Her warning came almost too late, as he was already deeply embroiled. Jesus knew Pilate to be a weak man, and almost expressed pity for him. Try as he might, Pilate could not extricate himself from this horrendous situation.

Dwight D. Eisenhower told how as a youngster he used to play cards with his family. One day he drew a series of lousy hands. Finally he threw his cards down in disgust, and said, "I quit!" His mother said to him, "Dwight David, in this life God deals the hand, and you have got to play it!" He said that that word carried him through many a difficult situation. We are not required to be winners, but we are obliged to play the hand that was dealt us to the best of our ability.

As a man of great personal ambition, who regarded success in his career as the most important thing, Pilate was in a no-win situation. He had the wrong priorities: first himself, then his job, third his family. God did not even figure into it. Isn't this a wiser set of priorities? First God, second myself, third my family, then my work. Be very careful not to let anything get between you and God. If anything does, it becomes an idol. And God hates idols. They will all ultimately be destroyed, and also those who cling to them.

A VICIOUS CHANGE OF ACCUSATION

"*Upon this Pilate sought to release him.*" John 19:12

Jesus is the friend of sinners. He proved himself on this occasion to be Pilate's friend. Pilate had asked, "What is truth?" Jesus had just revealed to him the truth about his situation. His position as governor was given him by God, to whom he was accountable. His life was involved in sin, but there were others whose sin was greater. Jesus was speaking the truth to him in love. Pilate could see himself in the mirror of God's Word, Jesus. He desired Jesus to be free. He had no personal animosity against him. Those standing by could release Lazarus from his grave bands, but Pilate would prove to be incapable of releasing Jesus. The one thing he sought to do he could not do. He could govern the nation, but he could not release an innocent man. Extraordinary!

"The Jews cried out, `If you release this man, you are not Caesar's friend; every one who makes himself a king sets himself against Caesar.'" Remarkably yet viciously, the Jews had suddenly changed their charge against Jesus. Prior to this they had claimed that Jesus was guilty of a religious offence, blasphemy. That charge was outside Pilate's area of responsibility. But now without warning they accused Jesus of the political crime of making himself out to be a king. Jesus had steered clear of the political arena, and had even advocated paying taxes to Caesar. His enemies though had no concern for ethics. To them the end justified the means.

Pilate got the message. His position was already insecure. Should the Jews leak the word to Caesar that he had tolerated an upstart king in the colonies, his position would be speedily forfeited. Should he lose his job, he might be forced into a nervous breakdown or worse. Several years later he did get recalled to Rome, from whence he was demoted to Gaul, where tradition says he committed suicide.

❦

BEHOLD YOUR KING!

"**W**hen *Pilate heard these words, he brought Jesus out and sat down on the judgment seat at a place called the Pavement, and in Hebrew, Gabbatha."* John 19:13

Pilate's job was more important to him than Jesus. Unless Jesus becomes more important to us than our jobs, we cannot be his disciples either. Friendship with Caesar was what Pilate prized. He had come a long way from freed slave to governor. He could not jeopardize his future over misplaced concern for a religious fanatic. So he took his seat in the place of judgment. Pavement is hard. So is the way of the transgressor hard. He was about to be hard on Jesus that ultimately God might be lenient on us, if we accept Jesus as standing in our place. No more self-justification. We allow Jesus to justify us, who are by nature ungodly.

"Now it was the day of Preparation of the Passover (the day the Passover Lamb was to be sacrificed); it was about the sixth hour." The Romans reckoned time as we do from midnight til noon, twelve hours. So it was six o'clock in the morning, by Roman reckoning, which was utilized in this gospel. In Mark 15:25 Jesus was crucified at the third hour. The Jews divided the daytime into twelve hours. So in Mark's gospel, which reckoned time the Jewish way, Jesus was nailed up just three hours after sun-up, or about nine in the morning. So it was three hours between sentencing and execution, which demonstrates that they took the long way to Skull Hill, that many might see and fear the Roman justice.

"He said to the Jews, `Behold your king!'" Earlier he had said, "Behold the man!" Now he identified the man as their king, giving them a final opportunity of accepting him as such. It had become his judgment that Jesus really was their King. Thank God, they could not see it. Had they seen it, we would not have a Savior from sin. He would never have been crucified in our place, nor raised from the dead.

❧

NO KING BUT CAESAR

"*They cried out, 'Away with him, away with him, crucify him!'*"
John 19:15

The Jews and Pilate were like two pit bulls in a ring. Neither was inclined to give way. They each had bulldog tenacity. The Jews said in effect, "You may call him our king; we call him refuse, dung, the off-scouring of all things." They had hardened their hearts against him. Or was it God who had done so?

"Pilate said to them, 'Shall I crucify your king?'" What people have ever insisted upon crucifying their king, even one who never did them harm, but always good? "The chief priests answered, 'We have no king but God.'" We might have expected them to say that, inasmuch as from the beginning of their history as a people, they were a theocracy, ruled by God (presumably). It was their unique relationship with God that set them apart from all the other nations of earth. They held to the sovereignty of God over their existence as a people. But no, they blurted out (and it must have astonished even them to hear themselves say it), "We have no king but Caesar." In their zeal to dispose of Jesus, they put their national neck in the noose of the heathen emperor. Their theocracy they sold down the drain. As a people they rebelled against "their king" in A.D. 66. Four years later "their king" prevailed, and they ceased to exist as a nation, their capital city in ruins.

In the twentieth century the title Caesar was taken over by the Kaiser, whose replacement was Hitler. He sought to destroy the Jews in the holocaust. In Russia Caesar cropped up in the Czars (the same word), who were displaced by the Communists. Communism has battled against the existence of the Jewish nation from year one. The misfortune of the Jewish people for 1900 years may be traced to the confession of their chief priests on April 7, 30, "We have no king but Caesar." We are trapped by the words of our mouth. The wickedness of unbelief produced disaster. ❧

CROSS BEARING

"Then he handed him over to them to be crucified."

John 19:16

In 18:30 we read that the Jews had handed Jesus over to Pilate. Now Pilated handed Jesus back to them for the purpose of crucifixion. The Apostles' Creed states that Jesus "suffered under Pontius Pilate, was crucified, dead, and buried." Technically Jesus was crucified under the jurisdiction of Pilate, but our evangelist tells us that he was undertaking the dirty work of Jesus' own people. The Romans were the agents of the Jews, who oversaw the affair. The Jews had master-minded Jesus' execution. Strictly speaking it was their doing.

"So they took Jesus." The Jews now accepted Jesus as Pilate's gift to themselves. Ultimately every one will accept Jesus as Lord and Savior or as the enemy to be put to death. We cannot remain neutral where Jesus is concerned. "He who is not with me is against me." he said. "He who does not gather with me scatters." "And he went out, bearing his own cross." He went out of the governor's palace and presence, as years earlier he went out from his Father's throne into this world of woe. "Only his great eternal love could make my Savior go."

We have heard of Atlas, who bore the world on his shoulders. That is a pagan myth. But the story of Jesus bearing his own cross is actual and factual. Jesus had a cross that was his very own. It was made of wood. Jesus said, "If any man will come after me, let him deny himself and take up his cross daily, and follow me." All who see fit to follow Jesus have a cross not made of wood to take up every day. It is the cross of self-denial. Peter had denied Jesus, saying, "I do not know the man." He had disowned him. Similarly, to deny oneself is to disown oneself, by saying, "I do not own myself; I am owned by Another." I refuse to be held captive by my own ambitions, to be enslaved by money. I am owned by Jesus, purchased by his precious blood.

❦

NO DEAD HEAD HE

"*He went out, bearing his own cross, to the place called the place of a skull, which is called in Hebrew Golgotha.*"

John 19:17

We have all seen pictures of Gordon's Calvary just outside the Damascus Gate in Jerusalem. It has the appearance of a skull. What is a skull but a dead head, that cannot think, nor see, nor hear, nor smell, nor speak. At one time it was capable of doing all these things, but no more. My own head is destined for this predicament. Shakespeare has Hamlet hold up a skull, and say, "Alas, poor Yorick, I knew him, Horatio." It is a sobering thought.

But, praise God, there is one noble, glorious exception: Jesus. He was put to death on Skull Hill, but his skull did not get reduced to that of a dead head. His body experienced no trace of decomposition. After his resurrection his head was glorified. He appeared to John, as recorded in Revelation 1:14, in this way: "His head and hair were white as white wool, white as snow (alluding to his wisdom and purity); his eyes were like a flame of fire (these eyes will set the universe ablaze come the end of the age); and his face was like the sun shining in full strength" (vs. 16). The appearance of Jesus blinded Saul of Tarsus instantly, just as sun-worshipers in India are blinded over a period of time. Here we have portrayed the head of him who is our Head.

"The head of every man is Christ." I Cor. 11:3. This means that he is our Leader. He sees the future for us. He hears the messages that God has for us. He speaks to the Father in our behalf, and communicates what God would say to us. All who submit themselves to another head are following the wrong leader. Those who follow Moses, Mohammed, Buddha, Confucius are bound to fall in the wilderness. The head of our Guide is not an empty skull. On the contrary he has the skill to conduct us safely through this vale of tears into the land that is brighter than day.

❧

278

HOLY RETICENCE

"There they crucified him." John 19:18

There on skull hill they did something so horrendous that it is not depicted. It is too horrible to contemplate. Years ago Rev. Lino Hernandez Lopez took us through a museum in Mexico that was filled with crucifixes. Each crucifix was worse, if possible, than its companion on either side. It was a relief to leave and see the blue sky.

I had opportunity to converse with a clinical psychologist on the faculty of Carnegie Mellon University in Pittsburgh, Pa. He would have dissected the brain of Speck, who slew eight nurses in Chicago, had Speck been executed for his crime. I asked him how it was possible for Jesus to endure crucifixion, having refused the drugged wine that would have made the pain more bearable. How could Jesus stand it without lashing out at those who so cruelly afflicted him? I will never forget his answer: "It was a case of over-learning." Dearly beloved, I do not believe over-learning could get the job done. It was a miracle undertaken by One who himself was and is the greatest Miracle. Only God in human form could endure the cross, despising the shame, without expressing hostility to those who did it to him. I know that I could not have approached the cross even to look upon it. I am too squeemish. Thank God for the reticence of the four evangelists, and their reluctance to describe the gory details.

A man who was horribly burned spent four months in the hospital recovering. I asked him what was the worst thing about it. He said, "The pain in my heels pressing against the sheet." Jesus' heel was bruised upon the cross as foretold in Genesis 3:7. An amazing prophecy - the heel, not the heels. The bottom of one foot was nailed to the top of the other, so that only one heel rubbed against the vertical beam. Time and again Jesus straightened his knees to take the weight off of his nailed hands so that he could breathe.

❧

THE UNIVERSAL STORY

"*And with him two others, one on either side, and Jesus between them.*" *John 19:18*

We were attending the Passion Play at Spearfish, South Dakota. We could hear the pounding as the nails were being hammered through Jesus' hands and feet. Our three year old daughter looked up and said, "Why are they doing that to Jesus?" I answered, "Jesus is dying for our sins, for all the wrongs we have done." She responded, "I never did anything wrong." In other words, "Don't think you are going to pin that on me." It reminds us of pinning the tail on the donkey. No one wants to be the donkey.

This is the universal story. Jesus, on the center cross, represents my spirit, my inner self, which was created kin to God. Hebrews 12:9 speaks of him as the Father of our spirits. I, in my egocentricity, have crucified my inner being that was fashioned with the instinct to please God. I have placed my better self under a curse, denying it, rejecting it, impaling it. When I realize what I have done, as Paul did on the Damascus Road, I confess with him, "I (my ego) have been crucified with Christ." Galatians 2:20 My ego is represented by the criminal crucified beside him, who came to his senses and declared Jesus' innocence and his own guilt, and who was told that he would join Jesus in paradise. But what about the unrepentant criminal who writhed in agony on the other side of Jesus? He symbolizes my soul. That part of me persists in unbelief. This is why I must say, "I believe (my repentant ego does), help my unbelief." The good news is that the unbelieving part of me (a major portion of my soul, or personal unconscious) is also on a cross. It curses and carries on rebelliously much of the time, but it is doomed to die. I will wave goodbye to my sinful nature when I leave this body of death and go to be with Jesus in heaven. The conflict will be over forever. Praise God!

SOME TITLE

"**P**ilate *also wrote a title and put it on the cross; it read, 'Jesus of Nazareth, the King of the Jews.'" John 19:19*

Pilate took delight in rubbing salt into their wounds. That the Messiah should spring out of God-forsaken Nazareth was to them an impossible possibility. The Jews of Judaea held the Galileans in low esteem. Their attitude was like that of the residents of Dixie toward the Northerners after the Civil War, whom they termed "Damn Yankees." "Can anything good come out of Nazareth?" was proverbial.

"Many of the Jews read this title (depicting his crime) for the place was near the city." Why outside the city? Hebrews 13:11,12 explains: "For the bodies of those animals whose blood is brought into the sanctuary by the high priest as a sacrifice for sin are burned outside the camp. So Jesus also suffered outside the gate in order to sanctify the people through his own blood." He fufilled in this way the Old Testament typology. So what is our response to be? "Therefore (verse 13) let us go forth to him outside the camp (of traditional religiosity), and bear the abuse he endured." As he was rejected and cast out of the city by those who trusted in their own righteousness, let us steel ourselves to be similarly treated.

"And the title was written in Hebrew, in Latin, and in Greek." "Jesus is King" in the three significant languages of that region. He is King in Hebrew, the language of revealed religion. So he must rule over the realm that is regarded as the prince of the disciplines - theology (the study of God). He is King in Latin, the language of government and law. So he must ultimately control the governments of earth. He is King in Greek, the language of culture and civilization. The so-called sophisticated of society are superficial and uncouth, if they have not been touched by the Spirit of Jesus Christ the King (the One Who Is Able).

281

WHAT WAS JESUS' CRIME?

"*The chief priests of the Jews then said to Pilate, 'Do not write,
"The King of the Jews," but, 'This man said, I am King of the
Jews.'" John 19:21*

There is a world of difference between a pretentious
claim and a fact. A man in an insane asylum may assert that he
is God, but that does not make it so. "Jesus has claimed to be our
King, but he obviously is not. Where are his subjects? (If you
looked around, you could not see a disciple in sight.) Jesus our
King? Preposterous! We won't take such an insult lying down.
One simple change will satisfy." "This man said, I am King of
the Jews."

"Pilate answered, 'What I have written I have written.'"
Change may be the law of the universe, but this is the exception
that proves the rule. You can push a man only so far. This is
where I draw the line. It was providential, because it is written
in heaven: "You shall call his name Jesus, for he will save his
people from their sins." Matt. 1:21

His people were the Judaeans, the Jews. He died as
their representative. Their sins were visited upon him. At the
cross, justice and mercy have kissed each other, and mercy has
triumphed over justice. What was Jesus' crime? The title over
his head made it clear. He committed the crime of being the
King of the Jews. It was not what he had done; it was who he
was. He was David's greater Son. David in the Hebrew means
Beloved. David was the apple of God's eye. Any one who injured
David, scratched the pupil of God's eye and made him cry. If God
loved David so, how much more would you expect him to love his
eternal Son? Yet God loved the Judaeans so much that he sent
his Beloved into this world to die the death of the damned in
their place. The very people who said, "We will not have this
man to rule over us," will eventually say, "What are these
wounds on your back?" "The wounds I received in the house of
my family." Zech 13:16

THE GREAT GAMBLE

"When the soldiers had crucified Jesus they took his garments and made four parts, one for each soldier; also the tunic.'

John 19:23

To the victor, the spoils. For their dirty work the execution detail was rewarded by being granted the clothing of the victim. So one soldier took as his stipend Jesus' head dress, another took his sandals, the third took his girdle, and the fourth his mantle. These four items were of equal value. The fifth garment was his tunic, which was like a long shirt. It was the most valuable piece of clothing worn by a man. "But the tunic was without seam, woven from top to bottom." It reminds us on the one hand of the garment of the high priest which was to be torn when he heard blasphemy. On the other hand we think of the veil of the temple, which was four inches thick and without seam. When Jesus died, it was torn from top to bottom as by the hand of God, indicating that the Holy Spirit had vacated the Holy of Holies at the same time Jesus' spirit left the temple of his body. Now the way was open for mankind to enter into the divine presence through the sacrificial blood of the Lamb.

"So they said to one another, `Let us not tear it, but cast lots for it to see whose it shall be.'" It was a logical, natural decision that was divinely mandated. Without realizing it, they did this "to fulfill the scripture (in Psalm 22:19), `They parted my garments among them, and for my clothing they cast lots.'" They were gambling, as all of us must when we hear the story of the crucifixion. We are gambling not for items of attire, but for our eternal welfare. We will stake our all on Jesus and his death for us, or we will bet our lives that he was a sinner like us who got what he had coming. This is the greatest gamble. If we bet on Jesus, we will find that the lot has fallen for us in pleasant places. Psalm 16:6 If we bet against him, we shall not live to regret it. No, we shall rue it in what the Bible calls eternal death.

❧

THE SOLDIERS' ERROR

"**So** *the soldiers did this.*" *John 19:25*

The soldiers did what they had to do. They were under orders. The military is a noble and necessary profession. Soldiers came to the Baptist to be baptized, and asked him, "What shall we do?" He did not say return to civilian life. He said to them, "Rob no one by violence or by false accusation, and be content with your wages." Luke 3:14 There is nothing wrong with soldiering, but the soldiers here represent the type who look not to the man but to what the man is wearing. They were so absorbed in securing Jesus' garments that they were distracted from looking to Jesus himself. They would say the clothes make the man; he is what he wears. In our society we tend to look at the kind of car one drives, or the neighborhood one lives in. We judge by appearances, not by right judgment. No, the individual is of infinite and eternal value, whereas the things that are seen are transient and of temporal value.

James chapter two warns about making distinctions between the rich and the poor when they come to church. By showing respect to the rich and disdain toward the poor, "we become judges with evil thoughts." The poor tend to be rich in faith, whereas the rich are inclined to oppress us and drag us into court. They are tempted to measure everything by the all-muddy dollar.

In his death Jesus took the curse of poverty upon himself. Though he was rich beyond imagining, yet for your sake he became poor, that you through his poverty might become rich. Through faith in Jesus, we have become the King's kids. You can't tell who belongs to Jesus just by looking. We may appear as ordinary as an old shoe, but if we have the Spirit of Jesus within us, it does not appear what we shall be. When Jesus appears, we shall be like him and enter into our eternal habitations. True wealth is spiritual and not material. This the four soldiers could not see.

❧

THE FELLOWSHIP OF SUFFERING

"*But standing by the cross of Jesus were his mother, and his mother's sister, Mary the wife of Clopas, and Mary Magdalene.*"

John 19:25

Here we have the counterpart of the four soldiers. The four women did not look to the material, but to the person. They looked at Jesus, whom they loved. There are many who come to Jesus for what they may gain from him, but how many share in the cross, standing by him in his anguish and pain? Three of the four had the name Mary, "bitterness." All four participated in the fulfillment of Simeon's word to Mary recorded in Luke 2:35, "And a sword will pierce through your own soul also, that thoughts out of many hearts may be revealed." A sword thrust through one's soul produces intense emotional pain. As Jesus writhed in agony, they writhed with him.

The Lord told Ananias concerning the Apostle Paul, "I will show him how much he must suffer for the sake of my name." Acts 9:16. And suffer he did. Paul even got to the place where he could say concerning Jesus, "that I may share his sufferings, becoming like him in his death." Phil. 3:10. It became his ambition to participate in the cross that Jesus experienced.

I am reminded of a young man I called upon in a nursing home years ago. It was a substandard place, an old house. Near him were several old men waiting to die. The young man's fingers were gnarled like tree roots. His teeth were rotting. He was a victim of rheumatoid arthritis. I asked him how long he had been in this condition. "Since I was two," he said. "Is it painful?" I asked. "It hurts so much that I pray every day that I may die," he answered. When I asked him how old he was, he said he didn't know, but thought he was in his early thirties. He was about the age of Jesus when he died. He was one who fellowshiped with Jesus in his cross. And we complain when the bee stings. "Take your share of suffering as a good soldier of Christ Jesus."

❦

THE DISCIPLE WHOM JESUS LOVED

"When Jesus saw his mother, and the disciple whom he loved standing near, he said to his mother, 'Woman, behold your son!'"

John 19:26

The disciple whom he loved was John, son of Zebedee, our evangelist. He never mentions himself by name. But he was the one who could never get over the fact that Jesus loved him despite himself. Would that each of us could come into the same awareness. Put your arms around yourself just now, and imagine that they are the arms of Jesus embracing you in love. They are, you know, since your arms belong to Jesus, as members of his body. Keep doing it until you can love and accept yourself just as you are. We are commanded to love our neighbor as we love ourselves. So we are obliged to love ourselves with the love of self-acceptance and self-appreciation.

Some people hate themselves. Then they project their self-hate upon those around them. The person you can't stand is picking up the projections of those parts of yourself that you cannot tolerate. Jesus was the one who accepted himself with perfect acceptance. This made it possible for him to accept everyone. He spoke the truth in love to one and all. When he excoriated the religionists, he was speaking in love, trying to shock them into repentance. When we experience the shocks that flesh is heir to, let us consider the possibility that the Lord is trying to get our attention. Perhaps he is seeking to turn us to himself in a deeper way.

There is always compensation. His mother is losing her first-born, but simultaneously she is gaining a son, one who loved Jesus as much as she. Indeed, after the resurrection, all of the young men who followed Jesus became her sons, and all of the young women became her daughters. She became a mother-figure for the family of God. No wonder she is called blessed among women. Luke 1:42 In the male unconscious she like Sophia (wisdom) is the idealized anima (feminine for "soul" in Latin).

MOTHER AND SON

"Then he said to the disciple, 'Behold, your mother!'" John 19:27
Why did the mother of Jesus need John as a son? She already had four sons: James, Joses, Judas, and Simon. See Mark 6:3. In the first place her natural-born sons were not yet believers in Jesus. "For even his brothers did not believe in him." John 7:5. In this hour of sorrow she needed a son to lean upon who was at hand, and who looked to Jesus in faith. As the son of Mary's sister Salome, our evangelist was her nephew. When it says "from that hour the disciple took her to his own home," it is likely that she also had as companion her sister, the wife of Zebedee. We need our family when we pass through the fire of trial and the deep waters of adversity. Blood is thicker than water. The Greeks had a word for it: storge, that is to say, natural affection. We may not agree totally with our next of kin, but when the evil day comes, we are inclined to close ranks and stand shoulder to shoulder against the attack of the enemy. The death of a family member is an occasion for reconciliation on the part of estranged siblings.

A second reason why Jesus united Mary and John as mother and son was pointed out in the story of the wedding at Cana. There we saw that his mother is never mentioned by name in this gospel, because she is a symbolic figure. She represents the Old Covenant community of believers. John, on the other hand, is the spokesman for the New Covenant company. So this gospel is telling us that we Christians are expected to attempt to take under our wings the Jews who worship in temple and synagogue. We may differ from them, as mother and son invariably do, but we are honor-bound to be concerned for their welfare, and to do all in our power to shield them from the attacks of the devil, who seeks to do them in. We are to proffer them sheltering love. We are also called to tell them about their Savior, and ours.

❦

JESUS' GREATEST NEED

"*After this Jesus, knowing that all was now finished, said (to fulfill the scripture), 'I thirst.'*" John 19:28

"If anyone does not provide for his relatives, and especially for his own family, he has disowned the faith and is worse than an unbeliever," wrote Paul in I Tim. 5:8. He got that from Jesus, who provided for the heartfelt need of his mother, as he was enthroned upon the cross. Now he was free to express his own need. His greatest need was to fulfill all that the Old Testament had foretold about himself. Psalm 91:21 specified, "And for my thirst they gave me vinegar to drink." He had said to the woman at the well, "Give me a drink," but from her he got no drink, though he had given her a sip of living water. Now again he expresses his need for something to drink.

"A bowl full of vinegar stood there. (It was the sour wine that was the soldiers' cheap beer, called posca.) So they put a sponge full of vinegar on hyssop and held it to his mouth." The soldiers had no way of knowing that they were fulfilling a prophecy of David written one thousand years before they were born. In God's book, though, a thousand years is as one day. Furthermore they used the hyssop growing there to carry the sponge full of vinegar to his mouth. Little did they realize that the blood of the lambs sacrificed at the first Passover in Egypt was to be daubed on the doorposts with hyssop. In this way God foretold the use of hyssop in the sacrifice of Jesus, the Lamb of God, whose substitutionary death had been predestined before the creation of the world.

Everyone connected with Jesus during his days in the flesh in some way proclaimed the good news. Judas' gospel was the most glorious, "I have sinned in betraying innocent blood." Matthew 27:4 Because Jesus died without sin, he was permitted to carry our sin, that we might be spared the eternal consequences.

❧

THE ONE PERFECT WORK

"When Jesus had received the vinegar, he said, 'It is finished.'"
John 19:30

Jesus gives humanity the water of life, even the Holy Spirit in overflowing measure. What do we give him to drink in return? Vinegar. And yet he received the vinegar without spitting it out. We moan and groan over the shabby treatment we get from the world. But that is possibly the best they can do. Treated shabbily themselves, they pass it on. Vinegar was all the soldiers had, and they were thankful for that. Jesus was thankful for daily bread. He did not demand cake.

"It is finished," he declared. Mark 15:37 says he "uttered a loud cry." It was a victorious shout: "Tetelestai" in the Greek. It means, "It is perfectly perfected." His work was to die the death of the damned, the innocent for the guilty. His death was the one perfect work. It had been foretold before creation. It was perfect in its motivation, perfect in its result. It is the one perfect work in human history. It cannot be improved upon. All I need do to please God is to confess my faith in Jesus Christ and his sacrificial death for me upon the cruel tree. The password to heaven is this: I have accepted Jesus Christ as my Lord and Savior, and I believe that his death upon the cross has purchased my pardon for time and eternity. Upon hearing this the angels in heaven will sing, "Lift up your heads, O Gates! and be lifted up, O ancient doors! that this child, washed in the blood of the Lamb, may come in."

Daniel 9:24 gives Jesus' job description. It says that he is the one who will "finish the transgression, put an end to sin, atone for iniquity, bring in everlasting righteousness." Jesus' death was perfect in that it accomplished these four things. Under grace, which involves the giving and receiving of gifts, transgression has no meaning. The power of sin has been broken, and rebellion has been replaced by righteousness.

AN ASTONISHING DEATH

"*And he bowed his head and gave up his spirit.*".
                                             John 19:30

He had said with a shout of triumph, "It is finished!" He had finished the work the Father had sent him to accomplish. He did not say, "I am finished." As the eternal I Am, he would never come to an end. Then his head fell forward, and he handed over his spirit to his Father. That happened inwardly, invisibly. Outwardly he stopped breathing.

A man who lived to be 100 was asked the secret of his longevity. He said, "It is simple. Just keep breathing." It is one thing to keep breathing, but quite another to stop breathing of one's own volition. Yet that is just what Jesus did. It so startled the centurion, who was used to seeing people die, that he exclaimed, "Truly this man was (an innocent) Son of God," a divine being. Ordinarily the crucified lingered for several days before dying of asphyxiation. Gradually they became so weak that they could no longer draw a breath. Jesus died with a shout, as Old Testament worshipers departed from their worship with a shout. John Wesley with his dying breath whispered, "I praise God." What a beautiful way to go.

Where did Jesus go? Peter tells us in his first letter, chapter 3:19, that he went and preached to the spirits in the prison of Sheol to the most wicked generation who ever lived. He proclaimed his sacrificial death to those who drowned in Noah's flood, "that though judged in the flesh like men, they might live in the spirit like God." I Peter 4:6 If the most wicked who ever lived on earth heard the gospel, we may be sure all the others who preceded Jesus in death also heard. Come the judgment day, those who believed will be welcomed into heaven. When they appear before Jesus at the great white throne judgment, they may say, "I accepted your death as the one perfect sacrifice for my sin, and look to you as my LORD forever."

❧

GOOD FRIDAY

"*Since it was the day of Preparation, in order to prevent the bodies from remaining on the cross on the sabbath (for that sabbath was a high day)." John 19:31*

Let us be sure that we understand John's chronology. Jesus was put to death on the day of Preparation for Passover and for the sabbath. It was Friday. And Jesus writhed upon the cross for six solid hours, from 9 in the morning until 3 in the afternoon. This was time during which the Passover lambs were being sacrificed before the temple building, that they might be eaten during the Jewish passover meal after sundown that evening. Jesus fulfilled in his death that which was symbolized by the Exodus from Egypt. As the Jewish nation was liberated from the house of bondage more than twelve hundred years earlier, so the people of Jesus were freed from the guilt and power of sin by faith in his loving sacrifice. As the result Christians are assured that when they die trusting in Jesus, they immediately enter into the reality of the next day, even the sabbath rest of the people of God. It is not purgatory.

The day of Jesus' death we call Good Friday. Friday is named after the Nordic goddess Frig. In the Roman tradition her name was Venus, the goddess of love. It is more than chance that Jesus died on the day memorializing feminine love. Think of it. Jesus died writhing in agony upon the cross just as a woman writhes in child birth. Upon the cross Jesus gave birth to the new creation, the Church.

Was the shame and pain worth it? Isaiah 53:11 reads: "He shall see the fruit of the travail of his soul and be satisfied." Yes, it was more than worth it. Notice the proliferation of sixes. Jesus was crucified on the sixth day of the week. He was sentenced to the cross at the sixth hour, and endured it for six hours: 666. Six is as far as humanity can go. See Rev. 13:18, where the beast or antichrist bears this number. This is God's way of telling us that Jesus became "the man of sin" that we through our faith in him might become manifestations of his righteousness.

❧

BROKEN BONES

"The Jews asked Pilate that their legs might be broken, and that they might be taken away." John 19:31

Good Friday surely was a high day. It was the day upon which Jesus was lifted up and made prominent that he might draw all humanity ultimately to himself. For the Jews their sabbath was a high day, as it was also Passover as we have seen. In this gospel the seventh day of the week is the day of healing in answer to prayer. Because our Passover Lamb has been sacrificed on the sixth day, the day in which the Holy Spirit nurtures us through feasting our faith on his selfgiving love, we come to find that the Jewish sabbath is for us the day of healing par excellence. We may pray to God in the full assurance that the answers are forthcoming in God's own time.

It was essential to the Jews that the crucified be dispatched and buried, lest the land be defiled by their accursed overshadowing presence on their high and holy day. That they had defiled themselves by sending to his death the one Innocent Man who ever lived somehow did not trouble their conscience. This was an instance of straining out the gnat and swallowing the camel.

"So the soldiers came and broke the legs of the first, and of the other who had been crucifed with him." Their bodies would slump, resulting in their inability to catch their breath. Hence they would quickly die. Also think of the frightful pain produced. "But when they came to Jesus and saw that he was already dead, they did not break his legs." Thank God, Jesus was spared this additional pain and indignity, providentially of course. Have you ever experienced a broken bone? I did on the mortar range while taking infantry training. I could see the bone of my little finger, which I thought was destined for amputation. The chaplain said, "Son, thank God you are alive. I saw the whole thing." I wondered why it had to happen in the first place.

THE CREATION OF EVE

"**B**ut one of the soldiers pierced his side with a spear, and at once there came out blood and water." John 19:34

The Roman spear had a head on it about the shape and size of a man's hand. What a gaping wound it made in Jesus' side as it penetrated his body beneath his rib cage. Remember, not a bone of him was broken, not even a rib. The first Adam sustained a broken-off rib, out of which Eve was fashioned. The bride of the last Adam is being created out of something more precious than a rib, as we shall see. As the spear was withdrawn, there gushed out blood and water. The flow of blood we comprehend, but how shall we account for the flow of water?

I asked a funeral director how much pericardium fluid there is between the heart muscle and the membrane that encloses the heart. He said, "Usually about a cup." So the spear penetrated Jesus' heart, allowing the release of the clear watery serum in which the heart beats. This means that we have sure medical evidence that Jesus was indeed dead. The swoon theory which pretends that Jesus revived while in the tomb is forthwith ruled out of court.

"He who saw it (John the Evangelist) has borne witness - his testimony is true, and he knows that he tells the truth - that you also may believe." Believe what? That Jesus is the Anointed Savior, who fashions his bride out of his riven side, from which flowed the water of baptism and the blood of holy communion. We call them sacraments, mysteries. By availing myself in faith of the water of baptism and the cup that runs red, I identify myself with Jesus' efficacious death. His death has been made effective in me. I have become part of the new Eve, his bride, the Church. Eve means life. I have the life of God within me. May I allow it to flow to others and thereby flourish. We never know when the trumpet will sound, and we will experience the upward call of God. Then will begin the marriage supper in heaven.

❧

HE'S MY EVERYTHING

*"**F**or these things took place that the scripture might be fulfilled."*
John 19:36

The Bible is a unique record. Three-quarters of it is the Old Testament, the book of promises. One-quarter of it is the New Testament, the book of the fulfillment of those promises. The Bible is the record of a divinely guided history. It discloses that life has meaning and history a Master, even Jesus Christ. Innumerable Old Testament promises were fulfilled in Jesus' crucifixion. John now cites two of them.

The first is recorded in Psalm 34:20 - "Not a bone of him shall be broken." Doubtless his nose was broken from all the blows to his face, but the nose is not a bone. It was miraculous that he should sustain such cruel injuries without so much as one broken bone. Exodus 12:46 says concerning the passover lamb, "You shall not break a bone of it." Had Jesus endured one broken bone he could not have been the Lamb of God, our Savior.

"And again another scripture says, `They shall look on him whom they have pierced.'" Zechariah 12:10 In the Hebrew text the "him" is identified as "aleph tau." Aleph is the first letter and tau is the last letter in the Hebrew alphabet. This means that the One whom they looked upon, after they had pierced his skin with hundreds of wounds, was everything to them from A to Z. "He's My Everything" is the name of a song. The Jews and everyone else may sing it to Jesus. When Jesus returns to Jerusalem as King of the Jews, Zechariah 12:10 goes on to say, "They shall mourn for him, as one mourns for an only child." Chapter 13:1 continues, "On that day there shall be a fountain opened to cleanse them (his people) from sin and uncleanness." That fountain flows from Jesus' side. It will eventually sweeten even the Dead Sea, the lowest place on earth. Ezekiel 47:8 Its life-giving flow brings satisfaction even now to all who humble themselves acknowledging their need.

WITH A RICH MAN IN HIS DEATH

"*After this Joseph of Arimathea, who was a disciple of Jesus, but secretly, for fear of the Jews, asked Pilate that he might take away the body of Jesus, and Pilate gave him leave." John 19:38*

Everything that happened to Jesus in his death and burial fulfilled Old Testament scripture. Isaiah 53:9 is now being accomplished: "And they made his grave with the wicked (plural) and with a rich man in his deaths (plural)." We have already taken note of the fact that Jesus experienced three deaths (spiritual, physical, and locational). Now the rich man associated with his death and burial is identified as Joseph of Arimathea.

We were conducted by a guide in the Church of the Holy Sepulcher to the family tomb of Joseph, where few tourists go. It is near the tomb where tradition says that Jesus was buried. Our guide said that the place where Jesus was buried was regarded as so sacred that Joseph had himself and his family interred in another cave dug out of the rock behind the holy sepulcher. I picked up and brought home a stone from the family tomb. It is a shame to be a secret disciple, but most of the time we are, not for fear of the Jews, but for fear of ridicule from our peers.

Yes, "they made his grave with the wicked ones," the naturally rebellious - that's us. I have officiated at hundreds of funerals. It is a sobering experience to walk ahead of the casket to the grave. I invariably think that some day my body will be in the casket and someone will be walking ahead of my procession. I will not be in the casket, but on ahead. "He is not dead this friend, not dead; but in the path we mortals tread got some few trifling steps ahead, and nearer to the end, so that we too, once passed the bend, shall meet again as face to face this friend we fancy dead." A happy reunion is in store for believers. In the meantime, we feebly struggle, while they in glory shine.

❧

SECRET DISCIPLES

"*So he came and took away the body of Jesus.*"

John 19:38

As long as Jesus was living, Joseph hid the fact that he was a disciple. But as soon as he learned that Jesus was dead, he went public with his faith. It was the awareness that Jesus had died for me that smoked me out of my secret discipleship. Since Jesus had died for me, I reasoned that I must be willing to die for him. What better way to die than to die of fright telling others about him. Telling others did not cause me to die as I thought. Instead it confirmed me in my faith. Dying to self, we come alive in Christ.

By handling the dead body of Jesus, Joseph rendered himself unclean in the eyes of the law. He would not then be permitted to eat the Jewish Passover that evening. Jesus had become more important to him than the most sacred occasion of his religion. By the same token, if Jesus does not become more important to us than our religion, no matter how true it may be, we too cannot be Jesus' disciples. Christianity is not really a religion; correctly viewed it is a personal relationship with Jesus, a relationship in which we trust him and he proves himself trustworthy.

"Nicodemus also, who had at first come to him by night, came bringing a mixture of myrrh and aloes, about a hundred pounds' weight." Nicodemus represents the procrastinating type of believer. Three years earlier he had learned from Jesus the necessity of new birth. He kept postponing his commitment to Jesus, as some do their whole life long. When he saw Jesus lifted up on the cross, though, he too was obliged to come forward publicly. He expressed his love for Jesus by lavishing upon his body burial spices fit for the entombment of a king. Study the reference to the spices in Psalm 45:8 to appreciate the significance of what he did. It is too bad that he could not have expressed his love for Jesus before the cross, as Mary of Bethany did.

❦

THE DAY OF NURTURE AGAIN

"*Now in the place where he was crucified there was a garden, and in the garden a new tomb where no one had ever been laid.*"

John 19:41

The Jews did not embalm dead bodies as the Egyptians did. Instead they buried the dead before sundown. "Now in the place where he was crucified there was a garden, and in the garden a new tomb where no one had ever been laid." We are reminded of the garden where our first parents had their beginning. It was in the garden that they went astray. The Lord Jesus had carried in his own body the tragedy of man's sin and rebellion against God. He bore for the human race God's wrath against sin and for God man's hostility toward God. Jesus was the middle man. He had been engendered in a virgin's womb; now he would be buried in a brand new tomb.

"So because of the Jewish day of Preparation, as the tomb was close at hand, they laid Jesus there." God's Passover Lamb had been sacrificed and now buried on the appointed day, thus fulfilling scripture. We reiterate that it was on the sixth day of Holy Week that everything from the arrest to the burial of Jesus took place. The sixth day is the day of nurture. As we have given our attention to the Passion narrative, we may be sure that the Holy Spirit has satisfied our hunger and thirst after the love of God. Christ laid down his life for us and died for us while we were yet sinners. Out of his broken body but unbroken bone structure flowed to us the two sacraments that nurture our faith.

When the Apostle Paul went to Corinth, he decided to know nothing among them except Jesus Christ and him crucified. I Cor. 2:2 This is the message that seizes our attention and will not let us go. "When I survey the wondrous cross, on which the Prince of glory died, my richest gain I count but loss, and pour contempt on all my pride." Pride has become for us a dirty word. Instead we delight in the knowledge of God's saving love.

❧

SHOCKING NEWS FROM A GRAVEYARD

"*ℜ ow on the first day of the week Mary Magdalene came to the tomb early, while it was dark, and saw that the stone had been taken away from the tomb.*" John 20:1

The overall theme of this chapter is seeing the Kingdom of God. It parallels chapter 9, the story of the man born blind, who little by little came to see who Jesus really is. In the previous chapter we met Mary as one of the women standing by his cross. After his death she and the other women prepared spices and ointments for his dead body. While it was still dark, she saw by the light of the silvery moon that the enormous stone had been removed from the entrance.

"So she ran, and went to Simon Peter and the other disciple, the one whom Jesus loved, and said to them, 'They have taken the Lord out of the tomb, and we do not know where they have laid him.'" She assumed that his body had been victimized by grave robbers. "Peter then came out with the other disciple, and they went toward the tomb." (Aren't we all? The paths of glory lead but to the grave.) They both ran (the most exciting footrace in human history); but the other disciple outran Peter and reached the tomb first." The other disciple, John, was younger and fleeter of foot than Peter. Also, as the contemplative type, he drew conclusions from what he saw before Peter did. The man of action is more bold than the contemplative individual, but the latter perceives things the former misses. Every type of person enjoys advantages and disadvantages. So let us learn to accept ourselves as we are, and stop making cheap comparisons between ourselves and others. When we compare ourselves with Jesus, our pride will be a thing of the past. May our pride cease, and our delight in the Lord increase more and more.

What they were about to see on Easter morning was the threefold testimony of the empty tomb. "Let everything be confirmed by the mouth of two or three witnesses."

❦

THE MYSTERY OF THE FOLDED NAPKIN

*"**A**nd stooping to look in, he saw the linen cloths lying there, but he did not go in." John 20:5*

The first disciple to reach the most sacred place on earth stooped when he got there. To enter the Church of the Nativity in Bethlehem, one must stoop to go in through the very low door. If we are to gain anything from God, we must bow low and humble ourselves. The first thing John saw as he approached the tomb was the great stone rolled away from the entrance. It had been rolled back, we know, by the angel, because it was bearing witness to what was no longer true. His body had vacated the tomb even before the stone had been removed.

The second thing he saw was the linen cloths lying there undisturbed with the nearly 100 pounds of spices inside them, allowing them to retain something of their rounded appearance. He surmised, Mary is wrong; his body has not been stolen, but is still there within the grave bands. The word "saw" is blepo, which has reference to simply seeing the facts. So he did not go in.

"Then (compulsive) Simon Peter came, following him (as he had followed him into the courtyard of the High Priest), and went into the tomb; he saw (theorized upon) the linen cloths lying, and the napkin, which had been on his head, not lying with the linen cloths but rolled up in a place by itself. (But Peter did not comprehend the significance of what he saw). Then the other disciple, who reached the tomb first, also went in, and he saw (in the sense that he formed a clear idea of what had happened; the light was turned on within him) and believed." He believed the most astonishing fact ever thought or recorded. John son of Zebedee was the first disciple to believe that Jesus had been raised from the dead. Why? Because he had probed the mystery of the folded napkin. Do you have any idea as to why it should have had such an impact on him?

❧

PROOF POSITIVE

"**𝕱***or as yet they did not know the scripture, that he must rise from the dead.*" *John 20:9*

Do you know what scripture is referred to here? It is the scripture that Peter would quote in his prophetic utterance on the occasion of Pentecost in Acts 2:25-28. "For David says concerning Jesus (Ps. 16:9-11), `I saw the LORD always before me, for he is at my right hand that I may not be shaken; therefore my heart was glad, and my tongue rejoiced; moreover my flesh will dwell in hope. For thou wilt not abandon my soul (the soul of Jesus) to Hades, nor let thy Holy One see corruption. Thou hast made known to me (Jesus) the ways of life; thou wilt make me full of gladness with thy presence" (after the Ascension).

Peter and John did not know as yet that scripture. Even so, on the basis of the third testimony of the empty tomb, John believed that Jesus was alive. He was the most perceptive of the Twelve. He had noticed that Jesus had a particular way of folding up his napkin after a meal. Could it have been in the shape of a triangle, expressing thereby the triune nature of God? Most simply discard their napkins, allowing them to fall at random on the table, but not so Jesus. That particular napkin had been used to cover his head, clamping his jaws shut in death. But when Jesus rose from the dead in the wee hours of Sunday morning, his physical body was instantly changed into a spiritual body as he sat up through the grave cloths. Then, to make it clear that his body was no longer within, he picked up the napkin, folded it in his customary manner, and laid it in a place apart.

When John saw the napkin folded just so, something clicked within him. He knew what every human being must come to know, that Jesus is alive, raised from the dead. Nothing can ever be the same for us again. "Then the disciples went back to their homes," each reflecting in silence upon what he had seen: the testimony of the empty tomb.

WATER MADE WINE

"**B**ut *Mary stood weeping outside the tomb, and as she wept she stooped to look into the tomb.*" *John 20:11*

With Peter and John we have encountered on Resurrection Day the first two themes of this gospel: testimony and faith. Now we are going to encounter with Mary the next two themes: life and abiding. We are reminded of the wedding at Cana, when the wine had failed. Here with Mary there is no wine, no joy, but only tears, the water of sadness. As she stood by the cross, so now she is standing beside the tomb. She is the devoted one, the emotional one.

Suddenly she stooped to look into the tomb, "and she saw (theorized, literally or contemplated) two angels in white, sitting where the body of Jesus had lain, one at the head and one at the feet. (She evidently thought they were two young men and did not perceive that they were heavenly beings). They said to her, `Woman, why are you weeping?' (This is no time to weep, but to laugh and leap for joy.) She said to them, `Because they have taken away my Lord, and I do not know where they have laid him.'

"Saying this, she turned round and saw (theoreo) Jesus standing, but she did not know that it was Jesus. Jesus said to her, 'Woman, why are you weeping? Whom do you seek?' Supposing him to be the gardener (as was the first Adam), she said to him, 'Sir if you have carried him away, tell me where you have laid him, and I will take him away. (A remarkable feat for a lone woman, the logic of emotion). Jesus said to her, 'Mary.' (The shepherd knows his own sheep by name. Likewise the sheep knows the shepherd's voice and will not follow strangers.) She turned and said to him in Hebrew, 'Rabboni!' (which means Teacher)" - the greatest recognition scene in human history. She, the emotional type, was the first to experience him as alive, the Risen One. The water has become wine. The joy of the wedding is resumed, more joyous than ever.

❦

A NEW NAME WRITTEN DOWN IN GLORY

*"**J**esus said to her, 'Mary.'" John 20:16*

Her name was Mary Magdalene, out of whom the Lord cast seven demons. Since she was delivered of much, she therefore loved much. In the Greek manuscripts her name was pronounced Maria. Here, interestingly enough, Jesus calls her Mariam. He has given her a new name. It is now very similar to the name of Moses and Aaron's sister, Miriam, who celebrated with song and dance "the horse and rider thrown into the sea" at the Exodus. Jesus' mighty resurrection was foreshadowed by the Exodus from Egypt, here alluded to in her name change (which does not appear in the English text).

Have you heard the old spiritual song, "There's a new name written down in glory, is it mine, is it mine?" A new name is expressive of a new character, which we shall enjoy when we arrive in heaven. We shall be like Jesus in body and character. Praise God! Recognizing Jesus, Mariam addressed him by what she regarded as his most respected earthly title, "Rabboni!" It means more than Teacher, literally My Great One - the greatest teacher ever.

"Jesus said to her, `Do not hold me.' (Evidently she had fastened her hands upon him. Possibly she had prostrated herself before him and had grasped his feet. Then he explained why she should not hold him) `...for I have not yet ascended to the Father. (It won't be as it was before my resurrection; I am not to be physically apprehended.) But go to my brethren and say to them, I am ascending to my Father and your Father, to my God and your God.'" We have encountered with Mariam the theme of life, and now the theme of abiding. She cannot any longer abide with Jesus as she used to, because he is now in the process of returning to his Father (homecoming) as he had said he would. But now his Father and God is also the believers' Father and God. A new, more intimate relationship with the Creator is about to ensue.

❦

EXCITING INFORMATION

"**M**ary Magdalene went and said to the disciples, 'I have seen the Lord'; and she told them that he had said these things to her."

John 20:18

In the original her name change sticks. She is again "Mariam the Magdalene," from Magdala, a town on the western shore of Lake Galilee. She had a double motivation to go to the disciples. Jesus told her to, and also she was burning with the desire to let others in on the most exciting news ever given.

Bob and Barbara Boesch in Nepture, NJ had been led to accept Jesus Christ as their Lord and Savior late one night. They were Episcopalians. She had been allowing the Jehovah Witnesses to hold meetings in their home. The next afternoon I went by to visit her. She said, "This morning, after having invited Christ into my heart last night, I read the 20th chapter of John. I read how Mary Magdalene went and told his disciples, 'I have seen the Lord.' It dawned on me that Jesus really is alive. Like Mary I had to tell someone, so I ran (several hundred yards) to tell my neighbor that Jesus has been raised from the dead." Impression without expression leaves depression. Impression plus expression produces exhilaration. The word for "seen" here is horao, meaning experience or personal encounter. We know from Luke 24:11 that her words seemed to them an idle fairy tale, and they did not believe them. In those days the testimony of a woman carried no weight in a court of law. It had no value. Hysterical woman talk, they thought. For them to believe, it would be necessary to experience him themselves. This they were about to do.

"On the evening of that day, the first day of the week, the doors being shut where the disciples were, for fear of the Jews, Jesus came and stood among them and said to them, 'Peace be with you.'" He scared them spitless. They thought they were seeing a ghost. Their hearts were in their mouths, but only for a moment.

THE WAR IS OVER

"**O***n the evening of that day, the first day of the week...*"

John 20:19

Already on the first day of the New Creation we have encountered the four original themes of the gospel: testimony, faith, life, and abiding/ homecoming. We are prepared now to look for the fifth theme: new birth. Seek, and ye shall find.

"..the doors being shut where the disciples were for fear of the Jews..." They were terrified that the Jews like the gestapo would come for them as they had for Jesus, to nail them up. We may be sure that the doors were locked and bolted. Suddenly, unexpectedly they got the shock of their lives: "Jesus came and stood among them." How had he gotten in the room? He got in the same way he got out of the grave bands and out of the tomb. He had a spiritual body that is not subject to the laws of time and space. He could appear and vanish at will.

"He said to them, `Peace be with you.'" This was the customary greeting, like our "hello," though in this setting it meant infinitely more. His first word to his assembled disciples after his resurrection expressed his gift to them purchased by his sacrificial death upon the cross. "You have peace with God now. By my shed blood I have washed away all your filthy stains. The armistice has been signed in the blood of the cross. The war between God and man is over. Lay down your arms." In September 1945, the armistice between Japan and the U.S. was signed on the battleship Missouri. The war was officially over. Even so many Japanese soldiers on the islands of the South Pacific did not get the message. They were hiding out and continuing the war for many years. Nearly two thousand years have elapsed since Jesus revealed by his resurrection that the great war is over. Tragically more than half of the world's population has not yet heard the good news. Isn't it time we got the message out?

❦

JESUS REVEALS HIMSELF

"When he had said this, he showed them his hands and his side."
John 20:20

They thought he was a ghost, a disembodied spirit, until he showed them his nail-pierced hands and his side with the gaping wound. On his resurrection body he still bore the marks of slaughter, as he does on his ascended, glorified body. They are the eternal badge of his love.

"Then the disciples were glad when they saw (eido, when it came into clear focus for them that he was) the LORD." Prior to this they called him Teacher and Lord, but by Lord they meant merely Master, as though he were the Master and they were his slaves. Now for the first time they saw who he really is: the LORD. In the Greek it is the word KURIOS. It is a rendering of the Hebrew YAHWEH, the name of God that was regarded as so sacred that they refused to pronounce it. They spoke of it instead as The Name. It was the name given to Moses at the burning bush in Exodus 3:14, and means "I AM WHO I AM" or "I WILL BE WHAT I WILL BE." It could be paraphrased, "I am the One without beginning or end, The Eternal One." Since Jesus is alive again, it is now evident that he cannot be exterminated. He keeps coming back like a song.

"Jesus said to them again `Peace be with you.'" Through the blood of the cross they already had a peaceful relationship with God. Now they could begin to enjoy a little emotional peace - a completely different matter. "`As the Father has sent me, even so I send you.'" He had already imparted to them his pardon and his peace; now he bestows upon them his purpose. They have a purpose now in life - to make Jesus known, even as Jesus had made the Father known. This was their commissioning as his apostles, his sent out ones. A Christian organization called The Navigators has as their purpose: to know Him and to make Him known. That captures it, doesn't it? Lord, reveal yourself afresh to me, that I may be an inspiration to others.

❦

A NEW CREATURE IN CHRIST

"**W**hen he had said this, he breathed on them, and said to them, *'Receive the Holy Spirit.'*" *John 20:22*

They had already received his pardon, his peace, his purpose. Now they received his indwelling presence. We are taken back to Genesis 2:7, where it says concerning the first man made of dust, "and (God) breathed into his nostrils the breath of life." But the breath (Spirit) of God left him when he disobeyed by eating the forbidden fruit. Ever since humanity has been conceived in sin without the Holy Spirit within. Jesus is the only exception, as he was conceived in Mary's womb through the overshadowing of the Holy Spirit. His spirit and the Holy Spirit were both within him from the moment of conception: his spirit the candle, the Holy Spirit the flame. Proverbs 20:27

The Holy Spirit could not be given until after Jesus had been glorified by death and resurrection. See John 7:39. In his physical death Jesus exhaled and refused to inhale. Now as the Risen One he is privileged to exhale over his disciples. Indeed he breathed the divine breath of the Holy Spirit into each one of them, and they were born anew, born again, born from above. John 20:22.

Jesus had said to Nicodemus in John 3:3, "Unless one is born anew, he cannot see the kingdom of God." Having seen Jesus crucified, dead, buried, and now risen, and having received the benefits thereof, they were now privileged to get their candles lit. From this moment on they were no longer natural men but spiritual men. Their bodies were now temples indwelt by the Spirit of God. Their spirits (inner selves) were now impregnated by the Spirit of God. My spirit may be thought of as the ova or egg, and the Holy Spirit as the sperm. When the two unite, there is a new creation. We became new creatures in Christ when we made the infinite resignation. If we have not yet done so, isn't it time we did?

❧

THE ROYAL PRIESTHOOD

"If you forgive the sins of any, they are forgiven; if you retain the sins of any, they are retained." John 20:23

Jesus said this to his disciples who had now received new birth. If you have been born a second time, born of God, you also have become a priest. You are a part of that Royal Priesthood spoken of in I Peter 2:9 and in Revelation 1:6. You have been charged with the sacred task of telling the gospel story. Those who believe the good news you may invite to confess their sins. You may then assure those who do, that they have been forgiven at the cross. Those who do not believe will not confess their sins. You must tell them that their sins are upon their own heads, and that they will receive their eternal punishment for them.

John 3:31 says, "He who comes from above is above all; he who is of the earth belongs to the earth, and of the earth he speaks; he who comes from heaven is above all. He bears witness to what he has seen and heard, yet no one receives his testimony; he who receives his testimony sets his seal to this, that God is true." Now you too have been born from above, and you too will bear witness to what you have seen and heard. You have a built-in urge to do so. As with Jesus, comparatively few will believe your testimony. Those who do will praise God; the rest will mock.

"For he whom God has sent utters the words of God, for it is not by measure that he gives the Spirit; the Father loves the Son, and has given all things into his hand. He who believes the Son has eternal life; he who does not obey the Son shall not see life, but the wrath of God rests upon him." The wrath of God rests upon unbelievers. It manifests itself primarily in sexual promiscuity. If we do not allow Jesus to control us, our sinful urges will. Romans 1:24-32 goes into all that follows the rejection of the gospel in vivid detail.

❦

THE SKEPTIC

"*ow Thomas, one of the twelve, called the Twin, was not with them when Jesus came.*" *John 20:24*

Thomas was the melancholy type. As such he was a loner. He has many twins. I am one of them. The crucifixion of Jesus had shot him out of the sky. He had crashed to earth in total dismay. So the disciples of Jesus left him alone to eat his heart out in dispair? An impossible possibility. They sought out the strayed sheep. When they found him, "the other disciples told him, `We have seen (experienced) the Lord.' But he said to them, `Unless I see in his hands the print of the nails, and place my finger in the mark of the nails, and place my hand in his side, I will not believe.'" That was his way of saying, "You have all been hoodwinked. You cannot reason me into like-minded faith. Jesus himself will have to twist my arm to make me a believer. I am fed up with being disillusioned. The pain and grief are more than I can bear."

"Eight days later, his disciples were again in the house (where they had celebrated the Last Supper), and Thomas was with them. (They obliged the skeptic to stick with them.) The doors were shut (no mention, though, of the fear of the Jews, as faith and joy had crowded out fear), but Jesus came and stood among them, and said, `Peace be with you.' (When we gather in his name, we sense his presence by the peace he brings.) Then he said to Thomas, `Put your finger here, and see my hands; and put out your hand and place it in my side; do not be faithless, but believing.'"

Two observations: One, Jesus was establishing the first day of the week as the special occasion for corporate worship. Two, he was present, though unseen, when Thomas had laid down his three-fold requirement for faith. For centuries the church has referred to this occasion as "the eighth day." Eight in the gospel speaks of new beginnings. There is hope for us all.

THE DEEPEST HEALING OF ALL

*"**T**homas answered him, 'My Lord and my God!'"*
John 20:28

When Jesus offered Thomas the privilege of satisfying his demand to make tangible contact with the wounds in his hands and side, did Thomas avail himself of the opportunity? We are not told, but for Thomas to have done so strikes me as grotesque. I am persuaded that he fell on his knees before the risen Christ to worship and adore. His confession, "My Lord and my God!" is the climax of this gospel.

Mariam had called him, "Rabboni," my Great Teacher. He is that, but infinitely more. Mariam was the emotional type. She and those she represents are the first to experience Jesus as their Savior. Thomas, the skeptical type, takes the long way around, but when he arrives, he has a deeper grasp of who Jesus is: not only his Lord, but also his God in human form. Jesus did not say to Thomas, "Don't say that; it is blasphemy." On the contary, he said to him, "Have you believed because you have seen (horao, in the sense of experienced) me? Blessed (to be congratulated) are those who have not seen (eido, in the sense of getting a clear idea of me) and yet believe." This is the final beatitude in the gospels, and it pertains to those of us who have not encountered Jesus in as tangible a way as the first generation of believers. Our faith in Jesus does not arrive through the eye gate, but through the ear gate. Faith comes through hearing, and hearing through the preaching of Christ. Romans 10:17

In retrospect we see that beginning with The Arrest in chapter 18 we have encountered all of the seven themes. In chapters 18 and 19 (the Tribulation): theme 6, which is nurture. In chapter 20 (the Triumph) prior to the Thomas story: themes 1 to 5. Now with Thomas we see at work theme 7: healing. He received the deepest healing of all, when Jesus healed him of his unbelief. Amen. This gospel is a four-storied structure.

❧

WHY WAS THIS GOSPEL WRITTEN?

"Now Jesus did many other signs in the presence of the disciples, which are not written in this book." John 20:30

John has given us a sample of the many signs which Jesus did during his days of ministry. He has given us only seven miraculous signs. Do you remember them? The first was turning water into wine, the key sign at Cana, that sheds light on the others. The second was healing the official's son across the miles. The third was healing the man who was 38 years an invalid. The fourth was multiplying the loaves and fishes. The fifth was coming to his disciples upon the waves of the sea. The sixth was giving sight to the man born blind. The seventh and climactic sign was restoring Lazarus, four days dead, to life. In each instance he brought joy, as symbolized by the wine. He also fulfilled in each sign his word, "I have come that you may have life, and have it abundantly."

All the signs that Jesus did fell into one of the above categories. Telling more would have been superfluous. But why did John relate these seven? He tells us: "But these are written that you may believe that Jesus is the Christ, the Son of God, and that believing you may have life in his name."

This assertion confirms our interpretation of this gospel. It underlines the three beginning themes. First, testimony. As the Baptist gave his testimony in chapter 1:19-34, so these seven signs also testify to Jesus. Why the testimony? That you may believe, the theme in ch. 1:35-51, which teaches us how faith begins and develops. But what is the value of faith? "That believing you may have life in his name." The theme of life is the third theme. It was first manifested at the wedding at Cana. 2:1-12 So underlying this gospel there is an equation: testimony + faith = life. It releases more power than Einstein's $E = MC$ squared, which made possible the Atomic Age. It ushers in the Age of Glory.

THE STAGE IS SET

"*After this Jesus revealed himself again to the disciples by the Sea of Tiberias; and he revealed himself in this way.*" *John 21:1*

Chapter 20 developed the theme of new birth under the aspect of seeing the kingdom of God as promised in 2:3. Chapter 21 (the epilogue) continues the theme of the new creation from the standpoint of entering the kingdom, first mentioned in 2:5. It answers the question "What kind of life results from believing in the risen Christ?"

The circumstance is no longer Jerusalem but Galilee. The great redemptive events happened in Jerusalem (death, burial, and resurection), but we normally encounter Jesus in Galilee, which represents where we feel at home and carry on our daily activities. Mark 16:7 records the angel saying to the women, "Go, tell his disciples and Peter that he is going before you to Galilee; there you will see him, as he told you." So the disciples returned to their homes by the lake, where the narrative resumes.

"Simon Peter (always the lead-off man, as the first among equals), Thomas called the Twin, Nathanael of Cana in Galilee, the sons of Zebedee, and two others of his disciples were together." Notice that there were seven of them, five identified, two anonymous. Nathanael is the third one mentioned, reminding us of the third day, when the marriage took place in his old home town of Cana. Indeed, what happens in this chapter was anticipated by the sign that occurred there. The wedding at Cana is the key that unlocks the hidden meaning in chapter 21. When you think of it, you realize that 3 X 7 = 21. On the third day the wedding took place attended by Jesus and six disciples (seven all together). Again we are about to encounter the life manifested at the wedding, this time with seven disciples present. Jesus is the eighth one at hand, and eight is the number of new beginnings. The stage is set.

❦

THE SEVEN COLORFUL DISCIPLES

"**H**is disciples were together." John 21:2

Is it possible that even the chapter numbers are inspired? An intriguing suggestion. We saw yesterday the two perfect numbers conspiring to form 21: three, the number comprising the Godhead, as well as the day of the marriage, and seven, the sacred number saturating this gospel. The seven disciples in verse two remind us of the seven disciples with speaking parts in this gospel. Each one ties in with one of the seven themes.

First, Peter, whose testimony at Pentecost converted the 3000. Color him red (for blood). Second, John, whose faith brought him the closest of all to Jesus. Color him blue (sky/heaven). Third, Nathanael, to whom Jesus said he would see heaven opened, as began to happen on the third day at Cana, his home-town. Color him yellow (for the life-giving sun). Fourth, Judas, the devil who betrayed Jesus, sending him by way of the cross back home to his Father, with whom he abides in heaven. When Iscariot departs, the other Judas takes his place and asks the homecoming question. 14:22 Color them lavender, (blood-red/blue).

Fifth, Andrew, gifted at bringing others to Jesus (his brother, the lad with the sack lunch, the Greeks), reproducing after his kind, the fruitful one. Color him green (folliage). Sixth, Philip, to whom Jesus asked the nurture question, "How are we to buy bread, so that these people may eat?" 6:5 Color him purple, for the grape which we eat and drink. Seventh, Thomas, who was healed of his flagrant disbelief on the eighth day, the day of new beginnings. Thomas' twins are legion - for all of us, if honest as he, must say, "Lord, I believe, help my unbelief." The ordeals of life are designed to purify our faith. So color Thomas and us orange (red/yellow). Red speaks of dying daily; yellow of the miracle-working life of Jesus first manifested at Cana. With which one do you most identify?

GOING FISHING

"*Simon Peter said to them, 'I am going fishing.'*"

John 21:3

We have seen the bumper sticker, "I would rather be fishing."
It is a natural desire, especially for an inveterate fisherman.
Don't just sit there; do something, even if it is the wrong thing.
Just sitting around can drive you up the wall. So Peter is on his
way back to where he started out when Jesus called him from his
nets to become a fisher of men. After all, he does have the skill
to catch fish. He has yet to demonstrate any prowess in fishing
for men. Also he had failed the Lord so miserably that he doubts
if he has any future in the kingdom of God business. "They said
to him, 'We will go with you.'" The power of Peter as a leader
comes out here. As Simon Peter goes, so goes the church.

"They went out and got into the boat." As they entered
into the boat, so they are about to enter in a surprising way into
the kingdom of God, the divine activity. "But that night they
caught nothing." The wine has failed. They were snakebit. The
coin kept coming up tails. They were tired, miserable, frus-
trated.

"Just as day was breaking, (and the expectation of
catching any fish was about to be abandoned), Jesus stood on the
beach." He is a very present help in the time of trouble. "Yet the
disciples did not know that it was Jesus." The risen Christ has
a way of approaching us on our blind side. Actually he is always
with us. I will never leave you, nor forsake you, he has said.
"Jesus said to them, 'Children, have you any fish?'" "Children"
to grown men? They had been involved with him less than four
years, so spiritually speaking they have not yet gone to kinder-
garten. 'Have you any relish to put on your bread?'(literally)
"They answered him, 'No.'" Our life is without relish. We are
barely survivors. We have to confess our failure and our sin
before Jesus can do anything for us.

313

FAITH, LIFE, ABIDING

"**H**e said to them, `Cast the net on the right side of the boat, and you will find some.'*" John 21:6*

A minister behind the Iron Curtain was preaching on this passage. For quoting what Jesus said here to his disciples, he was arrested and sent to prison. The Communist officials accused him of telling the people that the reason they went to bed hungry at night was because they were fishing from the left side of the boat. If they would fish from the right side like the democratic nations, they would have plenty to eat.

They evidently believed that the stranger on the shore saw evidence of a shoal of fish on the right side of the boat, "so they cast it." Here is the theme of faith. If you believe the word, you obey it. Faith is acting on the word of God. "And now they were not able to haul it in, for the quantity of the fish." This expresses the next theme in the gospel, life. Suddenly there was so much life in the net that the seven of them together could not haul it aboard.

"That disciple whom Jesus loved said to Peter, `It is the Lord!' When Peter heard it was the Lord, he put on his clothes, for he was stripped for work, and sprang into the sea." Why did he do that? Because his fervent desire was to abide at Jesus' side. (Abiding is the next logical theme.) His goal was to be at home with Jesus. Once again John our evangelist perceives immediately that it is Jesus. Peter, as the more enterprising of the two, acts upon the information. Peter picks up knowledge through his five senses. John derives insight through his intuition. "But the other disciples came in the boat, dragging the net full of fish, for they were not far from the land, but about a hundred yards off." They rowed ashore in the little boat. Remember the spiritual song, "Michael, row your boat ashore, Allelluia"? We are approaching the shore where Jesus is: heaven. What a marvelous homecoming that will be!

❧

SUPERNATURAL PROVISION

"𝕎hen they got out on land, they saw a charcoal fire there, with fish lying on it, and bread." John 21:9

Jesus had prepared them a breakfast. As he had been their servant and washed their feet before his passion, so afterward he was still their servant. There was one notable thing about this breakfast: there was but one "opsarion", the Greek for a little fish. He surely did not intend to feed seven hungry men with one little fish. How did he get it? Did he tell it to swim to his hand? Or did he turn the stones there into bread and into one little fish? He could have or the devil's temptation was not real.

The answer to the question as to why only one little fish was provided is given in what follows: "Jesus said to them, Bring some of the fish that you have just caught.' He had forseen and foreordained the miraculous draught of fish which they had just secured. "We know that in everything God works for good with those who love him, who are called according to his purpose." Romans 8:28 He told them to bring "some of the fish" only. All of them would have fed a small army.

"So Simon Peter (the chief doer of God's word) went aboard and hauled the net ashore, full of large fish, a hundred and fifty-three of them." They were so astonished at the size of the catch that they made a count. Seventeen means "deliverance out of tribulation" on the basis of the law of first mention. Look at Genesis 7:11 and 8:4 concerning the flood and seventeen. Add up 1+2+3....all the way to 17 and the total is 153. In the Hebrew the number 18 means life. Jesus, their life and ours, told them exactly what to do in their frustrating situation. The result was deliverance out of tribulation. "And although there were so many the net was not torn." A second miracle. The gospel net is strong enough and large enough to hold all whom the Lord may bring. But some one has to cast the net.

❦

A SACRED BREAKFAST

"Jesus said to them, 'Come and have breakfast.'"

John 21:12

They were about to enjoy a sumptuous breakfast, dining upon the one little fish and the bread that Jesus had provided? In 14:22 Jesus had said, "He who believes in me will also do the works that I do; and greater works than these will he do, because I go to the Father." Their contribution to the breakfast expressed the far greater success their ministry would enjoy than had the ministry of Jesus. On the occasion of Pentecost one throw of the gospel net would catch 3000 converts. After more than three years of ministry, all Jesus had to show for it was 120 who would do what he said by staying in Jerusalem for ten days. "Now none of the disciples dared ask him, 'Who are you?' They knew it was the LORD." There was no idle talk. A reverent hush had seized them all.

A communion service was being conducted in a home. The daughter broke the silence, "Now, mother, drink your grape juice." There was none of that irreverence on the lake shore.

"Jesus came and took the bread and gave it to them and so with the fish." The fish which he broke and gave to them was the opsarion, the one little fish which he had provided. He made no use of the 153 large fish which they had just caught. We may assume that they ate until they were satisfied, as was true of the multitudes when he fed them. This implies that when he broke the loaf of bread and the fish, they multiplied in his hands. What has happened here? Jesus had come to them after their long frustrating night of toiling over the nets in vain. But, praise God, our labor is not in vain in the Lord. He gave them a word of instruction. They did as told, and suddenly, surprisingly, they enjoyed astonishing success. Large fish don't congregate in schools. Jesus had turned water into wine, hunger into spiritual and physical satisfaction. So this chapter has to do with entering the Kingdom, which we experience from time to time, when by God's grace victory is snatched out of immanent defeat.

A DOUBLE FAILURE

"**T**his *was now the third time that Jesus was revealed to the disciples after he was raised from the dead.*" *John 21:14*

There are eleven resurrection appearances recorded in the New Testament, but John is preoccupied with three. The first was on Easter evening to the ten apostles, when they received within themselves the testimony of the Holy Spirit. The second was a week later to the ten and Thomas, when Thomas expressed his faith in the deepest way possible, "My Lord and my God." The third was to the seven disciples by the lake, when Jesus disclosed that he makes possible the abundant life. To experience that life we must stay alert to the fact that he is able to manifest himself at any time, and that he frequently does so through strangers. If like little children we will humbly do what we are told, we may experience success in life that goes beyond our fondest expectations. He will give us our daily bread, and even add some relish - himself.

"When they had finished breakfast, Jesus said to Simon Peter, `Simon, son of John, do you love me more than these?" Why had Jesus addressed him by his former surname (son of John) instead of Peter? Was it because he had returned to his former manner of life as a fisher of fish? Had Simon experienced so many things (including spiritual birth) in vain?

By following Jesus at the beginning Simon had indicated that he loved Jesus more than his livelihood as a professional fisherman. He had even boasted that he loved Jesus more than his companions: "Though they all fall away, I will not." Do you love me more than fishing, more than these others do? Simon had been humbled, even abased. Not only had he failed Jesus worse than the others, he could not enable them to catch even one miserable fish, though he knew the lake like the back of his hand. He was a double failure: as a disciple and as a fisherman.

❦

PROVE YOUR LOVE

"He said to him, 'Yes, Lord; you know that I love you.'"

John 21:15

Lord, you can leave out the "more than these." I am finished with boasting and making pretensious claims. Never again will I trust in the flesh, or in my own natural abililty. "He said to him, `Feed my lambs.'" Express your love for me by feeding my little ones with the sincere milk of God's word. "A second time he said to him, `Simon, son of John, do you love me?'" I take your suggestion by leaving out all comparisons. "He said to him, `Yes, Lord; you know that I love you.' He said to him, `Tend my sheep.'" Show that you love me by shepherding (looking out for the welfare of) my little sheep (literally), a more difficult task than the first.

"He said to him the third time, `Simon, son of John, do you love me?' Peter was grieved because he said to him the third time, `Do you love me.'" He was grieved on two accounts. The first was because putting the question for the third time reminded him of the three times he had denied Jesus, a pain and a hurt that he could never forget. Though forgiven, from that time on he felt he was unworthy to be Jesus' emmisary. This was one of the reasons he was back fishing for fish.

The second cause for grief was because Jesus had changed the word he was using for love. In the first two questions, he used the word agape, which is used to express God's kind of love. Do you have the same love for me that I have for you, the love that is patient and kind, faithful, willing to endure all the consequences? Peter answered with the word phileo, which simply means "I am your friend." Now Jesus stepped down to Peter's assertion, and asked, "Are you my friend?" "And he said to him, `Lord, you know everything (you are the only One who does); you know that I am your friend.' Jesus said to him, `Feed my sheep.'" The most difficult task of all is to nurture the faith of   Jesus' mature disciples.

❦

NEW BIRTH AND NURTURE

*"**J**esus said to him, 'Feed my sheep.'"*   *John 21:17*

Earlier in the epilogue we had encountered the themes of faith, life, and abiding. Then, when Jesus served his disciples breakfast, we came to the theme of nurture. What has happened to new birth? Seek and you will find. In his conversation with Simon, son of John, Jesus has taken seriously the fact that Peter is back to where he started out, fishing for fish. Is it possible that Simon has failed Jesus so miserably that he feels he is no longer worthy to be an apostle? He has lost face. So in the presence of his peers Peter was privileged to confess his love for Jesus three times, once for each denial. In the process Simon is reborn as an apostle, and is entitled to be addressed again as Peter, man of rock. The devil had ground him to dust, to powder under his heel, but Jesus has reconstituted him as a solid stone in the presence of his companions.

Actually we are born again only once. But as our life unfolds we experience new birth, in a sense, again and again. How is Simon Peter, now restored, to demonstrate his affection for Jesus? By nurturing the lambs and the full grown sheep. So we get a double dose of nurture: Jesus feeds his disciples, and his disciples in turn feed the rest of the flock.

"Truly, truly, I say to you, when you were young, you girded yourself and walked where you would; but when you are old, you will stretch out your hands, and another will gird you and carry you where you do not wish to go." Jesus had prophecied Peter's death. As an old man, the story goes, Peter was fleeing from Rome. He encountered Jesus entering the city, and asked, "Lord, where are you going?" "To be crucified in your place." So Peter returned to the city, where he was crucified head downward, his feet pointing heavenward, because he felt unworthy to die as his Lord died.

THE ULTIMATE HEALING

"(This he said to show by what death he was to glorify God.)"
John 21:19

We have seen that Jesus prophecied to Peter that he would die in a way he did not will, by having his hands stretched out upon a cross. I can see him now, the blood rushing to his head as his feet point heavenward, acknowledging in this way his unworthiness to die as his Lord died. So he glorified God. As soon as he breathed his last, he was glorified by God, who immediately welcomed him into heaven. "And after this he said to him, `Follow me.'" Follow Jesus, Peter did from the cross into glory, which is the ultimate healing. Please note that in this chapter we have now observed themes two to seven, everything from faith to healing.

As far as we know Peter was the only one who ever glorified God by being crucified upside down. What Jesus said to him concerning what would happen to him in his old age, though, is a parable that applies to many of us. Should we live many years, we will stretch out our hands and be taken to a hospital or nursing home, where we will be cared for as though we were infants. Others will dress and undress us, and we will experience the indignity of bed pan and needle, of exposure, discomfort and pain. Is this not an expression of the cross? But, praise God, the way of the cross leads home to glory and heaven.

For a more detailed parable of growing old, examine Ecclesiastes 12, where "the keepers" are the hands, "the strong men" the legs, "the windows" the eyes, and "the dust returns to the earth as it was, and the spirit returns to God who gave it." My soul may be destructable (should I be sent to hell, God forbid), but my spirit, fathered by God, will exist forever with or without God. From him I will receive eternal life or eternal destruction, depending upon what response I have made to Jesus and his saving love. Lord Jesus, save me now, if I have never called upon you before.

"WHOSE TESTIMONY IS THIS?

eter turned and saw following them the disciple whom Jesus loved, who had lain close to the breast of Jesus at the supper and had said, 'Lord, who is it that is going to betray you?'"

John 21:20

Our evangelist could be called Jesus' right hand man, the friend who sticks closer than a brother. "When Peter saw him, he said to Jesus, 'Lord, what about this man?'" He had disclosed to Peter his fate, but what were John's marching orders? What would he come to? "Jesus said to him, 'If it is my will that he remain until I come, what is that to you? Follow me!'" It is no concern of yours what befalls this other disciple. Your sole responsibility is to fulfill your destiny in the service of God. In the final analysis I am answerable only for myself. Every individual will give his/her accounting to God.

"The saying spread abroad among the brethren that this disciple was not to die; yet Jesus did not say to him that he was not to die, but, 'If it is my will that he remain until I come, what is that to you?'" In the primitive Church the believers took seriously the promise of the coming of Christ for his Bride, the Church. They thought that it could happen at any moment. They hoped that it would occur in their generation. Obviously it did not. One by one the apostles died, until this disciple alone was left. Then at last, he died. It was not the will of Jesus that he should remain until the catching up of the Church.

"This is the disciple who is bearing witness to these things, and who has written these things." All that we have read from chapter one, verse one to this verse is the testimony of an eye witness. He and Andrew followed Jesus the second time they heard the Baptist say, "Behold the Lamb of God." This is the testimony. "And we know that his testimony is true." We have the witness of the Spirit in our hearts. Note: all seven themes are found in this chapter.

321

DON'T WRITE A BOOK

"𝔅*ut there are also many other things which Jesus did; were every one of them to be written, I suppose the world itself could not contain the books that would be written." John 21:25*

This gospel, we believe, was some thirty years in composition under the leading of the Holy Spirit. John was a master architect, and this testimony to Jesus is like a cathedral. In the prologue he laid a foundation. The seven themes are found in ch. 1:11-17. Upon the foundation he laid a structure four stories high: from chs. 1 to 11 two stories, then from chs. 12 to 20 two stories. In chapter 21, the epilogue, he puts a roof on the structure.

On Jan. 23, 1963 I was reflecting about the wedding at Cana occuring on the third day. It was the third day after Jesus had said to Philip, "Follow me," that it happened. I thought, "Could it also be the third day as we have it in Genesis chapter 1?" When I looked at the gospel on the basis of its motifs, it exploded in my face. I took our children's building blocks and started reconstructing the gospel episode by episode, arranging the seven themes in the shape of a cross. Every block fell into place almost of its own accord. I had a revival in my heart. But it lasted for only eight months. For I came to realize that no matter how hard I tried, I could get only a few to see what I saw. I had eaten the little scroll spoken of in Rev. 10:10. It was honey in my mouth, but bitterness in my stomach. For three and a half years I was sick of this gospel. But it propelled me into the power dimension of the faith. Only after I had experienced something of Pentecost could I again teach the fourth gospel.

I have written a little of what Jesus did for me through John's expression of the gospel. Doubtless everyone who has read it has been changed in some measure, and could write a book about it. But the world is too small to hold them, and also would run out of paper and ink.

❦

THE APOSTOLIC CHURCH

"*The revelation of Jesus Christ which God gave him to show to his servants what must soon take place.*" *Revelation 1:1*

Martin Luther said that the book of Revelation will either find you mad or leave you so. He did not understand it and so left it alone. A little girl was drawing a picture. When asked what she was drawing a picture of, she said, "Of God." "But no one knows what God looks like." She exclaimed, "They will when I've finished." Viewing Revelation from the perspective of John's gospel, we are amazed to see it come into focus. We may regard Revelation chapter one as the prologue in which we may find the seven themes when we look for them. Chapters two and three are the letters to the seven churches. We shall look at these letters from a double perspective: the seven themes in the gospel, and the seven kingdom parables in Matthew 13. We shall treat the seven letters as prophetic of the Church Age.

The first church, Ephesus, symbolizes the Apostolic Age from 30 to 98 AD. We assign 98 as an approximate date for the death of John, the last surviving original apostle. This church has successfully identified false apostles by testing their counterfeit message by the standard of the testimony of the original apostles. Already the church has fallen from its first love. The parable of the Sower in Matt. 13:3-9 points to the fact that this church has received the good seed of God's word that is able to produce a bountiful harvest.

As an old man John was carried into the church of Ephesus and was asked to bring a word from the Lord. He said, "Little children, love one another." They said, "Wonderful. Now give us another word from the Lord." He said, "Little children, love one another." "Marvelous. But can't you give us another word from the Lord?" He said, "That you love one another is the only word from the Lord you need."

❧

323

THE FAITHFUL CHURCH

"*And to the angel of the church of Smyrna write: 'The words of the first and the last, who died and came to life.'*" *Revelation 2:8*

The church of Smyrna symbolizes the Church Age from 98 to 312 AD. This was the persecuted church that kept the faith during the two centuries when Rome attempted to drive it out of existence. Then in 312 AD the Emperor Constantine became a Christian and declared the Roman Empire "Christian". The persecution immediately ceased. The key word to this church is "Be faithful unto death." Jesus identified himself as the one "who died and came to life." The word Smyrna in the Greek is myrrh, used in embalming the dead. Some in the church would be tested in prison for ten days, a number that speaks of trial and testing. There is no word of criticism. On the contrary, "He who conquers shall not be hurt by the second death." So the death to fear is not physical death, but the death of being thrown into the lake of fire after the judgment.

We have seen the emphasis on faith and faithfulness, the second theme. Also we should perceive the application of the second kingdom parable in Mt. 13:24-30, that of the wheat and the tares. The tares inevitably make life miserable for the wheat, but the wheat is to endure the presence of the tares. It is useless for the wheat to battle the tares. The two are to grow up together until the time of harvest, when the angels of God make the final separation.

In our day the wheat and the tares seem to be coming to fruition simultaneously. The wicked are becoming, if possible, more ruthless, while the believers are experiencing more and more of the power of the Spirit. When this gospel of the kingdom, fleshed out with signs and wonders attesting to the truth of it, is taken to all the nations, then Jesus, who is the beginning and the end, will come for his bride. Mt. 24:14 What a day of rejoicing that will be.

THE TRAGIC MARRIAGE

"**A**nd *to the angel of the church of Pergamos write: 'The words of him who has the sharp two-edged sword.'" Revelation 2:12*

"On the third day there was a marriage (gamos, in the Greek) at Cana in Galilee." John 2:1 Now in Revelation by the same writer the third church is Pergamos. It is more than a coincidence. It is the key to understanding this last book of the Bible. This church symbolizes the Church Age from 312 to 452 AD. It is The Married Church.

When Constantine declared his empire Christian, the persecution ceased and the need for faithfulness unto death also. Suddenly it became politically expedient to join the church, and so to score brownie points with the emperor. The result was that the world streamed into the church; everyone and his brother became nominally Christian. This happened despite the fact that 2 Cor. 6:14 says, "Do not be mismated with unbelievers." There existed for a century-and-a-half a mixed marriage, which produced vinegar, not wine. Some came to "hold the teaching of the Nicolaitans," clericalism, which pretends that there are first, second, and third class Christians.

The third kingdom parable of the mustard seed become a tree found fulfillment. Matt. 13:31-32 The growth of the church like that of a mustard seed seemed miraculous. It spread like a tree over the earth, so that the birds came to nest in its branches. But woe to him who cannot differentiate between the tree and the birds. The tree represents the kingdom of God; the birds speak of the nations of earth that shelter in its branches. No matter how long it nests there the bird never becomes a branch of the tree. There is no such thing as a Christian nation. The Church itself is the holy nation, and it is half sheep and half goats, half wheat and half tares. It is miraculous that the Church should flourish half slave and half free, though it dwells where Satan's throne is, the planet earth.

❧

THE TOLERANT CHURCH

"*And* to the angel of the church in Thyatira write: 'The words of the Son of God.'" *Revelation 2:18*

Thyatira symbolizes the Church Age from 452 to 1517 AD. When we look at the letter to this church from the standpoint of the fourth gospel theme of abiding/homecoming, we find that the shoe fits. In 452 AD Attila the Hun and his barbarian hordes had arrived at the gates of Rome prepared to sack the city. Pope Leo I went out to meet him and prevailed upon him to spare the city. The bishop of Rome had displaced the emperor, who was no more. The papacy was born. The papa of the Roman church now wore two hats: the sacred and the secular.

From 452 to 1517 AD, when Martin Luther nailed up his 95 theses and the Protestant Reformation began, the world and the church cohabited under one roof and one head. Under Constantine the marriage had taken place and been consummated. Now under Leo I the church and the world would settle in together for more than a thousand years in what has been called the Dark Ages. Our letter excoriates Jezebel for introducing immorality and idolatry and for refusing to repent. Jezebel means "without cohabitation." Is it possible that behind every statue of "the Virgin Mary" lurks a Jezebel demon? Jesus' mother cohabited with Joseph as his wife and bore him children.

The fourth kingdom parable tells of a woman who hid leaven in three measures of flour, till it was all leavened. Matt. 13:33 Leaven represents the corruption that produces pride and every other evil. The leaven that Jezebel brought into the church of Thyatira was the doctrine of "works righteousness." This heresy pretends that one can earn a right standing with God by good deeds, a complete denial of the message contained in the letter St. Paul wrote to the Christians at Rome. Some in Thyatira did not hold to this teaching but received the promise of the morning star. Always in the history of the Church there has been the saving remnant.

❦

THE TRADITIONAL CHURCH

"*And to the angel of the church in Sardis write: 'The words of him who has the seven spirits of God and the seven stars.'*"

Revelation 3:1

The church of Sardis symbolizes the Church Age from 1517 to 1900. We would expect the fifth church to illustrate the fifth gospel theme and the fifth kingdom parable in Mt. 13, and it does. The fifth theme is new birth. A Catholic monk by the name of Martin Luther was studying St. Paul's letters to the Romans and the Galatians and discovered the teaching that "we are justified by faith, not by works, lest any man should boast." It resulted in him going the way of Nicodemus and of the man born blind, who received his sight and was kicked out of his religion.

He had experienced the truth contained in the parable of the man who finds the treasure in the field (the gospel of grace) and in joy sells all that he has to purchase the field with the treasure. Matthew 13:44 As the plow had unearthed the treasure, so Luther's study of Paul had unearthed the good news that had been hidden from the Church for centuries.

It resulted in the Reformation, and the Counter-reformation within the church of Rome. But tragically the followers of Luther failed to pursue his probing of the Bible, which would have produced new revelations. Instead they spent their time consolidating what had been gained, and fell into scholasticism, legalism on a higher level. So the message to Thyatira applies to the Church (Protestant and Catholic) which has gone through the Reformation: "I know your works; you have the name (reputation) of being alive, and you are dead. Awake, and strengthen what remains and is on the point of death, for I have not found your works perfect in the sight of my God.... Repent." Much of what masquerades as Christianity is nothing more than churchianity. Tradition will save no one; Jesus Christ is the only Savior of man.

❧

THE CHURCH OF THE OPEN DOOR

"*And to the angel of the church in Philadelphia write: 'The words of the holy one, the true one, who has the key of David.'*"

Revelation 3:7

The letters to the sixth and seventh churches address the situation in the Church Universal from 1901 to the present day. The 20th century began with an outpouring of the Holy Spirit in Topeka, Kansas, at the school established by Rev. Charles Parham. Church history came immediately to a fork in the road. Each individual and congregation was presented with the alternative of becoming part of the church of Philadelphia or of the church of Laodicea. If we refuse to become a member of the Church of Brotherly Love, we are inevitably a member of the Vomited Out Church.

The sixth church is the church of the open door, because it is the beneficiary of the sixth theme and parable. The sixth theme is worship and witness (nurture) in the Holy Spirit. The Philadelphia church presents an open door to Jesus Christ and to the Holy Spirit, with a resulting open door into the mission field and heaven. It has little power (in the natural), yet "you have kept my word and have not denied my name." It has found by seeking for it "the pearl of great price," (Matt. 13:45-46) even the empowering of the Holy Spirit and the accompanying manifestations. See I Cor. 12:8-10.

It is learning that Jesus loves it. Because it has kept his word of patient endurance, it will be kept from the hour of trial which is coming upon the whole world. The Greek expression is literally "will be kept out of the hour of trial." How? By being taken out of the situation when the door in heaven is opened, and a voice like a trumpet says, "Come up here." Rev. 4:1 It will participate in the first fruits catching up of the church, as symbolized by the five wise maidens in Mt. 25, who have not only the lamp of the word, but ample supply of Holy Spirit.

❧

THE LUKEWARM CHURCH

"*And to the angel of the church in Laodicea write: 'The words of the Amen, the faithful and true witness.'*" *Revelation 3:14*

If the church of Philadelphia was lean and hungry, the church of Laodicea is fat and sassy. This is the lukewarm church, that is going to be spewed out of the Lord's mouth. All of its needs are met. In the natural it is rich, but in the things of the kingdom it is empoverished. It has not learned that it is living in the red, that it owes all men the opportunity to learn of Jesus Christ. Why is it in such a deplorable condition? Because the Lord stands outside its door, seeking admission. Its members are nominal Christians. They know about Jesus Christ, but they do not know him.

This is the church that needs to experience the seventh gospel theme. It needs healing, the healing that comes through this prayer: Come into my heart Lord Jesus; there is room in my heart for you. The seventh parable concerning the fishermen sorting out the fish applies. Matt. 13:47-50 The good fish were separated from the bad on the basis of Leviticus 11:12, "Everything in the waters that has not fins and scales is an abomination to you." Spiritualizing it, we see that to be acceptable to the Lord at the end of the age, we must have both the fins of the Holy Spirit's guidance and empowering, as well as the scales of the full armor of God's word, spoken of in Ephesians 6:14-17.

When the Lord says, 'Come up here,' the believers symbolized by the five foolish maidens in Mt. 25:1-13 will be left behind. No longer will they be able to afford the luxury of remaining lukewarm, because the antichrist will be on the scene. Then, if they turn hot, they will be persecuted to martyrdom. But, if they turn cold to Jesus Christ, they will take the mark of the beast in order to survive. It will be the unforgivable sin in that time-frame, and it will send them to hell. See Revelation 14:9-11.

❦

THE ASTONISHING DISMISSAL

"After this I looked, and lo, in heaven an open door! And the first voice which I had heard speaking to me like a trumpet, said, `Come up here.'"   *Revelation 4:1*

John was caught up by the Spirit into heaven, anticipating what the obedient Christians will experience bodily. There he witnessed the heavenly worship. In chapter 5 the scroll with the seven seals comes into view. It is the title deed to earth. Only Jesus is worthy to open it. When he opens the first six seals in chapter 6, he begins to divest the devil of his strangle hold on the earth. Not until the church of Philadelphia has been dismissed from the earth can the antichrist manifest himself.

This is explained by Paul in 2 Thess. 2:3 - for the day of the Lord's wrath "will not come, unless the rebellion comes first, and the man of lawlessness is revealed, the son of perdition (another human devil like Iscariot), who opposes and exalts himself against every so-called god or object of worship, so that he takes his seat in the temple of God, proclaiming himself to be God... And you know what is restraining him now, so that he may be revealed in his time. For the mystery of lawlessness is already at work; only he who now restrains it will do so until he is out of the way (literally, out of the midst, referring to the genuine believers, who hold back the antichrist as long as they are on earth). And then the lawless one will be revealed," whom Jesus will destroy by his return to the earth during the battle of Armageddon. But some eight years will elapse between the catching up of the church of Philadelphia and that battle.

The seven year tribulation period, occurs during the opening of the six seals in chapter 6. It is followed by the day of the Lord's wrath, which lasts just over a year. The events of this day are recorded in Rev. chapters 8 through 11, with the blowing of the seven trumpets. It will gradually become clear, since scripture interprets scripture.

❦

WORLD WAR III

"*ow I saw when the Lamb opened one of the seven seals, and I heard one of the four living creatures say as with a voice of thunder, 'Come!'" Revelation 6:1*
Some said it thundered when God spoke to Jesus in John 12:28. Jesus had prayed, "Father, glorify thy name." God thundered back, "I have glorified it, and I will glorify it again." Now another voice like thunder is summoning a white horse and its rider. We may be sure that in all that happens from this point on God is manifesting his glory. Our first parents committed high treason in the garden of Eden. By so doing they handed the control of this world over to the devil. As Jesus opens the seven seals, he is reclaiming the earth and its works for God.

In the profoundest sense the rider on the white horse represents the Lord himself launching his attack against the evil forces that are ruling the earth. The war between light and darkness has started. Viewed from earth the rider with his bow and arrows had the appearance of the Parthians, who for several hundred years gave the Roman armies fits. They were noted for fighting on horseback and for giving their enemies a parting shot. Their place of origin was northern Persia, today Iran. It is conceivable that this rider represents Islam declaring a jihad (holy war) against Israel and those who support her.

With the opening of the second seal came the bright red horse. Its rider was permitted to take peace from the earth. The rider's name is Gog, the chief angel over atheistic communism. It comes charging into Israel out of Russia in the far north. Ezekiel chapters 38 and 39 spell out the details. Its companions are Persia (Iran), Cush (Ethiopia), Put (Libya), Gomer's hordes (in Europe) and Bethtogarmah (Turkey). An act of God will destroy them on the mountains of Israel. World War III is now underway.

❦

THE HARVEST RAPTURE

"**W**hen he opened the third seal, I heard the third living creature say, 'Come!' And I saw, and behold a black horse." *Revelation 6:5*

The rider of the black horse is Famine. Food prices go through the ceiling. It will take a day's wage to buy a quart of wheat. But the oil and the wine are not affected. The mention of the wine reminds us of the wedding at Cana on the third day, when Jesus brought the joy of abundant life. With the opening of the third seal, we see scarcity. Why? Because the opening of the first seal did not bring the testimony to Jesus, as in the gospel, but the message of Mohammed, and the religion of the sword. The opening of the second seal did not bring faith but its opposite, communism and militant atheism, into the holy land.

When he opened the fourth seal the pale green horse appeared with Death its rider and Hades following. They unleash new terrors: pestilence and wild beasts. AIDS has been traced to the green monkey in Africa, and Lyme disease to infected tics. New diseases are already taking their toll. A fourth of the earth will make their home in Hades (some homecoming).

With the opening of the fifth seal we have an interlude in which to catch our breath before he opens the sixth seal. Then: a great earthquake. That which accompanies the earthquake is in complete agreement with Matthew 24:29-31, "Immediately after the tribulation of those days the sun will be darkened, and the moon will not give its light, and the stars will fall from heaven, and the powers of the heavens will be shaken; then will appear the sign of the Son of man in heaven (a cross?), and then all the tribes of the earth will mourn, and they will see the Son of man coming on the clouds of heaven with power and great glory; and he will send out his angels with a loud trumpet call and they will gather his elect from the four winds" - in what is called the harvest rapture. This occurs seven years after the catching up of the church of Philadelphia.

❧

OPPOSITE SIDES OF THE SAME COIN

"*When he opened the sixth seal, I looked, and behold, there was a great earthquake; and the sun became black as sackcloth, the full moon became like blood.*" Revelation 6:12

It is essential that we recognize that what happens when Jesus opens the sixth seal harmonizes perfectly with what he taught in Mt. 24:29-31. The two passages are opposite sides of the same coin. In both scriptures Jesus appears with power and great glory. Two things happen simultaneously upon earth: in Matthew the angels gather his elect to meet the Lord in the air, while in Revelation the unbelievers hide in the caves and among the rocks of the mountains, calling to the mountains and rocks, "Fall on us and hide us from the face of him who is seated on the throne, and from the wrath of the Lamb; for the great day of their wrath has come, and who can stand before it?" The opening of the sixth seal marks the end of the seven year tribulation period, and heralds the day of the Lord's wrath.

We have now encountered two raptures: "the first fruits" preceding the tribulation, and "the harvest" that concludes it. The fact of the two raptures will be confirmed to us when we examine chapters 12 to 14. In both John's Gospel and the Revelation we begin again in chapter 12. This is the basic truth underlying both books.

Chapter 7 discloses what transpires between the harvest rapture and the day of the Lord's wrath, which occurs with the opening of the seventh seal in chapter 8. Chapter 7:1-8 records the sealing of 144,000 Jews, a number symbolising all Israel. Paul writes about this in Rom. 11:25-27. "The Deliverer will come from Zion (the heavenly Jerusalem), he will banish ungodliness from Jacob, and this will be my covenant with them when I take away their sins." The Jews as a people will be sealed with the Holy Spirit that they may be Messiah's witnesses during the day of the Lord's wrath. The Church is now in heaven.

THE DAY OF WRATH AT LAST

"*After this I looked, and behold, a great multitude which no man could number, from every nation, from all tribes and peoples and tongues, standing before the throne." Revelation 7:9*

When the question was asked, "Who are these?" the answer was given, "These are they who have come out of the great tribulation, they have washed their robes and made them white in the blood of the Lamb." So these are the vast "harvest rapture" company that was caught up to God during the opening of the sixth seal. The seven year tribulation consisted of 3 1/2 years of tribulation, followed by 3 1/2 years of great tribulation.

The first fruits rapture occurs after the gospel has been preached to all nations. Mt. 24:14 When this has been accomplished, then he who is the Beginning and the End will come for the church of Philadelphia between Mt. 24:14 and 15. Then 3 1/2 years later the great tribulation will begin, when the desolating sacrilege (the antichrist) takes his stand in the temple in Jerusalem and demands that he be worshiped. "Then there will be great tribulation" (Mt. 24:21) for 3 1/2 years.

Chapter 8:1 says, "When the Lamb opened the seventh seal, there was silence in heaven for about half an hour" - a perfect definition of a Presbyterian prayer meeting, as has been said (hopefully tongue in cheek). What follows is a detailed depiction of the day of wrath. It turns out that the contents of the day of wrath is what transpires during the blowing of the seven trumpets. Chapters 8-11. Now one third of everything is destroyed. In 8:11 the star that fouls the rivers is Wormwood, which is pronounced in Russian Chernobyl. In connection with the blast of the sixth trumpet, the seven thunders sounded. He is not permitted to write down their significance. God keeps some surprises up his sleeve. We look through a glass darkly, do we not?

❦

ANTICHRIST'S COVENANT WITH ISRAEL

"*Then I saw another mighty angel coming down from heaven, wrapped in a cloud, with a rainbow over his head, and his face was like the sun, and his legs like pillars of fire." Revelation 10:1*

On the basis of the description given, it seems that this angel (messenger in the Greek) is none other than Jesus Christ himself. The little scroll open in his hand is possibly an expression of the original scroll, the title deed to earth, which is now nearly repossessed. It is exciting to hear that "in the days of the trumpet call to be sounded by the seventh angel, the mystery of God, as he announced to his servants the prophets, should be fulfilled." It is a way of saying that God's saving purpose for mankind will have been accomplished. The revelation John receives when he eats the little scroll was bitter-sweet. All who proclaim the gospel know something about this.

Chapter 11:1-3 tells about antichrist's covenant with Israel. John is told to survey the reconstructed temple of the Jews in Jerusalem. The presence of the altar means that they have been allowed to reinstitute their sacrificial system. This is in spite of the fact that Isaiah 66:3 says that "He who slaughters an ox is like him who kills a man; he who sacrifices a lamb, like him who breaks a dog's neck." No mention is made here of the lampstand, because during the first 3 1/2 years of the tribulation period many of those who were part of the lukewarm church have been ignited by the fire of God and burn brightly for God. So they are the lampstand.

For 42 months antichrist allows the Jews to worship in their temple, while the gentiles trample the outer court and the city. He has effected a working compromise. But then he breaks his covenant and enters the temple himself to be worshiped, at which point all hell breaks loose. The two indestructable witnesses will then prophecy during the great tribulation which follows.

❧

THE TWO LAMPSTANDS

"*And I will grant my two witnesses power to prophesy for one thousand two hundred and sixty days, clothed in sackcloth.*"

Revelation 11:3

Chapter 11 is a vignette of the seven year tribulation period, during which antichrist is in charge. For the first 3 1/2 years he seems to be a perfect gentleman, then he removes his mask and becomes like his father, a fire-breathing dragon. During the second 3 1/2 years (the great tribulation), the Lord's two indestructable witnesses minister in Jerusalem clothed in sackcloth - a summons to repent. During the first 3 1/2 years the former luke-warmers now turned hot were the lampstand. But when the antichrist suddenly became a roaring lion seeking someone to devour, he martyred them.

God will always have his witnesses though, so he raises up the two who come in the spirit and power of Moses and Elijah. "These are the two olive trees and the two lampstands which stand before the Lord of the earth." As olive trees, they have their own supernatural provision of holy oil (Holy Spirit). As lampstands they burn brightly for God on the streets of Jerusalem. Since there are two of them, their witness is ten times more effective than was that of the martyred lampstand. (One will put a thousand to flight, two ten thousand.) The fire of God's Spirit issuing from their mouths destroys their adversaries. By pronouncing their curses upon the unrepentant, they wreak the havoc of severe drought, contaminated water, and unspeakable plagues.

After 3 1/2 years antichrist is allowed to kill them, but he refuses them the dignity of burial. The whole earth will celebrate an unholy christmas for 3 1/2 days, when suddenly over world-wide television they will be seen to come back to life. Then they will be caught up to heaven in anticipation of the harvest rapture which will soon occur. Is the great earthquake in 11:13 the same as that occuring in 6:12?

❧

THE HALLELUIA CHORUS

"*Then the seventh angel blew his trumpet, and there were loud voices in heaven, saying, 'The kingdom of the world has become the kingdom of our Lord and of his Christ, and he shall reign for ever and ever.'" Revelation 11:15*

The seventh trumpet blast is also identified as the third woe. It signals the conclusion of the day of wrath. It is set to the music of the Halleluia Chorus. We are presented with the scene of heavenly worship that has been going on the whole time. "And the twenty-four elders who sit on their thrones before God fell on their faces and worshiped God, saying, 'We give thanks to thee, Lord God Almighty, who art and who wast, that thou hast taken thy great power and begun to reign.'" Notice that the anticipated 'and who art to come,' is omitted, since he has already manifested his great power and is about to reveal his full glory.

"The nations raged, but thy wrath came (it is a thing of the past, and something new is about to happen:) and the time for rewarding thy servants, the prophets and saints, and those who fear thy name, both small and great, and for destroying the destroyers of the earth." The believers are about to be rewarded. They are the builders and bringers of life. On the other hand the unbelievers are about to be destroyed together with the three chief destroyers whom they serve: the devil, the beast, and the false prophet.

"Then God's temple in heaven was opened, and the ark of his covenant was seen within his temple." The ark of the covenant on earth had within it the momentos of God's steadfast love: a bowl of manna, Aaron's rod that budded, and the two tablets of the law. Its counterpart in heaven contains, I believe, the sprinkled blood of the Lamb of God. "And there were flashes of lightning, voices, peals of thunder, an earthquake and heavy hail." Ch. 11 concludes in the same way as ch. 16. Chapters 12 to 16 are an overlay, which means we begin again.

THE SUN CLOTHED WOMAN

"**𝕬**nd a great portent appeared in heaven, a woman clothed with the sun, with the moon under her feet, and on her head a crown of twelve stars." *Revelation 12:1*

The Book of Revelation is the greatest mystery ever written. The Greek word musterion means 'an open secret.' The writer of Revelation assumed that the readers had a thorough understanding of the fourth gospel and of the entire Old Testament. As we have seen, chapter 12 in the gospel is the hinge, the place of beginning again. In John 12 to 17 we encountered the seven themes in the original order. Remarkably the same principle applies in the book of Revelation. Failure to see this vitiates a valid interpretation of the book. However, when we see it, everything becomes clear. The book is no longer a closed secret. On the contrary, it opens wide.

The key is to perceive that we begin again in chapter 12. We have seen this principle in the gospel. Now let us look for it in Genesis, in the story of Joseph. Genesis 37 tells of the two dreams of Joseph. Though they were different, they told the same story. The second merely reinforced the first. Genesis 40 tells of the two dreams of Pharaoh. In his interpretation of them, Joseph said to Pharaoh, "The dream of Pharaoh is one; God has revealed to Pharaoh what he is about to do." Gen. 4 t :25 "The doubling of Pharaoh's dream means that the thing is fixed by God, and God will shortly bring it to pass." Gen. 4i :32 The same assertion may be made concerning the book of Revelation. The doubling of John's vision, which is what occurs beginning in chapter 12, "means that the thing is fixed by God, and God will shortly bring it to pass."

Who is the sun clothed woman? She is woman as she was meant to be: Eve before the fall, and the Lord's mother in a symbolic sense, i.e. the Old and New Testament community of believers. She is what we aspire to be.

❦

THE MYSTERIOUS CHILD

"She was pregnant and she cried out in her pangs of birth, in anguish for delivery." Revelation 12:2

We have associated the sun clothed woman with Eve and the Lord's mother. She is Old and New Covenant Israel rolled into one. In a word she is the believing woman. Revelation 12 parallels John 12, in which we saw Mary of Bethany give her silent testimony to Jesus as she anointed him Messiah. The first day of Holy Week was the day of testimony/preparation. Similarly the first seven verses in Revelation 12 is testimony/preparation for all that follows in the second half of the book. This significant sign woman is pregnant with a male child, whom we identify as the church of Philadelphia for reasons about to be made clear.

"And another portent appeared in heaven; behold a great red dragon, with seven heads and ten horns, and seven diadems upon his heads." He is the devil. He wears seven kingly crowns, whereas the woman wears a stephanos, the laurel wreath won for victory in competition. She is not aspiring to wear a royal crown. She has no aspiration to be "the queen of heaven." "His tail swept down a third of the stars of heaven and cast them to the earth." Since stars symbolize angels, we are told here that one third of the angels joined him in rebelling against God. Possibly they were the Nephilim (fallen ones) who came in to the daughters of men, whose progeny were the mighty men that became so wicked in the days of Noah. Genesis 6:4

"And the dragon stood before the woman who was about to bear a child, that he might devour her child when she brought it forth; she brought forth a male child, one who is to rule all the nations with a rod of iron, but her child was caught up to God and to his throne." There is no mention here of crucifixion, death, burial, and resurrection, so this child cannot be Jesus Christ. It has to be the first fruits rapture company.

❧

SATAN'S FALL LIKE LIGHTNING FROM HEAVEN

"And the child was snatched up to God and to his throne."
Revelation 12:5

Jesus had said in Revelation 3:21, "He who conquers, I will grant him to sit with me on my throne," and in 2:26, "He who conquers...I will give him power over the nations, and he shall rule them with a rod of iron." He said this to Christians. Jesus ascended slowly into heaven, whereas this child was caught up in a quick violent grab (the verb always used for the rapture of the church). "And the woman fled into the wilderness, where she has a place prepared by God, in which to be nourished for one thousand two hundred and sixty days (3 1/2 years)." After the birth of Jesus, Joseph fled with the mother and child into Egypt, where tradition says they stayed for about 3 1/2 years. The woman is the Old and New Testament believing community whose ministry (teaching/ praying) evokes the generation of Christians which are ripe for rapture.

Ch. 12:1-6 has testified/prepared us for the faith/persecution theme that concludes the chapter. "Now war arose in heaven (the catching up of the church of Philadelphia has tipped the heavenly scales), Michael and his angels fighting against the dragon; and the dragon and his angels fought, but they were defeated and there was no longer any place for them in heaven. And the dragon...was thrown down to the earth, and his angels were thrown down with him."

Then it is disclosed how the first fruits company succeeded in conquering the Devil: "by the blood of the Lamb and by the word of their testimony, for they loved not their lives even unto death." That is the formula for victorious faith. In great wrath the dragon seeks to destroy the woman with a flood (war?), but she is divinely protected. Then he attacks her other offspring, the lukewarm church, many of whom have now been shocked into keeping the commandments of God and bear testimony to Jesus.

OFF WITH THE MASK

"*And the dragon stood on the sand of the sea.*" *Revelation 12:17*

Revelation 12 runs parallel with John 12. They both begin with the story of a signficiant woman: Revelation with the sun clad woman, John with the woman who "messiahed" Jesus for death and burial. Mary of Bethany prefigured and anticipated the portent woman, who is simultaneously in heaven and on earth. Both chapters contain the first two themes of the gospel: testimony/preparation, and faith/betrothal. After the catching up of the man child, a significant portion of the church of Laodicea which was left behind see the error of their ways, repent and betroth themselves to Christ by total commitment. The dragon takes his stand on the seashore to call forth his earthly counterpart.

We are now half-way through the seven year tribulation. Rev. 13:1 begins the great tribulation. The dragon, the originator of rebellion/ unbelief, is now poised to direct the counterfeit of the marriage at Cana. John 13 develops the theme of the great love story initated by Jesus on the third day. Rev. 13 introduces the product of unbelief, the opposite of life, which is eternal death.

"And I saw a beast rising out of the sea." As yeast rises, so does the beast out of the instability of the nations, typified by the sea. The beast's career began 3 1/2 years earlier, when as "a perfect gentleman," he brought "peace to the nations." But "when men say, peace, peace, then comes sudden destruction." Suddenly the beast takes his seat in the reconstructed temple in Jerusalem, demanding that he be worshiped as God. The religious Jews are as little inclined to worship him as they were Jesus. So all hell breaks loose. As Satan entered into Iscariot in John 13, so in Rev. 13 Satan entered into this second son of perdition. As a monster rising out of the sea becomes visible, so the antichrist allows his true nature to be seen.

❧

THE UNHOLY TRINITY

"*And I saw a beast rising out of the sea, with ten horns and seven heads, with ten diadems upon its horns and a blasphemous name upon its heads." Revelation 13:1*

To understand the beast, we must compare it carefully with the appearance of the dragon in ch. 12:3. They are similar, but not identical. The dragon had seven heads and ten horns, and seven diadems upon his heads. The beast differed in that there were now ten diadems upon its horns. All ten horns were on the seventh head. The seven heads of the dragon are the seven biblical empires: Egypt, Assyria, Babylon, Media-Persia, Greece, Rome, and finally the realm of the beast. The ten horns on the seventh head of the beast are identified in 17:12 as ten kings. They are to receive royal power for one hour, are of one mind and give over their power and authority to the beast. "They will make war on the Lamb, and the Lamb will conquer them." 17:14

"And the beast that I saw was like a leopard (the symbol of Greece), its feet were like a bear's (Media-Persia) and its mouth was like a lion's mouth (Babylon). (The characteristics of these three empires converged in it.) And to it the dragon gave his power and his throne and great authority. One of its heads seemed to have a mortal wound (it was assasinated when it demanded worship), but its mortal wound was healed (the devil raised it from the dead), and the whole earth followed the beast with wonder." For 42 months (the time of the great tribulation) it blasphemed God and destroyed the Christians. It was irresistable.

"Then I saw another beast which rose out of the earth (a stable environment); it had two horns like a lamb (imitating Jesus) and it spoke like a dragon. It personified the religion of the devil, forcing people to worship the beast. It produced signs, even making fire come down from heaven, an imitation of Pentecost. It completes the unholy trinity.

THE MARK OF THE BEAST

"**A**nd *by the signs which it is allowed to work in the presence of the beast, it deceives those who dwell on earth, bidding them make an image for the beast which was wounded by the sword and yet lived." Revelation 13:14*

What kind of image does the devil's religion coerce the people to worship? An image that talks. I humbly submit that the image is widely distributed in our day: the computer. In the language of ancient Babylon the numerical value of computer is 666. The master computer in Brussels, Belgium has been aptly nick-named The Beast. "Also it causes all (of every class in society) to be marked on the right hand or the forehead (with computer chips under the skin?), so that no one can buy or sell unless he has the mark, that is the name of the beast or the number of its name. This calls for wisdom: let him who has understanding reckon the number of the beast, for it is a human number, its number is six hundred and sixty-six."

Every time we buy something from the store, we should note that the three long bars of parallel lines that pass over the scanner are 666. Also let it be known that the human devil, Nero Caesar, who set fire to Rome and who sentenced St. Paul to death by beheading, had as the numerical value of his name 666. The antichrist, Mr. 666, will be such a devil, only he will be exceptionally brilliant. He will lead astray, if possible, even the elect. But, praise God, it will not be possible.

To recapitulate, Revelation 12 parallels John 12. So also Revelation 13 is the antitype of John 13. In John 13 Jesus expressed love to the uttermost by washing the disciples' feet and by giving the dipped morsel to Iscariot. In Revelation 13 the devil's man expressed his selfishness gone berserk, demanding that others serve him to the extent of worshiping him. He gains control over the world's economy, twisting arms, till people bend the knee.

❦

THE BRIDE IN HEAVEN

"Then I looked, and lo, on Mount Zion stood the Lamb and with him a hundred and forty four thousand who had his name and his Father's name written on their foreheads." Revelation 14:1

John chapter 14 developed the fourth gospel theme: homecoming. Don't be surprised that Revelation 14 does the same. First of all, it is essential to see that the 144,000 in ch. 7 is a totally different company from the 144,000 in ch. 14. In ch. 7 they were all Jews, who were sealed with the Holy Spirit for the purpose of being Christ's witnesses during the day of the Lord's wrath, when all who comprise the church are in heaven. The Lord comes as a thief in the night to snatch away his own. He comes as a thief, though he is not a thief. The thief comes to snatch away that which is not his own.

The 144,000 in ch. 14 are the church of Philadelphia, identified as the male child in ch. 12. How can we be sure? Because they have learned the song that only those who had been redeemed from ("out of" in the Greek) the earth could learn. 14:3 The Mount Zion here described is the heavenly Jerusalem, because the worship is "before the throne." This company is characterized as those "who have not defiled themselves with women, for they are chaste (virgins)." Once they have trusted in Jesus Christ, they do not engage in sexual immorality. Also they are virgins in the sense that they refuse to go whoring after other gods.

"It is these who follow the Lamb wherever he goes." They accept the Lord's guidance in what they will do with their lives and where. "These have been redeemed from mankind as first fruits for God and the Lamb." They are the "first fruits" company of Rev. 4, who experienced the "come up here," and have thereby been redeemed out of the world system, and carried into heaven. "And in their mouth no lie was found, for they are spotless." They are the bride, without spot, or blemish, or any such thing. Eph. 5:27

GET OUT OF TOWN BEFORE IT'S TOO LATE, M'LOVE

"Then I saw another angel flying in midheaven, with an eternal gospel to proclaim." Revelation 14:6

Here we have an interlude during which a dispensational change is indicated by angels. The first angel warns all on earth to "Fear God and give him glory, for the hour of his judgment has come." From now on divine judgment predominates. A second angel followed, saying, "Fallen, fallen is Babylon the great, she who made all nations drink the wine of her impure passion." The double fall of Babylon is detailed: in ch. 17 religious Babylon, in ch. 18 commercial Babylon. The love of money binds them together. A third angel warns humanity against worshiping the beast and its image and receiving its mark, which during this dispensation is the unforgivable sin that will send one to hell. Another voice blesses those who die henceforth trusting in the Lord.

"Then I looked, and lo, a white cloud, and seated on the cloud one like a son of man (Jesus), with a golden (victor's) crown on his head, and a sharp sickle in his hand." He is instructed from heaven to "reap... for the harvest of the earth is fully ripe." The seven year tribulation has accomplished its purpose by turning multitudes to the Lord. "So he who sat upon the cloud swung his sickle on the earth, and the earth was reaped." The harvest rapture that occurs with the opening of the sixth seal is again portrayed.

We now anticipate the day of the Lord's wrath. Another angel is instructed to "Put in your sickle, and gather the clusters of the vine of the earth, for its grapes are ripe." So the angel did so, and threw the vintage "into the great wine press of the wrath of God; and the wine press was trodden outside the city (of Jerusalem), and blood flowed from the wine press, as high as a horse's bridle, for two hundred miles." Here is a miniature portrait of the battle of Armageddon, the final event in the day of the Lord's wrath.

THE NEW BORN SINGERS

"**T**hen *I saw another portent in heaven, great and wonderful, seven angels with seven plagues, which are the last, for with them the wrath of God is ended.*" *Revelation 15:1*

Revelation 14 paralleled John 14 in the theme of homecoming. In John 14 Jesus told about his return to his Father in heaven from whence he would come to receive us to himself. In Rev. 14 we saw the church of Philadelphia (man child) in heavenly Zion under the symbol of the 144,000. Then we were privileged to get another glimpse of those who turned to Christ during the tribulation period caught up to meet the Lord in the air in the harvest rapture. They were pleased to join the first fruits company in heaven before the day of the Lord's wrath. We then saw the grapes of wrath trodden down in the battle of Armageddon. It is during that battle that Jesus actually returns to earth to establish his 1000 year reign.

Now in ch. 15 we anticipate the theme of new birth. Jesus had said to Nicodemus in John 3:2, "Unless one is born from above, he cannot see the kingdom of God." Now John sees another portent comparable to that of the sun clad woman: the seven angels with the seven plagues. "And I saw what appeared to be a sea of glass mingled with fire, and those who had conquered the beast and its image and the number of its name, standing beside the sea of glass with harps of God in their hands." These are the innumerable company in white robes who have come out of the great tribulation, whom he saw in 7:9-17. He saw them garnered for God in 14:14-16. Having received new birth from God through trusting in Jesus Christ, they have put on their heavenly bodies, and John was privileged to hear the song they sing.

Afterward the seven angels stepped out of the temple and received the seven golden bowls full of the wrath of God. The heavenly temple was closed to all by the smoke of God's glory until the seven plagues were ended.

EVIL MEETS IT'S COME-UPPANCE

*"**T**hen I heard a loud voice from the temple telling the seven angels, `Go and pour out on the earth the seven bowls of the wrath of God.'" Revelation 16:1*

John 16 developed the theme of nurture. The Holy Spirit nurtures us through the hearing and telling of the gospel. The Holy Spirit is the defense counsel of the believer but the prosecutor of the world. He convicts the world of sin, righteousness and judgment. Here the judgments about which he warned and about which the new born singers sang are poured out in wrath. In Revelation 16 we encounter the negative side of nurture: not bowls full of food, but bowls full of divine displesure.

The first bowl poured upon the evildoer issues in foul and evil sores. The second bowl turns the sea into the blood of a dead man, destroying all life there. The third does the same for the rivers and fountains. The fourth causes the sun to scorch the unrepentant with fire. The fifth brings darkness and gnawing pain, and still men refuse to repent. The sixth dries up the Euphrates allowing the kings of the whole world to assemble for battle on the great day of God the Almighty at Armageddon. The seventh results in a voice from the throne, saying, "It is done!" "And there were flashes of lightning, voices, peals of thunder and a great earthquake such as had never been since men were on the earth, so great was that earthquake."

We have come again to where we left off at the end of chapter 11, where, "The kingdom of the world has become the kingdom of our Lord and of his Christ." We have covered the ground a second time. "The great city (Jerusalem) was split into three parts, and the cities of the nations fell, and God remembered great Babylon, to make her drain the cup of the fury of his wrath. And every island fled away, and no mountains were to be found." And on it goes. And still men cursed God. Two-fold Babylon is about to be done in.

❦

THE GREAT HARLOT

"**T**hen *one of the seven angels who had the seven bowls came and said to me, 'Come, I will show you the judgment of the great harlot.'" Revelation 17:1*

John 17 develops the theme of healing in answer to prayer. Jesus prays for his church, not for the world, because the world system is to be destroyed: religious Babylon in Rev. 17, commercial Babylon in Rev. 18. The destruction of the two Babylons is a major step in healing the earth. The first Babylon is called the great harlot "who is seated upon many waters (symbolic of many nations), with whom the kings of the earth (the politicians) have committed fornication, and with the wine of whose fornication the dwellers on earth have become drunk."

This morning on TV a lesbian couple and a male gay couple told of their mutual love. The two men had had their marriage "solemnized" by a rabbi. In the ceremony they drank the cup of wine under the canopy. They were not drinking the Lord's cup, but the wine of fornication. Both couples are drunk on the wrath of God without knowing it. They are proud of their corrupt relationships. They have imbibed the religion of Babylon (confusion).

"And he carried me away in the Spirit into a wilderness (denoting the absence of blessing), and I saw a woman sitting on a scarlet beast which was full of blasphemous names, and it had seven heads and ten horns." We saw it rising out of the sea in 13:1. It is the antichrist and his bunch. "The woman was arrayed in purple and scarlet, and bedecked with gold and jewels and pearls, holding in her hand a golden cup full of abominations and the impurities of her fornication." She is arrayed in purple, scarlet, and gold, but she is missing the blue (faith), which was mandated in the veil of the temple. She has the ceremony men love, but where is her faith in the living God? She had placed her faith in the beast who is carrying her. It will be a short ride.

❦

THE MYSTERIOUS BEAST

"**A**nd *on her forehead was written a name of mystery: 'Babylon the great, mother of harlots and of earth's abominations.'*"

Revelation 17:5

"This is the way of an adulteress: she eats, and wipes her mouth, and says, 'I have done no wrong.'" Prov. 30:20 Yet adultery like harlotry is one of earth's abominations. It breaks covenant with God and one's mate. This woman is the religion of Babylon. "And I saw the woman, drunk with the blood of the saints and the blood of the martyrs of Jesus." Every time she seduces Christians to commit sexual sin, she toasts herself with their blood.

Martin Hlastan of Yugoslavia knows a young man who was a monk in a monastery. Another monk had sought to involve him in homosexuality. So he called in the Abbot, who said, "This too is love." Babylon rears her ugly head in all denominations. She is the mother of the goats, the chaff and the tares. Let us beware lest she become our mother.

"When I saw her I marvelled greatly. But the angel said to me, 'Why marvel? I will tell you the mystery of the woman, and of the beast with seven heads and ten horns that carries her.'" I do not pretend to grasp the mystery of the beast, but this is a stab at it. The beast is another Iscariot, whom Jesus called in John 17:12 "the son of perdition." "He was, and is not, and is to ascend from the bottomless pit and go to perdition (eventually, as Antichrist). And the dwellers on earth whose names have not been written in the book of life from the foundation of the world, will marvel to behold the beast, because it was and is not and is to come." Judas was a master of deception, as is this man. Could it be that the evil spirit which entered Judas in John 13:27 has now reincarnated itself in the beast, who enjoys a similar cunning? Those who believe in reincarnation have probably picked up the evil spirits which possessed the demonized ones who lived before them.

❧

THE RIDDLE OF THE EIGHTH HEAD

"*This calls for a mind with wisdom: the seven heads are seven mountains on which the woman is seated.*" *Revelation 17:9*

We have already identified the seven heads or mountains as the kingdoms of Egypt, Assyria, Babylon, Media-Persia, Greece, Rome, and Rome revived (still future). "They are also seven kings, five of whom have fallen (Pharaoh, Shalmaneser, Nebuchadnessar, Cyrus, Alexander the Great), one is (Domitian, the Caesar when John was writing), the other has not yet come (antichrist, who makes peace in the Middle East), and when he comes he must remain only a little while (for the first 3 1/2 years of the tribulation). As for the beast that was and is not, it is an eighth but it belongs to the seven and it goes to perdition."

When the peacemaker (antichrist) fulfills Mt. 24:15 and becomes "the desolating sacrilege" by demanding that he be worshiped in the temple, he will be killed with a sword (Rev. 13:3). But his wound will be healed, when the devil raises him from the dead. The devil is the great copy-cat. He takes delight in following the pattern established by God. As Jesus became a life-giving spirit after his resurrection (I Cor. 15:45), the beast will be a death-dealing devil after his resuscitation. He will then incarnate, in addition to his own human spirit, the spirit of perdition (destruction) that possessed Judas after he received the morsel from Jesus. John 13:27 He is now totally Satan's man with supernatural power. He is an eighth (a new beginning), though he belongs to the seven, and still appears to be the seventh head. But do not judge by appearances. He goes to perdition as the incarnation now of the evil one (Satan).

"And the ten horns that you saw are ten kings who have not yet received royal power, but they are to receive authority as kings for one hour, together with the beast." Are they the kings of 16:14 who will assemble their armies for Armageddon?

❦

THE END OF FALSE RELIGION

"**These** *are of one mind and give over their power and authority to the beast; they will make war on the Lamb, and the Lamb will conquer them.*" *Revelation 17:13,14*

The story of his conquering them is reserved for ch. 19:17-21. It is easy for the Lamb to conquer them, "for he is Lord of lords and King of kings (their Lord and King), and those with him are called chosen and faithful." If it is our ambition to be soldiers in the heavenly armies which will participate in that fateful war, let us make sure our call by our faithfulness.

"And he said to me, `The waters that you saw, where the harlot is seated, are peoples and multitudes and nations and tongues. And the ten horns that you saw, they and the beast will hate the harlot; they will make her desolate and naked, and devour her flesh and burn her up with fire." Why will they do this? "For God has put it into their hearts to carry out his purpose by being of one mind (he makes evil to serve him) and giving over their royal power to the beast, until the words of God shall be fulfilled." His words are not idle words that fall to the ground; they accomplish the purpose for which he sent them out.

"And the woman that you saw is the great city which has dominion over the kings of the earth." Here he identifies the woman as Rome. Peter in I Peter 5:13 does the same: "She who is at Babylon who is likewise chosen, sends you greetings." Ancient Babylon had been destroyed centuries earlier. So this Babylon was a code name for Rome. In Yugoslavia Martin Hlastan heard a Catholic priest ascribe thirty attributes to Mary which belong only to Jesus Christ. After each ascription of deity to Mary, the church said to her, "Pray for us." Catholic tradition pretends that Mary is "full of grace," in the sense that she enjoys excessive merit upon which others may draw. Scripture teaches that Jesus alone was without sin.

❧

AS UP-TO-DATE AS THE MORNING NEWSPAPER

"*After this I saw another angel coming down from heaven, having great authority; and the earth was made bright with his splendor.*" *Revelation 18:1*

Chapters 18 and 19 in John are the Passion Story, which occurred on Friday, the sixth day (nurture) of Holy Week. God uses the Passion narrative to nourish the life of God within us. Let us see if Revelation 18 and 19 do not fulfill the same function (nurture through the Holy Spirit).

This shining angel "called out with a mighty voice, `Fallen, fallen is Babylon the great!'" Religious Babylon has fallen victim to cannibalism. Now it is commercial Babylon's turn to fall. John 18:6 says, "When Jesus said to them, `I am he,' they drew back and fell to the ground.'" "Humpty Dumpty sat on a wall. Humpty Dumpty had a great fall. All the king's horses and all the king's men could not put Humpty Dumpty together again." Do you know why? Wrong king. Wrong horses. Wrong men.

Iscariot had a weakness for money. There was a commercial streak within him that prevented his total capitulation to Jesus Christ. It is important to realize that the coin of the realm that really counts is faith. The kings and the merchants have committed fornication with the mighty city Babylon. She thinks she sits as a queen forever, not knowing that her plagues will come in a single day, and she shall be burned with fire. The list of her merchandise begins with gold, silver, jewels and pearls, and concludes with bodies, that is human souls. Her great sin is to regard human souls as nothing more than bodies to be used and then discarded. Therefore in one hour she has been laid waste. "All nations were deceived by thy sorcery" (drug use and trafficking). It sounds as up-to-date as the morning newspaper. Her name? New York. London. Tokyo. St. Louis. "The love of money is the root of all evils." I Tim. 6:10 It must be uprooted and replaced by the love of God.

❦

THE JUSTICE OF GOD

"*And in her was found the blood of the prophets and of saints, and of all who have been slain on earth.*" *Revelation 18:24*

Diogenes was seen going through the cities with his lantern aloft, heralding, "Bring me an honest man." He went from city to city. Finally he came to our city, where he was heard to say, "Has anyone seen my lantern?" Jesus went to the city to be crucified. Paul went to the city to be beheaded, Peter to be crucified. Where can we go for safety? To the small town? "God made the country, man made the city, but the devil made the small town." You don't have to go to the city to find the slickers. Don't give way to despair though. Instead listen to Revelation chapter 19.

John 19:2 tells of Jesus' coronation upon earth: "The soldiers plaited a crown of thorns, and put it on his head, and arrayed him in a purple robe; they came up to him, saying, `Hail, King of the Jews!' and struck him with their hands." Revelation 19 speaks of his coronation in heaven. It is an astonishing contrast.

"After this I heard what seemed to be the loud voice of a great multitude in heaven, crying, "Hallelujah! Salvation and glory and power belong to our God, for his judgments are true and just; he has judged the great harlot who corrupted the earth with her fornication, and he has avenged on her the blood of his servants." It is enough to make one tremble. Think of the millions of mothers who have murdered their unborn infants, calling it a surgical procedure. What has become of mother love? Before they can receive the mercy of God, they must confess that they are murderers. The law may not protect a person before birth, but God does. "Let the little children come to me," said Jesus. That is where the unborn infants go when they are dismembered in the womb: to be with Jesus. Rachel, though, is still weeping for her children, because they are no more. Mt. 2:18

❦

THE CORONATION OF JESUS

"*Once more they cried, 'Hallelujah! The smoke from her goes up for ever and ever.'" Revelation 19:3*

Babylon's ruin is eternal with no hope of reconstruction. It's place will remember it no more. "And the twenty-four elders and the four living creatures fell down and worshiped God who is seated on the throne, saying, 'Amen. Hallelujah!" Many times I heard an evangelist say on the radio, "God is seated on his throne, and as long as God is seated on his throne everything is going to be all right." Then one time I really heard it. Over all the confusion of our times sits God upon his throne with the universe in the palm of his hand. Why not trust him, and praise him?

"And from the throne came a voice crying, 'Praise our God, all you his servants, you who fear him, small and great.'" Lift your voice just now, and say, "Praise God!" Become in this way a member of the tribe of Judah, which means the God praisers. "Then I heard what seemed to be the voice of a great multitude, like the sound of many waters and like the sound of mighty thunderpeals, crying, 'Hallelujah! For the Lord our God the Almighty reigns.'" Just now in our mind's eye may we glimpse Jesus, the Lamb of God, and on his head many diadems (kingly crowns). Truly "the kingdom of the world has become the kingdom of our Lord and of his Christ, and he shall reign for ever and ever." 11:15 "Let us rejoice and exault and give him the glory, for the marriage of the Lamb has come, and his bride has made herself ready."

At Cana on the third day, his six disciples saw his glory and believed in him with the faith of full surrender. On that day they anticipated what is now about to take place. They had made themselves ready by submitting to water baptism, whereby they were purified through faith in his shed blood. Now they were "clothed with fine linen, bright and pure" - the righteous deeds of the saints (the ministry they had undertaken in his service).

❧

THE RIDER ON THE WHITE HORSE

"**A**nd the angel said to me, 'Write this: Blessed are those who are invited to the marriage supper of the Lamb.'" *Revelation 19:9*

Many in our day come to the marriage supper of the bride and groom, not having attended the wedding. They think that the marriage is inconsequential, that only the party is important. They are in for a rude awakening when they die. Only those who have entered into a marriage covenant with Jesus Christ and have committed themselves exclusively to him will received life's most prized invitation: an invitation to the marrriage supper of the Lamb. What a blessing! "And he said to me, `These are true words of God.'" When we arrive at the banquet hall, all heaven breaks loose.

"Then I fell down at his feet to worship him, but he said to me, `You must not do that! I am a fellow servant with you and your brethren who hold the testimony of Jesus. Worship God.'" The only angels who accept worship are the Devil and his bunch. They have a star complex, which obliges them always to look for clinging vines to fawn over them. Watch out for humans who invariably seek adulation; they are part of the wrong outfit. Those who have received the invitation to the marriage supper also hold on to their testimony to Jesus. They never tire of telling others about Jesus and his love. Why is that? "For the testimony of Jesus is the spirit of prophecy." I Cor. 14:5 says: "I want you all to speak in tongues, but even more to prophesy." New Testament prophecy always builds up Christians because it centers in Jesus. If so-called prophecy fails this double test, forget it.

"Then I saw heaven opened, and behold, a white horse!" The last time we saw Jesus on the back of an animal, he was riding the foal of an ass, because he was coming in peace. This time he comes to wage war. "He who sat upon it is called Faithful and True, and in righteousness he judges and makes war."

THE LAST ROUND-UP

"**H**is eyes are like a flame of fire, and on his head are many diadems; and he has a name inscribed which no one knows but himself." *Revelation 19:12*

The rider on the white horse in 6:2 was given a stephanos, a laurel wreath - much preferred to a crown of thorns. But now our Rider as King of kings wears many diadems. His eyes have the power to set the universe ablaze. His inmost being, symbolized by his name, is too awesome to be known. "He is clad in a robe dipped in blood (his own?), and the name by which he is called is The Word of God" (through whom the cosmos was fashioned).

"And the armies of heaven, arrayed in fine linen, white and pure, followed him on white horses." Since they are wearing the garb of the bride, they must be his bride on their first significant outing. "From his mouth issues a sharp sword (his tongue) with which to smite the nations." One little word will fell them. "And he will rule them with a rod of iron; he will tread the wine press of the fury of the wrath of God the Almighty." This expresson takes us back to 14:19, the depiction of Armageddon. "On his robe and on his thigh he has a name inscribed, King of kings and Lord of lords."

"Then I saw an angel standing in the sun, and with a loud voice he called to all the birds that fly in midheaven, `Come, gather for the great supper of God." This is the earthly counterpart of the heavenly banquet. Chapters 19 in John and Revelation develop the theme of nurture: eating and drinking. Those on earth who rejected the invitation to the heavenly banquet will find themselves to be the food and drink of God's earthly supper for the birds of prey. Poetic justice. "And I saw the beast and the kings of the earth with their armies gathered to make war against" Jesus and his army. If they had read the Bible, they would have known better. Without knowledge the people perish.

THE EARTH EMPTIED OF PRIDE

"*And the beast was captured, and with it the false prophet.*"
Revelation 19:20

The false religion of Babylon that taught "works righteousness" (the harlot) has already been destroyed, but antichrist and his chaplain are yet to be dealt with. "These two were
thrown alive into the lake of fire that burns with sulphur." This
is "the eternal fire prepared for the devil and his angels" that
Jesus warned about in Mt. 25:41. "And the rest were slain by the
sword of him who sits upon the horse, the sword that issues from
his mouth; and all the birds were gorged with their flesh." So
ends Revelation 19.

John 18 and 19 told the Passion Story of Jesus which
occurred on Friday, the sixth day of Holy Week - the day of
nurture. Revelation 18 and 19 have in like manner nourished
our life of faith, as we witnessed in ch. 18 the final downfall of
Babylon, and in ch. 19 the two feasts: the marriage supper of the
Lamb in heaven, and its earthly counterpart for the birds. The
first was spiritual, the second was flesh.

Now we have come to Revelation 20, which we may label
The Triumph. John 20 recorded Jesus' triumph over sin, death,
and the grave. Rev. 20 reveals his victory over Satan, Death,
and Hades. John 20 begins with the testimony of the empty
tomb; Rev. 20 with the testimony of the earth emptied of the
Devil. "Then I saw an angel coming down from heaven, holding
in his hand the key of the bottomless pit and a great chain."
After death, Jesus preached the gospel there, and came forth,
flourishing the key. "And (the angel) seized the dragon, that
ancient serpent, who is the Devil and Satan and bound him for
a thousand years, and threw him into the pit, and shut it and
sealed it over him, that he should deceive the nations no more,
till the thousand years were ended. After that he must be loosed
for a little while." He who exalted himself is now abased. A
haughty spirit goes before a fall.

THE FIRST RESURRECTION

"*Then I saw thrones, and seated on them were those to whom judgment was committed.*" *Revelation 20:4*

  In John 20, after the testimony of the empty tomb, we saw the theme of faith, when John believed that Jesus was alive. Looking for the faith theme now in Revelation 20, we find it: "Also I saw the souls of those who had been beheaded for their testimony to Jesus and for the word of God, and who had not worshiped the beast or its image and had not received its mark on their foreheads or their hands." Talk about faith! These had demonstrated it to the extent of martyrdom during the great tribulation, when the guillotine was back in use.

  "They came to life again, and reigned with Christ a thousand years." After testimony comes faith and resurrection life. "The rest of the dead did not come to life until the thousand years were ended. This is the first resurrection." Remember how Jesus said in John 5:29 that there are two resurrections: the resurrection of life and the resurrection of judgment. The first occurs before the thousand year reign of Christ, the second afterward. "Blessed and holy is he who shares in the first resurrection! Over such the second death has no power (20:14 identifies it as the lake of fire), but they shall be priests of God and of Christ, and they shall reign with him a thousand years."

  This glorious prospect will strengthen the resolve of believers during the reign of antichrist not to take his mark, if fear of the lake of fire were not enough. "And when the thousand years are ended, Satan will be loosed from his prison, and will come out to deceive the nations which are at the four corners of the earth, that is, Gog and Magog, to gather them for battle; their number is like the sand of the sea." During the thousand years, the nations will serve Jesus under duress. They must be given a choice, just as our first parents in Eden were.

THE DEVIL'S FINAL DESTINATION

"*And they marched up over the broad earth and surrounded the camp of the saints and the beloved city.*" *Revelation 20:9*

What is occuring here illustrates Jeremiah 17:9, "The heart is deceitful above all things, and desperately corrupt; who can understand it?" One would have thought that the inhabitants of earth would have been as happy as clams at high tide. They were privileged to live during the Golden Age: no war, longevity approaching that of Methuselah, prosperity beggaring description. Above all they enjoyed the privilege of visiting Jesus in Jerusalem and the twelve apostles ruling over the twelve tribes of Israel. Even so, they were not satisfied, and yearned for a deliverer that they might get back to doing their own thing in their own way.

Their deliverer, the Devil, suddenly appeared and led them in "a peace demonstration" against the ruling regime in Jerusalem. They numbered in the billions. "But fire came down from heaven and consumed them." Evidently they had not gotten around to reading the sacred record, which plainly foretold the manner of their demise. How stupid can you be? "And the devil who had deceived them (his function all along in the economy of God) was thrown into the lake of fire and sulphur where the beast and the false prophet were, and they will be tormented day and night for ever and ever." Once a spirit, always a spirit. Spirits evidently share the nature of God, the Father of spirits, in that they cannot be uncreated.

So in this portion we have had the fourth theme, which is homecoming. The Devil has finally found his eternal home in the place prepared especially for him and his angels. Yesterday I was asked if it was possible for the Devil to repent. The Bible answers "no." As God is all light, he is all darkness, all evil. Read more about him in Isaiah 14:12-20, and in Ezekiel 28:11-20. They tell of his origin, nature and end.

❦

THE GREAT WHITE THRONE JUDGMENT

"**T**hen I saw a great white throne and him who sat upon it; from his presence earth and sky fled away, and no place was found for them." *Revelation 20:11*

"It is appointed for men to die once, and after that comes judgment." Hebrews 9:27 Jesus is seated upon the great white throne, because "the Father judges no one, but has given all judgment to the Son, that all may honor the Son, even as they honor the Father." John 5:22 Now there is no place to hide. We have come to the resurrection of judgment.

"And I saw the dead, great and small, standing before the throne (every one who has ever lived from Adam on), and books were opened (in which are recorded the details of every life). Also another book was opened, which is the book of life. And the dead were judged by what was written in the books, by what they had done (good and bad, and above all by what they had done with Jesus). And the sea gave up the dead in it, Death and Hades gave up the dead in them, and all were judged by what they had done."

Then an astonishing thing happened: "Death and Hades were thrown into the lake of fire." Death, the last enemy to be destroyed, is disposed of, as is the place to which it consigned the dead, Hades (the Greek name for Sheol, the realm of the departed.) "This is the second death, the lake of fire; and if any one's name was not found written in the book of life, he was thrown into the lake of fire." This means that no one will be saved from hell by his or her good deeds. It is essential that our name be found in heaven's register. We must confess our faith in Jesus Christ as our Lord and Savior to have our name inscribed in the Lamb's book of life. If we have read this far without having done so, we are without excuse, and are of all men most to be pitied. If we confess Jesus before men, he will confess us before his Father in heaven. If we fail to do so, he will deny us come the Last Judgment.

THE NEW CREATION

"Then I saw a new heaven and a new earth; for the first heaven and the first earth had passed away, and the sea was no more."

Revelation 21:1

At the Great White Throne Judgment we saw the vast importance of new birth, that we might be assured that our name is found in the book of life. New birth occurred for the first time on Easter evening as recorded in John 20. Then we saw Thomas healed of his blatant skepticism in the last event recorded in John 20. God's universe at the end of Rev. 20 received an immense healing when Death and Hades were eliminated from it, together with those defiled by the wickedness of unbelief.

Now in Rev. 21 and 22 we have come to the climax. They parallel John 21, which also had to do with entering the Kingdom of God. As all seven themes were found in John 21, so will they be seen in Rev. 21-22. First is testimony/preparation, as Revelation bears witness to the new universe come into view. Peter foresaw what has happened, and wrote of it in 2 Peter 3:7, "The heavens and earth that now exist have been stored up for fire... The day of the LORD will come like a thief, and then the heavens will pass away with a loud noise, and the elements will be dissolved with fire, and the earth and the works that are upon it will be burned up... We wait for new heavens and a new earth in which righteousness dwells." The sea, which separates people from one another, has been eliminated by the fire.

"And I saw the holy city, new Jerusalem, coming down out of heaven from God, prepared as a bride adorned for her husband." It is a prepared city for a prepared people. "And I heard a loud voice from the throne saying `Behold, the dwelling of God is with men. (This has been the goal from before creation.) He will dwell with them, and they shall be his people, and God himself will be with them; he will wipe away every tear from their eyes." What a beautiful picture of the Father's solicitude for his every child.

THE PERFECTED CHURCH

*"**And** he who sat upon the throne said, 'Behold, I make all things new.'" Revelation 21:5*

"In the beginning God said, 'Let there be light;' and there was light." Genesis 1:3 He spoke in faith and it happened. Now he speaks again, and everything is brand spanking new. "Also he said, `Write this, for these words are trustworthy and true.' (Here we have the anticipated second theme of faith. Having spoken in faith, he could now say:) `It is done!' (The renewal of all things is an accomplished fact.) I am the Alpha and the Omega, the beginning and the end. To the thirsty I will give from the fountain of the water of life without payment. He who conquers shall have this heritage, and I will be his God and he shall be my son." The inheritance of believers is the fountain of life (eternal youth).

Now hear what lot shall fall to the unbelievers: "But as for the cowardly, the faithless, the polluted, as for murderers, fornicators (those guilty of every kind of sexual sin), sorcerers (includes those involved in illicit drugs), idolaters, and all liars (and who is a liar but he who denies that Jesus is the Christ, the Son of God), their lot shall be in the lake that burns with fire and sulphur, which is the second death." Such a prospect, if faced, would drive one stark, raving mad.

"Then came one of the seven angels who had the seven bowls full of the seven last plagues, and spoke to me, saying, `Come, I will show you the Bride, the wife of the Lamb.'" Now we have come to the third theme, marriage/life. "And in the Spirit he carried me away to a great, high mountain, and showed me the holy city Jerusalem coming down out of heaven from God, having the glory of God, its radiance like a most rare jewel, like a jasper, clear as crystal." Did you realize that the new Jerusalem is actually the Church of which we are living stones? We are looking in a mirror.

❦

A CITY OF ASTONISHING BEAUTY

"**It** *had a great, high wall, with twelve gates, and at the gates twelve angels, and on the gates the names of the twelve tribes of the sons of Israel were inscribed.*" *Revelation 21:12*

So the glorified Church, now the habitation of God, is entered by way of the Old Testament people, who are part of it. "And the wall of the city had twelve foundations, and on them the twelve names of the twelve apostles of the Lamb." The lives and testimony of the apostles mark out the limits of the Eternal City. We must stay within the confines of what they said and did to enjoy eternal security.

When the city was measured, it was found to be four-square in length, breadth, and height: twelve thousand stadia (1500 miles). Twelve is the number of divine government and one thousand, perfect order. The wall measured 144 (12X12) cubits (250 feet high). It was built of jasper (diamonds), while the city was pure gold, clear as glass. It has infinite value, and nothing is concealed. The foundations of the wall were adorned with every rare jewel, flashing every color of the spectrum: deep blue, sky blue, emerald green, red and white, fiery red, golden, sea green, transparent green, purple, red, violet. "The twelve gates of the city were twelve pearls, each of the gates made of a single pearl." A pearl is formed in response to pain. By bearing one's pain bravely, one may be a gate by means of which others may gain access to the Celestial City.

After the marriage at Cana, Jesus took his disciples (Bride) home with him to the temple, his Father's house. When we get to heaven, though, we will see "no temple in the city, for its temple is the Lord God the Almighty and the Lamb." The kings of the earth shall bring into it the glory and honor of the nations. There all peoples will feel at home. "There will be no need of sun or moon, for the glory of God is its light and its lamp is the Lamb."

❦

THE TREE OF LIFE

"**B**ut *nothing unclean shall enter it, nor any one who practices abomination or falsehood, but only those who are written in the Lamb's book of life.*" *Revelation 21:27*

In Rev. 21 we have encountered testimony, faith, life, homecoming, and now new birth. "Unless a man is born anew, he cannot see (or enter) the kingdom of God" (in this instance, the heavenly Jerusalem). John 3:3,5 We have noticed that new birth is the prerequisite of being inscribed in the book of life.

We have come as far as Revelation 22, and are now looking for nurture and healing, which is exactly what we find. Rev. 22:1, "Then he showed me the river of the water of life, bright as crystal, flowing from the throne of God and of the Lamb through the middle of the street of the city (our drink); also, on either side of the river, the tree of life with its twelve kinds of fruit, yielding its fruit each month (our food)."

In Genesis 3:22 "the Lord God said, `Behold, the man has become like one of us, knowing good and evil; and now, lest he put forth his hand and take also of the tree of life, and eat, and live forever - therefore the Lord God sent him forth from the garden of Eden. He drove out the man; and at the east of the garden of Eden he placed the cherubim, and a flaming sword which turned every way, to guard the way to the tree of life.'" Now, praise God, we have been saved from the curse of the law that forbad eating of the tree of the knowledge of good and evil. That tree was forged into the cross, where the last Adam died, that we may now enjoy free access to the tree of life, eat, and live forever. How is that for nourishment! Furthermore, "the leaves of the tree were for the healing of the nations." Some of us have been called to be wounded healers. We can heal others, but not ourselves. There is a tree planted in the city that has foundations in eternity, the leaves of which will heal all of our inner wounds.

❦

COME, LORD JESUS

*"**T**here shall no more be anything accursed, but the throne of God and of the Lamb shall be in it, and his servants shall worship him."*
                                                                Revelation 22:3

The fatal flaw running through creation and through all the creatures in it has been healed. The curse has been lifted. Heaven and earth have been united. God is everywhere self-evident, and adored. That which the philosophers from time immemorial have aspired after has now become reality: "they (his servants) shall see his face." It is called the beatific vision, the goal of every creature. "And his name shall be on their fore-heads" - Father. "And night shall be no more; they need no light of lamp or sun, for the Lord God will be their light, and they shall reign for ever and ever" (literally, unto the ages of the ages). It is exciting to realize that each age has its unique characteristic. The previous age was characterized by sin and death, the current age by the power of Christ, the coming age by glory. The one constant amid all the changes is that God's servants will share the rule with him.

The rest of the book is postscript. "And he said to me, 'These words are trustworthy and true,'" something you can bank your life on. The refrain: "I am coming soon." When John fell down to worship the angel, he was forbidden to do so, and told, "Worship God." "I Jesus have sent my angel to you with this testimony for the churches."

There follows the threefold invitation, "Come." Then the warning: "if anyone adds (to this book), God will add to him the plagues described in this book, and if any one takes away from the words of the book of this prophecy, God will take away his share in the tree of life and in the holy city, which are described in this book." In conclusion Jesus says, "Surely I am coming soon." Since with the Lord a thousand years is as one day, we are nearing the third day.

❦

THE ACTS OF THE APOSTLES

"*The grace of the Lord Jesus be with all the saints. Amen.*"

Revelation 22:21

We end the year with the blessing of John. It has been said that the first thousand years of the Church belonged to Peter. He was appreciated especially in Rome. The second thousand years of the Church belonged to Paul, in that his teaching produced the Reformation. The third thousand years of the Church will belong to John, in that he was given to see while in exile on Patmos the thousand year reign of Christ, which may well begin within our generation.

Hopefully we have seen the seven themes articulated again and again. It is most interesting to see them in the Acts of the Apostles. In the gospel the Baptist prepared his disciples for the coming of Jesus. In Acts Jesus prepares his disciples for the coming of the Holy Spirit. In the gospel Jesus gathered six faithful disciples about him; in Acts the number of believers comes to 120. The marriage at Cana becomes the miracle of Pentecost, as Jesus transforms the water of their natural speech into the wine of supernatural utterance.

Then as Jesus takes his own ones home with him to his Father's house, Peter calls the 3000 who were cut to the heart to come home to God by repenting and being baptized into his family. The subject of new birth underlies the story of the man crippled from birth, who clings to Peter and John as a new-born clings to its mother. Then when the apostles are arraigned before the ruling council, they proclaim Jesus under the anointing of the Holy Spirit; they ate while the rulers were convicted. Forbidden to speak or teach in the name of Jesus, they held a prayer meeting. The place was shaken, and they were all filled with the Holy Spirit and spoke the word of God with boldness. In other words, they were healed of any trace of fear. Here is the seventh theme, healing in answer to prayer. So Acts is structured after the manner of John.

❦

Impact Books, Inc. is pleased to recommend the author's personal presentation of this material, which causes the Gospel to truly "come alive."

Gordon Dean Johnson welcomes the opportunity to present the Gospel to groups using his seven-fold key format, as he reconstructs the narrative of the gospel with *The Glorious Cross*.

This powerful, visual, "show and tell" presentation can be made to any size group and takes about one hour to complete.

He also does a similar visual presentation utilizing the Book of Revelation.

You may write to Gordon Dean Johnson, in care of

7100 Cheshire Lane,
St. Louis, MO 63123

IMPACT BOOKS, INC.

Announces

The Exciting New Power for Deliverance Series:

Power for Deliverance; Songs of Deliverance
Power for Deliverance From Fat
Power for Deliverance for Children
Power for Deliverance From Childlessness

Lives have already been changed by the powerful truths and revelations contained in these books as the author has taught them over the past seventeen years. These deliverance tools have been tested in the crucible of prayer room battles to free lives from Satan's control. You have tasted in this book the kind of dramatic accounts and truths which are to be found in the other volumes in this series.

Each book is just $5.95. When ordering add $1.50 postage and handling for the first book and $.50 for each additional title.

Available at your local Christian bookstore, library, or directly from:

IMPACT BOOKS, INC.
137 W. Jefferson
Kirkwood, MO 63122

POWERFUL NEW BOOK
BY SAME AUTHOR . . .

This new book is unique because it offers real help for the suffering women who have already had abortions. This book is full of GOOD NEWS!

It shows how to minister to them, or may be used by the women themselves as it contains simple steps to self-ministry.

Millions of women **have had abortions**: every one of them is a potential candidate for the type of ministry presented in this book. Every minister, every counsellor, every Christian should be familiar with these truths which can set people free.

$3.95 + $1.00 Shipping/Handling

IMPACT BOOKS, INC.
137 W. Jefferson, Kirkwood, Mo. 63122

Powerful Help on Cassette

Are You Saved? Have You Been BORN AGAIN? Do you even know for sure what is meant by these questions?

If not, we strongly recommend that you send for the tape
HOW TO BE SAVED, or BORN AGAIN!

To receive this informative tape, which can change your life . . . just as it has for thousands of others, when they have heard the message contained on the tape and responded to it. . . .

Simply send your name and address along with $5.00 to cover all costs to:

IMPACT BOOKS, INC.
137 W. Jefferson
Kirkwood, MO 63122

NOTE: If you honestly cannot afford to pay for the tape, we will send it to you free of charge.

THE HEAVENS DECLARE . . .

William D. Banks

More than 250 pages!
More than 50 illustrations!

- Who named the stars and why?
- What were the original names of the stars?
- What is the secret message hidden in the stars?

The surprising, **secret message** contained in the earliest, original names of the stars, is revealed in this new book.

The deciphering of the star names provides a fresh revelation from the heart of **the intelligence** behind creation. Ten years of research includes material from the British Museum dating prior to 2700 B.C.

A clear explanation is given showing that early man had a sophisticated knowledge of One, True God!

$6.95 + $1.00 Shipping/Handling

ALIVE AGAIN!

William D. Banks

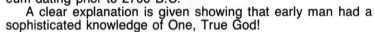

The author, healed over twelve years ago, relates his own story. His own testimony presents a miracle or really a series of miracles — as seen through the eyes of a doubting skeptic, who himself becomes the object of the greatest miracle, because he is Alive Again!

The way this family pursues and finds divine healing as well as a great spiritual blessing provides a story that will at once bless you, refresh you, restore your faith or challenge it! You will not be the same after you have read this true account of the healing gospel of Jesus Christ, and how He is working in the world today.

The healing message contained in this book needs to be heard by every cancer patient, every seriously ill person, and by every Christian hungering for the reality of God.

More than a powerful testimony — here is teaching which can introduce you or those whom you love to healing and to a new life in the Spirit!

$4.95 + $1.00 Shipping/Handling

FOR ADDITIONAL COPIES WRITE:

137 WEST JEFFERSON
KIRKWOOD, MISSOURI 63122